Graduate Study
and Research
in Physical Education

Graduate Study and Research in Physical Education

Walter P. Kroll, P.E.D.
Department of Exercise Science
University of Massachusetts

Human Kinetics Publishers, Inc.
Champaign, Ilinois

Publications Director
Richard Howell

Production Director
Margery Brandfon

Editorial Staff
Jean Ford

Typesetter
Sandra Meier

Text Design and Layout
Denise Peters and Lezli Harris

Cover Design and Layout
Jack Davis

Library of Congress Catalog Number: 82-81057

ISBN: 0-931250-31-5

9 8 7 6 5 4 3 2 1

Human Kinetics Publishers, Inc.
Box 5076
Champaign, Illinois 61820

Contents

A Note
From the Publisher

Graduate Study and Research in Physical Education is a revised edition
of *Perspectives in Physical Education* which was first published in 1971
by Academic Press. It is not customary for the publisher to write a fore-
word to a book he publishes, but there is a story about this revised edition that I wish to tell.

Two years ago my colleague John Loy wanted to use the original edition for an introductory graduate seminar, only to learn the book was
out of print and not to be reprinted. One day when John was lamenting
this sad state of affairs to me, he suggested that our company reprint it. I
began pursuing the idea immediately, for both John and I thought
Walter Kroll's book to be an enormously important contribution to the
field.

First I contacted Walter about the possibility of re-issuing the book; he
was more than pleased. Then I sought some reviews to consider what
revisions would be necessary. The result of that exercise convinced me
more than ever about the value of this book. To a person, it was agreed
that little in the book needed to be revised. A few tables, recent events,
and statistical supplements were added, but the essence of the book is unchanged from the original edition. It's difficult to improve on what is
likely to become a classic.

The original title, *Perspectives in Physical Education*, always seemed
to me to be nondescriptive. The book is an essential orientation to
graduate study and research in physical education and thus we titled it
just that. We hope the title change does not create any confusion, but we
felt strongly that the previous title was inadequate.

I believe this book is essential reading for students entering graduate physical education for several reasons. Graduate programs in physical education today emphasize teaching students the knowledge of one or more subdisciplines of the field, such as exercise physiology, biomechanics, or sport psychology. Students also are given extensive instruction in research methods and statistical techniques so they can join the small army of researchers who are discovering knowledge about human movement and sport. Yet, all too often, students embark on graduate education while not really understanding what graduate education is. Kroll's book provides an insightful introduction. He describes the emergence of physical education as a *discipline* and the distinction between the discipline of physical education and the profession of physical education.

With perceptiveness, Kroll helps entering graduate students obtain a perspective about the past research in physical education and how the current subdisciplines emerged. This provides a vital foundation from which scholars-to-be can move forward in the pursuit of more knowledge.

Graduate school is the first time many students are exposed to science and the scientific method. Kroll's text contains three excellent chapters on these topics, discussing them not in the abstract but within the context of physical education.

An astute professor of many years, Kroll knows that one of the more difficult problems for graduate students is learning to ask good questions for investigation. Kroll offers sage advice about investigating meaningful problems. Then students are given assistance on how to write research proposals and completed reports.

Graduate Study and Research in Physical Education is an indispensable book for beginning graduate students. In the interim from its first publication, nothing of which I am aware has appeared to replace it. Human Kinetics is proud to re-publish this important contribution to the field, written by one of the profession's leading scholars.

Rainer Martens,
Publisher
Human Kinetics Publishers

Foreword

The transition from undergraduate study to graduate study causes "cultural shock" for many students. Newly admitted graduate students quickly discover that they are required to play a different academic game. This game has a different set of objectives, more stringent rules, better qualified players, more demanding coaches, a greater degree of competition, more sophisticated equipment, and last but not least, this game has a highly uncertain outcome wherein each player has more at stake. Thus, beginning graduate students must learn new skills, master new strategies, adapt to new equipment, develop new styles of play, adjust to new player-coach relationships, and most of all, cope with anxieties resulting from the problematical chances of victory or defeat.

Although students entering graduate school in all fields of study must acquire new academic lifestyles, there is little doubt that the transition from undergraduate study to graduate study is especially traumatic for students in physical education. This transition is made difficult because of the Dr. Jekyll and Mr. Hyde syndrome that is unique to physical education. On the one hand, undergraduate physical education majors are typically exposed to professional preparation programs that emphasize the educational aspects of teaching and/or coaching. On the other hand, graduate students in physical education are typically exposed to more discipline-oriented programs that stress research and the scientific study of the diverse parameters of physical activity.

To make matters worse from the students' perspective, in reality the situation is not as clear-cut as stated in the latter case. Many graduate programs in physical education are both paranoid and schizoid in their efforts to sort out the profession versus discipline bases of their degree requirements. This sociological ambivalence at the program level induces psychological ambivalence at the personal level which compounds the trauma of transition from undergraduate study to graduate study of students in physical education.

The preceding observations strongly suggest that prospective master and doctoral candidates in physical education are sorely in need of a "game book" that would help them learn the rudiments, rules, and relevances of the new game in which they are about to participate. To my mind, there is no better "game book" available for such students than Professor Kroll's *Graduate Study and Research in Physical Education*. For 10 years I have encouraged all of my graduate advisees to buy a copy of Dr. Kroll's book and I have made his text required reading for several graduate seminars that I have taught. In view of the very favorable reactions of my students to Professor Kroll's book, I am pleased that Human Kinetics has published a revised edition of it.

By way of further introduction, I wish to state three personal tenets about the education of graduate students and to suggest why I think *Graduate Study and Research in Physical Education* should be mandatory reading for all students pursuing graduate study in physical education.

First, I assert that all graduate students should be able to clearly articulate what their field of study is about. Thus, I believe that the present book is a very important one, for to date it represents the most successful effort to answer the question: "What is American physical education?" Interestingly, Kroll attempts to answer this question by implicitly proposing in a rather Hegelian manner an inverted-U hypothesis regarding the historical development of physical education in American universities. In brief: (a) he states the *thesis* that nearly 100 years ago a few innovative individuals were motivated to try to establish a science of physical education, (b) he then sets forth the *antithesis* that the majority of leaders in physical education at the turn of the century sought to align physical education in particular with education in general and thus establish a profession of physical education, and finally, (c) he posits the *synthesis* that in recent years a few leading individuals and institutions in physical education have returned to the original motivation and once again are trying to establish physical education as an academic discipline with a focus on the scientific study of physical activity.

Secondly, I contend that all graduate students should be familiar with the history, major problems, and academic standing of their field of study. Accordingly, I believe that the present book is relevant for beginning graduate students because it provides a thorough overview of graduate study at a university, the origins and problems of professional preparation in physical education, and the past and present status of research laboratories and research productivity in physical education. A knowledge of these matters will help students to better understand the harsh criticisms made of graduate study in physical education and will help prepare students for their future professional roles in which they will share the responsibility of finding solutions to the difficult problems facing physical education.

Thirdly, I hold that all graduate students should have a working knowledge of philosophy of science, research methodology, and scientific writing. Hence, I believe that the present book is most useful for new graduate students because it clearly introduces novice researchers to such key topics as the following: (a) dimensions of science, (b) basic steps in the scientific method, (c) categories, characteristics, and uses of scientific explanation, (d) kinds of scientific problems and types of experiments, (e) identification and evaluation of research topics, and (f) substance, structure, and style of writing research reports.

Finally, I note that a special bonus of *Graduate Study and Research in Physical Education* is that it is just as interesting as it is important. The book is well and succinctly written, it is marked by numerous passages of understated and somewhat satirical humor, it contains several pithy moral maxims and many provocative illustrations, and it is filled with fascinating facts about the "roots" of physical education. Because of its broad embrace, the book can, no doubt, serve many purposes. But I believe that it will be good value for the price if it only serves to inform students of the differences between a discipline and a profession and to challenge students to determine to what degree physical education is either.

John W. Loy
University of Illinois
Urbana-Champaign

Preface

To say that physical education is experiencing rapid change and growth is merely to say that physical education is part of the twentieth century. But it seems reasonable to suggest that physical education is in the midst of something more than just normal growth pains due to the population increase and the explosion of knowledge and technology. Historically a part of education, physical education shares the changes sweeping across educational theory and practice. Goals and objectives, trends and fads, curriculum revisions and professional problems of physical education have always been inextricably interwoven with those of the education profession, but today an undeniably new movement is afoot in physical education. Although quietly developing at first, the new movement is mushrooming into a full-blown giant almost brash and discourteous to traditional concepts of physical education.

This new movement is, of course, that associated with the establishment of physical education as an academic discipline. Visionaries involved with this new movement see physical education as something more than just an area of study whose major responsibility is the training of teachers and coaches to conduct games and sports in the public schools; more than just an area where graduate education and research have the responsibility of producing better teachers and coaches to conduct more games and sports for more and more of our citizens. Such rebels against tradition also see physical education as concerned with the nature and meaning of human movement in its many forms, with the establishment of a science of exercise, and with inquiry into the why rather than solely the how of physical activity.

One of the origins—or one of the consequences—of this new movement has been an enormous increase in the emphasis and prestige given to research. This new emphasis, furthermore, has been primarily upon scientific research rather than just an increased production rate of the kinds of research previously done by physical educators. No longer is poor research excused because it was done by physical educators for physical education consumption and was "good enough." As a result of strong demands for excellence in research, major changes have occurred in the programs of study being offered in physical education. Undergraduate and graduate course prerequisites have broadened, graduate course offerings bear strange new titles, and research laboratories are springing up that are as well equipped as many in the basic sciences.

No wonder that new graduate students often find themselves in a different academic world from that they expected. Most undergraduate programs in physical education have by necessity concentrated upon preparation of a competent, well-prepared practitioner with sound professional qualities. When the student appears for graduate work it seems appropriate to expect more of the same kind of preparation, but that is now seldom the case in many of the newer quality programs of graduate study. Instead of a laboratory section to sharpen officiating skills, analysis of oxygen content of gas samples collected on sedentary subjects from a nursing home is the laboratory project. Instead of a professional-level discussion about new rule changes and likely modifications in strategy due to such rule changes, the sport in question is analyzed for different role models in a sport sociology course. Instead of a thesis topic dealing with a practical teaching or coaching problem, the new graduate student is reviewing foreign scientific periodicals searching for information on a topic that never existed until this decade.

Traumas like these cause bewilderment, and many students flounder about aimlessly until they either drop out or catch on to graduate study. This book was written to soften the crushing blow of graduate study and scientific research upon new graduate students. It was designed to introduce the graduate student to a new world of academic effort so that even if the goals are not accepted, the challenges will be understood. In many ways the contents of this book make explicit the many implicit standards and operating codes in graduate study. Terms such as research, science, and scientific method have been used so loosely that few persons in physical education adequately understand their meaning. Indeed, few appreciate fully the meaning of an academic discipline and what the changes currently being proposed for physical education entail.

Both those who teach and those who take courses in research methods, scientific foundations, seminars dealing with professional problems and curriculum issues, or independent research may find this book useful. Judging from student reactions during its development, the book may serve both academic and humane purposes. An understanding of graduate study and scientific research seems to help orient students in the right direction and relieve some of the confusion about what is going on in graduate school. Once students find out the rules of the game they can better direct their energies into productive channels, and with the heritage of competitive spirit, these students are more likely to prove not only good enough for physical education, but good enough to support us all in the academic jungle. For now, more than ever before, being sincere and dedicated is not enough. We must also be right.

Graduate Study at a University

Every state in America is proud of the institutions of higher learning within its borders, whether the institution be public or private. Great universities in our country reflect not only the accumulated intellectual strength of our nation but the esteem that society holds for knowledge and the pursuit of new knowledge. These seats of learning are composed of an august community of scholars whose major responsibility is to preserve, transmit, and improve the vast amounts of knowledge entrusted to their keeping. For many obvious reasons, universities are looked upon as the academic backbone of our nation and are charged with the responsibility of making highly important contributions to society in several different ways. Over the years, outstanding universities have gradually assumed a threefold responsibility to society and are recognized for their contributions to society through teaching, service, and research. Such a threefold obligation adequately embodies university activities although the relative balance and emphasis to be given each of the three responsibilities is even now not fully established. The relationships of these three obligations continue to be examined closely not only by the university structure itself, but by the federal and local government agencies, society in general, and lately by the students themselves.

The talent reservoir represented by learned faculty members is considered to be an important and unique resource of society. Society frequently calls upon this resource for service functions encompassing a wide range of activities from loaning out audiovisual aids to acting as consultant to foreign countries. University service functions are thus seen in the diverse areas of economics, politics, culture, the military,

1

agriculture, and, indeed, in almost every area of importance to society. The university of today is not an isolated white tower serving as a haven for scholarly recluses, but a functional and full-fledged partner in America's efforts to achieve greatness. This concept of a service function for a university has been called an American phenomenon of higher education that is unique in modern histories of education (4, page 387). The idea of an educated gentleman was borrowed by America from the English. The German philosophy of scholarly research for its own sake was absorbed as well. However, to these two traditional functions of a university America added the simple democratic and practical concept of a service function to the responsibilities of a university.

Because of an obligation not only to preserve knowledge but to transmit knowledge as well, universities are great teaching centers. Available knowledge is structured into formal courses of learning for efficient transmission to citizens of our society. Programs of study have been developed in as many different areas as society has deemed necessary in the past, and, as both knowledge and society change and advance, in almost as many new areas. Preparation for service to society finds individuals studying at institutions of higher education in a multitude of subject matter concentrations. Each of the subjects being taught has, in some manner or another, passed the inspection of society as knowledge worthy of preservation and transmission. The teaching responsibility of a university thus reflects one more aspect of its commitment to society, from which it draws its strength and support.

Teaching and service responsibilities, however, are not the unique function of today's great universities. Other institutions of higher education also assume these obligations and one finds a variety of service and teaching functions being carried out by community colleges, liberal arts colleges, technical institutes, and state colleges throughout America. All things considered, it seems fair to say that the most unique contribution of the great university lies in the new knowledge it produces through the scholarly research efforts of its distinguished faculty. Teaching and service functions are no less important at a great university and are never negated or given second-class roles. However, it is to great universities that society looks for the unique contribution of new knowledge. Without a continuous search for new knowledge, both the service and teaching functions would deteriorate and result in less than adequate progress toward the goal of a better society.

To many persons this unique and crucial responsibility for production of new knowledge translates roughly into programs of graduate study and associated research activity. Undergraduate programs are typically viewed as important for the transmission of knowledge already available, while graduate programs represent advanced study in an area of endeavor with the goal in mind of not only transmitting greater amounts of knowledge but of training individuals to become producers of needed new knowledge. Production of new knowledge is to be expected from the faculties of these great universities and from the products of advanced study in graduate education programs. Graduate education thus produces additions to the talent reservoir of learned scholars and to the reservoir of knowledge yet to be realized. If we can accept the conclusions of a report by the American Council on Education, the criterion of a successful graduate education program seems to be associated to a large degree with the quality of new knowledge it produces, as evidenced by the number of research contributions its faculty has achieved (7).

Although graduate education programs and production of new knowledge through research are seen as the more unique responsibilities of great universities, teaching and service functions continue to be important obligations. In many respects the presence of graduate study programs, faculties of highest academic competency, and on-going research activities all interact to magnify the potential of universities for teaching and service contributions. Dilemmas frequently trouble administrators when teaching, service, and research responsibilities must be weighed as to importance, priority, and emphasis. Criticisms of higher education as well as changes in higher education commonly revolve around the issue of what the balance of these three major responsibilities should be for optimum effectiveness of operation.

In a rapidly changing world, knowledge as well as the needs of society are in a state of flux. The balance of teaching, service, and research functions established today may not be satisfactory tomorrow. When any of the three functions fails to reflect developments in society, its status may change from that of seemingly proper emphasis to a condition where it then seems under-emphasized or over-emphasized with respect to the other functions. In either case, critical reaction is likely to occur, drawing attention to the new imbalance and deteriorating effectiveness of programs. It may even be the case that the relative emphasis to be given the functions has no stable pattern and that continuous revision and change in emphasis actually constitutes an inherent characteristic of the system.

In the following sections of this chapter an attempt will be made to present a brief summary of some of the important forces influencing the development of graduate study and research at universities. Examination of some of these past influences may provide a better understanding of the complexity of the problem that faces higher education today. The role of such pertinent factors in influencing decisions made today may be clarified if we can appreciate the potency of their effects in the past.

EARLY SCIENCE AND HIGHER EDUCATION

Major universities of today encourage research by their faculties, sponsor research projects with funds secured either locally or from private and governmental agencies, and actively recruit productive scholars for their staffs. A responsibility for research is accepted as an essential obligation by universities almost to a fault; for example, some critics claim universities are involving themselves too much with research and are failing to fulfill their teaching and service responsibilities. Such emphasis upon research, however, is a relatively recent phenomenon and, in many respects, reflects changes in science as a whole as much as it does changes in universities.

Originally universities assumed no responsibility for research whatsoever, and any research activity on the part of its faculty members was strictly avocational and sometimes even secret. Sir Robert Boyle, for example, formulated his laws about the elasticity of gases using tubes strung out around stairways rather than in a well-equipped laboratory specifically designed for his research activities. Sir Francis Newton performed his classic investigations at home. Galileo once wrote Kepler that in his role as professor his responsibility was only "to hand down the accepted opinions of the past" (23, page 218). It comes as no surprise, then, that the earliest colleges in the United States were not established to promote research (or science for that matter). Harvard in 1636 and Yale in 1701 were founded primarily to offer the basis for professional training in the ministry and were patterned after such aristocratic institutions in England as Cambridge and Oxford. In fact, many of the Harvard College statutes were lifted word-for-word from the Elizabethan statutes of Cambridge.

Although it cannot be denied that the earliest colonial-era colleges were formed in order to provide clergymen, other factors were also important. Settlers in America were equally intent upon recreating and preserving Old World culture and academic tradition. In addition, a growing society needed well-educated men for various civil duties and public leadership. Preparation for the ministry, however, was definitely the primary force behind the establishment of the first American colleges. Of the first nine colleges established in America, all but one had charters directing the training of students for the ministry. Most of the faculty members were clergymen themselves and it was not until about 1750 that laypersons began to exert much influence in college affairs.

For almost a century after their founding, early colleges provided a curriculum with emphasis upon classical languages, literature, and philosophy. Greek and Latin, of course, were important because of their role in the professions of medicine, theology, and law. Modern subjects, such as science, history, or government, had to win their places a little later in the traditional curricula of Western Europe. Course work in the natural sciences, mathematics, modern foreign languages, and the English language did not assume much importance until after 1765 (17, page 15). Gradually, however, ecclesiastical control of higher education was diminished as the population spread over the land and communities became less homogeneous as far as religion was concerned. Eventually the function of a college was seen to include "all the sciences useful to us and at this day, be taught in their highest degree" (17, page 26).

As the United States grew and became more mechanized, the demand increased both for more college-level study and for advanced study on a graduate level. Major factors contributing to such demands included the rise of interest in agriculture and the need for specialized knowledge in both business and the professions. Agricultural interests, in particular, were instrumental in securing passage of the Morrill Act of 1862 establishing land-grant colleges for the benefit of agricultural and mechanical arts. At that time, the study of such subjects was considered beneath the dignity of institutions of higher education already in existence. When viewed in retrospect, the effect upon higher education due to this development was of a considerable magnitude.

Carmichael (5, page 67) contended that the real beginning of serious development of science and technology in American universities was due to the Land Grant Act of 1862. As both Carmichael (5, page 21) and Berelson (2, page 12) pointed out, graduate education in the United States owed its development to the rise of science and technology in colleges and universities. Science and technology brought with them the recognition and acceptance of research as a necessary university function. Accelerated development of the graduate school resulted, therefore, because of the newly accepted research function given impetus by inclusion of science and technology in the curricula of institutions of higher education. Even more than the accelerated development of graduate schools has resulted since the new science and technology introduced a philosophy of utilitarianism, and even great universities "bowed to the idea of applying learning to social needs" (2, page 13). Only then did the university see its role as one encompassing teaching, service, and research.

An article by Daniels (12) analyzed the growth of science in the United States and drew an interesting parallel between the growth of science and the growth of higher education as a whole. He showed that by 1880 science was firmly established in almost 400 American colleges and universities. At about the same time, however, science was also abandoning the tenet that its primary goal was the production of useful knowledge. Scientists were now embracing the idea of a pure-science ideal, one of science for science's sake, and were uneasy about the fact that their positions in colleges and universities required heavy teaching loads and provided so little time or encouragement for research.

Daniels argued that the rise of professional scientists—scientists whose true vocation was research—saw many American scientists studying at

German institutions because only there was advanced study congruent with their new philosophy of science for science's sake with a great emphasis upon research. The attitude of individuals who had adopted the new pure-science ideal was undoubtedly mildly antagonistic to undergraduate programs where the emphasis was still mostly upon useful knowledge for application to practical problems. New scientists became more interested in the advancement of science and not in the diffusion of knowledge or the application of scientific knowledge for the good of society. The developments in science, therefore, coincided with the rising demand for higher education (and particularly graduate study) in the United States and constituted a potent force in the development of graduate education curricula.

In effect, science, having established itself as being important because of the useful knowledge it produced, having become well established in American higher education, and having contributed to a rising demand for more of such useful knowledge, now began to disengage itself from the mundane world of practical applications of knowledge and sought the vision of a pure science. Graduate education programs along the pattern of German institutions must have had great appeal to this new breed of scientists as one way to allow the pursuit of their new objective.

Prehistory of the Useful Knowledge Concept

From its earliest beginnings, scientific research had to be defended and a case made for its existence and support. Initially science was an avocational pursuit as reflected by the necessity for famous scientists like Newton and Galileo to conduct their research at home or on their own time. Considerable caution was also necessary not to interpret scientific facts as being in conflict with religious dogma and, for several generations, science had to be reconciled carefully with theology. One of the forceful arguments used in defense of scientific research was that it produced *useful* knowledge and thus served humankind.

Religious dogma held that absolute truth was unrealizable to human beings. The Greeks were among the first to take the diametrically opposed view that it was possible for human beings to achieve knowledge. They held that the acquisition of knowledge would furnish the power to "sustain and unite man forever with the ultimate being" (6, page 3). Nature was thus conceived of by the Greeks as a paradigm of general ideas converging to a meaningful end. Hence, from its earliest beginnings, the search for truth was justified on the basis that knowledge would be useful and enable human beings to become one with the gods.

Later one finds medieval humans living in an orderly and comfortable universe, deriving knowledge from two sources: reason and revelation.

Since it was believed the scheme of creation was known, the Scriptures were looked upon as containing divine revelation inaccessible to reason. Aristotle's work embodied the highest discoveries that human reason was capable of achieving. In this era, science was of little importance. How things happened could be of no consequence when one could concern oneself with the problem of why things happened and be certain that the answer would be flattering to the human ego.

Since it was accepted that humans could profitably investigate nature, they began to do so through philosophical speculation and metaphysical insight. Rationalism was perhaps the keynote of intellectual endeavor in the period preceding the seventeenth century, along with two other strong undercurrents—the rise of mathematics and an instinctive belief in a detailed order in nature (30, page 39). Rationalism, the belief that the avenue to truth was predominantly through a metaphysical analysis of the nature of things and that such analysis could determine how things acted and functioned, was dealt a stinging blow when people began comparing speculative truth with empirical observation of reality. It was only when faith in the omnipotent purposefulness of natural phenomena began to fade that the scientific method of inquiry became of any importance. Until such time there was no need for systematic searching for the truth nor any doubt that all truth could be achieved.

Empirical scientists became fond of asserting that science did not explain, but described (27, page 392). This descriptive view of science seems to have originated as a reaction against the tenet that knowledge of ultimate reality could not be obtained from the unordered sense-datum experiences of the external world. It also indicated that empirical science was breaking away from rationalism and any requirement that science channel itself into finding truth compatible with preconceived paradigms of nature.

In the time between the fall of rationalism and the rise of empirical science there exist some illustrative examples attesting to the clash of these doctrines. Newton (1642-1727) said his formulas merely described the way in which bodies behaved and he did not seek to explain the causes of that behavior. If pressed, Newton could retort that everything happened by the will of God (28, page 46). Before Newton, Kepler gave the reason for phenomena being as they were—that they fulfilled certain mathematical relations. By discovery, these mathematical relations could provide an insight into the purpose that guided the Creator.

Just how potent the conflict between empirical science and theological doctrine was can be appreciated by the case of Galileo Galilei (1564-1642). The Inquisition forced Galileo to renounce the Copernican theory in 1633 under threat of torture. In his *Letter to the Grand Duchess Christina*, Galileo attempted to depict a compatible relationship between science and theology. According to Galileo, empirical science could serve to clarify those aspects of theological doctrine that were vague, and would never support findings contradictory to the Scriptures. Because of his belief that the earth followed an orbit around the sun instead of vice-versa, Galileo was forced to live a secluded life and carefully weigh announcement of any scientific finding against prevalent theological doctrine.

With the more convincing defeat of rationalism, however, the tone of empirical science began to change. The first followers of Newton had disarmed criticism by saying that theoretical physics had no obligation to offer a causal explanation of nature. Why things happened was of no concern to science, only an adequate description of nature was required. Newton contended that the basis of science was observation and experiment. Mathematical deductions were to be made and tested. With this concept of its function, science could form an independent and encapsulated system, borrowing nothing from rationalism or metaphysics and owing nothing in return.

Hence, the first historic break of scientific endeavor from speculative philosophy was made with some caution not to attack too dramatically the concept of God or of human importance in the scheme of creation. In order to safeguard their existence, scientists disengaged from mystical explanations, from explanations in terms of the value-loaded "why," and instead became occupied with observing and describing nature in mathematical terms. That this was a subtle means of renouncing rationalism on the part of the scientist and a safe way to go can be appreciated if one considers how much more resistance to Newton's discoveries there would have been if he had been forced to reconcile his work with rationalistic ideals.

According to Daniels (12), both religion and science were eventually freed of the necessity to explain each other's principles. Scientists no longer felt the need to interpret scientific findings in order to show how such findings corroborated religious beliefs. Daniels considers this condition to have been clearly visible by the mid-1870's and cites this date as the beginning of "a changed image of the scientist and his role in society." The new change was for science to disavow the obligation to produce useful knowledge for practical application.

Pure or basic research, then, and not the production of useful knowledge via applied research, began to emerge as the important function of science. Science was to rid itself of any requirement that it justify its activities on any grounds other than a pursuit of knowledge and an understanding of nature. Insistence on the production of useful knowledge, it was thought, could hinder such a fundamental purpose of science, and the prestige of practical research began to fade. The ideal of a pure science began to reach its zenith in our generation although, throughout its rise, the concept has been questioned and condemned and questioned and upheld. Even today one can hear the arguments over the merits of pure versus applied research being discussed as budgets for the financing of scientific investigation are set.

GRADUATE STUDY IN EDUCATION

The short treatment of the development of science in higher education provides some help in understanding the problems and goals of graduate education in modern universities. Against the background of science, one can also trace the development of professional education (pedagogy), for it is interwoven with science. Early programs for the preparation of teachers were not esteemed very highly by academicians. Indeed, nineteenth century opposition to pedagogy was strong enough to result in the establishment of normal schools apart from the liberal arts colleges. Pedagogy, like agriculture and mechanical arts, was viewed as a practical or utilitarian pursuit. Hence, pedagogy was definitely of inferior quality when compared to the academic subject matter areas of the liberal arts.

According to Berelson (2, page 28), the uneasy acceptance of education as a field of undergraduate and graduate study was analogous to the resistance initially experienced by science in its quest for an academic niche in the university setting. Classical traditionalists fought against the acceptance of science into the curriculum "on the ground of inappropriate subject matter and method for 'true learning.' " When the professions sought admission into the hallowed halls of ivy, they found the now established sciences aligned with the academic arts in the attempt to block their admission. Such an alliance was quite ironical, to say the least. Science had forcefully employed the argument of useful knowledge to gain its own foothold in higher education. Once science had established itself, it gradually de-emphasized the role of useful knowledge, and fostered its own style of "true learning" in the form of a pure-science ideal. Fields of utilitarian identity were now considered in a poor light on the basis of the same arguments that science had once used in its own defense. Part of this frowning upon utilitarian pursuits by the sciences was undoubtedly due to the rise of scientific insistence upon freedom of inquiry and the negating of any major responsibility for practical research designed to produce useful knowledge.

Today, of course, large universities have somewhat reluctantly accepted utilitarian fields of study on their campuses and one finds a broad spectrum of subject matter specialties being offered at many colleges and universities across the country. Amalgamation is not complete, however, and one still sees medical schools, law schools, and dental schools located at off-campus sites. Several technical institutes still exist as autonomous institutions offering the highly specialized training necessary for engineering. One must remember that the original reason for their location away from the regular campus was, in most instances, due to the academic resistance to their being considered an integral part of the true center of academic learning.

A large university now finds itself composed of diverse specialties and the concept of a multi-university is a popular one. No wonder then that the multiple responsibilities for education and training have resulted in a number of different kinds of degrees being offered. By 1959, 393 different kinds of master's degrees were being awarded (14, page 27), and in 1961 almost 200 institutions were conferring 36 varieties of the doctor's degree (9, page 2). In physical education alone we see the Ph.D. in education with a major in physical education, a Ph.D. in physical education, an Ed.D. in education with a major in physical education, a doctorate in physical education (D.P.E.), and a physical education doctorate (P.E.D.). If one were to add the degrees in safety education, recreation, health, and outdoor education and all the combinations possible, the number of different kinds of degrees and degree programs would be considerable just for one area of study.

In some respects, graduate programs can be divided roughly into two major orientations. On the one hand are those programs leading to scholarly degrees, and on the other hand, those leading to professional degrees. Scholarly degrees place great emphasis on in-depth study of the subject matter content to produce a new generation of scholar-researchers and a supply of well-trained teachers. Professional degrees emphasize intensive training in the professional specialty, the application of knowledge to professional practice, and the supply of well-trained teachers. In the case of scholarly degrees, emphasis is, thus, upon the acquisition of knowledge in order to produce new knowledge via scholarly research. Professional degrees, likewise, emphasize the acquisition of knowledge but for the slightly different purpose of applying such knowledge in professional practice and improving the quality of professional service.

Scholarly degrees are associated with academic disciplines (or the sciences) while the professional degrees are, of course, linked with the professions. One distinction between the two, that has been forwarded to contrast the two different types of graduate program, is that scholarly degrees prepare students to be producers of knowledge while professional degrees prepare students to be consumers of knowledge, capable of applying such knowledge in the professional situation. Unfortunately, such a simple distinction between basic purposes is much easier to accept than it is to implement in actual programs of study.

Criticism of Professional Education

Although most physical educators are aware of the criticisms leveled against professional programs in physical education, few are aware of the severe criticism of education's graduate study programs. Only a small percentage are, likewise, aware of the critical rumblings going on in other professions. A brief consideration of some of these criticisms may show that the task of balancing scholarly research content and professional-competency content is not unique to physical education and education.

The education of nurses, for example, has seen a marked shift from hospital schools of nursing to nursing schools affiliated with universities. Between 1959 and 1966, 91 hospital schools of nursing went out of existence. An additional 59 such diploma nursing schools announced their intentions of closing down in 1966. The consequences of having nursing schools affiliated with colleges instead of hospitals were called deplorable by Thomas Hale, M.D., who was an executive vice-president of a medical center hospital. Collegiate training was said by Hale to emphasize theoretical aspects at the expense of practical necessities in nursing education. Hale criticized graduates of such nursing schools as being incapable of ". . . giving safe bedside care, giving treatments and medications. . . ." In short, Hale concluded, the nursing student, because of a drastic reduction in the number of hours of nursing practice, ". . . does not know how to nurse patients."

In similar tones, the medical profession itself has been doing some sharp soul searching. As a profession, medicine has seen a dramatic increase in the emphasis given to it as an academic discipline and to research. As one might expect, one of the results has been a decrease in the emphasis of medicine as a profession obligated to give service to human beings through its practice. Respect given to the theoretical researcher in medical schools and concurrent downgrading of the practitioner have contributed to the decline of public respect for physicians. Physicians have "lost sight of the whole man to whom we as physicians were obligated" (21, page 1). The inventor of the heart-lung machine, John H. Gibbon, Jr., M.D., similarly complained that physicians today do not know how to treat their patients. Writing in the *Medical Tribune* of February, 1966, Gibbon contended that part of the cause of such an unfortunate development was the over-emphasis upon research in medical schools. He declared that the "Ph.D. scientist has no place in a medical school, teaching medical students" because these scientists transmit their attitude of scientific detachment to the medical students in their classes.

Comments such as these do much to exemplify the difficulty involved in any attempt to combine the two roles of a competent professional person and a competent scholar-researcher. Too much emphasis on research results in too little emphasis on professional obligations to practice. Also, as recognized by the Association of American Medical Colleges, the linking of medical schools to universities has resulted in an adoption of university standards. The result has been a rise in specialization and research emphasis akin to an academic discipline. This result brings with it the danger of a loss in professional competency.

By far the most attention, however, has been given to recent criticisms of the profession of education. Due to many causes, apprehension over the quality of education in America caught the public's eye in the early 1950's. Only a historian or a prophet would undertake to pinpoint the exact causes of society's new interest in academic excellence. Some experts voice the opinion that burgeoning public school enrollments that necessitated massive amounts of additional tax money were easily the most important factor. Others point to the increased demand for scientific and technological training in a modern society, which required a marked revision of traditional curricula, as a potent force in the public's new involvement with the schools. Most authorities agree that the launching of the Russian "Sputnik" jolted American complacency and caused widespread concern over the quality of education in the United States.

Whatever the exact causes, society began an appraisal of academic excellence in education that has since raised many controversial issues to prominence. Two of the first publications to attract national attention were the books *Quackery in the Public Schools* by Albert Lynd (19), and Arthur Bestor's *The Restoration of Learning* (3). Most of the sharp criticism that followed employed Lynd's technique of citing ludicrous theses and course titles from the field of education to ridicule the quality of programs of study in professional education.

Of these two publications, Lynd's was geared to popular consumption. Words such as "pedagese" and "educationese" were used throughout the book to portray education in comical and trenchant terms. As was to be the case with most future critics of education, Lynd also included comic reference to physical education:

I should be hard put to nominate my choice for the most interesting piece of Educational research. There is provocative material in the vast field of physical education. Somebody at Syracuse University won his Master's degree through a thesis, *A Survey of the Requirements for the Master's Degree in Physical Education.* (That is one more example of Educationism contemplating its own navel.) Another Master came by that dignity with *Effects of Coaching on Acquisition of Skill in Basketball Free Throw*, by grant of the University of Wisconsin. A lady Doctor of Columbia University Teachers College wrote her thesis on *Games Preferences of 10,000 Fourth Grade Children* (19, page 89).

In other sections, Lynd charged education with needless proliferation of course work. Many such courses, he charged, were "Box Office Courses" that were good sellers with little academic challenge or necessity. Among the examples of such courses was a social dance service course that could be taken either for credit or noncredit. Lynd's comments about the dance course included the observation that "The charge was probably less than the cost of similar lessons at Arthur Murray's. The scholar who gave the course was ranked Assistant Professor of Education, Columbia University" (19, page 137). At another point Lynd cited the vast number of courses in education that include "a philosophy of" in their title. He knocked the University of Pittsburgh's course in Philosophical Bases of Health and Physical Education and cited the course Analysis of Current Systems and Trends in Football as one that must have been "briskly unphilosophical" (19, page 150).

Unlike Lynd, Bestor's contribution, *The Restoration of Learning*, was a distinctly more serious undertaking so far as style of writing was concerned. Indeed, Bestor's book deserves careful reading because it so wonderfully represents a somewhat archaic Old World philosophy of higher education. For example, Bestor views the present decay in academic quality as being "one of the evil legacies of the free-elective system into which the college curriculum disintegrated at the end of the nineteenth century" (3, page 62).

In another passage, which will be quoted here, Bestor exemplifies the position that the academician has held not just for generations but for centuries. The argument forwarded by Bestor concerning utilitarianism was, in fact, the same argument used by early academicians against the introduction of the natural sciences and by later protectors of the intellect against the inclusion of engineering. Although the passage to be quoted does not mention physical education specifically, Bestor at another point does definitely cite physical education as one of the "ancillary tasks." Bestor (3, page 73) writes:

> The pseudo-subjects that wormed their way into the curriculum under these circumstances were not offered for the purpose of advancing fundamental knowledge. They were frankly proposed as a means of preparing groups of students for certain specified jobs. Several of the courses, if viewed merely as optional supplements to the standard program, could be defended on utilitarian grounds. A student, alongside his serious academic work, might profitably pick up some practical training in accounting or pedagogy or public speaking or home economics or library cataloging. The difficulty was that teachers of these supplementary, vocational courses began to aspire to higher recognition. With fatuous disregard of intellectual realities, university administrators permitted the development of departments and even colleges devoted to these academic byways, and eventually students were permitted to take degrees in them.*

*From *The Restoration of Learning* by Arthur Bestor, Knopf, 1956. Used with permission of Alfred A. Knopf, Inc.

Apparently emboldened by the success of earlier criticisms in gaining widespread attention and having had to endure little in the way of organized retaliatory efforts, later critics of education spared no derogatory adjective in their pointed appraisals of the educational establishment. Of these later precentors, James D. Koerner rates as one of the severest and most outspoken critics of education. His comments suffered from no lack of clarity as he branded course work in education as being dull, ambiguous, and incontestably puerile. Such intellectual impoverishment, Koerner lamented, was due to the markedly inferior intellect of the faculty in departments of education. Koerner also viewed attempts by education to engage in scientific research as further contributing to the deterioration of the education that teachers received. Such a feeble attempt, according to Koerner "encourages the pernicious belief that their teaching can be based on some kind of exact or scientific foundation" (18, page 201).

A good share of Koerner's criticisms concerned the training that faculty members received in their graduate work in education. He called attention to the point that education faculty members have completed very little work in the liberal arts at the undergraduate level and almost none at the graduate level. Instead, Koerner stated, the education major spends his time in methods courses and "other trivia of education." One of the necessary steps to be taken, he thinks, is to abolish undergraduate majors in education. Nonacademic subjects (which include physical education, art, music, industrial arts, and home economics) are said to require so much time in education courses that graduates of such programs can hardly be said to have received a college education.

James Conant (10, page 201) gave no less indictment of work in physical education:

> If I wished to portray the education of teachers in the worst terms, I should quote from the descriptions of some graduate courses in physical education. To my mind, a university should cancel graduate programs in this area.*

A statement on graduate education in physical education was transmitted to Dr. Conant on August 17, 1964 in rebuttal. The letter was prepared by the president of the National College Physical Education Association for Men (NCPEAM), who worked with the American Association for Health, Physical Education and Recreation (AAHPER) Professional Preparation Panel in formulating the response. Forwarded with the letter was a copy of the May 1960 issue of the *Research Quarterly* of which it was felt: "No other single document will provide a better

---

*From *The Education of American Teachers* by James B. Conant. Copyright McGraw-Hill, 1963. Used with permission of McGraw-Hill Book Company.

introduction to the kind of research which is being produced in our graduate programs.'' The *Research Quarterly* issue referred to, of course, was the supplement on The Contributions of Physical Activity to Human Well-Being. Dr. Conant must have been highly impressed at the quality of work that the publication represented for physical education. Of course, two of the six chapters in the publication were written by non-physical education people. Then, too, the first chapter on The Contributions of Physical Activity to Physical Health had found it necessary to cite three former articles of the *Research Quarterly* out of the total 118 references used. Conant could not help but be impressed by such a notable display of intellectual strength by physical education.

The point of major importance, however, in these criticisms was that the content of the knowledge being acquired in graduate education courses was nonacademic; in other words, it was not really knowledge at all, but simple methodology and skill techniques. One is never quite sure what Koerner's proposal for change entails other than major reduction in education course requirements. Although Koerner proposed that education courses related to academic disciplines—such as psychology, history, and philosophy—should be taught by instructors from these disciplines, he never quite decided what these courses would then include that was different from those taught by educationists. Although Koerner contended there was so little worthy of serious study in. education, he spent all of his time for about two years studying the curriculum and administration of education.

Turmoil in the Schools

The loud public laments over the inferior intellectual quality of professional preparation in education were not without repercussions in many quarters. As might be expected, changes in teacher certification practices were sought by an aroused public to prevent any further admission of poorly qualified teachers into the public schools. An excellent series of papers by Hendrick (16) chronicles the activities in California over the controversial Fischer Bill concerning revision of teacher certification that was passed in 1961. Many observers believe that developments associated with the passage of the Fischer Bill have had a great impact upon the thinking of physical education leaders across the country. Some even contend that the real impetus for moving toward an academic discipline of physical education came from the embarrassing position that the profession was forced to take during the Fischer Bill deliberations.

Hendrick's account catalogs the numerous charges, counter-charges, and defensive arguments occurring during the time that the people of California were pondering the need for revision of teacher certification practices. The atmosphere prevailing was one that decried the poor academic preparation of teachers and the number of courses of dubious value required in education. Many of the emotion-laden arguments, furthermore, once again brought athletics and physical education into the limelight of public attention for ridicule. One newspaper editorial, for example, groaned about the fact that many children were being taught foreign languages, mathematics, or physics by teachers who had majored in physical education. A report in the *San Francisco Chronicle* on March 30, 1961 contained a harsh satire titled "Goodbye, Old Football Coach" that lambasted the professional establishment for permitting a condition to exist in which about one-third of the school administrators in the state were physical education majors.

The kinds of criticism heard in California were no different from those being aired on the national scene. For a host of reasons, society was sold on the need to further academic excellence in the schools. In order to accomplish such a feat it apparently was deemed necessary to de-emphasize nonacademic areas and chastise professional education preparation. Among the casualties at the public whipping post were the traditional nonacademic scapegoats: athletics, home economics, speech, art, business education, music, agriculture, and vocational education. Some of these groups attempted defenses against public castigation while others chose to suffer in silence. None could, of course, deny that they were practical or emphasized the practical as an end objective. Utilitarianism was congruent with the nonacademic and to argue for practical services to society was an admission of a lack of academic content.

Crucial points of the legislation passed involved the definition of an academic subject matter area. In the act itself an academic subject matter area was defined as referring "exclusively to the natural sciences, the social sciences (other than education and educational methodology), the humanities, mathematics, and the fine arts." The State Board of Education was given the authority to decide which subject areas qualified as academic subject matter areas. In order to be considered an academic subject, the following criteria were suggested:

(1) that there be an orderly and logical sequence;
(2) academic courses be prerequisite for successful achievement in the subject in question;
(3) intellectual development be emphasized;
(4) scholarly literature and research facilities be emphasized;
(5) understanding and application of theoretical principles be emphasized in laboratory work; and
(6) knowledge and understanding be gained from study in one or more of the academic subject matter areas.

Qualifying as an academic subject matter area was important because of the new certification requirements. The Fischer Act established five types of credentials in education: (1) a standard teaching credential with specialization in elementary, secondary, or junior college teaching; (2) a standard designated subjects teaching credential; (3) a standard designated services credential; (4) a standard supervision credential; and (5) a standard administration credential. At first glance, the types of credentials being given do not seem damaging to any of the traditional-type certification practices. The difference in the situation revolved around the definition of an academic subject matter area.

Under conditions of the act, a standard teaching credential was authorized only when a candidate presented a degree with a major or minor in an academic subject. School administrators, in addition, were now required to show specified amounts of graduate work in academic subjects in order to obtain certification. Physical education, along with several other teaching areas, was classified as nonacademic. Such a classification was considered to be a rebuke of status in the profession and relegation to second-class citizenship.

After passage of the act several of its provisions began to cause difficulties. For one, new certification requirements were blamed for an increasingly troublesome shortage of elementary school teachers. The new legislation required elementary school teachers to obtain a baccalaureate degree with either the major or minor in an academic subject matter area. Because elementary education was not considered an academic subject, it was virtually eliminated as an area of concentration. At any rate, a modification of the 1961 law became necessary in 1965; and for a period of about 90 days in 1967, credentials were issued based upon certification requirements in existence prior to the 1961 law, in order to relieve some critical teacher shortages.

At the present time, the new certification requirements continue to cause many frustrating difficulties for the State Board of Education in California. Assembly bill number 1269, introduced to the California legislature, would wipe out requirements for an academic major or minor and restore education as a valid area of concentration for future teachers. Hendrick pointed out that some of the vigorous support for the Fischer Act had now dwindled in the face of realities. He cited the *Los Angeles Times* as one apparent reversal when, under the heading "California's Supply of Teachers," it stated that "inflexible application of rules" could serve to "jeopardize essential staffing." Although previously a strong proponent of academic excellence and certification reforms, the article now stated "the goal of better teaching will not be served if future idealistic standards force faculty shortages" (16, page 399).

Regardless of how one views the developments, the fact remains that the pointed criticisms of professional education have caused a good deal of soul searching in higher education as well as in the public schools. Some of the proposals for change appear drastic and tinged with sensationalism. Many of the severest critics certainly fit the comment made by Paul Woodring, education editor of the *Saturday Review*: "in the interests of style, truth was often sacrificed and many of the sharpest criticisms hardly seem substantiated by the actual facts" (31, page 63).

As is true of most forms of criticism, however, the public reacts most strongly to the initial barrage of criticism and does not often bother to listen to defensive arguments couched in less dramatic tones. The situation is much like the plight of a man who is arrested on some charge of breaking the law. Even if he is acquitted of the charge, his reputation still bears the scar of suspicion. Education, much like any profession, is often forced to make important decisions without the benefit of substantial and definitive evidence. Although alternative policies might also lack a firm factual basis for support, alternative decisions seem more desirable if present policies are deficient.

PREPARATION IN AN ACADEMIC DISCIPLINE

At this point, speculation about possible deficiencies in graduate study programs for an academic discipline is quite commonly very close to actuality. Any graduate program must provide for an optimum balance among teaching, service, and research emphases according to some goal. If, as in the case of medical and nursing education, a program over-emphasizes the scholar-research component, then some deficit may arise in the service obligation. Such a deficiency in a profession could be disastrous. A similar deficiency can result, however, in a program designed to produce an individual prepared to work in an academic discipline. In the case of those Ph.D.'s prepared in an academic discipline who find employment as professors in institutions of higher learning, an extreme emphasis upon the scholar-research component may jeopardize the extent and quality of their teaching and service obligations. A point frequently overlooked is that an academic discipline located in a university setting has both a teaching and a service commitment *as well as* a commitment to scholarly research.

Teaching versus Research

Teaching is called a profession. Scholarly degree programs in an academic discipline train researchers. However, somewhere around 60 to 70 percent of the Ph.D.'s in academic disciplines find themselves employed as college teachers (25, page 108). Here, however, is the oddity. If there has been one dominant and lasting criticism of graduate education, it has been that too much attention has been given to the preparation of scholar-researchers and too little to preparation for college teaching. Hence, the question of the amount of emphasis to be given to professional preparation for teaching and to in-depth preparation for the scholar-researcher has given rise to considerable, and often bitter, debate.

Note that the question of balance between teaching and research emphasis can be asked of both scholarly and professional degree programs. A professional degree assumes that the possessor can be a consumer of research and has acquired necessary knowledge for the practice of his or her profession. How much basic knowledge is necessary, however, and how much research competency is required for a professional to be an adequate consumer of research are questions that need to be answered. In order to be a consumer of research—research of the kind that produces new knowledge—one must know something of research techniques and important research questions. A consumer of knowledge who lacked such competencies could hardly be expected to be able to read and understand research. In addition to the research techniques and strategies, the question may also be asked of how much basic knowledge a professional must acquire in order to perform satisfactorily in a chosen profession and to understand the significance of new research findings? If the decisions reached for the composition of a professional education program are inadequate, the end-product professional will be less than satisfactory.

However, the same kind of unsatisfactory result can occur in a program of study for an academic discipline. Although the amount of emphasis given to the scholar-research component is understandably greater in a discipline than in a profession, can teaching and service commitments be glossed over in a discipline or not? A university expects a triad of responsibilities—research, service, and teaching—and the question arises as to whether or not university professors can legitimately deny any teaching or service obligations and contend that their role is to produce new knowledge. Many of the criticisms leveled against the modern university would seem to imply a failure of the university to accept a more proportionate commitment to the problems of society. Other criticisms suggest inadequate dedication to teaching responsibility and lack of interest in the student as an individual. Some of the critics voicing such opinions hold that an undue emphasis upon research is the causal factor.

A former United States Commissioner of Education, Earl J. McGrath, contended that the present emphasis in universities upon research is incompatible with the essential purposes of undergraduate education.

McGrath (20) holds that as graduate schools grew in importance, the quality of undergraduate education deteriorated. Because the emphasis in graduate work was solely on a narrow specialization of subject matter and research, individuals prepared under such a system were incapable of performing as undergraduate education instructors. The research-scholar was said to be unable to impart synthesized knowledge in a broad and sometimes survey-like frame of reference which was much more to be desired in undergraduate education than a narrow specialized knowledge. Instead, the scholar-researcher instructors used courses to identify prototypes capable of doctorate-level work in their own narrow field of interest.

McGrath is not alone in the position that one of the major defects in the present Ph.D. programs is their incompatibility with the basic needs of imparting broad knowledge and intellectual skills deemed necessary for the college teacher. Berelson (2), recognized as one of the staunchest supporters of the integrity of the Ph.D., fully acknowledges that the problem of college teaching versus university research represents "some direct and lasting conflicts of interest." In one study conducted by Berelson, he asked respondents to agree or disagree with the statement that emphasis upon research in universities was resulting in poorer preparation of college teachers. Three-fourths of the college presidents and more than one-third of the graduate faculties agreed. Interestingly enough, among professional fields 44 percent agreed, while only 30 percent agreed in the arts and sciences.

According to Murray (22), whenever teaching responsibilities vie with research activities for attention, research wins. Since universities encourage research publication with salary increases and promotion in rank, it is not hard to see why such a choice is frequently made. The flight from teaching responsibility is also seen by Cooper (11) as an expected phenomenon since faculty members seek prestige by research accomplishments. Lighter teaching loads, the viewing of undergraduate teaching as a chore and a bore, and the writing of graduate course proposals in a specialty area testify to the migration upward, away from teaching and undergraduate students, to the pinnacle of all research and no students.

University employment represents a paradox to many faculty members. As Caplow and McGee (8) have pointed out, the faculty member in higher education is hired to teach, but gains prestige primarily through production of research publications. Caplow and McGee's study suggested the number of faculty members who regarded teaching duties as an obstacle to their success was increasing and discernible at every major university considered. Responsibility for instruction thus tends to fall more and more into the hands of faculty members who have failed to distinguish themselves in their discipline by research activities.

Which position is right? The argument that faculty members are likely to neglect and de-emphasize teaching responsibilities in order to provide time and energy for research and publication is encountered too frequently to be dismissed simply as escape rationalization by scholar-researcher incompetents. Similar dissatisfaction with incompetent undergraduate teaching has been voiced for several generations and the criticism must be accepted as possessing some degree of validity. Nonsense criticisms do not survive so long. All the arguments being heard currently were also expressed during the earlier part of the 1900's when traditional German programs of higher education were being widely criticized (4).

Critics of graduate study in the academic disciplines thus contend that products of such programs have neither the ability nor the desire to teach. As a reward for scholar-researcher productivity the academician seeks relief from teaching responsibilities, particularly undergraduate course work unrelated to research interests. Top research-scholars are also likely to be off-campus quite frequently acting as consultants, giving addresses and papers at various conferences, or on research leave. Such developments have seethed on some campuses until students have taken their own action to seek relief by publishing guides to teachers and courses and campaigning for the awarding of tenure to good teachers. Some have even taken the advice of John Fischer (15) to "raise a little more hell."

Staunch defenders of the scholar-research emphasis in graduate study use one very simple and strong argument against the criticism that an over-emphasis upon research results in an inability to teach effectively. They simply deny such a criticism is true. Indeed, they argue that just the opposite is true and that the best researchers are also the best teachers. A distinguished dean of a school of physical education wrote a stirring plea for near abandonment of professional degrees in physical education and urged university administrators to replace teachers, coaches, and administrators with scholar-researchers in as many positions as possible. He saw little chance for a deleterious effect upon the quality of teaching from such a strategy because "teachers who do research are better teachers" (26). The argument is also voiced that the best teaching cannot "be done by the retailing of secondhand information by a faculty whose own horizons are limited to other people's textbooks" (1).

Certainly, excellent teaching skills alone cannot overcome outdated subject matter, and the students' expectation that their professors be knowledgeable authorities must also be considered. Professors who teach at the graduate level and who sponsor student research in the form of master's theses and doctoral dissertations must not only possess research competency but should exemplify it by their own production of research. The argument, therefore, that good teachers are only found among those who cannot, or do not, produce scholarly research is just as ridiculous as the argument that all researchers are poor teachers.

Lee A. Dubridge, former president of the California Institute of Technology, contends that the tradition of teaching without research prevented American universities from becoming ". . . the great fountainheads of new knowledge which the British, German, and French universities had become" (13). World War I revealed this striking deficiency, and fortunately, by the time of World War II, American universities had truly become great scientific centers. Dubridge also notes that undergraduate education programs were vastly improved because of the expansion of both graduate study and research activities on university campuses.

Although Dubridge was quite firm in his stand that undergraduate education was not being neglected and that the "flight from teaching" criticism was sheer fantasy, it is interesting to note some other points in his paper. First, he suggested that the great awakening to the need for research in American universities was associated with a lightening of teaching loads for those talented in basic research. Second, the long-awaited expansion of graduate study and research brought about a different responsibility for the typical university professor, and the new professor ". . . no longer carries the formerly impossible burden of undergraduate teaching." Impossibly heavy teaching loads, Dubridge noted, led to bad teaching because professors had no time to do research.

Arguments in defense of a professionally oriented program of graduate study and arguments on behalf of a scholar-research prototype are equally persuasive. Few could deny the premises and even fewer would be able to suggest fully acceptable compromises. The balancing of professional versus academic discipline graduate study is likely to be an interesting juggling act for some time, increasing rather than decreasing in difficulty. As suggested previously, the task of continuous revision and change may be a perennial and inherent characteristic of the system. If it is, then continuous criticism of residual deficiencies in either of the programs of graduate study is also an inherent characteristic, and periods of tranquility are not likely to occur very often.

As was the case a few years ago (24, 29), the reporting of deficiencies and suggested solutions can be expected to come from many quarters. Society is interested in the university and can be expected to react when its demands are not being met. As Schaefer (25) predicted back in 1951, "such an avalanche of criticism and suggestion" cannot be withstood for very long before changes are made. Since the needs and demands of society change, the university must be ready to respond with program modifications as quickly as possible to prevent criticism. Past history suggests that such a feat has seldom been accomplished and only a true optimist would expect anything different in the future.

Criticism and changes have manifested themselves in most aspects of higher education whether it be graduate or undergraduate programs, professional or academic discipline. Whatever security and complacency physical education might have enjoyed, nestled close to the bosom of education, was severely threatened when education itself was sharply lambasted for academic deficiencies. It is no understatement of fact that recent criticisms of education in general and physical education in particular reached a wide audience. Across the country both education and physical education have been, voluntarily and involuntarily, closely scrutinizing the nature of their courses of study. Any fair assessment of the present state of affairs must conclude that major revisions are in store for many programs of study in both education and physical education.

It is in this educational arena that new graduate students in physical education find themselves. Mostly protected and naive about such massive controversies, new graduate students are now faced with the necessity of preparing themselves to tackle the solutions of the difficult problems confronting physical education. In their previous educational experiences, any discussion of professional problems occurred among their own kind; for instance, with faculty and student groups sharing a dedicated belief in the value of physical education. Such experiences did much to nurture enthusiasm and deeper commitment to the profession. Graduate-level study, however, now asks them to consider the viewpoints of outsiders—individuals and groups who do not share a quasi-mystical belief in the value of physical education.

For some graduate students the harsh criticisms of education and physical education will be viewed as being unfair and cruel. To these products of physical education the only defense needed would be to brand unfair critics as being "against physical education." Others, however, will weigh the content of such criticisms with an impartial set of criteria. Any criticism evaluated as possessing some validity will be identified and the means for amelioration of the deficiency sought. It is to these latter products of graduate programs that the advancement of physical education will be entrusted. If physical education is to continue and prosper it will undoubtedly need more than a fair share of intellectual talent to guide its destiny in an ever-changing and challenging world. To be sincere and dedicated is simply not enough. One must also be correct.

REFERENCES

1. Ashton, John W. Your university: its progress and urgent needs. *Your University* 9: 1-4; July 1964. Bloomington, Indiana: Indiana Univ. Alumni Association.

2. Berelson, Bernard. *Graduate Education in the United States*. New York: McGraw-Hill, 1960.

3. Bestor, Arthur. *The Restoration of Learning*. New York: Knopf, 1956.

4. Brubacher, John S., and Willis Rudy. *Higher Education in Transition*. New York: Harper, 1958.

5. Carmichael, Oliver C. *Graduate Education: A Critique and a Program*. New York: Harper, 1961.

6. Cassirer, Ernst. *The Problem of Knowledge*. New Haven: Yale Univ. Press, 1950.

7. Cartter, Allan M. *An Assessment of Quality in Graduate Education*. Washington, D.C.: American Council on Education, 1966.

8. Caplow, Theodore, and Reece McGee. *The Academic Marketplace*. New York: Basic Books, 1958.

9. Chase, John L. *The Number and Kinds of Earned Doctor's Degrees Awarded by United States Institutions in 1961-62*. Washington, D.C.: Department of Health, Education and Welfare, Office of Education, 1964.

10. Conant, James B. *The Education of American Teachers*. New York: McGraw-Hill, 1963.

11. Cooper, Russell M. The college teaching crisis: has the graduate school done right by the college teacher? *Journal of Higher Education* 35: 6; January 1964.

12. Daniels, George II. The pure-science ideal and democratic culture. *Science* **156**: 1699-1705; June 30, 1967.

13. Dubridge, Lee A. Research and teaching—the total academic contribution. *Educational Horizons* 43: 4-17; Fall 1965.

14. Eells, Walter C., and Harold A. Haswell. *Academic Degrees*. Washington, D.C.: Department of Health, Education and Welfare, Office of Education, 1960.

15. Fischer, John. Is there a teacher on the faculty? *Harper's* **230**: 18-28; February 1965.

16. Hendrick, Irving G. Academic revolution in California: a history of events leading to passage and implementation of the 1961 Fischer Bill on teacher certification. *Southern California Quarterly* **XLIX**: 127-166; June 1967. Part II: 253-295; September 1967. Part III: 359-406; December 1967.

17. Horton, Byrne I. *The Graduate School: Its Origins and Administrative Development*. New York: New York Univ. Bookstore, 1940.

18. Koerner, James D. *The Miseducation of American Teachers*. Boston: Houghton Mifflin, 1963.

19. Lynd, Albert. *Quackery in the Public Schools*. Boston: Little, Brown, 1953.

20. McGrath, Earl J. *The Graduate School and the Decline of Liberal Education*. New York: Teachers College, Columbia Univ., 1957.

21. Milch, Elmer. Physicians have lost sight of the whole man. *Medical Tribune* 6(81): 1, 16; July 7, 1965.

22. Murray, R.K. The effect of a university's graduate program on its undergraduates. *Journal of Higher Education* 32: 260-264; May 1961.

23. Ornstein, Martha. *The Role of Scientific Societies in the Seventeenth Century*.

Chicago: Univ. of Chicago Press, 1928.

24. *Report of the President's Commission on Higher Education*. Washington, D.C.: Government Printing Office, 1947-48.

25. Schaefer, Robert J. The function of graduate schools: claims and counterclaims. *Harvard Educational Review* **21**: 107-114; Spring 1951.

26. Staley, S.C. Keys to advancement in physical education. *The Physical Educator* **18**: 83-88; October 1961.

27. Stebbing, L.S. *A Modern Introduction to Logic*. New York: Crowell, 1930.

28. Sullivan, J.W.N. *The Limitations of Science*. New York: New American Library, 1949.

29. University committee on the preparation of college teachers. *The Preparation of College Teachers*. Chicago: Univ. of Chicago Press, 1947.

30. Whitehead, Alfred N. *Science and the Modern World*. New York: Macmillan, 1954.

31. Woodring, Paul. The active voice. *Saturday Review* **XLVI**: 63; November 16, 1963.

Origins of Professional Preparation in Physical Education

2

There is some value in examining the earlier origins of the professional preparation of physical educators. Undergraduate programs generally precede graduate programs, and consideration of the forces affecting one may offer keener insight into the forces fashioning the other. Tracing the development of an idea or theme is a difficult undertaking and is made even more hazardous because the history of our professional beginnings is so poorly understood. Unlike a history of science or a history of government, the history of major ideas in physical education is still characterized more by a series of descriptive rather than interpretive endeavors. In this instance, hindsight is almost as risky as the prediction of the future.

The following sections will take up the origins of professional training for teachers of physical education and the origins of a scientific or quasi-academic discipline of physical education. Following this, a chapter will be devoted to the first graduate study programs in physical education and to considerations of current developments in graduate education. The material presented is factual, although interpretation of the facts cited is subject to the usual qualifications attached to any subjectively derived conclusion. Few great authorities could be cited in defense of many of the conclusions, both implied or specifically stated. A good many of the conclusions forwarded possess no virtue other than representing one possible set of interpretations of the facts available, and perhaps, in being ideas on topics that have never before been formally considered in physical education circles.

EARLY BEGINNINGS OF EDUCANTO
IN PHYSICAL EDUCATION

The appeal of a healthy body and possession of awesome physical prow-ess has been a long persisting phenomenon in our culture. George Barker Winship, for example, was motivated to take up a regimen of hard physical training because a bully had intimidated him during his school days at Harvard. His article "Autobiographical Sketches of a Strength-Seeker," which appeared in the January 1862 issue of the *Atlantic Monthly*, probably expresses a motivation for the acquisition of strength that characterizes thousands of today's youth even though it was written over a century ago. Later, upon completion of his M.D. degree at Har-vard in 1857, Dr. Winship opened his famous Washington Street gym-nasium in Boston and thrilled countless thousands with his impressive ex-hibitions of heavy lifting. Other individuals, later to achieve prominence in physical education, owed some of their interest in physical activity to the excitement associated with being a circus acrobat. Among these acrobats one can count such notable figures in American physical educa-tion as Dudley Allen Sargent, William G. Anderson, and Clark W. Hetherington.

In the middle of the nineteenth century most gymnasiums were thought of as hang-outs for a robust but rowdy clientele. The typical gymnasium was frequented primarily by circus performers, prize fighters, strength-seeking fanatics, local strong boys, and an interesting assortment of other physical prima donnas. Directors of these early gym-nasiums often doubled as custodians and generally reflected their clientele in appearance and social standing. Having been drawn from the ranks of gymnasium users on the basis of superior performance abilities, they commonly appeared in spangled circus tights and glamorous robes when giving instruction or demonstrating their wares.*

Fortunately, the universal appeal of a healthy body and physical well-being also reached individuals with other motivations. Many of the early and more important pioneers in physical education recognized exercise

---

*See, for example, L.L. Doggett's book, *History of the Boston Young Men's Christian Association*, Boston: Y.M.C.A., 1901, in which some descriptive material is available con-cerning the early gymnasium directors around 1875: The chief leader during this period was Professor Du Crowe as he was called. He was a circus performer, slack-wire walking being his specialty. Nearly all the work was of the "circus kind, being intended for display." The early instructors wore flesh-colored tights and spangles, and performers for prominent cir-cuses, which were then popular throughout the country, found their way into the Boston Gymnasium (page 50). In other sections reference is made to the fact that many of the peo-ple "who frequented the exercising hall were not men of elevated character" and that "there is evidence that some were of dissolute habits."

and wholesome health practices as entwined modalities of great potential for the achievement of a better life. To a large degree, however, even the more prominent early leaders viewed exercise primarily as a medium through which attainment of a Christian health goal was made possible. Physical activity was as much—or more—a vehicle for achievement of a clean and long life free of sin and corruption as it was a primary goal. Among the individuals present, for example, at the 1885 founding of the Association for the Advancement of Physical Education were many who were more closely identified with interests other than physical exercise per se. Dio Lewis, who frequently appeared wearing an iron crown decorated with stars and stripes, was a dedicated temperance apostle and believed that ". . . dumbbell exercises preserved a sinless nature" (7, page 48). William Blaikie, a New York City attorney, lectured widely not only on the value of exercise but on temperance as well. His widely renowned book, *How To Get Strong and Stay So*, would be classified as physical culture by today's standards. Another original charter member was Helen C. Putnam who, in addition to being head of the Vassar College gymnasium, was a prominent crusader for women's suffrage.

Drawn together by a fraternal interest in the cause of exercise and hygiene, early members of the Association for the Advancement of Physical Education overcame rather remarkable differences in background preparation and worked hard to forward their mutual cause. Whatever their differences, the appeal of exercise was capable of uniting diverse interests under one shield. Judging by stated aims and objectives in the association's several constitutions, the group was, at first, primarily interested in meeting together for a mutual exchange of information and inspiration in order to extend the experiences of gymnastics, games, and athletics into the education of children and youth across the country. By 1920, the formally stated purpose of the association included the promotion of universal physical education, well-prepared teachers, and adequate programs. Finally, in 1952, the association clearly depicted its predominant ties with education by stating that its aims were ". . . consistent with the aims of general education." Today, the association reportedly conducts its professional activities in symbiotic harmony with the National Education Association of which it is a well-esteemed department.

It seems reasonably clear that the association demonstrated a strong inclination for identification with education from the very beginning. At the founding meeting in 1885, the list of topics to be considered included methods of teaching, a comparison of the German, American, and English systems, and normal classes. Dudley Sargent of Harvard asked who, where, and what physical educators were to teach. T.J. Wilkie of the Brooklyn Y.M.C.A. declared that normal classes were an imperative necessity because of the continuous and urgent demands for trained teachers, and Reverend Edward Anderson of Norwalk, Connecticut urged foundation work during the childhood years. At the 1886 conference, W.C. Joslin spoke on "Physical Training of Public School Children" and decried the fact that so many schools failed to provide time for calisthenics. He called for the physical training of boys and girls so that they could grow up "lithe, free-limbed, erect and joyous, moving with the grace, ease and elasticity which we attribute to the young gods."

In 1887, the association adopted a resolution recommending inclusion of physical culture classes in school programs. This resolution was, in fact, the first ever adopted by the association and contained an ambitious provision to present the resolution to all the boards of education in the United States. Later it was moved that the resolution also be presented to the National Social Science Association, the American Teachers' Association, and the American Educational Society. In part, the resolution noted that physical training was "a most essential factor in the education of the child with reference to his intellectual, moral, and physical nature." The resolution on physical education was presented to the conference by C.G. Rathman of the North American Turnerbund of St. Louis and was unanimously adopted.

Several years later, Luther Gulick proposed the formation of a committee to decide upon a suitable degree program for the profession and to actually propose a course of study to be approved by the association. Gulick's proposal for such an important committee was preceded by his paper at the same conference in 1890 titled "Physical Education—A New Profession." The 1899 conference of the association, hailed as the first truly national convention because of the membership represented, chose as its theme "Physical Training in the Educational Curriculum." Topics discussed at the conference included certification standards for teachers, compulsory physical education in the schools, and the need for more and better training schools to ensure increased production of well-prepared teachers of physical education. The 1899 conference also saw establishment of the Committee of Fifteen which, for several years, was to work for more adequate recognition of the value of physical education in the public schools. The 1909 conference repeated the 1899 theme and emphasized "Physical Education in the Public School Curriculum" as an issue of utmost concern. In 1913, the rebellious Middle West Society of Physical Education and Hygiene adopted a theme of "Professional Training of Physical Educators." The 1914 American Physical Education Association convention in St. Louis had an almost identical theme of "Preparation of Teachers of Physical Education."

Such activities of the association certainly support the thesis that inclusion of physical education programs in school curricula was an early and important objective. Certain events outside the American Physical Education Association, however, were probably more important factors in contributing to the rapid expansion of physical education programs in the public schools. One of these developments seemingly had its origin at the 1880 convention of the German Turnvereine held in Indianapolis, at which the organization decided to work toward the introduction of physical education in the public schools of the country. Prior to this time, the Turnvereine limited its membership to those of German descent and employed the German language in virtually all of its activities. As a result, some negative sentiment developed against such a German-American sect within a liberty-conscious American society; another outcome was that Turner activities were largely unknown outside the membership circle. Soon afterwards, however, agitation by its members was largely responsible for the establishment of physical education programs in the cities of Kansas City, Chicago, Davenport, Cleveland, St. Louis, and Sandusky. Between 1885 and 1890 each of these cities established physical education as a regular school activity and hired prominent graduates of the Turner-sponsored Normal College of the American Gymnastic Union.

The first state law prescribing public school physical training was passed in Ohio largely as a result of the vigorous efforts by Turners. Coupled with concurrent efforts by local teachers' associations and societies affiliated with the American Physical Education Association, Turner efforts were also evident in most of the eight states passing legislation concerning compulsory physical education between 1915 and 1918. The year 1918 saw the establishment of the National Physical Education Service, which was to exert an important influence throughout the country in efforts to pass state legislation in favor of compulsory physical education in the schools.

Under the auspices of the Playground and Recreation Association of America (later called the National Recreation Association), the National Physical Education Service acted to educate the general public concerning the value of universal physical education programs. The service worked persuasively and successfully, providing copies of model laws, sending special representatives to lobby for legislation, and helping to develop efficient programs of physical education in the schools after legislation had been passed. Between 1919 and 1925, twenty-two more states passed legislation favorable to universal physical education. The National Physical Education Service was instrumental, both directly and indirectly, in helping to mold a favorable public opinion toward physical education and promoting legislation in each of these states. Such successful efforts soon resulted in a swift demand for qualified teachers, and during the years from 1920 to 1927 the number of schools in the United States offering professional preparation in physical education jumped from 80 to 150.

Contacts by the Physical Education Association with professional education itself were also visible at a very early time. One of the original founders of the Association for the Advancement of Physical Education, E.M. Hartwell, conducted a survey on physical education in the United States for the United States Bureau of Education that was published in 1885. Later, by invitation of the National Education Association, Hartwell was to serve as chairman of a department conference on hygiene and physical education at the Chicago World's Fair. The National Education Association had also formally recognized physical education as an acceptable subject in a school curriculum in its 1891 *Proceedings*. After some serious consideration of affiliation with the Playground Association of America and the American School Hygiene Association, the American Physical Education Association finally consummated its ties with education by becoming a department in the National Education Association in 1937. The name of the organization was also changed at that time to the American Association for Health and Physical Education, at last giving formal recognition to a health theme with which it had long been involved.

As efforts by the association and other interested agencies to implant school programs of physical education showed signs of success, the problem of supplying such programs with capable teachers grew proportionately. It became obvious very quickly that implicit in the rather prolonged and concerted efforts to initiate such programs was acceptance of the need and obligation to consider optimum programs for the preparation of well-qualified teachers. In the very early days of physical education, directors of gymnasiums came from many diverse backgrounds, a situation that could no longer be tolerated if the advancement of physical education was to continue in acceptable channels. Soon physical educators were coming from two major sources, medical schools or proprietary-type normal training schools with no collegiate (and hence no academic) affiliation. Only Oberlin College with a one-year Normal Course in Physical Training for Women even came close to claiming true academic recognition at the collegiate level. Most of the textbooks dealing with the history of these early developments in professional training have leaned rather heavily upon Delphine Hanna's article "Present Status of Physical Training in Normal Schools" which appeared in the *American Physical Education Review* 8: 293-297; 1903. Tables 2.1 and 2.2 contain summaries of the normal school training programs and summer schools of physical training as compiled by Miss Hanna in 1902-1903.

Although not included in Miss Hanna's survey, credit for the earliest formal preparation of physical education teachers in America is usually given to Dio Lewis, who opened his Normal Institute for Physical Education in 1861. The first course lasted from July 5, 1861 to commencement exercises on the 5th of September, with seven men and seven women completing the course of study. Lewis' public gymnasium, open to men, women, and children, at 20 Essex Street in Boston was the site of his Normal Institute and, as was the custom with later schools of this type, could boast of a distinguished faculty. In addition to Dio Lewis, who served as Professor of Gymnastics, the faculty included three medical doctors: Thomas H. Hoskins, Professor of Anatomy; Josiah Curtis, Professor of Physiology; and Walter Channing, Professor of Hygiene (4, pages 260, 261). Dio Lewis and his biographer are said to have disagreed on how many students actually completed a full course of study at the school. Lewis stated that more than 250 persons had earned a diploma, while his biographer indicated the number to be 421 men and women. In 1868 the institute closed after having offered ten-week courses starting each January and July, and Lewis devoted himself to other pursuits until his death in 1886.

Following the demise of the Normal Institute for Physical Education in 1868, a decided lull in the preparation of physical education teachers occurred. Only the German, Turner-sponsored Normal School of the North American Gymnastic Union existed so far as formal preparation of the teachers was concerned, and its influence was not of great proportions. Throughout its early years the location of the school jumped about from New York City (1866-1867, 1869) to Chicago (1871) and back to New York (1872-1873) before finally settling in Milwaukee for an extended stay from 1875 to 1888. Because it was primarily committed to the preparation of leaders for the Turnvereine, its activities were largely unknown to all but those within the organization. Sargent's establishment of his Sargent Normal School of Physical Training in 1881 broke the dry spell and marked the beginning of a rather rapid growth in the number of both normal schools and summer schools of physical training as evidenced by the data in Hanna's report of 1903 (see Tables 2.1 and 2.2).

Most of the normal and summer school programs for the preparation of physical education teachers followed the precedent set by Dio Lewis by utilizing distinguished professors of anatomy, physiology, hygiene, and medicine as instructors. The Harvard Summer School of Physical Education, for example, offered theory courses in anthropometry, applied anatomy, personal hygiene, physical diagnosis, physiology, prescription of exercise, and treatment of spinal curvature during its 1888 session. Of the three physicians assisting Sargent in the teaching of theory courses, one finds the name Dr. Edward H. Bradford of the Harvard Medical School (10, page 408). Throughout its years of operation, the Summer School was noted for the quality of its faculty in both theory courses and practical work. According to Van Wyck, who wrote a concise history of the Harvard Summer School of Physical Education, Dudley Sargent firmly believed that a successful teacher of physical

Table 2.1

Location	Name of institution	When established	Length of course	Name of director
Milwaukee, Wisconsin	Normal School of the North American Gymnastic Union	New York City, 1886-9 Chicago, 1871 New York City, 1872-3 Milwaukee, 1875-88 Indianapolis, 1889-91 Milwaukee, 1891	10 months	Geo. Wittich
Cambridge, Massachusetts	The Sargent Normal School of Physical Training	1881	1881-1902, 2 years 1902, 3 years	D.A. Sargent, A.M., M.D.
New Haven, Connecticut	The New Haven Normal School of Gymnastics	1885-92, Brooklyn Normal School of Physical Education 1892-1900, The Anderson Normal School of Gymnastics 1901, The New Haven Normal School of Gymnastics	2 years Graduate Courses in Massage and Medical Gymnastics	E.H. Arnold, M.D.
Springfield, Massachusetts	The International Y.M.C.A. Training School	1886	3 years	J.H. McCurdy, M.D.
Oberlin, Ohio	Oberlin College, Normal Course in Physical Training for Women	1886	1886-92, 1 year 1892-1900, 2 years 1900, 4 years	Delphine Hanna, A.M., M.D.
Boston, Massachusetts	Boston Normal School of Gymnastics	1889	2 years	Miss A.M. Homans
Boston, Massachusetts	The Posse Gymnasium	1890	1890-2, 1 year 1892-7, 1 and 2 years 1897, 2 years	Baroness Posse
Chicago, Illinois	The Secretarial Institute and Training School of Y.M.C.A.	1890	2 years	H.F. Kallenberg, M.D.
New Orleans, Louisiana	Department of Normal Physical Education, Newcomb College	1892	2 years	Miss C.G. Baer
Philadelphia, Pennsylvania	Philadelphia Normal School of Physical Training	1895	2 years	H.S. Wingert, M.D.
Milwaukee, Wisconsin	The Burnham Normal School of Physical Training	1895	2 years	Miss S.M. Burnham
New York City, New York	New York Normal School of Physical Education	1898	2 years	W.L. Savage, M.D.

[a]Data from Delphine Hanna. Present status of physical training in normal schools. *American Physical Education Review* **8**: 293-297; 1903.

Normal Schools of Physical Training in the United States as Reported in 1903[a]

Literary requirements for entrance	No. of teachers employed	No. of students enrolled 1902-3		No. of graduates		No. of graduates teaching		Certificate diploma or degree
		Male	Female	Male	Female	Male	Female	
High school diploma	7	8	9	216	4	159	—	Diploma
High school diploma	20	—	74	—	215	—	172	Diploma
High school diploma or equivalent	12	2	36	6	208	6	156	Diploma
High school diploma or equivalent	15	45	—	83	—	64	—	Diploma
College entrance requirements	4 Special 27 from College Faculty	—	29	1-yr. course 2-yr. course 4-yr. course	10 35 1	—	25	A.B. degree and diploma normal course
High school diploma or equivalent Probation 1 month	18	2	66	7	255	7	155	Diploma
High school diploma or equivalent	18	2	38	11	200	11	140	Diploma
High school diploma or equivalent	5	8	—	27	—	23	—	Diploma
Graduate academic courses	4	—	9	—	24	—	10	Certificate
High school diploma or equivalent	12	14	12	14	39	12	20	—
High school diploma or equivalent	3	—	12	—	12	—	10	Certificate
High school diploma or equivalent	13	—	38	—	27	—	27	Diploma

Table 2.1 (Cont.)

Location	Name of institution	When established	Length of course	Name of director
Berkeley, California	University of California	1898	4 years	W.E. Magee
Lincoln, Nebraska	University of Nebraska	1899	4 years	Raymond G. Clapp, M.D.
Bloomsburg, Pennsylvania	State Normal School	1902	2 years	A.K. Aldinger, M.D.
New York City, New York	Columbia University, Teachers College, Department of Physical Education	1903	2 years	T.D. Wood, A.M., M.D.

education not only needed to "possess ability as a performer" but ". . . that it was important for teachers of physical training to have a thorough knowledge of the elements of anatomy and physiology and great emphasis was therefore placed on instruction in these subjects" (10, page 415).

At least for the period of time covered by Miss Hanna's report, all programs for the preparation of physical education instructors gave attention to an obviously needed competency—the ability to perform and teach specified exercises and physical activities. However, in addition to such traditional practitioner skills, a satisfactory background in anatomy, physiology, hygiene, and elements of medicine was also considered important. Then, as now, it was clearly apparent to most of those concerned with teacher preparation that practices in physical education had to be based upon an adequate foundation of knowledge and theory. Curricula of physical education showed an evident emphasis upon physical training, posture, remedial exercise, and exercise for its body building and health-giving effects. Professional preparation of teachers to handle such responsibilities attempted to produce individuals with proper backgrounds in physical training regimens, remedial exercise prescription, and a health-oriented philosophy toward physical education.

Around the turn of the century, another factor emerged which had rather significant effects upon physical education. A comprehensive treatment of the impact of this factor upon the profession is given by Lewis (5). According to Lewis, the growth of athletics had a profound effect not only upon school-sponsored programs, but upon the nature of

Normal Schools of Physical Training in the United States as Reported in 1903[a]

Literary requirements for entrance	No. of teachers employed	No. of students enrolled 1902-3		No. of graduates		No. of graduates teaching		Certificate diploma or degree
		Male	Female	Male	Female	Male	Female	
College entrance requirements	8	2	9	15	21	12	17	Bachelor degree and certificate
College entrance requirements	—	4	16	—	—	—	—	Bachelor degree and certificate
High school diploma or equivalent	7	8	—	—	—	—	—	Diploma
—	—	—	—	—	—	—	—	Bachelor diploma in physical education (as work develops, courses for graduate degrees will be developed)

professional preparation of physical educators as well. Not only did the popularity of athletics change the content of physical education service curricula in the schools, it was equally responsible for "a philosophical revolution" as "educationists replaced medical men in positions of leadership."

After a faltering student-sponsored beginning, around the turn of the century athletics emerged as a phenomenon of such overwhelming potency that it swept aside traditional academic resistance against its presence in educational institutions. Public sentiment virtually forced the schools to provide a base of operations for athletics. One of the direct effects of such public support of athletics was the widespread adoption of sport activities in the school curricula of physical education. From a remedial exercise and calisthenic focus in 1900, the school curriculum evolved, by 1930, into a program that was practically all games and sports. Even though marked differences existed in specific types of professional preparation in physical education, the public as well as school administrators could not (and did not) differentiate between an athletic specialist and a physical educator. A degree in history, mathematics, or the like, coupled with athletic experience and competency, was deemed sufficient preparation for the coach of athletic sports in the schools. Although both athletic specialists and physical educators might complain about each other's lack of professional competency, an uneasy but tolerable coexistence was not impossible in the public school setting.

At the college level, however, the residency of coaches in departments of physical education caused more than just amazement at the imposed shotgun wedding of physical education and athletics. In addition to the

Table 2.2

Summer Schools of Physical Training in the United States as Reported in 1903[a]

Location	Name of school	When established	Length of course in weeks	Name of director	Literary requirements for entrance	No. of theoretical courses	No. of practical courses	No. of teachers employed	No. of students enrolled 1902 Male	Female
Chautauqua, New York	Chautauqua School of Physical Education	1886	6	J.W. Seaver, M.D. W.G. Anderson, M.D.	High school diploma or equivalent	8	15	10 Faculty 16 Instructors	23	55
Cambridge, Massachusetts	Harvard Summer School of Physical Education	1887	5	D.A. Sargent, A.M., M.D.	High school diploma or equivalent	4	4	44	40	90
Bay View, Michigan	Bay View Summer University	1887	5	—	None	Mixed (theory and practice in same lesson)		2	40	35
Cottage City, Massachusetts	Martha's Vineyard Summer Institute	—	5	Miss Charlotte Carne	—	—	1	1	—	50
Lake Geneva, Wisconsin	Secretarial Institute and Training School of Y.M.C.A.	1889	4	H.F. Kallenberg, M.D.	High school diploma or equivalent	9	9	8	83	—
Boston, Massachusetts	Posse Gymnasium Summer School	1890	4	Baroness Posse	Good general education	5	6	2	—	8
New Haven, Connecticut	New Haven Normal School of Gymnastics	1885	5 Med. 1 Play 4 Gym.	E.H. Arnold, M.D.	Normal school graduates	4	1 4	1 3	—	11

Location	Institution	Year		Director	Entrance requirement					
Monteagle, Tennessee	Monteagle Summer School of Physical Education	1898	5	C.G. Baer	High School diploma or equivalent	9	10	4	1	10
New York City, New York	Summer Session Columbia University	1899	6	J.C. Egbert W.L. Savage, M.D.	None	Mixed (theory and practice in same lesson)		5	20	68
Ypsilanti, Michigan	State Normal College	1895	6	Mrs. Fannie Cheever Burton	High school diploma or equivalent	4	4	1	—	130
Berkeley, California	University of California	1900	6	W.E. Magee	None	—	2	2	25	80
Ann Arbor, Michigan	University of Michigan	1900	—	C.T. Teetzel	—	—	—	—	—	—
Madison, Wisconsin	University of Wisconsin	1898	6	J.C. Elsom, M.D.	High school diploma or equivalent	3	3	3	15	10
Peru, Nebraska	State Normal School	—	—	Mrs. E. Graham	—	—	—	—	—	—
Terre Haute, Indiana	Indiana State Normal School	—	—	J.P. Kemmell Miss E.M. Love	—	—	—	—	—	—

[a]Data from Delphine Hanna. Present status of physical training in normal schools. *American Physical Education Review*, **8**: 293-297; 1903.

new glamour and spectacular budgets, the appearance of athletics was responsible for a remarkable transformation in the faculty composition of physical education departments. Reflecting the philosophy of health, calisthenics, and remedial exercise, in 1908 almost two-thirds of all the directors of college physical education departments possessed a medical degree. This number dropped to 7 percent by the 1920's. One study showed that 199 college directors had been appointed primarily on the basis of their athletic credentials. Also, less than one-fifth of the directors sampled in one survey had majored in physical education at the undergraduate level, and about 85 percent of another sample of college directors were successful football coaches. In Savage's study (8) of 63 head football coaches at leading collegiate institutions, only 2 of the 55 who enjoyed faculty status in departments of physical education had a bachelor's degree in physical education.

Thus, as physician directors of college physical education departments declined in numbers, they were replaced by individuals competent in athletics, regardless of their area of formal academic preparation. Although professionally trained and oriented physical educators were present on such staffs, athletic coaches possessed the largest amount of influence and control. Such athletic affluence was bound to have some influence on the future professional preparation of physical educators. Collegiate institutions were, by 1930, rapidly replacing summer schools and proprietary-type normal schools as the more esteemed route for professional preparation. The "ideal image" of a physical educator in such college departments was now to be influenced by the clamor of school administrators for expert athletic coaches and the receptive philosophy of athletically oriented directors in control of professional preparation departments. Because of such influences, Lewis suggested in his penetrating analysis, programs for the professional preparation of physical educators had become congruent with the preparation of athletic coaches. Indeed, several observers have concluded that by 1930, the major emphasis in undergraduate major programs was definitely upon coaching courses and sport skill curricula.

Only a comprehensive treatment of the history of professional training in physical education could do justice to the complex task that faced those charged with the responsibility for decision making about teacher preparation curricula. Our purpose, however, has been only to show that strong motivation for an association with education existed right from the very inception of an organization dedicated to the advancement of physical education. The material selected for consideration argued the thesis that a general adoption of professional education standards for the preparation of physical educators resulted due to (a) the successful implantation of universal physical education laws and the resultant obligation to meet teacher certification standards, and (b) the tremendous rise in demand for coaches of athletic sports and the parallel growth of athletic influence in professional departments of physical education.

ORIGINS OF A SCIENTIFIC BASIS FOR PHYSICAL EDUCATION

Strong sentiment existed from the very beginning of the Association for the Advancement of Physical Education to link physical education directly to education. No more proof of this thesis is needed than that provided in the preceding section and its account of early conference themes and the explicitly stated purposes of the association. The motivation for involvement and identification with the education profession has, indeed, been one of the few enduring traits characteristic of association activities from its beginning to the present time. From the very beginning as well, however, there was evidence that more than just an unimportant minority in the association was working for the development of physical education on a path parallel to that of medicine and the biological sciences. A number of important leaders among the association membership seemed to be suggesting at least a dual path of educational and biological emphasis for physical education. Although never having been completely abandoned, emphasis upon a biological science foundation eventually became displaced as a major force in physical education. Instead, educational aspects assumed a dominant role and the idea of a scientific basis for physical education lost its vigor and became relegated to a status of secondary importance. Education, in effect, became the primary basis for physical education and preparation for physical education became synonymous with preparation for education. In this section an account will be given briefly concerning the origins of a scientific basis for physical education.

To begin this brief account of the origin of a scientific emphasis in physical education, it seems only fitting to start with Edward Hitchcock, who is credited with being the "first physical educator in America to apply the science of anthropometry to physical education" (6, page 203). The claim that Hitchcock was thus the first scientific worker in physical education merits acceptance on the basis of several convincing arguments: (1) He was the first individual in the United States to have held professorial rank in physical education at a collegiate-level academic institution; (2) he was the first officially recognized director of a physical education program in a college in the United States; and (3) he was undoubtedly the first among physical educators to systematically collect anthropometric data for scientific purposes and to receive recognition for such efforts. Accordingly, it seems reasonable to accept the conclusion that Hitchcock "laid the foundation for the scientific approach and investigation by physical educators of that early era, and, by so doing, he contributed materially to the establishment of physical education as a profession" (11, page 167).

It should be pointed out, however, that the practice of taking anthropometric measurements before and after a schedule of physical training as a means of assessing improvement in the physique was not an idea uniquely attributable to Hitchcock. Although some historians allow that Hitchcock may have become acquainted with the value of anthropometric measurements during his trip to England and contact with Archibald Maclaren (9, page 416), it seems more probable that Hitchcock merely formalized a practice already widely used in the United States. Such a practice is probably as old as any among the ranks of strength and physique enthusiasts, and evidence that body measurements were commonly taken in gymnasiums prior to Hitchcock is quite bountiful. An article written by Thomas W. Higginson appeared in the March 1861 issue of the *Atlantic Monthly*. Under the title of "Gymnastics" the article commented upon several aspects of physical training practices in gymnasiums of the era. In one particular section, Higginson states:

> The first effect of gymnastic exercise is almost always to increase the size of the arms and the chest and newcomers may commonly be known by their frequent recourse to the tape-measure. The average increase among the students of Harvard University during the first three months of gymnasium was nearly two inches in the chest, more than one inch in the upper arm, and more than half an inch in the fore-arm.

Since both Hitchcock's career at Amherst College and his extended collection of anthropometric data began in 1861, it is obvious that he was not the first to think of using such measurements to assess the effects of physical training programs. The comments by Higginson just quoted indicate that the assessment of anthropometric changes was quite a common practice in gymnasiums of the era. Indeed, the acclaim bestowed upon Dudley Sargent for his own anthropometric data collection efforts at Harvard must be similarly tempered inasmuch as such a practice was being followed well before his arrival in 1879. However, most authorities classify the anthropometric data collection efforts by Hitchcock and Sargent as the first systematic measurement work in physical education, and they are rightly pointed to as the first research efforts of any formal nature by physical educators. By 1900, emphasis upon anthropometric work had diminished and interest in strength measurement absorbed most of the data-collecting researchers of the period. Babbitt noted in 1903 that so far as anthropometric physical examinations were concerned, "we are possibly wasting too much time in the endless routine of an almost clerical character." He must have spoken for the majority of the profession for even Edward Hitchcock agreed with him (1, page 282).

These efforts by Hitchcock and Sargent for the collection and subsequent use of anthropometric data were by no means isolated examples of the desire to base physical education on a sound scientific foundation. At the organizational meeting of the American Association for the Advancement of Physical Education, for example, the desire to advance scientific knowledge was shown by the formation of a committee of the association on statistics and measurements. By 1891, the association had seen fit to bestow honorary membership status upon several individuals respected for their scientific accomplishments: H.D. Bowditch, M.D., a noted physiologist and dean of the Harvard Medical School; and two pioneers in anthropometry from England, F.S. Galton and Charles Roberts. Galton was a friend of Edward Hitchcock and presented a paper on anthropometry at the Boston convention held in 1889. It was fitting, of course, that two individuals in anthropometry were so honored since the majority of scientific work being done in physical education in the United States was in the same area. More importantly, however, is the implicit affirmation of the value and need for scientific contributions and research efforts that the bestowing of honorary membership status represented.

One of the more prominent individuals in the profession to speak out for a scientific emphasis was Thomas D. Wood. Noted more for his efforts as a pioneer health educator and innovator of a system of natural gymnastics, Wood nevertheless made one of the first and most explicit pleas for a science of physical education. In later years (1901-1932) at Columbia University, his desire to establish a science of physical education apparently waned and he devoted his energies to problems of teacher preparation and broader aspects of educational methodology. During his early years at Stanford, however, he was one of the first to campaign for a scientific emphasis in physical education. In a speech given at the International Congress of Education at Chicago in 1893, Wood began by stating that: "The great need in physical education today is the scientific spirit." Shortly thereafter he stated his idea about a science of physical education:

There is today, in an embryonic and crude form, a science of physical education; and for the sake of the honorable future, the idea of the science should exist first in the minds of the profession, and then in the minds of laity. The science of physical education should take the place of the so-called systems of physical training. We can conceive of a system or series of definite exercises, arranged to produce a desired effect upon a given person, or upon a class of persons; but the only adequate name for a department of human knowledge and of research is that of science (12).

Other leaders in the association besides Wood saw the need for the development of a sound scientific foundation upon which to build the future of physical education. One of these was a tireless worker by the name of Luther Halsey Gulick of the Y.M.C.A. Training School at Springfield, Massachusettts. Gulick was one of the first to speak out on the need to give careful consideration to programs for the preparation of physical educators and to suggest that a physical educator was more than just a skilled technician or teacher. In an early article entitled "Physical Education: A New Profession," which appeared in the 1890 *Proceedings of the American Association for the Advancement of Physical Education*, he declared that the current modes of entry then being utilized for admission to the field of physical education were inappropriate. A medical physician, Gulick noted, was inadequately prepared to conduct educative gymnastics properly. In a similar manner, the study of psychology and pedagogy alone would not provide an adequate basis upon which to understand and conduct activities which were so involved with physiology and medicine.

Gulick went on to state that the opportunity for new and worthy scientific investigation was available in physical education more than in any other profession. Because the scientific aspects of physical education were so poorly developed, he believed it to be an obligation of every physical educator to "expect to do scientific work which will be not merely original with him, but original to the world." Such original scientific work was necessary in order to provide an adequate scientific foundation "for the use of those who come afterward." An idea such as this, spoken over three-quarters of a century ago, displayed an insight into the problem of professional training that is as poignant today as it was then. Nowhere is Gulick's insistence upon the obligation to conduct scientific research of an original nature better appreciated than in his founding of the original Academy of Physical Education. In order to qualify for membership in the academy, an original piece of research had to be produced that was pertinent to the problems of physical education. In addition, members were further obligated to report a new piece of original research each year or suffer loss of membership in the academy. The major, if not sole, purpose of the academy was to promote an increase in the scientific investigation of problems in physical education (see Chapter 5, pages 143-148, for a discussion of the academy and Gulick's activities).

It seems clear that Gulick as well as others were concerned about the manner in which the preparation of physical educators was being accomplished. If, as Gulick claimed, neither an excellent medical education nor the study of psychology and pedagogy was worthy of consideration as a model for professional preparation, what, then, was to be acclaimed as an optimum program? His dissatisfaction with either of the two commonly used modes of entry into physical education and the position forwarded that only a combination of essential talents in these two channels could suffice for a true profession of physical education was thus clearly expressed. Gulick, furthermore, did not look upon the Y.M.C.A. Training School with which he was affiliated as "an academic institution" (3, page 165). This attitude, plus his statements about the inadequacy of the study of psychology and pedagogy alone, would seem to indicate that he did not hold much hope that an ideal program of professional preparation would come out of the normal training schools, for which he lacked high respect. The question of whether or not a medical degree was an essential requirement for physical educators remained a controversial issue for many years, as did the wisdom of placing the future of the profession in the hands of normal training schools.

Let us now return our attention to Thomas D. Wood, whom we have considered previously, and his contention that the development of a science of physical education was essential to wholesome growth of the profession. Wood not only professed such a belief, but, in 1892, was able to install successfully an academic four-year degree program at Stanford University leading to an A.B. degree in physical training and hygiene. For some reason, this academic program was not reported in the survey conducted by Delphine Hanna in 1902-1903 (see Table 2.1). In defense of Miss Hanna's work, it must be noted that such an omission was likely excusable when one considers the communication problem that must have existed at that time. Less excusable, however, is the fact that this program has not been acknowledged in standard reference texts on the history of physical education even though the existence of the program was reported in our own professional literature in 1939 (2). DeGroot's article appeared well before the publication dates of many of our standard history texts, and it would seem that entirely too much dependence has been placed by historians upon Miss Hanna's survey as an adequate and comprehensive summary of early professional preparation programs.

The degree program developed at Stanford University by Wood is of special and important interest for several reasons. First, it effectively dispels the idea that the University of California in 1898, the University of Nebraska in 1899, and Oberlin College in 1900 were the only academic institutions offering four-year bachelor degree programs in physical education. Second, the program at Stanford University affords an insight into the manner in which a proponent of the science of physical education set about to accomplish such an objective. In addition, the Stanford program was under the direction of a man whose roots and allegiance were strong in both health and physical education. Information about the program can thus allow some opportunity to assess the means by which a combined health education and physical education major was to be produced. Lastly, if neither a medical education nor a teacher education was deemed adequate for a professional preparation paradigm, then one could evaluate the worthwhileness of a combination of such emphases into one academic degree program.

A Department of Physical Training and Hygiene existed at Leland Stanford Junior University from its very inception in 1891. In addition to

Professor Wood, two other staff members were listed in the department: Miss Ellen L. Lowell, a Sargent School graduate who was also in charge of physical training for women; and Walter O. Black, a Springfield Y.M.C.A. Training School product. The 1891-1893 *Register* of the University showed the following courses to be available in the department:

(1) Hygiene. a. Personal and General Hygiene. b. Sanitary Science. c. Treatment in emergency, or "first aid to the injured." Two hours a week. Complete course each semester. Professor Wood. Open to all students.

(2) Physical Training. Three exercises a week, through the year. Professor Wood, Miss Lowell, and Mr. Black.

Open to all students, under the advice of the medical director. Credit will be given for systematic prescribed work in physical training as for laboratory and shop work, three hours of exercise to be equivalent to one hour's work of recitation; the possible three exercises a week to be taken on three separate days, arranged according to the work of the student. Individual and class work, with and without apparatus.

(3) Physical Training and Hygiene. a. Hygiene: Personal and General Hygiene; Sanitary Science; School Hygiene; Physical Conditions of Childhood. Two hours a week, first semester. b. Theory of Physical Training: Bodily Mechanics; Physiology of Exercise; Anthropometry; Charting and Tabulation of Statistics; Examination of Special Sense Organs; History of Gymnastics and Description of Gymnastic Systems; Medical Gymnastics. Two hours a week, second semester. Professor Wood. c. Practice in Physical Training: Individual and Class Work; Developing Appliances; Calisthenics; Swedish and German Exercises; Health Gymnastics, with and without Apparatus; Gymnastic and Athletic Games. Five exercises a week, through the year. Professor Wood, Miss Lowell, and Mr. Black.

Intended for those who expect to teach these subjects (page 73).

One interesting feature of the first year's program at Stanford was that it showed a clear separation of course work into a "service" program and a "professional" program. Thus, course (1) in hygiene was open to all students while the hygiene course (3), Physical Training and Hygiene, was "intended for those who expect to teach." The content of each of these courses was similar in many respects and the differentiation appears to be one that is recognized today primarily through the titles of service or professional course emphasis. The courses made available for the school year 1892-1893 were considerably modified, with more courses being offered for an in-depth study. The *Stanford Register* for 1892-1893 listed three courses open to all students [courses (1), (2), and (3)] while course (4) in School Hygiene was "open only to students in the Department of Education and others who expect to teach." Thus, in addition to a service and a professional major-course concept, the idea of a professional theory course designed for nonmajors was introduced. The four courses open to all students or to nonmajors who expect to teach were:

(1) Gymnastic Exercises. Individual and class work, with and without apparatus. Three hours a week, through the year. Professor Wood, Miss Lowell, and Mr. Black.

Open to all students, under the advice of the medical director. One hour of credit will be given for systematic prescribed work in physical exercise, and three exercises a week to be taken on separate days arranged according to the work of the student.

(2) Personal Hygiene. Two hours a week, through each semester. Complete course each semester. Professor Wood.

Open to all students. Course 2 is designed to give the student practical knowledge upon matters pertaining to the care of the health, and treatment in emergencies, or "First Aid to the Injured."

(3) Advanced Hygiene. Two hours a week, second semester. Professor Wood.

Open to all students who have completed course 2. Course 3 will take up the study of general hygiene and sanitary science. Students will prepare papers upon assigned topics.

(4) School Hygiene. Two hours a week, first semester. Professor Wood.

Open only to students in the Department of Education and others who expect to teach. The subjects studied will include: physiology and hygiene of the nervous system; personal hygiene of school children; location, architecture, and surroundings of schoolhouses; lighting, heating, ventilation, and furniture of schoolrooms; hygiene of instruction; school diseases; physical training in schools, and the examinations and measurements of children.

It can be seen from the descriptions of these four courses that another distinctive feature appeared in the Stanford program, the idea of prerequisites for a course. Course (2) was an official prerequisite for course (3) and, although not so stated, it would appear from the course numbering that courses (2) and (3) were both prerequisites for course (4). By far the most distinctive feature of the 1892-1893 department description, however, was the fact that an A.B. degree in physical training and hygiene was available. In addition to courses (2), (3), and (4) described above, the following courses were designed for degree candidates in the department and "for special students in this department":

(5) General Anatomy and Physiology. (See course 1 in Physiology.)

(6) Animal Physiology. (See course 2 in Physiology.)

(7) Applied Anatomy and Physiology. Two hours a week, through the year. Professor Wood.

Course (7) takes up the study of human anatomy and physiology from the standpoint of physical training.

(8) Physical Education. Two hours a week, second semester. Professor Wood.

Course (8) includes the special physiology of exercise and bodily mechanics, history of physical training, and the study of the various "systems of physical culture."

(9) Physical Training. Six hours of exercise a week, through the year. Professor Wood, Miss Lowell, and Mr. Black.

Course (9) includes individual and class exercises; use of developing and other apparatus; calisthenics; light and heavy gymnastics; health and medical gymnastics, with and without apparatus; gymnastic and athletic games.

(10) Special Courses of instruction and training are laid for advanced and special students according to the needs and qualifications of each individual. Such courses include instruction and practical work in anthropometry, charting and tabulation of statistics, physical examinations, diagnosis, special tests, prescription of exercise, medical gymnastics, fitting of gymnasiums, etc. Special investigations in the laboratory and gymnasium are to be taken up by advanced students as rapidly as they are able to do such work. This includes investigations into the physiology of special exercises, testing of physical conditions and specific effects of various exercises upon the nervous system, heart, and lungs, and the various bodily functions. Professor Wood.

Courses (5) and (6) were given in the Department of Physiology and Histology. Course (5), General Anatomy and Physiology, met for two lecture hours a week and had a laboratory requirement of seven and a half hours each week throughout the school year. It was designed to provide a scientific foundation for advanced course work in the department. Course (6), Animal Physiology, met for a one-hour lecture each week and had a laboratory requirement of five hours a week throughout the year. It was described as "an experimental course in physiology based upon Foster's *Physiology* as the text." Special note should be made of the fact that course (8) included a study of the various bodily processes. Besides being ample evidence of the desire to develop a scientific attitude among students majoring in physical education and aid in the development of a scientific foundation for physical education practices, the program shared an emphasis with a program at Harvard University which will be considered shortly.

An examination of the contents of this very early "major program" for health and physical education is of interest on several counts. In addition to the obvious value of studying the Stanford program because of its historical significance, a comparison of courses and semester-hour allocations can be made with similar programs for undergraduate majors in vogue today. The Stanford program is easily seen to have included many courses which are still being offered today and was definitely designed with the idea of preparing a well-qualified teacher of physical education. Even with a strong commitment to professional preparation of a teacher, however, it possessed a distinctive scientific flavor. Based upon present day practices of semester hour valuation, the program required six semester hours in the hygiene area; four semester hours in applied anatomy and physiology; and two semester hours in course (8) which emphasized history of physical training, a study of various exercise systems, and special exercise topics. The courses in the Department of Physiology and Histology, General Anatomy and Physiology, and Animal Physiology, amounted to a sixteen semester hour requirement in the science area. Only course (9) in physical training can be classified as an activity class and its six hour a week requirement for the entire year gave four semester hours credit. Course (10), special courses, had no actual number of credit hours listed. Class schedules noted that hours and days would be arranged, however, and the nature of the course makes it reasonable to estimate that it would carry about three semester hours credit.

A breakdown of semester hour credits thus shows that the Stanford program required six hours in health, sixteen in a basic science, six in physical education theory courses, four of physical activity work, and about three for special work of an investigative nature. In all, approximately 35 semester hours were required, of which almost half were in a basic science. Notably absent from the program were courses commonly required today in administration, separate curriculum courses at the elementary, junior and senior high, and college levels, philosophy, recreation, child growth and development, and specific athletic coaching courses in the major sports or athletic training. The content of course (10) suggests the availability of emphasis in the area of tests and measurements. Since the physical education emphasis accounted for thirteen semester hours of credit while health required only six, it seems safe to conclude that the program was designed to produce a physical educator with a substantial health competency rather than vice versa. Although a major in the department was designated by the letters "HYG," it did not mean the degree was in hygiene. The name of the department was Hygiene and Physical Training, and majors were designated by HYG because it represented a simple means of abbreviating the department title.

Although the degree program at Stanford University was available in

1892, the first individual to graduate from the department did not do so until 1897. On Wednesday, May 26, 1897, at the Sixth Annual Commencement of Leland Stanford Junior University held in Encina Gymnasium, Walter Wells Davis of Maynard, Iowa received his Bachelor of Arts degree. His A.B. degree was awarded in Hygiene and Organic Training, as the department was then named, although alumni directory records have followed the practice of simply listing the degree as A.B., Hygiene, '97. According to the *Stanford University Alumni Directory and Ten-Year Book of 1891-1931*, Walter Wells Davis had previously earned a B.S. degree from Upper Iowa College at Fayette, Iowa in 1893. Mr. Davis, with an A.B. degree awarded in 1897, thus predated the initiation of four-year degree programs at the University of California, the University of Nebraska, and Oberlin College.

After finishing his degree at Stanford under Wood, Davis traveled across the country and completed a Ph.D. degree at Yale University in 1901. His work at Yale is probably familiar to any researcher who has ever studied the phenomenon of cross-transfer or cross-education, although it is doubtful whether anyone recognized Davis as the first degree recipient in health and physical education from Stanford University. Davis' two lengthy articles on "Researches in Cross-Education" appeared in the 1898 and 1900 volumes of *Studies from the Yale Psychological Laboratory*. Both of these articles are virtual classics in the field and have since been cited in countless research investigations as one of the earliest demonstrations of the cross-transfer phenomenon in the United States. Davis' findings were cited in three other classics in the field of cross-transfer, with lengthy discussions of his work in Scripture's article on "Cross-Education" in *Popular Science Monthly* 56: 589-596; 1900; in Wissler and Richardson's "Diffusion of the Motor Impulse" in the *Psychological Review* 7: 29-38; 1900; and in Anderson's paper on "Studies in the Effects of Physical Training," which appeared in the *American Physical Education Review* 9: 265-278; 1899.

Anderson's article stated that Davis was a member of the elective class in physical education at Yale University, indicating that Davis took some of his work in physical education while at Yale. Davis went to a position at Iowa College in Grinnell, Iowa as Director of Physical Training, and then to Lehigh University in Pennsylvania as an Associate Professor of Physical Education. He later served as Principal of Schools at Columbus, Washington and from 1916 to 1942 he was Supervisor of Health and Physical Education for the Seattle, Washington school system. In 1923, he published an article in the *Elementary School Journal* entitled "The Questionnaire Method in Health Education" and in 1930, an article entitled "Underweight Children in Seattle" in *Hygeia*. On the basis of his professional career, Davis must be said to have made successful use of his academic preparation as a health and physical education major at

Stanford University.

Wood remained at Stanford University until he accepted a position at Columbia University as Director and Professor of Hygiene and Physical Education in 1901. His stay at Stanford, however, was not without some important accomplishments. Although not listed in Hanna's survey (see Table 2.2), Wood directed a Summer School of Hygiene and Physical Training for teachers at Pacific Grove, California in July of 1894. In 1893, he had attracted to his staff Celia Duel Mosher who was destined to go on and be recognized as one of the pioneer women in the profession. That same year the name of Clark W. Hetherington was added as an assistant in the department. Although Hetherington elected to take his degree in psychology while working for Wood at Stanford and later take up work in psychology at Clark University, he eventually became one of the great leaders in the "new physical education" and established himself as an outstanding figure in American physical education. In addition, it was at Stanford University that Wood originated and helped to popularize the concept of natural gymnastics or a natural program of physical education as contrasted to the rigidly formal European gymnastic systems.

As noteworthy an accomplishment as the degree program at Stanford University was, Wood had a counterpart on the east coast who was even more imbued with the need to establish a scientific basis for physical education. This man—George Wells Fitz of Harvard University—was not only instrumental in establishing an academic four-year degree program at Harvard, but he also developed what appears to have been the first formal physical education research laboratory in the United States. Details about Fitz himself and the research laboratory at Harvard are discussed in a later chapter (see pages 173-183), but it is recommended that this later material about Fitz be read in conjunction with the information about to be presented. It is felt that only then can there be a full realization and appreciation of Fitz's activities at Harvard and his rather remarkable efforts to establish a scientific basis for physical education.

Scattered throughout the published proceedings of early association conferences are remarks by Fitz that testify to his strong scientific orientation toward the problems of physical education. In many such instances reported in the proceedings, Fitz showed himself to be an outspoken critic of the energies being expended in continual and emotion-laden arguments about which of the competing systems of physical training was the best for physical education. He said numerous times that such debates could serve no purpose until factual evidence was produced, through scientific research, for every one of the extravagant claims made by proponents of the various systems of physical training. Only with actual evidence substantiated by scientific research could any assessment of the competing systems of physical training ever be accomplished, Fitz declared, and until such evidence was available, such debates were nothing more than an exchange of opinions about facts not in evidence.

Quite often, the comments made by Fitz seemed tinged with sarcasm, impatience, and irritation. Events transpiring at the seventh annual meeting of the Association serve quite well to illustrate Fitz's attitude toward such debates and his strong argument for scientific work. The 1892 conference held in Philadelphia scheduled a discussion group to speak on the topic "What constitutes a rational and a practical course of professional traning for directors and teachers of physical training?" Dr. C.E. Ehinger of West Chester Normal School in Pennsylvania was to speak on public and private normal schools; Dr. William G. Anderson was assigned to talk on summer and Y.M.C.A. schools and gymnasiums; and Dr. George W. Fitz of Harvard was to cover colleges and universities. The panel was apparently moderated by the association president, Dr. Edward Mussey Hartwell, who was, at that time, Director of Physical Education of the Public Schools of Boston. The talks given, reactions from the floor, and Fitz's reply coming toward the end of the activities are of considerable value in exemplifying the advanced philosophy of George Wells Fitz.

The position adopted by Dr. C.E. Ehinger at the symposium was not unexpected since he represented the West Chester Normal School and was genuinely convinced of the importance of pedagogy. He declared that "normal schools are preeminently the most suitable places" for professional preparation because securing a place in the school curriculum could best be accomplished by teachers of regular subjects. Reflecting his pedagogical outlook on the trend of modern education and the prevalent whole-child philosophy, he cautioned that normal schools could not be obligated to the preparation of special teachers of gymnastics. Instead, he considered it necessary only to instruct normal school graduates well enough to "fit them to give instruction systematically" in physical training. Even then it appeared that the knotty issue of breadth versus depth in teacher training curricula was present. After further declaring that "the disciplinary value of a well regulated drill can hardly be overestimated," Ehinger deviated from his assigned topic and became enmeshed in the then current controversy over which system of physical training was best suited for physical education programs.

After Ehinger opened the door to discussion of systems of physical training with his remarks, Colonel Francis W. Parker was allowed to comment from the floor. Parker gave a rousing commentary on the value of the German system of physical training "which was born and nourished by the unrivaled pedagogical, educative spirit of German philosophers and teachers." Although Parker did not claim that the German system was the best, he did note that (1) Germany had the first claim to a science of education as well as more books on education than the United

States; (2) the German Turnen was a system of perpetual research and perpetual progress appealing to genuine students; and (3) that German Turners were in the vanguard of liberty, having saved Missouri for the Union as well as quelling riots in Cincinnati. He then modestly ended his comments by humbly asking members of the association not to make a decision as to which system of physical training was best until the German Turnen was adequately studied. Although Parker was not listed as a participant of the discussion panel, his supposedly extemporaneous talk from the floor was longer than any of the scheduled speeches. Colonel Parker, incidentally, was not an unimportant figure in the association and neither were his comments atypical of the kind of arguments used in debates on systems of physical training. At the end of the Philadelphia conference, Colonel Parker was elected one of the three vice-presidents of the association. Luther Halsey Gulick, a prominent and important leader, was one of the unsuccessful candidates for a vice-presidency.

When it came William G. Anderson's turn to speak on summer and Y.M.C.A. schools he must have felt it necessary to comment on the various systems himself. Only brief attention was given to the value of summer schools of physical education and none at all to Y.M.C.A. schools and gymnasiums. After pronouncing summer schools to be valuable even if they were too short and defending the practice of the Chautauqua summer school, which he sponsored, for awarding certificates, he spent most of his allotted time in an examination of the merits and claims of merit for Delsarte, German, and Swedish systems of physical training. He counseled wise use of any and all systems so long as they were expertly taught by enthusiastic teachers. One of the important contributions of summer schools of physical education, Anderson added, was that proponents of different systems were exposed to other systems, allowing the possibility of cross-fertilization of ideas.

At this point, the moderator disallowed a request from the floor for an opportunity to comment on Anderson's speech and called upon George W. Fitz to speak on the four-year course in physical training at Harvard University. The message that Fitz conveyed in his talk was not unlike other comments he had made at numerous other conferences. As seemed to be his style, he was blunt and made his point very quickly.* Fitz asked, "What right have we to theories?" He then proceeded to ridicule statements about the theory of physical training and the theories of different systems which had been solemnly debated. His plea was for scientific

---

*In 1896, for example, Fitz commented on all the physiological theories that had been imported with the various systems of physical training: "They are very simple, entirely logical, very superficial, delightfully fantastic, and mostly absurd." (See *Report of the Tenth Annual Meeting of the American Association for the Advancement of Physical Education*, 1896, page 178.)

work to establish the basis for physical education rather than continued efforts in making groundless assumptions about physical training systems. To Fitz, the assumptions being bandied about in arguments concerning advantages and disadvantages of various physical training systems were of no significance since none of them was based upon established fact. The degree program at Harvard University that Fitz had organized was designed to prepare teachers "who are thoroughly trained in scientific methods of work, who have fundamental knowledge which will enable them to make successful teachers of physical training."

Although textbooks on the history of physical education fail to mention the four-year program at Harvard, documents clearly show that a Department of Anatomy, Physiology, and Physical Training existed at Harvard University from 1891 until August of 1898. The department was administratively housed in the Lawrence Scientific School, which began in 1847. The Lawrence Scientific School was the fourth such school for professional and scientific study established at Harvard, with the medical school in 1782, the law school in 1817, and the divinity school in 1819 preceding it. In 1898, the words "physical training" were deleted from the department title although the stated aims of the course of study remained unchanged. After Fitz's resignation in 1899, however, the aim of the program was also changed so as to exclude the purpose of preparing individuals for work in physical education. It can only be surmised that, once Fitz had left, the motivating force for such a purpose also left, or that Fitz left because provision for preparation of physical educators had been deleted. During the years from 1891 to 1898, however, the Department of Anatomy, Physiology, and Physical Training offered an academic four-year degree program leading to a B.S. degree from the department at the Lawrence Scientific School of Harvard University.

There is little doubt that the B.S. degree program offered in this department under the direction of Fitz was not only intended to prepare physical educators, but also to prepare physical educators with a sound scientific background in anatomy and physiology. In the 1891-1892 announcement of the Lawrence Scientific School, for example, this description of the course of study is given on page 222:

> This course is intended to afford a special training for those who wish to fit themselves to take charge of gymnasium or to give instruction in physical exercises. It may advantageously be pursued by students who intend to study medicine or who need a systematic education of the body.

By the following year, 1893, the department had crystallized a sound and stable set of objectives for the course of study. The aims of the department and the nature of the courses offered in this curriculum seem worthy of presentation here in their entirety (see Table 2.3). In many respects

Table 2.3

Departmental Aims and Course of Study Presented to Implement Them Department of Anatomy, Physiology, and Physical Training, Lawrence Scientific School, Harvard University, 1893

Description of Courses in Physiology, Hygiene, History of Physical Education, Applied Anatomy, and Anthropometry, Athletics and Gymnastics

The aims of this department are as follows:

1. To prepare persons who, with or without a subsequent training in medicine, may intend to seek employment as directors of gymnasiums or instructors in physical training.
2. To educate youths who may need to take particular care of their bodily health, and therefore should have a knowledge of the subjects taught in the course as well as systematic training in the care of their bodies.
3. To afford in the first two years a suitable general training for young men who may desire afterwards to pursue the study of medicine. The course of these two years has been approved by the Medical Faculty. Students completing this course (four years) will be able to enter the second class at the Medical School and graduate in three years.

A large and well-equipped laboratory has been organized for the experimental study of the physiology of exercise. The object of this work is to exemplify the hygiene of the muscles, the conditions under which they act, the relation of their action to the body as a whole affecting blood supply and general hygienic conditions, and the effects of various exercises upon muscular growth and general health.

The work in the gymnasium gives a systematic and thorough bodily training, and at the same time a familiarity with and drill in the exercises needed for future teaching. Associated with this is the study of human anatomy analytically and synthetically leading to an understanding of the body as a working machine, and the inter-relation of its parts. The students are taught to measure persons and to classify them into types. Corrective exercises are studied and applied.

The course includes studies in biology, physics, chemistry, English and French or German, and thus affords a considerable amount of general culture.

the program would seem worthy of emulation today, either in part or in whole.

Several noteworthy features of the Harvard program merit comment. First of all, one of the stated aims of the department noted that the course of study was designed to prepare individuals for positions as directors of gymnasiums or instructors in physical training. This in itself was not unusual, but the phrase "with or without a subsequent training in medicine" did represent something out of the ordinary. An aim such as this implied that, although a medical degree might be desirable, it was not essential for adequate professional preparation of a physical

Table 2.3 (cont.)

(1) The Elementary Physiology of and Hygiene of Common Life, Personal Hygiene, Emergencies. Half-course. One lecture and one laboratory hour each week throughout the year (or three times a week, first half-year). Dr. G.W. Fitz.
This is a general introductory course intended to give the knowledge of human anatomy, physiology and hygiene which should be possessed by every student; it is suitable also for those not intending to study medicine or physical training.
(2) History of Physical Education. Half-course. Lecture once a week and a large amount of reading. Drs. Sargent and G.W. Fitz.
The student is made acquainted with the literature of physical training; the history of the various sports is traced and the artistic records (statuary, etc.) studied.
(3) Physiology of Exercise. Experimental work, original work and thesis. Laboratory work six hours a week. Dr. G.W. Fitz.
This course is intended to introduce the student to the fundamental problems of physical education and to give him the training in use of apparatus for investigation and in the methods in such work.
Course (3) must be preceded by the course in General Physiology at the Medical School, or its equivalent.
(4) Anthropometry. Measurements and Tests of the Human Body, Effects of Age, Nurture and Physical Training. Lectures and practical exercises. Half-course. Three times a week (first half-year). Dr. Sargent.
This course affords systematic training in making measurements and tests of persons for the purpose of determining individual strength and health deficiencies. Practice is also given in classifying measurements, forming typical groups, etc., and in determining the relation of the individual to such groups. This course must be preceded by the course in General Anatomy at the Medical School, or its equivalent.

educator. At the time, of course, it was expected that directors of a gymnasium would hold an M.D. degree while assistants or instructors could be normal-school products. Since the Harvard degree was not linked to any requirement for acquisition of a medical degree or a normal-school certificate, it effectively established a new means for respected entry into the profession. Rather than traditional medical degrees or normal-school training certificates, a distinct four-year academic degree program was now available for physical education. The same thesis, of course, was probably implicit in the Stanford degree program, but Harvard's program explicitly stated such a policy and preceded the Stanford program by one full year. Luther Gulick had contended that physical education was best served by neither a medical degree nor a teaching education but by a special program designed for itself. The Harvard program would seem to have fitted Gulick's desires admirably. Second, the course of study provided for instruction in biology, physics, and chemistry to be followed by applied science courses in the department. Such a science

Table 2.3 (cont.)

(5) Applied Anatomy and Animal Mechanics. Action of Muscles in Different Exercises. Lectures and Demonstrations. Half-course. Three times a week (second half-year). Dr. Sargent.

The muscles taking part in the different exercises and the mechanical conditions under which they work are studied. The body is considered as a machine. The development of force, its utilization and the adaptation of the different parts to these ends are made prominent in the work.

This course must be preceded by the course in General Anatomy at the Medical School, or its equivalent.

(6) Remedial Exercises. The Correction of Abnormal Conditions and Positions. Lectures and Demonstrations. Half-course. Twice a week (second half-year). Dr. G.W. Fitz.

Deformities such as spinal curvature are studied and the corrective effects of different exercises observed. The students are trained in the selection and application of proper exercises, and in the diagnosis of cases when exercise is unsuitable.

(7) Gymnastics and Athletics. Dr. Sargent and Mr. J.G. Lathrop.

Systematic instruction is given throughout the four years in these subjects. The students attend the regular afternoon class in gymnastics conducted by Dr. Sargent, work with the developing appliances to remedy up their own deficiencies and take part in the preliminary training for the various athletic exercises under Mr. Lathrop's direction. Much work is also done with the regular apparatus of the gymnasium.

emphasis was strong enough to be approved by the Harvard Medical School faculty to the extent that after four years of study in the department students could "enter the second class at the Medical School and graduate in three years." In addition to the courses in biology, physics, and chemistry, it was also necessary for students to take courses in general anatomy and general physiology at the Medical School. According to the *Annual Reports of the President and Treasurer of Harvard College for 1891-1892*, students in the program were obliged to spend their third year of study in the Medical School. These courses in basic related sciences were prerequisites to courses in the department in physiology of exercise, anthropometry, and applied anatomy and animal mechanics. The department course in physiology of exercise, with six hours of laboratory work each week throughout the entire year, was designed to permit the opportunity for experimental work of an original nature on the fundamental problems of physical education. Thus, Fitz's often-expressed contention that scientific study was needed before curriculum controversies in physical education could be settled was given a sizable portion of time in the program for realization. In addition, an experimental laboratory was established to allow such investigative studies upon "the effects of various exercises upon muscular growth and general health."

Figure 2.1. James F. Jones, B.S., Harvard, in Anatomy, Physiology, and Physical Training, 1893. Photograph courtesy of the Biscoe Collection of Photographs, Marietta College, Marietta, Ohio.

One would be obliged to conclude that the Harvard program embodied a strong scientific, biological, and medical orientation. Few undergraduate major programs of today could match the strong science core required at Harvard back in 1891. As vigorous a scientific program as it was, it should be noted, however, that preparation in the basic sciences alone was not considered sufficient. Then, as now, it was realized that the problems in physical education required specific course work designed to apply the knowledge of the basic sciences. Thus, even though general physiology was taken at the Medical School, a course in physiology of exercise was deemed essential. Although general anatomy was taken at the Medical School, courses were offered in anthropometry and in applied anatomy and animal mechanics. In essence, then, Fitz saw a strong preparation in the biological sciences as being essential for the preparation of a scientifcally grounded physical educator. He did not—and this point bears emphasis—see such basic science preparation as a substitute for specific course work designed for scientific investigation of the fundamental problems in physical education.

The first individual to be graduated from the Department of Anatomy, Physiology, and Physical Training of the Lawrence Scientific School at Harvard was James Francis Jones (Figure 2.1). According to the Harvard Commencement Program of 1893, page vi, Jones received a B.S. degree with cum laude honors in Anatomia, Physiologia, Corporis Cultu, the Latin title of the departmental major. The 1893 date of his graduation makes him the first such recipient of a bachelor's degree from an academic four-year program in the United States. Upon graduation, he returned to Marietta College, Marietta, Ohio, where he had previously been a student, to take up a position as Instructor in Physiology, Hygiene, and Director of Gymnasium. The Marietta College *Olio* of October, 1893 congratulated the school because "at last Marietta has a Department of Physical Culture." A gymnasium was also reported as forthcoming and great expectation was expressed for the "physical upbuilding of the college." Thus did the first degree recipient in scientific physical education begin his career. To Marietta College goes the distinction of having hired the first academically prepared physical educator in the United States.

The degree program at Harvard began in 1891 and continued to graduate students with B.S. degrees in anatomy, physiology, and physical training until 1899. Beginning in 1900, the title of the department was changed to "anatomy and physiology," and no mention was made again, in the statement of purpose, referring to preparation for positions in physical education. As previously noted, Fitz had resigned in 1899. Nine persons, however, received B.S. degrees in anatomy, physiology, and physical training before the program changed. In addition to Jones, the following individuals were listed as degree recipients from the department in Harvard Commencement Programs: Thomas J. Manahan, Richard Grant, Howard F. Holmes, Edward W. Rich, and Roger Spaulding; Charles H. Tozier—cum laude honors; Charles Moline and Robert J. Graves—magna cum laude honors.

REFERENCES

1. Babbitt, James A. Present condition of gymnastics and athletics in American colleges. *American Physical Education Review* **8**: 280-283; December 1903.

2. DeGroot, Dudley Sargent. Physical education in California—1854-1900. *Journal of Health and Physical Education* **10**: 67-68, 125; February 1939.

3. Gulick, Luther II., and James Naismith. Normal physical training. *Physical Education* **1**: 165-166; October 1892.

4. Leonard, Fred E., and R. Tait McKenzie. *A Guide to the History of Physical Education*. Philadelphia: Lea and Febiger, 1927.

5. Lewis, Guy. Adoption of the sports program, 1906-39: the role of accommodation in the transformation of physical education. *Quest* **12**: 34-46; May 1969.

6. Rice, Emmett A., John L. Hutchinson, and Mabel Lee. *A Brief History of Physical Education*, 4th ed. New York: Ronald, 1958.

7. Riordan, William G. Dio Lewis in retrospect. *JOHPER* **37**: 46-48; October 1960.

8. Savage, Howard J. *American College Athletics*. New York: Carnegie Foundation for the Advancement of Teaching, 1929.

9. VanDalen, Deobold B., Elmer D. Mitchell, and Bruce L. Bennett. *A World History of Physical Education*. Englewood Cliffs, New Jersey: Prentice-Hall, 1953.

10. VanWyck, Clarence B. The Harvard Summer School of Physical Education. *Research Quarterly* **13**: 403-431; 1942.

11. Welch, J. Edmund. *Edward Hitchcock, M.D., Founder of Physical Education in the College Curriculum*. Unpublished dissertation. Nashville: George Peabody College for Teachers, 1962.

12. Wood, Thomas D. Some unsolved problems in physical education. *Addresses and Proceedings of International Congress of Education, Chicago* **3**: 621-623; 1893.

Graduate Study in Physical Education

3

Graduate study, as anything resembling a major factor in the advancement of physical education, is still a rather recent development. Even though the number of colleges and universities offering undergraduate and graduate degree programs has grown tremendously, a sizable percentage of the personnel in departments of physical education do not hold an advanced or terminal degree. An uncomfortable number of collegiate institutions still select faculty members on the basis of technical skill competencies such as coaching record or activity specialization. Many job descriptions in higher education, for example, relegate the possession of a doctor's degree to optional or secondary-factor status. Possession of technical practitioner skill competencies, thus, tends to outweigh a preference for academic or intellectual qualities in a good number of instances. Whether such a state of affairs with regard to the balance of technical skills and academic preparation on a staff can or should be changed remains open for debate. It seems obvious that a heterogeneous staff composition is dictated in many departments of physical education because of the multiplicity of responsibilities for professional service, and in such instances, the question of proper balance in staff preparation is strictly an academic exercise.

Our immediate past history also shows many faculty members in higher education holding advanced degrees in other subject matter areas. Such obvious mismatches between training and position responsibilities were considered stop-gap measures made necessary by sweeping demands for such positions to be filled quickly. The expectation was, of course, that properly trained individuals would eventually occupy such positions in departments of physical education. Of late, however, possession of an advanced degree in an allied specialty has assumed a position of elevated prestige in some departments of physical education. Such a situation is indeed interesting as it must qualify physical education as one of the few fields where direct and specific study of its own subject matter is deemed inappropriate.

The situation is not much better in the public schools. Because of the important influence of interscholastic athletics, instructors for boys' physical education programs are more often selected on the basis of coaching vacancies than on the needs of the physical education program per se. Where the number of coaches needed is greater than the number of physical education teachers, head coaches of major sports often receive the major assignment for the teaching of physical education classes. Coaches of minor sports and assistant coaches find it necessary to teach in other subject matter areas while waiting their chance to advance up the ladder, eventually to qualify for assignment in their major area of specialization and to teach physical education. Either because of a change in career goal aspirations or financial considerations, many public school teachers of physical education elect to pursue advanced graduate study in another area of specialization outside of physical education. Among the more common choices for such later specialization are educational administration and guidance and counseling. After a few summers of employment outside of the profession, others elect to leave the teaching profession completely and find business and industry attractive as a means of earning a livelihood. The net effect of all such factors is to dissipate professional energy and hinder development and advancement of physical education, since the presence of individuals intent upon utilizing the profession for personal motives makes the task of fully committed workers in the profession very difficult.

The mosaic pattern of degrees, areas of specialization, transitional career goals, and ill-defined professional objectives found among physical educators in schools and colleges is matched by equally nebulous programs of graduate study. Graduate programs in physical education can be called many things, but standardized is not usually found on any list of applicable adjectives. An area of graduate specialization at one school may require an entirely different set of courses than the same specialization at another school. Another remarkable feature is the swiftness with which specialization areas at just one school can change without any concurrent effects upon budget, laboratory facilities, staff, or any of the other usual items associated with a particular specialty. Ever since their appearance, graduate programs in physical education have demonstrated this remarkable capacity for continuous adjustment and change. Dramatic course additions and deletions occur with such regularity as to challenge all curricula for speed of metamorphosis.

Understanding the purpose of advanced study is important to beginning graduate students in physical education as well as to the profession as a whole. This is particularly true today when somewhat radical new graduate programs, designed for an academic discipline of physical education, are being initiated and traditional professional education programs are being subjected to critical evaluation. More different kinds of graduate programs probably exist today than at any other time in the profession's history, and the prospects are for even more variation in the immediate future. These changes in programs of preparation, undergraduate and graduate alike, will eventually affect both the nature of the profession and the services it provides to society. Awareness of these changes and their possible causes seems necessary for proper evaluation of their desirability and possible effects.

In the previous chapter, the beginnings of formal programs of study for physical education specialists were considered. An attempt was made to show that sentiment existed among early leaders in physical education for at least two kinds of emphasis in professional training programs. One of these emphases was tied to the profession of education and stressed the need for adequate training in teacher education. The other emphasis linked the development of physical education practitioners more to the line of training afforded in medicine and the biological sciences. Early in the 1890's, attempts were made at Stanford University and at Harvard to combine the pedagogical and the scientific research emphases into four-year academic degree programs. In this chapter, consideration will be given to the beginnings and later developments of graduate study in physical education. As will be seen, the first overlap between undergraduate and graduate programs of study in physical education occurred at the turn of the century.

GRADUATE STUDY BEGINS AND SCIENCE LEAVES

The beginning of graduate study in physical education is associated with a master's program offered at Teachers College, Columbia University in 1901 and a program at Oberlin College of Ohio that conferred its first master's degree in physical education in 1904. The year 1924 saw both New York University and Teachers College, Columbia University offering the first Ph.D. programs in education with a major in physical education. A short time later (1929), both the University of Pittsburgh and Stanford University offered the first Ed.D. degrees in education with a physical education concentration. These beginnings of graduate study were hailed as legitimate advances toward academic respectability and acceptance of physical education as a working partner in higher education. Although the profession of education still labored to escape a second-class citizenship image in universities, Columbia University was, after all, one of the original 14 charter members of the elite and prestigious Association of American Universities. Graduate degree programs in physical education linked with such a respected university certainly represented a giant stride forward toward an enhanced educational status for physical education.

Without underestimating the importance of undergraduate teacher-education roots, the first doctoral programs of graduate study did much to seal the fate of physical education as an integral part of education and to set in motion the absolute and nearly complete professionalization of physical education. The slim chance that physical education might have followed a path closer to the biological sciences, or at least a parallel course of professional education and a biological science orientation, quickly dissipated under the influence of such a close association and identification with college departments of education. Having been accepted in education departments, physical education was rightly expected to conduct itself in accordance with educational doctrine. Sincere and dedicated physical educators may have over-responded to this obligation.

Graduates from educationally oriented doctoral programs were bound to become future leaders of prominence, if for no other reason than the simple fact that doctoral degree holders would be prime candidates for positions of importance in college and university departments of physical education. Although athletic specialists might effectively control many departments administratively, the responsibility for professional training of students majoring in the field would still fall primarily upon the non-coaching members of a departmental faculty. Since the training of these doctorate people was to be fashioned within departments of education rather than the biological sciences, the philosophical basis of physical education was destined to be compatible with that of professional education. From that point on, any scientific orientation in physical education would find itself subservient to professional education dictates. The twig was decisively bent toward education and not toward the sciences.

By the time of the first graduate programs in physical education, many leaders must have been convinced that the beneficient goals of a healthy body and a vigorous life could best be achieved by a full-scale development of physical education as a teaching profession. Clark W. Hetherington, for example, stated quite unequivocally that physical education was a teaching profession "first, last, and all the time" (11, page 209). Allegiance to education, after all, made good sense. In the first place, an alliance with education provided a logical home for a group with the zealous intent of transmitting a physical culture philosophy to major segments of society. By reaching the young through a slot in the school curriculum, such an objective might be realized if there be any truth in the "bending of the twig" adage.

Second, some disquieting challenges to physical education as the sole guardian of health and physical exercise had begun to appear. By 1908, the Playground Association of America had already surpassed the older American Physical Education Association in both membership and financial resources. The medical profession was still encouraging health in the schools but was now suggesting more direct attacks on health problems and the establishment of distinct hygiene courses in the schools. Hence, a program of physical exercise slipped in importance as a health promoter. At the 1910 convention, for example, the association found it necessary to make a concerted attempt at convincing school administrators that although hygiene was valuable it should not be allowed to take the place of physical education course work. The 1910 conference was held in conjunction with the National Education Association's (NEA) Department of Superintendents and the American School Hygiene Association, making dialog on the topic quite meaningful.

It must also have been apparent to many physical educators that individuals with medical degrees would soon begin to diminish in both numbers and influence among the professional membership. Early M.D. programs were less than four years in length, hardly considered equivalent to a college degree by many, and, like other professional schools during that time, did not enjoy a high level of respect. A dramatic revision of medical education came about, however, upon the appearance of the Flexner report. Published in 1910, the Flexner report was a study of medical education sponsored by the Carnegie Foundation for the Advancement of Teaching (6). As a result of the report, many low-standard medical schools closed immediately, and the majority of schools still in operation soon adopted rigid requirements for admission, including several years of premedicine study as we know it today. With such lengthy schooling now required of physicians and an associated rise in the prestige of medicine, the influx of medical doctors into physical education work was destined to dwindle.

There is some evidence that physical educators were aware of these sweeping developments in medicine. The *American Physical Education Association Review* of January 1914 carried a news note about the fall in medical school enrollments and the closing of some 16 medical schools the previous year. In this same issue, a report appeared from a committee on teacher training formed by the Middle West Society of Physical Education and Hygiene. Chaired by Charles H. Judd, Ph.D., who was Director of the School of Education at the University of Chicago, the committee recommended that each institution training physical educators be visited, investigated, and that ". . . a classification [be] set up similar to the classification of medical schools made by the American

Medical Association" (12, page 21). It is also worthwhile to note that no technical courses in medicine were recommended as part of a minimum training program for professional physical education teachers. The committee reported that this issue was made ". . . a subject of explicit discussion and the omission is deliberate." Such action would seem to suggest that the role of a physical educator was being defined more as an educator and less as a health worker charged with the traditional responsibility of administering physical examinations. Education and not medicine was beginning to exert the most powerful influence when attempts were made to identify the professional tasks of a physical educator.

A diminished influence of medicine in the profession of physical education was probably not only inevitable but also desirable. Physical education was making notable strides in establishing itself as a distinctive field of endeavor and, apparently, some feeling was present that a "medical doctor" and "physical educator" were neither synonymous nor compatible terms. It was being recognized that advanced study in physical education would be necessary, and that a medical education was not an adequate solution to such a need. For example, data from the November 1921 *American Physical Education Review* showed that, by 1920, departments of physical education existed in 199 colleges and universities. The department head in 187 of these institutions had faculty status, with 157 holding the rank of full professor. In commenting on these data, Leonard and McKenzie noted that personnel seeking careers in physical education at the college level would be at a disadvantage in measuring up to usual academic standards for faculty appointment and promotion unless they were able to show postgraduate education comparable to that in other academic subjects. Their position on medicine as preparation for a career in physical education suggested that a medical degree was losing its attractiveness. Leonard and McKenzie stated: "A course in medicine, which has seemed to many the natural portal of entry to the new profession, cannot be viewed as anything but a makeshift solution of the problem, and until this need is met in some more adequate way it must be difficult for the department of physical education to win and hold a status equal to that of others long established" (16, page 289). Physical education was ready for its own unique graduate study programs and the field of education was the most likely prospect through which to accomplish this breakthrough.

At any rate, a base of operation in teacher training departments and an affiliation with the National Education Association did offer one way of achieving universal physical education programs for all youth. At the same time, an association with education could serve as a protective umbrella against competitive agencies attempting to assume responsibility over physical education functions. At least as physical education existed in the schools, a voice in teacher training curricula offered a means of exerting control over the nature of physical education to be transmitted and the type of training a physical educator would receive. Alliance with education, however, also brought with it an obligation of allegiance. It is under this allegiance to education that physical education as we know it today has been fashioned. An allegiance to education has been the most singularly important factor affecting the development of physical education in our modern era. Much like a puppet on strings, whenever education moved, so did physical education.

According to several authoritative sources, the "new" physical education owed its origin to such men as Thomas D. Wood, Clark W. Hetherington, and Jay B. Nash. Both Rice (21, page 272), and VanDalen et al. (24, page 424) cite Thomas D. Wood and Clark W. Hetherington as powerful influences in the original establishment of a move toward natural physical education. In 1910, Wood published his important paper on "Health and Education" (27) in which he impugned the traditional programs of physical education in existence as being too concerned with the physical. More emphasis was needed, Wood contended, upon the effects of physical activity upon attitudes, disposition, and personality. In addition, Wood called for natural and enjoyable activities of a spontaneous nature more closely related to human life. Programs of physical education, Wood declared, had to be both psychologically and physiologically sound in order to be pedagogically acceptable. His words were consistent with the fast-developing idea of social education in American educational circles and were well received by those dissatisfied with the formal German and Swedish systems of physical education prevalent at the time.

Hetherington's contribution was an article titled "Fundamental Education" in which the term "new physical education" was coined, and it emphasized the principle that physical education was education through, and not of, the physical (10). Weston (26, page 218) refers to the "great trinity" of Wood, Hetherington, and Nash as originators of the new physical education movement. Both Rice (21, page 273) and VanDalen et al. (24, page 424) added the name of Jesse Feiring Williams to the list of pioneer proponents of the new physical education. From that time on, physical education has been identified as a medium for educational developmentalism. Its philosophy has since been congruent with the educational philosophy that emphasized the idea that the experience of doing was more important than what was being done and that social education was an essential objective of education.

As one of the foremost proponents and leaders of the new physical education movement, Clark W. Hetherington occupied a position of great influence. As Professor of Physical Education in the School of Education at New York University, he was in charge of graduate work and was instrumental in fashioning one of the first two Ph.D. programs of graduate study in physical education. Hetherington outlined his underlying philosophy for graduate work in physical education in a two-part article published in the *American Physical Education Review* (11). One of his major points was that the problem of designing an acceptable professional training program could only be accomplished through the technique of job analysis. Thus, he contended that it was necessary to ascertain the services provided by physical educators and then devise necessary training programs in a professional curriculum in accordance with such service tasks.

Job analysis, according to Hetherington, was the "approved method in the organization of any professional curriculum." It was quite clear that application of the job-analysis technique was to forge professional training programs upon the anvil of services rendered in the public schools by physical educators. Hetherington definitely thought of physical education as a teaching profession as he unequivocally stated: "Physical education is a teaching profession; it is that first, last and all the time." Furthermore, he contended that school men would judge physical education by its effects upon children in the public schools, and that "school men will determine, ultimately, the status of physical education in this country, and the status of the profession." It seems quite evident, on the basis of such definitive and poignant statements, that Hetherington's approach to graduate programs of physical education was distinctly bent toward educational developmentalism—strictly in line with, in accord with, and swearing allegiance to professional education upon which the status of physical education depended.

Based upon the job-analysis technique, Hetherington outlined four basic functions of physical educators that had to be encompassed in the design of both undergraduate and graduate professional training programs. The first function involved the acquisition of technical skills and included: (a) personal skills in pertinent activities, (b) special methods of teaching skills, and (c) general principles of teaching or leadership. A second function involved the administration of activity programs, necessitating a course or courses in administration as well as a course or courses encompassing the care and protection of children. This latter portion of the second function made necessary the consideration of legal responsibility, accident prevention, and health supervision. A third function of a physical educator dealt with the realization of aims or objectives, to be covered via a course on objectives and principles of teaching. Finally, the scientific procedure was listed as a fourth function, and was subdivided into two major categories: (1) "the knowledge of and the classification of children according to tendencies, capacities and needs, and (2) the knowledge of or the ability to formulate a program of activities to meet the tendencies, capacities and needs" (11, page 210).

Translated into actual course work and credit prescription for an undergraduate major, the function of technical skill would require: (a) four years of training in the techniques of the activities, (b) special methods—10 points, and (c) principles of teaching—4 points. In addition to these undergraduate professional courses dealing with technical skills, a set of ". . . essential professional sciences or so-called theory courses" were prescribed to round out a ". . . standard undergraduate curriculum in physical education": (d) Principles of Physical Education—4 points, (e) Nature and Function of Play—2 points, (f) Growth and Development of Children—2 points, (g) Introduction to the Physical Examination and Tests—4 points, (h) Kinesiology—2 points, (i) Physiology of Exercise—2 points, and (j) Special Adaptation of Corrective Exercise—? points.

Unlike undergraduate study, the program of graduate professional training was to be distinctive in preparing for the ". . . full functions of the physical educator in positions of large responsibility." Based once again upon the proven technique of job analysis for defining professional training programs, Hetherington described the following five major positions where ability in the full functions of a physical educator were represented:

> The positions where the ability is needed to render the full functions of the physical educator are represented (1) by the head teachers or teaching administrators or directors in charge of large elementary schools or playgrounds, junior or senior high schools, normal schools, colleges, etc.; (2) by the supervisors of teachers in elementary schools and playground systems; (3) by directors in institutions for the handicapped and defective; (4) by overhead administrators in school and playground systems; and (5) by those in charge of professional training in teacher training institutions. The larger competence for these positions is gained either by experience or by graduate training or both. The larger competence is essential if physical education is to secure its objectives and some cities and states now legally require the experience or graduate work or both (11, page 264).

Although Hetherington had presented explicit apportionment of course work and time for an undergraduate professional-training curriculum based upon vital service functions, no such plan was similarly presented for the graduate curriculum. This lack of an equally well-defined graduate program was probably due to the novelty of the situation. As Hetherington clearly stated, it would require some time to organize a formal course of study for the Ph.D. degree. Since his article was written the same year the authorization for the Ph.D. degree at New York University was granted, it would be naive to expect a clearly defined graduate curriculum to have been ready so quickly. Other than negating the advisability of skill courses for graduate credit and noting that six courses in administration had been proposed (for example, community organization and public recreation), Hetherington's most explicit references to graduate work concerned the matter of scientific procedure in physical education.

Hetherington emphasized the need in physical education for ". . . theorists or scholarship and research specialists to teach the distinctly professional scientific courses" (11, page 264). In the first category of a scientific procedure in physical education he defined a need for tests to classify individuals according to differences in tendencies, capacities, and needs. The other major category of a scientific procedure in physical education was seen as complementary to the first. Having classified individuals according to needs, it was then necessary to classify activities as to the contributions each could make to the previously defined needs. According to Hetherington's paper, a laboratory to investigate these problems was being planned at New York University, and he stated quite emphatically that a competency in the scientific procedure in physical education ". . . must become the supreme aim in the training of every physical educator who takes a position of independent responsibility" (11, page 266). Having been associated with Wood while at Stanford University, Hetherington clearly accepted the need for critical scientific analysis of activities in physical education. Indeed, Wood himself had appealed for a scientific approach in physical education and called for the establishment of a science of physical education. Wood's position definitely included the need for physiological (or a physical emphasis) research as well as research in the psychological-education domain. In one paper, for example, Wood applauded the establishment of an exercise physiology laboratory and encouraged other laboratories to be similarly developed (28).

Thus, the vision of a new physical education must certainly be said to have maintained recognition of a biological heritage for physical education. As was true of many of the early leaders, both Wood and Hetherington appreciated the need for both scholarly and scientific research in physical education. Although their idea of a scientific procedure and a science of physical education was probably not congruent to usual definitions of a discipline, preservation of a scientific base for the professional conduct of physical education *could* have led to such a development. Much like the history of science, useful research could have led to a pure-science ideal for research activities in physical education. In some manner, however, the scientific procedure and a scholarly research emphasis, as postulated, were apparently translated to mean research compatible and congruent with—and only with—educational dogma. Rather than moving toward a pure-science ideal, the outlook in physical education traveled in the opposite direction. Useful knowledge and applied research were the ultimate goals and any vigorous development of the content domain of physical activity was to be frowned upon.

In a thoroughly charming article titled "The Research Specialist and

His Role in Teacher Education," a noted professor of education at New York University spelled out in unmistakable terms what scientific procedures eventually came to mean in an educationally oriented profession of physical education. Granted the fact that this article appeared in the *Research Quarterly* more than ten years after Hetherington's position paper on graduate study, it is interpreted here to exemplify an attitude toward research that has characterized physical education ever since its union with education. The genesis of such a research attitude would seem best credited to the annexation of physical education to the yoke of educational philosophy. The following quotes from the article are offered without further comment:

> The criterion of its worth will be the degree to which it has immediate application—value to the problems of education people.

> Education being an applied field, will find many of its problems best answered by research expertly conducted in its related areas, e.g., physiology, sociology, etc. Some problems will be peculiar to education and consequently become the province of research on education. Such problems will center around activities, methods, facilities and equipment, and administration.

> That the research conducted by or through such a person must have demonstrated educational value.*

Regardless of original intent, graduate programs in physical education quickly assumed the characteristics of their new guardian. Educational goals and educationally oriented definitions of scholarly research became the guidelines for development of physical education. According to Rice's account of the natural movement in physical education, Teachers College, Columbia University was ". . . the center from which the new movement in physical education has radiated" (21, pages 272, 273). Rice also stated that Williams played a key role in the development of the natural movement (the new physical education) and ". . . in showing that the new physical education is in close harmony with American educational theories." Such a statement seems based upon strong evidence, and elicits little debate from history. It is interesting, then, to examine how a Ph.D. program was translated into course work at this fountainhead of the new physical education and to contrast its philosophy with that propounded by Hetherington at New York University.

With permission, the transcript of one of the first Ph.D. products from Teachers College was examined. Needless to say, the actual program that was eventually developed must have undergone many changes from the course of study initially prescribed for a Ph.D. in physical

*From Lloyd (17). Used with permission of American Association for Health, Physical Education, and Recreation, Washington, D.C.

Table 3.1

Courses Taken in an Early Ph.D. Program

Catalog listing	Course title	Point value
Ed.	Philosophy of education	8
Ed.	Educational psychology	6
Ed.	Practicum: application of psychological statistical methods to education	8
Ed.	History of education	3
Phys. Ed.	Problems in hygiene and physical education	3
French	Educational French	2
Ed.	Major course for superintendents of schools	12
Ed.	Introductory course in mental tests	4
Ed.	Criticism and supervision of instruction in elementary schools	3
Ed.	Psychology of the elementary school subjects	3
Ed.	Foundations of method	3
Ed.	Seminar: educational psychology	4

education. The list of courses to follow, however, does offer some evidence of just how harmonious a graduate program in physical education was with American educational theories. Thus, the actual courses taken by a very distinguished early Ph.D. in physical education are as shown in Table 3.1.

It seems evident that the orientation in both of the first Ph.D. programs was definitely toward professional education. Through the years, the job-analysis technique has continued to be used as an identifier of needed new graduate work. Each time a new service function was demanded of a physical educator the job-analysis approach swiftly identified another course to be offered. Unfortunately, the job-analysis technique has constituted a stronger force in fashioning graduate curricula than was the accumulation of new knowledge. As is acknowledged in any sensible evaluation of the technique, the job-analysis approach seldom guarantees that optimum practices will be identified. Rather, job analysis depicts current demands for services resulting from present human needs. As a tool for developing graduate work, Hetherington fully realized that the job-analysis technique had to be coupled with careful scientific work that established a suitable knowledge structure. With concurrent growth of reliable knowledge, ideas gleaned from a job-analysis technique could be modified intelligently to help enhance progress in the profession as a whole. This seems not to have been accomplished.

IMPACT OF EDUCATIONAL ORIENTATION
UPON PHYSICAL EDUCATION

Because of their early association with teacher education, graduate programs in physical education were heavily laden with professionally oriented course work essential for the development of sound educational methodology. As an integral part of the education profession, physical education was obliged to concentrate upon the necessary and important problems involved in the transmission of subject matter in the teaching situation. Less time and effort, unfortunately, was then available for developing a factual basis for the subject matter content of physical education itself. To a considerable extent, this early and close identification with the profession of education has had a seemingly stultifying effect upon physical education's capacity to develop fully its own identity.

Unlike teachers prepared for other subject matter areas, physical education has had no specific discipline area developing its unique domain of knowledge. Most subject matter areas can point to a parent discipline as the fountainhead for their source of knowledge. Teachers of mathematics, for example, receive their academic preparation in mathematics departments and are taught by mathematicians. Departments of mathematics develop their subject matter content as an academic discipline and create new bodies of knowledge in mathematics for transmission. After sufficient academic course work in the discipline of mathematics, students are then given the professional skills necessary to teach mathematics. Physical education, on the other hand, has been faced with the dilemma of preparing teachers for a subject matter area that has no counterpart as an academic discipline.

Physical education has understandably had considerable difficulty in wrestling with the necessity for developing its own subject-matter knowledge structure and simultaneously preparing teachers. Any honest appraisal of the situation must conclude that, by far, the majority of effort has been expended along lines characteristic of the education profession. Much less energy has been spent in activities aligned with the emphasis typically found in an academic discipline—scholarly research and production of a structured knowledge system. Because of its widely based core of professional services, physical education has often contended that it is eclectic and required many disciplines as a knowledge source.

Rightly or wrongly, the physical educator's graduate program of study has contained massive slices of education course work in administration, curriculum, history and philosophy of education, teaching methods, and current professional problems. The understandable goal of including such requirements was to insure the acquisition of the capabilities necessary for a professional educator and was reflected in the methods approach needed in a profession. Since these courses were designed for education in general, and did not deal with topics specific to physical education, mirror-images of these courses appeared under a physical education title. In addition, a wide variety of teaching responsibilities resulted in the need to offer even more methods courses in order to endow the physical educator with the know-how to teach all kinds of assigned subject matter courses.

Examples of such graduate programs are easy to find among schools offering graduate degrees in physical education, particularly when the department of physical education is housed administratively within a college of education. An Ed.D. program at a major university, for example, required each doctoral candidate in physical education to complete a number of field courses in education and to successfully pass the Graduate Record Examination in Education. The field courses represented one survey-type course in each of the departments in the college of education: administration, curriculum and instruction, educational psychology, history and philosophy of education, and special education. When the doctoral candidate was examined for capabilities as an educator during the preliminary orals (taken after completion of all field courses), members of the examining committee would frequently prescribe further course work in one or more of the departments. A student who escaped completion of field courses with only the required fifteen semester hours of credit would be considered very lucky.

The reasoning behind the requirement of field courses was certainly sound. A doctorate degree in education with a major in physical and health education surely necessitated that competency be demonstrated in education per se. A minimum of one required course in each of the departments in the college and a passing grade on the Graduate Record Examination in Education was, therefore, a reasonable standard. However, the physical and health education department also offered (and most of its students took) similar course titles in its own area. Thus, courses were available in administration, curriculum, philosophy, and history from the viewpoint of physical education alone and for health education alone in curriculum and administration. Before receiving their Ed.D., doctoral candidates would probably take 15 or more semester hours in education field courses and another 12 to 15 semester hours in similar course titles in physical and health education.

Certainly, sound arguments could be forwarded for the perpetuation of such a curriculum design. Course content could undoubtedly be shown to be nonoverlapping and possessed of essential scholarly composition pertinent to the profession. Too often, however, such course sequences in a professional curriculum are appraised differently by outsiders who are unaware of professional realities. To such critics, a sequence of courses such as those just described would fit remarkably the charge of needless proliferation, major duplication with only minute differentiation, and the need to "vague up" course content to fill out semester hour time requirements.

Assuming doctoral-level study requires about 60 additional hours beyond the master's degree, this is quite a large share for educationally and professionally oriented course work. If the doctoral dissertation carries 12 to 15 semester hours credit, somewhere around three-fourths of the entire semester hour allocation is gone. If the field courses in education require 15 hours credit, another 15 hours credit for similar course titles in physical and health education, plus 15 hours for the dissertation, then only 15 hours remain for further work representing in-depth preparation in the subject matter area of physical education itself. It is understandable that, after one or two courses in statistics, very little need existed for more than survey-type courses in other areas of physical education. The pie had to be sliced up in so many pieces that none of the pieces could be expected to be very large.

Contributing even further to the dilemma of duplication and proliferation of course work has been the inability of physical education to forward a definitive consensus of its major focal point of interest. Perhaps another result of its close allegiance to education, physical education has always embraced a set of objectives that reflected the traditional whole-child philosophy of progressive education. Perusal of any set of objectives will show that physical education claims contributions to health and organic development, social and emotional development, cultural and aesthetic experiences, recreational and leisure time activities, outdoor education and nature study, and, indeed, to as wide and diverse a range of goals as would be found in any set of volumes extolling the virtues of education in toto.

With so phenomenal a scope of operations, it has been difficult for physical education to define clearly a primary set of distinguishing characteristics. Although historically identified with exercise, physical development, and physical fitness, the influence of broad educational goals threatens even this component of physical education. Witness the statement "You begin by realizing that sweat need not be the common denominator of all physical education classes" (20, page 56), and the recent JOHPER article titled "Is Physical Fitness Our Most Important Objective?" (25). When the public uproar over the physical unfitness of our youth was at its height, the physical education profession responded by depreciating the old-fashioned concept of physical training as being an obligation of modern physical education. AAHPERD's professional journal responded to the national charge for attention to physical fitness with articles on total fitness, fitness through camping, recreation fitness, emotional fitness, and fitness for what? The profession seemed quite set upon preserving its commitment to a broad set of educational goals, and refused to allow the physical fitness movement to take over.

The professional posture of physical education has traditionally accepted the responsibility for physical fitness as an important obligation. Recent developments would seem to suggest, however, that the role of physical fitness is something less than a major and dominating theme in the profession. The whole-child approach seemingly discourages any establishment of priorities and strongly dictates that equal emphasis must be given to the entire gamut of educationally oriented objectives. As a result, physical fitness has had to take its place alongside a whole string of desirable outcomes supposedly derived through participation in physical activity.

Lack of a universally accepted central theme and central core of interest for physical education has also resulted in a poorly defined public image. One of the not too startling outcomes of an inadequately defined domain of interest has been the recent challenge of physical education as the guardian of physical fitness. Since physical education seems none too concerned over physical fitness as a major and dominating theme for its entire profession, it is not unexpected that a number of groups would eventually express dissatisfaction with physical education's management of physical fitness.

Most physical educators, for example, have warmly welcomed the research and writings of Hans Kraus, M.D., as an ally in their attempts to educate the public concerning the values of physical fitness. His work with the Kraus-Weber tests brought national attention to the physical unfitness of American youth with subsequent federal action in the establishment of the President's Council on Youth Fitness. Along with his thesis of hypokinetic disease, there can be no doubt that Kraus' work is more than complimentary to the role of physical fitness as a desirable health adjunct. However, note the following excerpt from an article of his:

> Adequate physical exercise for all age groups is the main preventive measure (sic. against hypokinetic disease), and programs should be established under the leadership of specialists in physical medicine and rehabilitation (14).

In line with such an obvious position by the medical profession of assuming the responsibility for physical fitness is the statement by Thomas P. Anderson of the Dartmouth Medical School, who decried "leaving the national approach to physical fitness in this country to athletes and coaches instead of by physicians and physiologists" (2, page 350).

As strong interest continues over the role of cardiovascular fitness in heart disease, workers in many fields—physicians, physiologists, nutritionists, pharmacists, and cardiologists—are now giving major attention to the many factors involved in heart disease, and this includes the factor of physical exercise. The physical therapy profession is carefully exploring plans to establish a discipline worthy of graduate degrees up to and including the Ph.D. degree. In attempts to define its boundaries, physical therapy is seeking to establish discipline provinces, and exercise is seen as one of their basic modalities of treatment. Corrective therapy is a growing professional group primarily composed of personnel oriented in adapted physical education, and they view exercise in rehabilitation as one of their specific tools. Applied physiologists are expanding their interest into realms heretofore unattended exept for intermittent, and often inept, efforts by physical educators. Since physical education has not always (and apparently has not even now) openly and unashamedly embraced the full responsibility for physical fitness, it may find the problem solved—by default to other qualified groups publicly soliciting rights to physical fitness. It may be an old-fashioned idea that physical training is a major responsibility of modern physical educators, but to several rather respectable groups there seems little to be embarrassed about in calling physical fitness their own.

The question of what should be done about the role of physical fitness in physical education is certainly an important one, but this topic was not raised in the hope of finding an acceptable answer. The issue of property rights to physical fitness was merely used to illustrate the lack of a carefully defined domain of subject matter content in the profession of physical education. Without such a defined domain, physical education has been forced to shuffle about within the borders of a wide, diverse, all-encompassing, and ever-changing set of objectives germane to education in general. It is not too difficult, then, to understand the vexing maze encountered in prescribing an orderly sequence of course work for graduate study in physical education. A wide, diverse, and all-encompassing set of educational objectives necessitates a wide, diverse, and all-encompassing set of courses. Since no agreement can apparently be reached about priorities and major and unique responsibilities, there can be little hope for agreement as to the optimum composition of graduate study programs.

The knotty problem of defining physical education as a recognizable entity distinct from an educational panacea has been made even more complex by other crucial developments. Physical education itself was being considerably broadened in complexity by a somewhat implicit acceptance of other service responsibilities within the educational establishment. Being intimately concerned with organic vigor, physical education tacitly accepted the responsibility of teaching health. As might be expected, satisfactory execution of professional health responsibilities demanded preparation in the health area. As the health education movement matured and prospered, the importance of health in the schools was increased, and the demand came for better training in health. State certification practices, however, have tended to view health and physical education as *one* subject matter area rather than two distinct teaching areas. Health educators fought, by the means available to them, for more time in the curriculum. If a separate major or minor in health education were not feasible or practical in a financial sense, then they took the obvious course of action and fought to reduce physical education course work in the major program. Many fought for an equal 50-50 split in the semester hour allotment for an area major, and the result has been an uneasy alliance between physical education and health education in many schools. Undergraduate and graduate programs alike have faced the uncomfortable and perplexing task of preparing an individual for two teaching areas with a semester hour allotment hardly adequate for one subject matter area alone.

Later, recreation needs expanded and recreational leaders became a marketable commodity. For good measure, safety education (particularly driver education) and adapted physical education were added as necessary ingredients of a well-prepared physical educator and the pot brewing the professional physical educator had to be stirred up frequently via periodic curriculum evaluations and reevaluations to keep the concoction from overflowing. As if the job-analysis technique for definition of major programs had not already done enough to ensure an impossible program of studies, coaching of athletics and athletic training roles similarly demanded specialization advances. Currently we are privileged to see the entrance of several more course developers who are making their presence felt. Physical education for the mentally retarded, movement education, and perceptual-motor training programs are mushrooming into existence all over the country. Each is guaranteed, by past historical precedents, to result definitely in at least a workshop course for undergraduate or graduate credit, to have a good chance at winning a specific course at the undergraduate or graduate level or both, and to be the people's choice for an area of specialization with a core concentration of five to six courses.

For a host of acceptable and logical reasons, all of these important professional responsibilities are loosely incorporated into the "one" subject matter area broadly conceived of as physical education. Can one be surprised to learn that a summer session seminar never got off the first topic for consideration: What physical education means to me. To prepare a professional capable of handling so many responsibilities requires some modicum of time and course work in each of the areas. One small example may serve to illustrate how added responsibilities can serve to multiply courses offered in professional programs of physical education. In 1928, N.P. Neilson (19) examined 28 college catalogs and listed the courses required or offered for the preparation of physical education teachers. Totaled, some 671 different courses were included in his list, which must suggest that agreement on a standard curriculum in physical education could initiate some interesting staff discussions.

With such breadth and scope made necessary, it is a small wonder that both undergraduate and graduate major programs have been forced to give relatively superficial treatment to any one area. So much has needed to be done in so many essential areas that only broad generalization and a smattering of exposure could be allowed in any single area. Physical educators had so many important responsibilities that specialization in only one or two areas would be seen as detrimental, and could result only in unforgivable deterioration in the execution of their professional obligations. Few students have ever completed the catalog major as listed at the time of admission. Instead, systematic course-evaluation would reveal a set of glaring deficiencies in the current major curriculum. Many such deficiencies would be bound to show up because the cluster of responsibilities to which a physical educator becomes obligated is staggering, and the job-analysis technique of curriculum development would identify each and every teaching need. If this did not result in a curriculum change, then the appearance of new faculty members on the staff would. New faculty members with their own unique and inimitable set of professional values—what physical education means to me—would campaign for their ideas, dedicated to the proposition of saving the majors from a deficient and watered-down professional preparation. So noble an obligation to humankind could not be denied, and only a major revision of the curriculum could suffice. As one professor put it, any major who could decipher the revised and new major requirements would deserve to graduate.

Within the profession, enormous turmoil has prevailed in a struggle to blanket new and more demanding obligations with the same-sized cover of major semester hour allocations. Too much emphasis on an in-depth approach had to be avoided and the result has been attention to "how to do it" competencies. Skill development and methods courses best matched the job-analysis technique of curriculum development and any intellectual considerations had to be given delayed consideration. Many graduate programs still offer course work that, more than anything else, simply represents the making up of undergraduate deficiencies. The rule of thumb is quite simple. If the job-analysis technique uncovers a service function not present in the curriculum, then some new course work must be set aside or allotted to its coverage. If all the worthwhile job functions cannot be worked into a single undergraduate time schedule, they can be taken at a later date for graduate credit.

How many college catalogs show countless courses that can be taken for undergraduate *or* graduate credit? One institution offers a course on methods of teaching badminton and tennis which can be taken for undergraduate or graduate credit of three semester hours. "We are interested in excellent teaching" is their motto. Coaching clinics offer semester hour credit for attendance, which many students submit as work toward a graduate degree. If students present an undergraduate deficiency for some course, they may find that it is allowable to take a graduate course with the same title in its place and ameliorate the undergraduate deficiency while at the same time receiving graduate credit. Whether such practices are legitimate or not is for some higher authority to decide. These examples are cited mainly to exemplify the effects of a wide and diverse set of professional responsibilities upon major curricula, both undergraduate and graduate.

In moot testimony to the observation being discussed here, that physical education has emphasized its relationship to educational outcomes at the expense of discovering its own identity, are the textbooks used in introductory physical education courses. An inspection of these textbooks would show that the majority of them devote almost exclusive attention to the role of physical education in an educational setting, either in the schools or in other institutional settings. The physical educator is pictured as a professional educator contributing to all the objectives of education through the modality of physical activity. Yet the course work and competencies prescribed for professional preparation seldom highlight the nature of the subject matter itself; in other words, an understanding of physical activity in its own right is notably absent. Instead, such texts typically treat physical activity as an educational medium capable of contributing to educational objectives without any need to establish the validity of such a premise.

Such an observation about undergraduate textbooks and the usual content of introductory courses is not an indictment. It is, rather, only an observation pointing out the major emphasis prevalent in undergraduate programs of study in physical education. Such programs give legitimate attention to the professional obligations of physical educators that are likely to be encountered when they assume roles of educators. This same observation, however, raises the disturbing question of where the personnel needed to define the scientific basis of physical education will be found if all majors are groomed for roles as professional educators. Rather than having too many chiefs and not enough Indians, physical education produces too many Indians and not enough chiefs.

Consider now the usual definition given for physical education. No physical educator is complete until a personal definition of physical education is formulated. In one of the more accepted introductory texts the following definition of physical education is given:

Physical education, an integral part of the total education process, is a field of endeavor that has as its aim the improvement of human performance through the medium of physical activities that have been selected with a view to realizing this outcome (4, page 16).*

Such a definition is certainly acceptable and would be similar in theme to any definition of physical education ever proposed. It depicts physical education as an integral part of education and as making contributions to a set of objectives which are nearly perfect and also nearly impossible to achieve.

However, an emphasis upon a strictly educational focus simply fails to give due consideration to the subject matter content of physical activity itself. Leaders have demonstrated an implicit acceptance of the naive notion that the subject matter content of physical education is already known and requires only transmission of necessary content through skills classes and methods courses. The incredible situation seems analogous to preparing a clergyman without any in-depth study of theology. Preparation for the ministry, in this case, would require only courses along the lines of: (1) the relationship of the church to society, (2) counseling in church work, (3) methods of delivering inspiring sermons of a noncontroversial content, (4) professional organizations, (5) administration of church affairs, (6) the law and the church, (7) nontaxable fund raising ideas, and any number of other course titles descriptive of a job-analysis approach to the professional activities of clergymen.

This analogy is, of course, unfair. Any program of study for the ministry would include an in-depth study of theology itself since theology is the subject matter content of this profession. Likewise, any program to prepare physical educators contains ample allotments of course work to master the subject matter of physical activity. Or does it? Implicit in the previously cited definition of physical education is a well-structured knowledge system of physical activity. The definition clearly included the point that the educational objectives would be achieved "through the medium of physical activities that have been selected with a view of realizing these outcomes." Whose responsibility is it to define the nature of physical activity so that proper selections can be made?

If the vast majority of emphasis in physical education is upon professional education aspects, there seems little hope for an adequate study of physical activity itself. Any definition of physical education as an integral part of education thus calls for the development of a body of knowledge about physical activity in order for professional education responsibilities to be fulfilled. How can professionally oriented educators, using the physical activity medium, select the activities optimal for achievement of physical, mental, emotional, and social objectives if little is known about physical activity itself? On what basis can a

---

decision be made when the need arises to select activities designed to develop self-confidence and aggressiveness in a timid youngster? Which activities (if any) really do contribute to acquisition of leadership? The basis for such decisions in the past, of course, has been mostly the opinions of a committee charged with establishing policies for educational practices.

Of little amazement to observers of these phenomena, physical education failed to develop an acceptable body of knowledge upon which to base its professional practices. Since both society and state certification of teachers demanded breadth and scope rather than an intensive in-depth preparation, the profession obligingly attempted to meet any and all of the demands imposed upon it. So many fires needed water doused upon them that few individuals in the profession could afford to concern themselves about the supply of water itself. Gradually, however, it is being realized that the profession may have responded too well to the demands made upon it and has attempted to do too much. The result has been inadequate preparation of a professional in many areas—a jack-of-all-trades and master of none syndrome. The conclusion seems inescapable that the job-analysis technique has simply failed to work.

TIME OF REASSESSMENT

Leaders in physical education have begun to examine the results of past efforts and some are generally dissatisfied with what they have found. Attention is being given to the organization of the profession and to the wisdom of trying to produce a multifaceted product in an amount of time hardly adequate for only one facet of endeavor. Each of the content areas present has expressed discontent and is demanding a greater share of the training time in order to produce an acceptable professional product. From such internal wranglings, many recommended programs have ensued to prepare specialists in a single area instead of the total physical educator.

The inability of physical education to study itself in-depth also meant that very little in the way of scholarly research activity could be expected. Whether a result of the harsh criticisms that have jarred education or a realization brought about through its own maturation, physical education today realizes, to a fuller extent than ever before, the importance of preparing specialists in research. Whatever the cause, physical education is taking a long and critical look at its programs of graduate study and seeking a better balance of emphasis between professional and discipline areas. Several bugle calls to action on this front by Staley (23) and by Daniels (5) called attention to the lack of research in physical education and to the criticism that the field was understandably receiving. None of the arguments used was new or novel, but the articles faced the issues squarely and did much to reflect and draw attention to a wave of growing sentiment for change in physical education.

Both Staley and Daniels claimed that our image as technicians and practitioners responsible for utilitarian service programs was due to a failure to properly exploit the potential for research that existed. Franklin Henry's article (9), sandwiched in between those of Staley and Daniels, contained sharper and more pointed criticisms. Henry decried the condition in which physical education found itself, that is, of being a subject for which teachers were prepared but which was not recognized as a subject matter field in its own right. His case for an academic discipline of physical education contained few compliments to traditional undergraduate physical education major programs which were composed of methodology courses and other nonintellectual pursuits.

These articles, along with many others that could be cited, were public laments about the quality of the scholarly research content present in the field of physical education. They undoubtedly were an impetus to numerous changes in both undergraduate and graduate study programs across the country. Although suggesting need for a concerted move into research, their proposals for actual changes in graduate course work and programs of study were veiled and hidden in the shadows of a plea for motivation toward research. Little more can be said for the report by the Graduate Education Conference sponsored by AAHPERD to establish guidelines for graduate education (1). Assuming that the quality of scholar-research content should be raised, the question of importance becomes—how?

Founders of the AAHPERD Kinesiology Council have proposed to examine the structure of an academic discipline associated with the study of human movement (3). They suggested that kinesiology consists of two major divisions, one that can be called general kinesiology and the other, which involves the study of specific human movements, to be classified as applied kinesiology. Under general kinesiology one would find five major subdivisions: (a) physiological kinesiology, (b) psychological kinesiology, (c) mechanical kinesiology, (d) maturational kinesiology, and (e) structural kinesiology. The second major classification, applied kinesiology, would represent application of the principles of general kinesiology to specific motor activities.

At the present time, the kinesiology council does not recommend a separation of the academic discipline of human movement from traditional physical education, where traditional physical education is defined as "skillful practitioners in the educational application." Like previous efforts to identify the basis of an academic discipline, the council has an interesting start in renaming traditional course work and research areas in traditional physical education with a kinesiological nomenclature. The council will, hopefully, move on to identifying the body of knowledge more definitively, as it seems doubtful that a change in course titles will transform traditional physical education into an academic discipline of human movement.

Some definitive work in this direction was initiated by the American Academy of Physical Education (18) in 1962, and the Big Ten's body-of-knowledge project (29). The latter is attempting to define the composition of an academic discipline in physical education, and gives some promise of developing a concrete set of topical areas from which graduate study programs might fruitfully be organized. At last report, attention was being given to the possibility of five areas of specialization: (a) exercise physiology; (b) biomechanics; (c) motor learning and sports psychology; (d) history, philosophy, and comparative physical education and sport; and (e) administrative theory. Unlike several other classification schemes, specific subject matter content for each of the areas is to be developed.

Larson (15) has presented a carefully delineated educational scheme for the training of personnel in the activity sciences. Assuming that physical education does cross the Rubicon and seek to prepare workers in the academic discipline model, concrete recommendations must be available for the actual design of graduate study programs. Larson's plan for the activity sciences is a decided start toward this desideratum. He depicts two tracks in the activity sciences, one for the scholarly research specialist and the other for the practitioner. The plan is complete with possible semester hour credit allocations from bachelor to doctoral degrees. For the specialist degree of a research-scholar, the curriculum calls for a double major from the bachelor's to the doctor's degree. One major is to be in an appropriate science or philosophy and the second major in a designated component of the activity sciences. The first major can be selected from biology, psychology, sociology, physical science, philosophy, history, or education. This major is to be coupled with one in the activity sciences which comprises five components: health sciences, biokinetic sciences, socio-cultural sciences, therapeutic sciences, and the safety sciences.

A fair consensus of these attempts to define the dimensions of an academic discipline of physical education is that the potential for scholarly research seems magnificently available in a number of areas. Granting that the potential is there, however, does not mean the same thing as contending that a discipline exists (as all concerned know full well). Indeed, the question might be asked as to why such potential has not been adequately mined during the time (over three-quarters of a century) that the association has been in existence? It is to be noted with careful attention that the job-analysis approach, which fashioned the profession, is absent in the plans for an academic discipline. The best way to define a discipline may very well be simply to be a discipline—by doing all the things required of a discipline. At the very least, physical education is in an interesting position. Most disciplines give rise to professions, and not vice versa. Our current mad dilemma finds us putting a discipline veneer on the professional body, and the analogy seems to be that the offspring is giving birth to the parent.

THE BASIC MODEL
FOR GRADUATE STUDY IN PHYSICAL EDUCATION

The presence of a variety of graduate study programs in physical education and the various recommendations for sometimes radical change suggest the existence of disjointed and haphazard efforts with only a vaguely defined goal. In actuality, the new programs being suggested and initiated, and the old programs being revised or abandoned represent neither disjointed nor haphazard processes. Such efforts reflect the response of physical education to new factors influencing it. A basic pattern or model is discernible and the complexities of change and growth can be put into proper perspective. To see this pattern, one must understand the relationships among physical activity, the profession of physical education, an academic discipline of physical education, and several related basic disciplines. Whatever differences exist between various proposals and recommendations for change in physical education graduate programs all revolve around these basic components.

Physical Activity

Physical activity constitutes a phenomenon that is as broad and varied as the sum total of humankind's history of human movement endeavors. Our motor activities represent expressions of our physical and competitive nature, yield expressions of aesthetic values, involve us in social and cultural aspects of society, and affect us in both physical and psychological dimensions. As a focal point of interest, physical activity includes considerably more than just those activities traditionally taught by physical educators in a school setting. At the present stage of development, it is seen to include sport in its broadest sense and subtends play, dance, games, sports, exercise, and athletics. The strongest common bond between these physical activity components is the muscular exertion involved and the natural desire in human beings for muscular activity in nonutilitarian pursuits, both competitive and noncompetitive.

A complete list of all the physical activity components to be considered pertinent and legitimate has not yet been forwarded. Because of physical education's long historical association with athletic activities and the school, the sports emphasis is likely to receive major consideration at first. There is good reason to expect, however, that the defined composition of physical activity will gradually change and broaden in scope. Many sports go virtually unstudied because they have not commonly been included within the sphere of traditional physical-education activities in the school setting. Thus, horse racing, car racing, boating, children's play, and marksmanship have seldom been considered legitimate components for universal attention. Yet activities like these share the common criteria for inclusion in the domain of physical activity, and as the profession and academic discipline of physical education mature, such activities are likely to come in for consideration.

Unlike the attitude held by those who established the Association for the Advancement of Physical Education in 1885, there is no requirement that physical activity be defined within the borders of a health-oriented temperance movement. This means that restricting the study of physical activity only to those pursuits which are health giving, character building, and capable of giving sustenance to educational goals is no longer an oligarchic mandate. Physical activity in all its forms and variations is not to be subjected first to a moral judgment as a qualification before entry is granted into the domain of physical activity for study. A discipline concerned with physical activity can suffer no such restriction in its academic pursuits, for if it did it would cease to be a discipline. Entry into the domain of physical activity is enjoined by only one criterion: whether or not the object of interest is a form of physical activity as defined. A profession can make moral judgments about phenomena within the domain of physical activity as it seeks to select appropriate activities for the fulfillment of professional responsibilities. However, the set of criteria employed by the profession cannot also be imposed upon a discipline setting out to structure a knowledge system within the domain of physical activity.

The Profession Associated with Physical Activity

The existence of diverse forms of physical activity naturally creates a demand for expert conduct of some of these activities and leads to the development of a group of individuals who are skilled in the administration of physical activity. Such skilled technicians do not necessarily have to be professional in the true sense of the word profession.* Conduct of

*The reader is asked to accept these statements about a profession, for the time being, as something close to the truth. Chapter 4 will show them to be reasonably accurate.

many forms of physical activity is still handled today by nonprofessionals. Thus, major league baseball and professional football are managed and coached by individuals who are highly skilled but who are not true professionals. Such individuals are capable of conducting these activities with trade- or business-like skills and competencies to the degree that society accepts their performance. Only physical education comes close to qualifying as a profession concerned with physical activity.

The role of the profession of physical education today is primarily restricted to activities in school settings and is greatly controlled by teacher certification standards. If the value of the profession is made clearer, it is not unreasonable to expect an expansion of the professional role into more segments of society. For example, numerous exercise gymnasiums that are commercially operated offer many forms of physical activity traditional to physical education. Many of these health spas are operated by personnel characteristic of the gymnasium directors of yesteryear. As a service to society, these gymnasiums might be better staffed by professional physical educators than the personnel currently in charge. Similarly, many coaches of school-sponsored athletic teams have had little or no preparation as physical educators. As a profession, physical education must eventually consider the wisdom of allowing such physical activities to be conducted by nonprofessionals. It may very well be true that physical education or society, or both, may eventually demand that such activities be conducted competently and educationally by qualified professionals instead of by skilled technicians.

One point to be borne in mind is that, whether a profession concerned with physical activity exists or not, the phenomenon of physical acivity will persist. Any history of mankind shows that play has been an omnipresent phenomenon and, from at least the time of the Greeks, coaches and athletic trainers have existed. The importance that society attaches to the conduct of such activities serves as the motivating force for the development of a profession. If society decides that physical activity can be conducted satisfactorily by skilled technicians or by unskilled citizens on their own, then the reason for the existence of a profession charged with such a responsibility is negated. Thus, physical activity as a definite entity can be defined for a discipline to study without the requirement that a profession exist to utilize the knowledge generated by the discipline. Also, in the same manner, the physical activity can exist without either the profession or the discipline.

Academic Discipline Aspects of Physical Activity

An academic discipline concerned with physical activity may exist even if a profession of physical education does not. Such a discipline would seek to understand physical activity from many perspectives and to develop a body of knowledge appropriate to the content domain. For proof, the situation can be compared to any other content domain. Physics, for example, could exist as a science even if no profession of engineering were available to apply the knowledge generated by physicists. English would still exist as a discipline even if teachers of English disappeared from our schools. Physical education, however, has always had a professionally oriented responsibility and many today still cannot accept the concept of an academic discipline of physical activity without insisting that it produce useful knowledge for the benefit of a profession of physical education.

Most of the proponents advocating increased scholarly research activities in physical education do so with the fervent conviction that it is essential for the benefit of physical education as a profession. The major theme seems to be that an academic discipline of physical education will be charged with the responsibility of developing the knowledge structure upon which the profession of physical education can rest and advance. Such pragmatically oriented advocates of the academic discipline would also require that the research produce only such knowledge. Now the question seldom recognized as a legitimate one is that of whether or not a discipline so restricted to the production of useful knowledge can ever be considered to be a true discipline. As we shall see later, a true discipline does not need to produce knowledge useful to society. Indeed, such a requirement is antagonistic to the pure-science ideal considered previously. It may very well be true that much of the current movement to enlarge scholarly research efforts in physical education is evidence not of the desire to create a discipline but of the desire to enhance a true professional status.

Discussions of the future of physical education and new programs of study currently consider the existence of a core of physical activity, a profession of physical education, and an academic discipline of physical education as being mutually essential. Thus, the discipline must exist to nurture the profession and the profession must exist to give a reason for the discipline to exist. Although such a situation need not be necessary, most current developments implicitly operate within this frame of reference. Conceptually, the system may be defined with physical activity as the central core and focal point for both the profession and the discipline. A profession of physical education has the responsibility for the conduct of suitable programs of physical activity and is responsible for research and scholarly activities designed to improve the quality of its practices and services to society. An academic discipline of physical education conducts advanced and more basic research and scholarly activity, pertinent to the basic core of physical activity.

Acceptance of such a model for the relationship of the profession to the discipline of physical activity has many points in its favor. Such a model, however, should not be used by the profession as an excuse not to conduct any research of its own. The profession must not contend that the production of knowledge and answers to pressing questions is a function to be performed solely by the discipline. If the profession were to do this, then the discipline would be obliged to produce only useful knowledge. Unfortunately the discovery of knowledge cannot be effectively programmed to produce only useful results. Indeed, some of the best and most sophisticated research efforts by the discipline might not have useful applications for many years, for several generations, or ever. The pursuit of knowledge must be guided by the demands of the knowledge structure being developed in the domain and by the curiosity of the scientist. The demands of practical problems may have to be answered by the profession itself or by a combined mission-oriented type of cooperative endeavor.

The monumental task of formally defining the content domain of an academic discipline of physical education lies ahead. Even a comprehensive definition of physical activity, upon which the discipline is to focus, is not enough. A definition of the academic discipline must be available so that implementation of training programs for specialists in the discipline can be developed. Most of the present attempts at advancing research in and scholarly study of physical education as an academic discipline have sometimes sought merely to transfer established disciplines and their study techniques over to a physical-activity focus. Thus, we see an avalanche of courses being drawn from the roll call of established disciplines: psychology of, physiology of, history of, sociology of, philosophy of, and so on right down the list of new "academic" courses in physical education.

Few would argue that several disciplines are closely related and pertinent to the focus of interest upon physical activity as an area of scholarly investigation. It is for this reason that a transfer and application of investigative strategies from related disciplines into a physical activity focus is both understandable and desirable. Ignoring well-established bodies of knowledge in pertinent disciplines, or a refusal to take advantage of proven research strategies simply does not make sense. At the same time, two important points need to be given ample consideration: (1) the content domain of an academic discipline of physical education cannot be fully and adequately defined at this time; and (2) a full scale transfer of all related disciplines in one simultaneous and sweeping reform can be of little value.

First, since it can be discussed quickly, let us consider the wisdom of defining the content domain for the academic discipline of physical education. What role is foreseen for studying the play of animals in an academic discipline of physical education? One of the earliest pioneers in the Association for the Advancement of Physical Education spent several years of intensive study on animal play, compiling notes apparently with the intent of writing a book on the topic. His writings included a book, *A Philosophy of Play*, that contained many references to the play of animals as a basis for understanding the phenomenon of play activities among human beings (8). Should a study of play be restricted to humans or not? If so, what of exercise physiology that presently makes considerable use of animal experiments in attempts to explore more adequately exercise physiology in humans? How indeed should restrictive boundaries be established for this physical activity focus?

Several definitions of an academic discipline of physical education have been forwarded. Each constitutes an important and necessary contribution, and all are essential if actual programs of study are ever to be implemented. Identification of the essential components, however, must be viewed as temporary and perhaps even inaccurate constructs necessary for immediate action. Since a discipline of physical activity barely exists, such definitive constructs must be accepted only as good beginnings and not final evaluations. Fifty years ago, a science of nutrition did not exist. Today the science of nutrition encompasses topics never before known to human beings. In a like manner, the discipline of physical education must be free to develop its own destiny in regard to a substantive domain. Topical areas of importance, as yet unknown, must not suffer restrictive influences generated from decisions made too early as to the composition of the discipline.

Consider now the second point. What would be the result if graduate programs suddenly saw transplants of course work from related disciplines appearing on a large scale within graduate curricula? Owing to the wide variety of disciplines related to physical activity, there would be a wide variety of transplanted courses in full foliage. If only one course were required for each of the related disciplines the result would again be a broad, thin, and diluted curriculum. Just as in the case of planning an adequate professional curriculum, the problem of breadth versus depth again looms as a problem.

Fraleigh (7), for example, has suggested five key concepts in his model of an academic discipline in physical education, all of which have, as a perspective, an entity that we shall loosely define as physical activity. These five key concepts are: (a) biological development; (b) political, social, and economic forces; (c) expression; (d) learning; and (e) applied mechanics. Certainly such an attempt at defining the content domain for an academic discipline of physical education possesses considerable merit, and Fraleigh's model seems sufficiently adequate for at least qualified acceptance. The breadth of key concepts encompasses most of the areas of interest likely to be pursued with much diligence by capable investigators. Although still obligated to stand as a target for suggestions of revision, the model holds much promise for surviving with a discernible parentage.

Now, however, the nagging question arises as to how such an adequate conceptual model can be translated into real-life graduate study programs. Fraleigh suggested that the methods of inquiry for this conceptual model would necessarily include approaches from both the objective and subjective dimensions of existence (7, page 39). There are many who share Fraleigh's conclusion that the combination, in one discipline, of all the methods of inquiry included in the arts, sciences, and humanities could result in a discipline of exceptional stature. A discipline that combined the methods of both science and the humanities would indeed possess virtue. However, how realistic is it to expect that physical education could produce a discipline that the rest of humankind has failed to realize ever since the dawn of time? Could one program of study in the academic discipline of physical education produce a competent and productive Ph.D. in each and every one of the five key-concept areas?

One answer is that no single program of study can be fashioned that could do justice to all of the areas depicted in any conceptual model for an academic discipline of physical education. Some priorities have to be established and some choices have to be made. Larson's plan (15) for the scholarly research scientist represents one strategy for making a choice among the alternatives available. His scheme calls for graduate work in five areas of an activity science: health, biokinetics, socio-cultural, therapeutic, and safety. This concentration in the activity science is to be coupled with a second and equally emphasized major in some related discipline. Thus, Larson's model for the academic discipline of physical activity includes acquisition of a broad preparation with course work and competency provided for in five defined content-areas of the discipline. The companion major in a related discipline is assigned to provide an adequate in-depth preparation with which to exploit the breadth of preparation in the activity sciences. This plan for graduate study has considerable merit and many proponents.

Like Fraleigh's model, however, Larson's plan could be criticized on the basis that little in the way of in-depth preparation could be realized when the academic discipline of physical activity contains five components. Several of the methods of inquiry and key concepts forwarded by Fraleigh could be suggested as needed for some or all of the five areas outlined by Larson. Thus, Larson's health area could be further differentiated by Fraleigh's biological, learning, expression, and political—social—economic key concepts. Holders of this viewpoint would allow that the definition of an academic discipline proposed by Larson was acceptable, but that requiring preparation in all components of the activity sciences was not. Every one of the five component-areas could not be singularly well developed through intensive study, and products of such a graduate program might find it necessary to rely rather heavily on their companion major in a related discipline in order to make scholarly contributions.

Such a criticism of Larson's plan would be likely to lead to the idea that preparation in all of the content areas of the discipline of physical education is undesirable and that still further specialization is needed. This thesis was offered by Kenyon (13), who suggested the adoption of a "controlled empirical inquiry" approach in which several discipline-like subfields are developed encompassing the breadth of the entire discipline collectively. Rather than attempting to develop a single discipline, Kenyon recommended a collection of several such subfields "loosely affiliated in a consortium of movement studies." One can envision products of such a plan for graduate study as being reasonably well prepared and capable of scholarly contributions within the subfield discipline. Once again, however, a commitment to an adequate in-depth preparation carries with it a criticism that the breadth of preparation necessary for a well-proportioned frame of reference toward physical activity is lacking.

Viewed with measured caution, the several contributions offered as a definition for the academic discipline of physical education seem endowed with reasonable adequacy and palatability to major segments of the profession. The several actual and deduced graduate study programs, however, seem less successful in charting a route out of the wilderness presented by the depth versus breadth dilemma. Difficulties with the depth versus breadth strategy for both professional education and academic-discipline oriented programs of study present decision makers with several uncomfortable alternatives. Figure 3.1 can help illustrate the conceptual model involved in such necessary decision making and can suggest some further issues that need to be considered as well.

Depicted in Figure 3.1 is a central core representing physical activity, two concentric circles representing first the profession of physical education and then the academic discipline of physical education. Finally, a sharp triangle is depicted representing the content domain of a related basic discipline with its overlaps. Regardless of how it is defined with respect to composition, physical activity is seen as occupying a position around which both professionally oriented physical education and an academic discipline of physical education revolve. The focus of interest, be it profession or discipline, remains on this physical activity eye. Pertinent and related disciplines are seen as wedge-shaped content domains piercing through successive layers of concentric circles. As the related-discipline wedge passes through to the center, it diminishes in size of overlap, first with the discipline of physical education, then with the profession of physical education, finally with the physical activity focus.

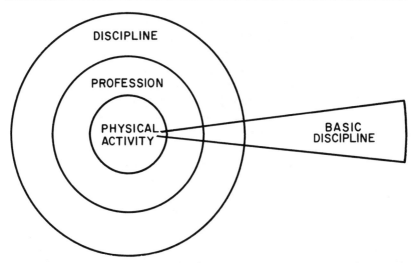

Figure 3.1. Relationships of physical activity, the profession and academic discipline of physical education and a basic discipline.

Such an attrition reflects the content domain orientation of the related discipline. Although certain aspects of the content domain of the related discipline do, indeed, overlap with a discipline of physical education, less of it overlaps with the profession of physical education, and even less of it overlaps with the physical-activity focus.

Consider, for example, the case of physiology as one of the basic disciplines important to the model presented for conceptualizing graduate study in physical education. Certainly physiology as a discipline is concerned with some topical areas which are of little or no concern to physical activity, the conduct of physical activity by a profession, or the academic discipline of physical education. However, the physiology of exercise is of concern, and physiology—the discipline—may then overlap within the boundaries of the proposed model. In the academic discipline of physical education, this overlap could represent special interest in the problems of physiology of exercise, heat mechanisms, metabolism, and so on. The overlap, however, is not complete between the discipline of physiology and the discipline of physical education. Only in a limited range of topics would the two areas find congruence of interests, and the two fields would still remain more unalike than the same.

The basic question to be asked in the development of programs of graduate study in the academic discipline of physical education is, then: How much of physiology—the discipline—does one need to be competent in that part of the academic discipline of physical education called physiology of exercise? An answer is needed for all such overlaps of basic disciplines within the sphere of the physical education discipline. This task by itself will cause considerable debate, but the same kinds of decisions must also be made for the overlap within the professional sphere.

One might argue that an individual interested in physical acivity as the focal point must be prepared completely in the discipline of physiology in order to be competent. This may be true, and if it is, then the Ph.D. in biophysics must present Ph.D. competencies in both biology *and* physics. More likely, the solution lies in selecting appropriate amounts of preparation in the related basic discipline, and then supplementing such basic preparation with specific preparation in the content area of the academic discipline of physical education.

When seen from this vantage point, several alternatives for models of graduate study in physical education are possible. One might decide, for example, that the best way to develop the knowledge system within the academic discipline sphere of physical education is to seek individuals with complete preparation in a basic related discipline. If such completely prepared disciplinarians then focus their attention on physical activity, physical education will prosper and advances will be made in both the profession and the discipline of physical education. On the other hand, complete preparation in the basic discipline may not be considered essential. Physiological psychologists, for example, do not first become threefold Ph.D.'s in physiology, neuroanatomy, and neurophysiology. A selection is made of necessary competencies in these areas, and intensive study is then focused upon the specific content area of physiological psychology.

Another important and critical point to be remembered is that once a basic discipline pierces the academic discipline domain of physical education and there is an overlap, the basic discipline's overlap is then amenable to the principles of that domain. When physiology overlaps physiology of exercise, for example, the academic discipline of physical education evaluates the overlap from a new frame of reference—that of the physical-activity focus. Maximal oxygen uptake may have been researched adequately so far as the physiologist is concerned, but the physical-activity focus now asks how much can other factors affect its role in performance? How important is personality in overcoming oxygen uptake deficiencies in running a mile? Could the presence of spectators, for example, motivate performers with an inferior level of oxygen uptake such that they would run farther and faster than performers with superior oxygen uptake? How do racial background, sociological factors, previous competitive experiences, skill, and the importance attached to successful performance interact with the physiological oxygen-uptake factor? Which activities require or develop good oxygen uptake, or both?

When questions such as these are asked, the basic discipline of physiology is seen to be inadequate in the academic discipline of physical education even though there is overlap. The discipline of physical education asks other questions and looks differently at physical activity. To demand that graduate programs of study in physical education prepare individuals completely in *all* the basic disciplines overlapping its content domain is almost to demand the impossible. Selection of necessary competencies from other disciplines is seen to be complicated and difficult, but absolutely necessary.

Since no graduate study program can hope to endow an individual preparing for work in the discipline of physical education with complete preparation in all the pertinent disciplines, the pattern becomes one of delimitation and selection. The task of developing adequate and successful programs of study in the discipline of physical education will not be easy. A variety of programs and a greater variety of successes and failures will undoubtedly occur. A variety of diverse programs, in fact, may well serve best to assess which approach (or approaches) promises the best success. Whatever changes are suggested and new programs are evolved, they all represent some definition or redefinition of the amount and kind of emphasis to be allotted to the constituent areas diagrammed in Figure 3.1. Diverse as they may seem, they all have a definable pattern and a discernible, although elusive, goal.

Graduate programs designed to prepare professional physical educators have similar tasks of definition and selection. The basic discipline of physiology penetrates through into the domain of the profession of physical education as well as into the discipline of physical education. As shown in the diagram, there is less overlap within the professional sphere. The profession must concern itself with a greater variety of study topics and cannot afford to emphasize one topic more than another. A profession must consider a more general approach since it has the responsibility of conducting the actual programs of physical activity.

In the profession, consideration of exercise physiology is certainly important. It must, therefore, give proper attention to such topics as heat training, injury management, physical fitness, fatigue, and rest. Such topics reflect the exercise-physiology component in physical activity. However, the profession must *also* give attention to other essential components in physical activity as well. Hence, consideration of motor learning, educational goals and objectives, proper selection of activities for different age levels, efficient management in the conduct of activities, and a host of other topics must be evaluated properly in order to conduct optimal programs of physical activity. Deletion, over-emphasis, or dilution of any of the pertinent components could bring about deleterious effects. By necessity, then, a program of graduate study for a profession must have greater breadth than a program of graduate study for a discipline.

The difficult decisions to be made must balance necessary breadth against essential depth of preparation. Superficial knowledge of pertinent exercise physiology may be quite costly, but if better preparation in exercise physiology is achieved at the expense of preparation in motor learning the cost may be even greater. Contemporary critics of education point to the lack of depth in graduate programs, but amelioration of this deficiency often brings with it the possible deficiency of a lack of essential breadth. An individual completely prepared in the basic discipline of physiology may not be the best prospect for the conduct of physical-activity programs. He or she would lack necessary skills and competencies essential to the professional conduct of a physical activity program. Indeed, this individual is not likely to be interested in such a responsibility and may even ridicule such efforts.

Thus, the basic model for programs of graduate study can be seen as a struggle between depth and breadth of preparation. Because the focus of both the profession and the discipline is toward physical activity, graduate-study programs of each must reflect the essential components of its content domain. Since physical activity is complicated and comprises a number of essential components, graduate study will find it difficult to contend with its complexities. Denial of any essential component's existence would amount to a denial of the true character of physical activity. The task of deciding upon proper emphasis for defined areas and actual definition of the essential component areas is, indeed, complex and fraught with pitfalls; but it is both an inevitable and continuing task for all of higher education.

AN ACTUAL PROGRAM

Intriguing as all the new developments are for graduate study in physical education as an academic discipline, the real test comes in implementing actual programs. Certainly, a sample program can afford opportunity for criticism, a starting point for further revision, analysis of objectives, and so forth. Considering the number of factors to be given attention, any program of graduate study seems a creditable achievement. A specific example, however, with concrete advantages and visible deficiencies may help to crystallize thinking and channel attention to specifics and away from vague generalizations.

A program of graduate study leading to a Ph.D. in an area of specialization called exercise science has been developed at the University of Massachusetts. In planning the program, it was decided that preparation of a generalist who was both capable in the professional aspects of physical education and a research scholar as well was too ambitious an undertaking. Instead, the program was devised to prepare individuals skilled as research scholars, and no efforts were made to produce simultaneously skilled practitioners in professional aspects of physical education.

Unlike several Ph.D. programs in the midwestern United States, it was decided that the major portion of the course work should be focused on subject matter germane to human movement in games, sports, and physical activity in the broad sense. Such a decision meant that Ph.D. students in the program would take more course work taught by research specialists in these areas and take less of their course work in outside disciplines. Some graduate programs, for example, offering a Ph.D. in physical education find students taking only two or three courses in physical education. The rest of the graduate program is taken, say, in biochemistry or in physiology. Credentials of such products thus show six to nine semester hours credit in subject matter pertaining to physical activity per se, and 60 to 90 hours in outside disciplines. Although such programs have many advantages, their products must consider problems in physical activity avocationally or at some later date.

The New England approach decided that considerable subject matter content in physical activity already existed that required direct study. Thus, specific course work should be taken *inside* the discipline with needed course work outside the discipline taken as cognate areas. Requiring cognate areas instead of minors reflected the idea that courses in outside disciplines should be selected to contribute best to the program in the exercise sciences. Too often, courses for a minor are set up to reflect minimal competencies needed in the area of minor specialization and do not equally enrich the area of major concentration. Naturally, some disciplines might set up minors that would directly complement the major area of specialization in the exercise sciences, but the idea of cognate areas helped guarantee such a desired outcome.

Exercise science was seen as constituting the knowledge system or subject matter domain basic to human movement in games, sports, and physical activity. Human movement represented such a unique and unstudied phenomenon that no program of study could be synthesized adequately by selection of seemingly pertinent courses from outside disciplines with some semester-hour quota system. No matter how judiciously the selection of course work from other areas is made, a body of knowledge cannot be developed and structured through the avocational interests of scholars from other disciplines. The breadth and depth of human movement cannot be identified by the patching together of bits and pieces of related topics randomly and haphazardly investigated in other areas. Scholarly investigation of human movement must focus directly upon the phenomenon with systematic and organized efforts.

By necessity, such scholarly study of human movement will borrow from other related disciplines just as other developing disciplines have done in the past. Astronomy, for example, utilizes the instruments and principles of physics. Physics, in turn, rests heavily upon mathematics. Early research in the area of perception was done by physiologists and physicists. Psychologists now study perception as well, and contributions come from all three disciplines. Psychology itself developed out of philosophy. Psychiatry and clinical psychology coexist although each studies the same content area. Anthropology, psychology, and sociology are all concerned with the study of the human. Differentiation among these three occurs only when the perspective of study is considered; for instance, the kinds of different questions each asks about human beings.

Such examples demonstrate well the axiom that nature knows no subject matter boundaries. Many disciplines operate in overlapping subject matter domains and frequently the overlap results in the emergence of a new discipline. Biophysics, for example, represents such a development. A biophysicist is less than a biologist and less than a physicist, but as a biophysicist has no peer. Concern that a discipline cannot be born unless it can possess a *unique* body of knowledge is not a critical issue. Overlapping of disciplines reflects only the multiple efforts required in the pursuit of knowledge, and disciplines have long functioned in symbiotic harmony. Territorial rights are less important than territorial development.

The Ph.D. program eventually developed had a commitment to research-scholar emphasis in three major divisions of the broader term of exercise science: (1) biomechanics; (2) exercise physiology; and (3) motor integration. Emphasis and likely content in the first two components requires little further explanation, but the content of motor integration does. Simply defined, motor integration might be likened to the physiology of motor learning *and* exercise physiology from the viewpoint of the nervous system. Motor integration is seen as basic to future emphasis on typical motor learning content work and affords a bridge not only between exercise physiology and motor learning but between exercise physiology and biomechanics as well.

All students in the Ph.D. program for the exercise sciences would take course work in each of these three areas and then specialize in one (and with counseling, perhaps two) of the areas. By decision of the graduate faculty, certain competencies (to be reflected in course work) would be required of all Ph.D. candidates in exercise science regardless of final specialization. Required courses would include introduction to research, measurement theory, seminar, and a dissertation. Prerequisites to the course in measurement theory require undergraduate credits in tests and measurements, elementary statistics, and a computer science course; graduate prerequisites include elementary statistics and design of experiments course work. These general requirements were seen as providing a reasonably adequate basis for proper use of statistics and the computer in experimental studies.

Further course work for specialization in exercise science was to be chosen from these alternatives:

Biomechanics
   Mechanical analysis of human motion
   Biomechanics
   Kinesthetic form
   Joint torque analysis of human movement

Exercise Physiology
   Instrumentation theory
   Experimental physiology of exercise
   Metabolic adaptations to exercise
   Exercise and the cardiovascular system
   Respiratory physiology and the exercise response

Motor Integration
   Motor integration practicum
   Human fatigue
   Kinesthesis

Cognate areas were defined for each of the major divisions of the exercise science major. Each specialty might have several cognate area possibilities depending upon the major topical area in the specialty to be emphasized. The cognate area, however, had to enrich and complement the exercise science major rather than constitute an acceptable minor in the related discipline.

Viewed on the basis of the present stage of possible development, the program seems to offer good preparation for experimental work in the exercise science field. So far as the humanities offerings are concerned, the program is seen as minimal but essential in order to preserve the total outlook toward physical activity. Course work in basic disciplines—such as physiology, engineering mechanics, and psychology—is not maximized, which may or may not be a mistake and a shortcoming. The true and final test of the program (as with all such programs) will be the productivity of the scholar-researchers it purports to produce.

Perhaps the exercise science specialty is still too broad or perhaps it is not broad enough. To the developers of the program, it represented the consensus of opinion as to what could reasonably be accomplished with optimum efficiency. Course work in traditional and professionally oriented physical education was deliberately omitted. Advanced courses at the graduate level in administration, principles and objectives, curriculum development, supervision, and school-related problems were seen as professional and educational in nature and thus unsuited for a graduate program intent upon evolving into a model representative of an academic discipline of physical education. Notably absent as well are courses representing the content of related physical education areas such as health education, recreation, dance, and safety education. No denial of the importance of these fields in professional education is intended by such deliberate omission. Also, no claim is made that these areas do not exhibit strong and essential bonds with professional physical education. These first cousins to physical education as well as the current patriarch of education were omitted for the simple reason that they represent professional ties. An academic discipline of physical education could be developed, it was believed, only by shedding the professional harness and pursuing an independent course.

The position adopted thus reflects a sharp move away from extensive breadth in a graduate program. It was deemed difficult enough to prescribe an in-depth preparation in the academic discipline of physical education alone without attempting to pay academic homage to all the revered members of the loosely knit family that are embraced collectively within the professional robes of physical education. Indeed, definition of a program for preparation in an academic discipline of physical education had already necessitated several painful decisions as topical areas of obvious relevance were eliminated. Inclusion of another half-dozen professional service areas would have served only to dilute the value of the program beyond acceptable limits. As the program stands now, the course of study is considerably more specialized than many previous graduate programs labeled academic and scholarly. At the same time, it is also less specialized than some new programs that require almost complete specialization and preparation in a related discipline. Developers of the program decided, however, that further specialization would work to hinder necessary breadth when the focus upon physical activity was to be passed through the lens of an exercise science emphasis.

The program does not, of course, claim to constitute an adequate and complete model for an academic discipline of physical education. What it does do is make several difficult priority decisions about some probable components within the discipline domain. With its major emphasis upon biomechanics, exercise physiology, and motor integration, it was forced to exclude the social, cultural, and philosophical analysis of physical activity as a dominant study area. In so doing, a strong commitment was made to develop adequate competencies in statistics, experimental design, computer usage, and, in fact, to a complete empirical investigative method of inquiry. The emphasis is upon quantitative rather than qualitative analysis, upon the mechanisms of physical movement associated with physical activity rather than the uses and meanings of physical activity. In order to accomplish even such a limited set of goals, the program was forced to exclude, but not negate, the value or existence of several other legitimate components within the discipline domain. By and large, those excluded areas were exemplified by subjective and qualitative approaches as a method of inquiry. These excluded areas, however, were not totally exempted from consideration and recognition even in a program heavy with quantitative emphasis upon the mechanisms of physical movement. Indeed, these areas were partially identified and loosely named a sport in culture area to which all students would receive some exposure. Although certainly not a clean dichotomy, a separation into an exercise science and sport in culture areas paralleled a decided difference in method of inquiry. Since it is extremely doubtful that human capacities can handle optimally combinations such as biomechanics and philosophy or exercise physiology and comparative sport, the artificial dichotomy imposed between the exercise sciences and sport in culture recognizes the reality of both interest and likely competency clusters.

However, the program of studies outlined does contain some breadth as well. This breadth is provided for through a threefold attempt to understand physical activity: biomechanics, exercise physiology, and motor integration. It is possible, therefore, to study physical activity from more than just a consideration of lever systems alone, from the action of physiological systems alone, or from the nervous system alone. Exercise and physical activity comprise at least these three major components and to the extent that this is true, the graduate program has breadth. What, then, of motor learning and skill acquisition? Is skill not a factor in exercise and physical activity? What of motivation, personality, anthropometry, growth and development, and countless other pertinent and important topical areas? The answer to such disturbingly legitimate questions is, of course, that the program is deficient in these respects. However, any program devised must face the crisis of decision and live with the resultant set of advantages and disadvantages. Even with the full exclusion of professional aspects and related first cousins of subject matter interest, the program of study for an academic discipline of physical education is still beset with the breadth versus depth dilemma. The only comfort available is to consider what the situation would be if inclusion into a graduate program were also necessary for the professional aspects of education, adequate representation of related service subjects such as health and recreation, and an expressed goal of attacking all such problems philosophically, historically, sociologically, scientifically, and, indeed, with all methods of inquiry known to humankind. Strange as it seems, many graduate programs of the past have attempted to do just that and have claimed success.

Academic Discipline(s) of Physical Education

The development of an exercise science graduate degree program at the

University of Massachusetts in 1969* represented a radical departure from traditional graduate degree programs in physical education. The program accepted nonphysical education as well as physical education undergraduate majors, did not require teaching credentials or courses in education either as prerequisites or for program completion. Students entered from diverse academic discipline backgrounds with no allegiance to teaching or education, only a commitment to research and scholarly expertise in the particular knowledge domain of exercise science. Many observers charged the program was disloyal to its physical education roots. By 1980, however, many other universities had initiated graduate program specialization in discipline-based areas; some sought and achieved a name change from physical education for the department and the degree.

Beginning in 1974, AAHPERD underwent important organizational changes which, among other significant developments, resulted in the establishment of the National Association for Sport and Physical Education (NASPE). As one of its features, NASPE sponsors ten academies charged with the responsibility for the knowledge base of physical education. The ten academies are adapted physical education, curriculum, exercise physiology, history, kinesiology, motor development, philosophy, sport art, sport psychology, and sport sociology. Several of these academies complement scholarly societies initiated by other groups of scholars in various disciplines interested in sport and physical activity. The North American Society for Psychology of Sports and Physical Activity (NASPSPA), the Philosophic Society for the Study of Sport (PSSS), and the North American Society for Sport History (NASSH) were already formed and active before the NASPE academies were organized.

Thus, the search for a scientific basis for physical education practices begun by George Wells Fitz in the 1880's and eloquently called for again by Franklin Henry in 1964 erupted into existence during the 1970's and exists in a stage of development farther advanced than ever before. The current movement for an academic discipline of (or for) physical education exists with striking similarities in Australia, England, Canada, and Japan. New graduate students and new professionals have a most exciting future before them. The next decades promise to be the most challenging and potentially the most rewarding for physical education, sport, and physical activity—the profession and the discipline.

---

*The Department of Exercise Science in the School of Physical Education was created officially in 1971 under the chairmanship of Harry K. Campney, Jr. The Ph.D. degree was initially titled human movement, which was later changed to a degree in exercise science when the Department of Sport Studies offered a Ph.D. in sport studies.

REFERENCES

1. American Association for Health, Physical Education and Recreation. *Graduate Education in Health Education, Physical Education, Recreation Education, Safety Education, and Dance.* Washington, D.C.: American Association for Health, Physical Education and Recreation, 1967.

2. Anderson, Thomas D. A lesson from the Greeks on exercise. *Archives of Physical Medicine and Rehabilitation* **45**: 350; July 1964.

3. Barham, Jerry N. Toward a science and discipline of human movement. *JOHPER* **37**: 65, 67-68; October 1966.

4. Bucher, Charles A. *Foundations of Physical Education,* 8th ed. St. Louis: Mosby, 1979.

5. Daniels, A.S. The potential of physical education as an area of research and scholarly effort. *JOHPER* **36**: 32, 33, 74; January 1965.

6. Flexner, Abraham. *Medical Education in the United States.* New York: Carnegie Foundation for the Advancement of Teaching, Bulletin No. 4, 1910.

7. Fraleigh, Warren P. Toward a conceptual model of the academic subject matter of physical education as a discipline. *Proceedings, National College Physical Education Association for Men* **70**: 31-39; 1967.

8. Gulick, Luther H. *A Philosophy of Play.* Boston: Scribner's, 1920.

9. Henry, Franklin. Physical education: an academic discipline. *JOHPER* **35**: 32, 33, 69; September 1964.

10. Hetherington, Clark W. Fundamental education. *American Physical Education Review* **15**: 629-635, December 1910.

11. Hetherington, Clark W. Graduate work in physical education. *American Physical Education Review* **30**: 207-210, 262-268; 1925.

12. Judd, Charles II. Report of the committee on resolutions concerning the kind and extent of facilities and courses needed to meet the demands of the country for well-trained physical educators. *American Physical Education Review* **19**: 19-21; 1914.

13. Kenyon, Gerald S. On the conceptualization of subdisciplines within an academic discipline dealing with human movement. *Proceedings, National College Physical Education Association for Men* **71**: 34-45; 1968.

14. Kraus, Hans. Preventive aspects of physical fitness. *New York State Journal of Medicine* **64**: 1182-1185; May 15, 1964.

15. Larson, Leonard A. Professional preparation for the activity sciences. *Journal of Sports Medicine and Physical Fitness* **5**: 15-22; March 1965.

16. Leonard, Fred E., and R. Tait McKenzie. *A Guide to the History of Physical Education.* Philadelphia: Lea and Febiger, 1927.

17. Lloyd, Frank S. The research specialist and his role in teacher education. *Research Quarterly* **9**: 33-37; December 1938.

18. Metheny, Eleanor, et al. Physical education as an area of study and research. *Quest* **9**: 73-78; December 1967.

19. Neilson, N.P. A curriculum for the profession and preparation of physical education teachers for secondary schools. *Research Quarterly* **2**: 217-226; March 1931.

20. Oberteuffer, Delbert. Evaluating the college physical education program. *Proceedings, National College Physical Education Association for Men* **67**: 56-60; 1964.

21. Rice, Emmett A. *A Brief History of Physical Education.* New York: Barnes, 1929.

22. Rice, Emmett A., John L. Hutchinson, and Mabel Lee. *A Brief History of Physical Education,* 4th ed. New York: Ronald, 1958.

23. Staley, S.C. Keys to advancement in physical education. *The Physical Educator* **18**: 83-88; October 1961.

24. VanDalen, Deobold B., Elmer D. Mitchell, and Bruce L. Bennett. *A World History of Physical Education.* Englewood Cliffs, New Jersey: Prentice-Hall, 1953.

25. Weiss, Raymond A. Is physical fitness our most important objective? *JOHPER* **35**: 17, 18, 61, 62; February 1964.

26. Weston, Arthur. *The Making of American Physical Education.* New York: Appleton, 1962.

27. Wood, Thomas D. Health and education, Part I. *Ninth Yearbook of the National Society for the Study of Education.* Chicago: Univ. of Chicago Press, 1910.

28. Wood, Thomas D. Some unsolved problems in physical education. *Addresses and Proceedings of International Congress of Education, Chicago* **3**: 621-623; 1893.

29. Zeigler, Earle F., and King J. McCristal. A history of the Big Ten body-of-knowledge project in physical education. *Quest* **9**: 79-84; 1967.

The Dimensions
of a
Profession

The term "profession" has several meanings. It is commonly used in reference to one's employment, occupation, or calling, and thus differentiates between activities by which a livelihood is earned and pursuits that represent avocational leisure-time interests. Quite often, someone may be described as a professional if that individual devotes considerable time and effort to some pursuit and displays exceptional skill and talent above and beyond ordinary or average performance. Designation as a professional, in this instance, may seem appropriate even if a livelihood is not earned via skill and talent. In athletics, an amateur may be classified as a professional if an award or financial compensation in excess of specified limits has been accepted.

An important distinction exists, however, between a profession and mere job activities that provide paychecks. A true profession possesses several important characteristics that distinguish it from straight vocational pursuits. Status as a profession is attractive enough to be sought after by many occupations not traditionally thought of as professions. Although theology, law, and medicine are historically classified and known as learned professions, other occupational groups are seeking the means by which to be similarly recognized. Of late, education has campaigned diligently for such status and both nursing and physical therapy are contending that they are professions, rather than occupations requiring skilled technicians.

A profession comes into existence owing to some specific need of society for a particular kind of service. When society was simple, its needs were simple and required only a few simple professions. Modern society, however, is more complex and demands many different kinds of services. Very often these services require extended periods of formal preparation before an individual can acquire the knowledge and skills necessary to perform satisfactorily. When the amount of training and quality of service reaches a certain level, one often finds that the specialty claims status as a profession. In most instances, when a college degree is required in a specialty, the occupation claims fulfillment of all criteria necessary for designation as a profession.

Many occupational groups are today claiming that they are true professions, and several recurring arguments are used by members of such occupations. Although some of the arguments used by such groups sound similar, different groups do not always use the same arguments, indicating some uncertainty about the actual criteria for a profession. As we have seen previously, graduate education is involved with the complex task of achieving a balance between professional and academic discipline emphasis in courses of study leading to advanced degrees. Physical education itself is seen to be moving from its implied status as a profession to the ranks of an academic discipline. Because of such developments, it seems important to define the distinguishing characteristics of a profession as accurately as possible in order to be sure of just what arguments are involved.

CRITERIA FOR A PROFESSION

Fortunately, there are several sets of criteria upon which the judgment of what comprises a profession can be made. Of the many lists of such criteria, there seems to be common agreement as to just what constitutes a profession. Differences may exist in exact nomenclature, but, in general, the meaning of the criteria lists exhibits mutual agreement on major issues. Boone (4) listed six major characteristics that differentiate a profession from a business or trade. A few years later, Flexner (6) gave another set of criteria. Although both lists are quite similar and either would suffice, Flexner's list is more commonly cited and his criteria have been selected for consideration.

(1) The activities involved are essentially intellectual in character.
Mere possession of a useful skill is a necessary but not sufficient condition for qualification as a member of a profession. Intellect must guide the application of a useful skill. A trade may require even more skill and dexterity than a profession, but the single requirement—possession of a set of skills, no matter how difficult acquisition of the skills may be—does not qualify the trade to be a profession. What skill to use, why to use it, and when to use it are

more important than simply *how* to execute the skill. This does not mean that a profession may not require possession of useful skills, only that such skills must be guided by the intellect. A dentist or a surgeon must certainly possess considerable physical skill but, more importantly, the dentist and surgeon must diagnose the necessity for application of such skills or must choose from a variety of possible skills that could be employed.

(2) A profession is practical.

Although intellect dominates, the practice of the profession serves useful ends that are of social significance. Pursuit of a pure-science ideal is alien to the profession, which must focus upon its responsibilities to society and not allow itself to become completely abstract. As Flexner put it, a profession could not be ". . . merely academic and theoretic. . . ."

As was seen earlier in the discussion of graduate study, medical schools cannot allow the study of medicine to become purely a scholar-research activity. The practice of medicine to maintain and restore the health of the individuals in a society cannot be eliminated as a sacrifice to a pure-science ideal. The acquisition of knowledge is highly important—more important, perhaps, than technical skill—but the knowledge must be applied to the practical and socially important responsibility to which the profession is obligated.

(3) A continuous flow of new facts and ideas comes from the laboratory and the seminar.

A profession cannot remain static in the quality of its services to humankind. New and relevant knowledge produced in disciplines pertinent to the profession must be acquired and application made to professional practices. Implicit in this Flexnerian principle is an obligation on the part of the profession to examine the basis of its practices to ensure their quality.

If the practices presently employed are relatively unsuccessful, then the profession seeks to find new and better techniques. An examination of practices inevitably requires research and a profession thus finds itself obligated to conduct research, sponsor research, or both. An eternal question thus arises as to how much acquisition of an intellectual nature and how much research to examine the basis of its practice can be nurtured before the profession becomes too academic and theoretic with resulting deterioration in its practical service to society.

At the very least, a profession is obligated to assimilate the new knowledge being produced by others and to evaluate present professional practices in the light of such new knowledge. If new knowledge suggests that an accepted practice is, in reality, unsatisfactory or even hazardous, then the practice must be modified or eliminated. An obligation to develop a new practice to take the place of the old then becomes apparent. Often, this development of a new practice requires additional basic knowledge that is not yet available. The profession may merely await production of this needed knowledge by others, or, as is frequently the case, it may seek to produce this new knowledge itself.

(4) Self-organization.

(5) Capable of communication.

These two criteria concern the internal organization or mechanics of the professional practice itself. In order to provide its useful and important services, the profession must organize itself for greatest efficiency of operation. Individuals allowed to become members of the profession must be capable of administering its practices; hence, selection of professionals, educational training, and continued assessment of competency for retention in the profession become necessary internal activities.

A code of ethics is developed, satisfactory and unsatisfactory practices are identified, proper educational training experiences are organized, candidates are examined to ensure professional competency and are so identified (licensed), while incompetents in the profession are identified and eliminated. Thus, approved programs of medical education are offered, degrees and licenses to practice granted, and unethical practices admonished by the profession. Because a profession provides useful services to society, society itself may become involved in such aspects.

It should be noted that the fact that members of some occupations require a license or approval by society to perform their skills does not mean that the occupation is automatically a profession. Barbers, hair dressers, and plumbers may need to be licensed by some governmental agency to ensure society's control over injudicious practices even though such occupations are not usually classified as professions. Qualifying as a profession requires more than self-organization and recognition by society that a useful service is being performed. To qualify as a profession *all* the criteria of a profession must be satisfied, not just one or two.

(6) Altruism.

The last, but by no means least, characteristic of a profession is that its motivation for existence is altruistic; i.e., it has a regard for and a devotion to the interests and welfare of others. A profession exists not for itself but for the benefit of others. Administration of its useful and important services to society is the major objective, and not development of a powerful and influential organization. A profession exists for the contributions that it can make to humankind and not for what contributions humankind can make to the profession.

Altruism is frequently translated to mean that a profession can never deny its services to society in order to advance its own interests. Physicians, for example, may not refuse medical attention to patients needing it in an effort to demand greater support from society. Teachers may not refuse to teach in efforts to secure higher salaries. Society generally frowns upon the denial of any services essential to it, however, and the fact that laws prevent "strikes" does not qualify an occupation as a profession. Sanitary workers may see an injunction processed to prevent loss of their services but this does not mean sanitary workers are a professional group.

Attention to material things by a profession is being seen more frequently in modern society. Teachers and even physicians have withheld some of their services in attempts to improve certain aspects of their profession. Paramount in such actions was the expressed desire to improve the profession so that the profession could adequately or more adequately serve society.

PHYSICAL EDUCATION AS A PROFESSION

Undergraduate education programs in physical education are predominantly professional in nature. Most of these programs prepare physical educators for teaching and other service-related positions. The terms profession and professional conduct are used so frequently by faculty members in these departments that students avow being professionals by mere dint of repetition. A true physical education major is professional and assumes all the necessary professional obligations expected. A very interesting learning experience with somewhat surprising results occurred recently when students in an undergraduate junior-level course for physical education majors were asked to state what being professional meant to them. Being professional meant, in part, at least:

being dedicated and hard-working
being unselfish and hard-working
getting paid by the month instead of by the hour
not getting paid for any overtime work
not swearing, smoking, or drinking in public

good grooming; shirt and tie rather than sweatshirt; high heels instead
of flats
being underpaid and overworked but not complaining
never criticizing a fellow worker
having a college degree
"a professional is an amateur who got paid too much money"
"being a member of AYFER"
These statements were not artificially manufactured and were actually
culled from student responses to the question of what being professional
meant to them. The statements represent, of course, only a minority of
the total number of responses elicited from the students and in no way
represent a majority view. Acknowledging this, one would still be hard
pressed to contend that some of these points are not emphasized in
undergraduate major programs. Certainly, just the opposite of these
statements is not true. Being professional, of course, must mean more
than what is implied in this interesting (but prejudiced) set of student
responses.

The set of criteria suggested by Flexner for a profession is widely used
and generally accepted. Articles have been written, books have been
published, and conferences, seminars, and symposiums have been conducted on the question of whether or not teaching is a profession. Proponents of today who are moving to establish a discipline of physical
education assume that physical education is already a profession because
of its bonds with education. Before a discipline of physical education is
postulated, however, it might be well to consider whether physical education fulfills the criteria necessary for a profession.

Physical education apparently has a core of special skills that constitute practical, useful, and important services to society. Among these
skills are special techniques and abilities in games and sports, programs
of physical fitness, knowledge of rules and strategy, etc. Demands from
society for its instruction and participation in such activities seem to
satisfy the practical criterion. However, mere possession of a set of skills
is not enough. Are the activities of physical educators essentially intellectual in character? Are our skills guided by the intellect or not? Consider
for a moment the following situations:

(1) At a certain college town, an English professor specializing in
western folklore managed a little league baseball team to two successive
championships. He jokingly asked the chairman of the department of
physical education for men if there were a position available for him.
Naturally, the English professor could not be appointed. He seemed to
know a great deal about teaching baseball and did teach such skills successfully to young boys. Even though a position in the department was
open for a baseball coach who could be assigned activity courses in soft-
ball and baseball as teaching responsibilities, the English professor just

did not qualify. He was not a professionally trained physical educator. Important questions to be answered are: In what ways would a professionally trained physical educator have performed differently if assigned the task of teaching baseball to little leaguers, and in what ways would the English professor have been deficient as a staff member in the department of physical education?

(2) Many undergraduate major programs in physical education require that students be competent to teach swimming. Activity courses for majors in swimming tend to be offered universally because the teaching of swimming is considered a rather essential ability in a well-prepared professional physical educator. In order to qualify as a teacher in the public schools, of course, the physical educator must have earned a college degree and have met all of the other requirements for a teaching certificate. Swimming programs in municipal parks and other youth agencies, however, also conduct learn-to-swim classes, and the instructors of these classes are not obliged to be physical education major students or to possess a college degree.

In what ways would a professionally trained physical educator teach a learn-to-swim class differently than an 18-year-old just out of high school with a water safety instructor (WSI) certificate?

(3) The chairman of a physical education department has an opening on his staff for a faculty member whose responsibilities would include the teaching of several sections of golf as well as the coaching of the varsity golf team. The chairman, of course, wants to hire the best qualified individual possible for this vacancy because of his strong commitment to carry over sports in the well-balanced physical education curriculum he is developing. After the applications are received, it is found that a professionally prepared physical educator and a top ranked professional golfer are the only candidates for the position.

Which of the two candidates would you hire if you were the department head? If you were to be a student in the golf classes or a member of the golf team? How should you explain to the professional golfer that you decided to hire the physical educator?

(4) A highly successful high school football coach has a bachelor's degree in business administration. He was an all-American football player in college, noted for his dynamic leadership ability, and said to be possessed of the rare talent of being able to develop each athlete to his maximum potential. After assuming the head coaching position at a large university that had a losing record for several years, he quickly produced a team that went undefeated throughout the season and won a major bowl game. This team was named number one in the nation and he was given an award as the year's outstanding football coach.

In what ways would a professionally trained physical educator have performed differently if given the same coaching assignment?

Any argument suggesting that the difference between a professionally trained physical educator and the individuals in the situations cited is that a professional could do more things at the same time, for example, teach baseball, swimming, golf, and football rather than just one of them, is not much of an argument. Even our professional physical educators specialize in particular skill areas; we see some who specialize in dance, others in team games, and so forth. However, carpenters are still in the trade category even if they can point to the fact that they know how to drive in tenpenny nails as well as sixpenny nails, that they can saw two-by-fours as well as one-by-sixes.

An argument to effectively dispel the connotation of a trade must not cite the possession of useful skills *alone*. To argue that possession of teaching skills or of skills themselves is the hallmark of a professional physical educator is to argue on the basis of only *one* of the criteria of a profession. An analogous argument would be for labor unions to profess professional status because they are self-organized, perform a service important to society, and are definitely practical.

To qualify as a profession, physical education needs *most* to establish the fact that its emphasis is on the intellectual aspects in the performance of its skilled and practical service to society. Rather than emphasizing its proficiency in *how* to teach certain skills, it must show the intellectual process involved in deciding whether to teach them at all. Is golf worth teaching? What happens to people when they participate in golf? In which activities should a young boy participate if the desired outcome is to develop self-confidence and more aggressiveness? Are isometrics and weight training equally good as strength developers? Is strength necessary for successful performance? If so, in which activities is it necessary? Is warm-up necessary? Will sit-ups reduce my waistline?

Practices, Knowledge, and Research

A profession must examine the basis of its own practices. It must produce *not only* successful practices, but the best practices. It must produce new practices, new applications, practices of broader and more important usefulness. It must not merely pass along from one generation to another an unchanging bag of tricks of the trade that have been relatively successful; a profession must pass on to the next generation better practices to the end-goal of producing the best practices for the best results in order to ensure the best possible service to society. A profession must not only be successful, it must be as successful as possible. It must, in fact, be even more successful than society demands since the profession and not society knows the true limits of its capabilities.

The responsibility to improve continuously and to expand the scope of

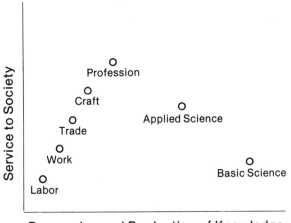

Possession and Production of Knowledge

Figure 4.1. Relation of service to society and the possession and production of knowledge.

important services to society is an essential characteristic of a profession. A profession must keep pace with advances in knowledge pertinent to its core of practices. This requirement necessitates not only the possession of pertinent knowledge already available, but also the ability to absorb relevant new facts as they are made available by related disciplines. Such an obligation frequently calls for the profession to seek out new facts on its own and finds the profession assuming the responsibility of a research capacity in order to dig out the facts deemed necessary in the profession but not in the related disciplines. An obligation to possess and produce new knowledge, however, can, in more than one way, lead to changes in the service to society that a profession delivers. If one were to plot a pair of axes at right angles to each other having as respective components (a) a continuum indicating the possession and production of knowledge, and (b) a continuum of the amount of service to society expected or produced or both, an interesting concept develops. Figure 4.1 suggests the nature of the concept that such a scheme might represent.

"Labor" implies more gross physical exertion and less skill than "work." Work is a less strenuous occupation than labor, but physical exertion is still the dominant feature. In a trade, however, manual or mechanical dexterity rather than gross physical effort is of more importance as a distinguishing characteristic. A craft is often synonymous with trade but really implies a trade requiring considerable skill, more experience, and more knowledge. One can see the implication that, as the requirement for gross physical effort decreases, the amount of knowledge required for successful performance in the occupation increases.

Note that basic science is placed lower on the ordinate representing service to society than a profession even though a basic science is depicted as requiring more knowledge. An argument could be raised contending that science's service to society may merit an equally high or a higher position on the ordinate than a profession. A "pure" science, however, just as an academic discipline, is defined as theoretical and is neither obligated nor expected to produce practical knowledge. The knowledge produced may be useful to society, but the obligation to make use of such useful knowledge belongs to the professions.

Although a profession is pictured at the highest point on the ordinate representing service to society, it is also somewhere in the middle so far as possession and production of knowledge is concerned. Certainly, the amount of knowledge that a profession possesses helps it to make a better contribution to society via improved practices. However, if a profession chooses to emphasize the knowledge continuum too strongly its contribution to society may be diminished. Physicians, after all, must stop studying sometime and start applying their knowledge and skill in medical practice. On the other hand, if a profession merely stresses acquisition of mechanical skill in a physical or manual sense, it may likewise contribute less to society because of a diminished amount of knowledge and intellect that is available to guide its practices. No matter how skilled the surgeon might be at the task, bloodletting is no longer accepted as a medical treatment. Situated at the apex of such a conceptual triangle, a profession will frequently vacillate and slide down either one of the two sides of the triangle depending upon the argument for change being used.

In one respect, it is easier to be on either side of the apex than it is to be situated precariously at the top. The quality of a discipline is judged primarily by its discoveries of new knowledge and its more astute interpretation of knowledge. The quality of a profession is judged primarily by its services to society. A discipline can afford to wait until it has a complete set of facts neatly explained by a tight and precise theory before making any decisions. A profession, however, must make decisions and act even it if does not have all the knowledge necessary for the best practice.

A scientist may say that the cause of cancer is still unknown and then retreat back into the laboratory for further study and experimentation, but a physician must treat cancer in a patient depending only upon what knowledge is available. A scientist may say that not enough is known about the phenomenon of warm-up and its relationship to motor performance, and then offer poignant critiques of the research methodologies used to study the topic. A professional, unfortunately, must decide one way or the other; either a warm-up is given or it is not. Either way, the professional is forced to make a decision. The only other alternative is to abandon the professional obligation entirely and not face the necessity of making a decision. If the decision made is shown later to have been a correct one, the professional is happy. If not, an error of omission or commission will have been committed. A professional thus has two chances to be wrong and only one to be right. The scientist does not take any chances.

A profession thus finds itself in a rather precarious position perched at the top of the apex. It must possess a hard core of skilled practices based upon an adequate amount of knowledge. A move in either direction could jeopardize the quality of its services to society and promote stinging criticism. Yet, a profession is obligated to move increasingly higher on the service ordinate. To do so requires quite a feat of balance as it must move upward while simultaneously increasing both possession of knowledge and skill in execution of practices. Imbalance in either direction gives birth to deterioration of purpose, and life at either side of the triangular base must often seem attractive and less complicated. As McGlothin (11, page 40) put it, a profession "sits like the god Janus, looking forward and back" at the same time.

PROFESSION VERSUS DISCIPLINE

A later chapter will consider in some detail the nature of an academic discipline. The present chapter on a profession, however, requires that some minimal conception of a discipline be possessed by the reader in order to afford a contrast for several aspects of a profession that need to be made. Any definition of an academic discipline is likely to be tainted by a number of deficiencies. A definition of an academic discipline can endure such deficiencies so long as its advantages are considerable. The definition of an academic discipline as forwarded by Franklin Henry seems fully sufficient for our purposes at this point:

> An academic discipline is an organized body of knowledge collectively embraced in a formal course of learning. The acquisition of such knowledge is assumed to be an adequate and worthy objective as such, without any demonstration or requirement of practical application (7, page 32).*

Such a definition of an academic discipline is congruent with the ideas developed concerning the rise of the pure-science ideal discussed in Chapter I. An academic discipline is interested in knowledge for knowledge's sake alone. It concerns itself with understanding, account-

---

*From Henry, F.M. (7). Used with permission of American Association for Health, Physical Education, and Recreation.

ing for, explaining, and predicting phenomena in its designated domain. It is not, however, obligated to consider control of such phenomena or to implement the application of knowledge produced for practical use. A discipline can forsake such complications to a profession and to society.

Several basic differences between an academic discipline and a profession can be seen to exist. In an academic discipline, the primary motivation is the acquisition of knowledge per se. Important knowledge is knowledge that contributes to further understanding of the theoretical system of the content domain in which the academic discipline operates. A profession, on the other hand, has an altruistic motivation and an important advance means a significant stride forward in the quality of its services for the good of mankind.

The difference in motivation between an academic discipline and a profession apparently reflects itself in the personalities of the individuals selecting careers in one or the other. Several studies have shown that research scientists tend toward a stereotype quite different from workers in a profession. One biographical analysis of over 2000 scientists (research professionals) mostly from National Aeronautics and Space Administration installations showed that successful scientists had very high levels of self-confidence and were very dedicated to their work, "often to the exclusion of other hobbies, interests, and even family activities" (13).

Another study among the many that could be cited seems particularly well suited to illustrate personality differences between individuals entering a profession and individuals electing careers in an academic discipline. This study was done on a group of honor winners from a talent search for science, and contrasted those seeking a career in science with those entering engineering. To many people, engineering seems highly loaded with scientific emphases and only moderately different from a science. Any differences demonstrated between two such groups may be assumed to be even more true if a contrast was made, say, between future scientists in an academic discipline and future teachers in the profession of physical education.

Future engineers (N = 110) and future scientists (N = 164) were studied from a sample of 504 award winners of a science talent search. All were freshmen or sophomores in college at the time they completed forms designed to identify characteristics and background factors which differentiated them from each other and from a control group of 78 students in education. Results showed that future engineers were decidedly more socially oriented than future scientists. They accepted social responsibilities and American social ideals, looked upon science as being for the benefit of humankind, and liked to associate with people and be of service to them. Future scientists were characterized by nongregariousness, found satisfaction in nonsocial activities that were complex and intellectual, and were more interested in understanding natural law than in solving problems of society (10).

Included among the list of items that significantly discriminated future scientists and future engineers from each other and both groups from the control sample of education students were the following:

Professional
  likes to assume responsibility
  likes scouting activities
  had been elected an officer in student government
  never questioned the soundness of religion
  questioned the use to which science is put
  thought science was for human use
Scientists
  preferred not to enjoy play and pleasure with other people
  disliked community service with children
  not active on any athletic teams
  in case of disaster decided that people should be saved in order of their
    worth to science
  believed in a material cause for all events
  kept no domestic pets at home

If such a list is a reasonable estimate of the type of individuals likely to elect entry into the academic discipline of physical education and the profession of physical education, it becomes difficult to decide which set of characteristics is "best" for physical education whatever it is to become. Previous attempts in other areas have found little success in endeavoring to use the machinery of higher education to manufacture an individual who possesses the desirable characteristics of both an academic discipline and a profession. These sets of distinguishing characteristics seem to be mutually exclusive sets so far as career choices are concerned. Yet, physical education finds itself considering the establishment of an academic discipline that would be substantially unlike the traditional profession of physical education. Whether physical education can successfully divide itself into two parts—one an academic discipline and the other a profession—and still stand has yet to be considered seriously. Could the personnel necessary for the work of a discipline be successfully recruited out of the ranks of the profession or not? How will the academic discipline of physical education with a pure-science frame of reference relate to the profession of physical education?

As was discussed in Chapter 2, most of the alternatives available have been advocated for graduate study programs in physical education. The penetrating analysis by Staley (12) called for the elimination of professional degrees and production only of research-scholars. Larson's plan (8) for activity sciences proposed two tracks, one for the practitioner and one for the specialist. Proponents of the kinesiological sciences called for the establishment of an academic discipline that could stand alone, apart from teacher preparation in physical education, but did not recommend that "the two fields be immediately divorced from each other" (2).

One thing is certain, however, and that is that a major segment of physical education is pushing for the establishment of physical education as an academic discipline. Whether this development represents a flight mechanism in response to some of the intolerable problems associated with the professional aspects of physical education, or reflects wholesome growth and long awaited maturation, remains, as yet, relatively undecided. Any decisions made will most certainly affect everyone now involved with physical education, but also students and citizens who are consumers as well.

Fortunately, physical education has the advantage of being able to consider developments in at least two other areas for help in working out its profession and discipline trends. Problems in one of these other two areas—medicine—was considered earlier under problems in graduate education for a profession. It was seen that medicine, as a profession, showed a marked tendency to become more research-scholar oriented and found criticism of such a shift to be disruptive to its professional obligations to society. We may now consider developments that are seemingly just the opposite. Psychology calls itself an academic discipline. Some critical issues in psychology may help us to see the situation developing in physical education in a slightly different and broader perspective.

Psychology and Its Discipline—Profession Aspects

When the American Psychological Association (the APA) was founded in 1894, its constitution stated that its objective was the advancement of psychology as a science. Bear in mind, by the way, that psychology, thus, got underway about ten years later than the Association for the Advancement of Physical Education which was founded in 1885. By 1930, a group of psychologists had organized a rival group called the American Association of Applied Psychology (AAAP). While the APA was still devoted to the advancement of psychology as a science akin to physics or chemistry, the AAAP was composed of members concerned with the application of psychological knowledge as a profession.

The two associations were eventually combined after World War II, but the rift between professional and disciplinary sentiments continued, mostly because of a tremendous demand for psychological services of a clinical nature. One of the apparent compromises made was reflected by a dent in the pure-science ideal, as training programs were begun to produce a combination scientist-professional. In 1947, for example, the APA Committee on Training in Clinical Psychology concluded that the dissertation should be retained in order to deveop a "research-oriented professional person" (1).

From the model of a psychologist as a scientist, therefore, a second model now appeared of a psychologist as a combination scientist and professional. Several more conferences have been held by psychologists to consider the kind or kinds of graduate education that psychologists should receive. Some assessment had to be made, naturally, as to what the end product of graduate education should look like. As late as 1962, however, the marriage of the professional psychologist and the scientific psychologist was still not far from divorce.

In 1962, Levy (9) contended that the requirement that graduate education produce a professional product imbued with scholarly-research capabilities was simply not being realized. If insistence upon scholarly-research contributions in the form of publications in psychological journals were still demanded, then the status of a very large portion of all psychologists would certainly be in doubt, for very few professional psychologists were publishing any research. Levy's attempt to see if "reality and fantasy [have] been kept innocent of each other" led him to suggest that rethinking about the Ph.D. programs in psychology was in order.

Much like Cook's earlier paper (5), Levy concluded that the attempt to produce a combined professional and scientist was not without its considerable share of problems. Professionals complained of an over-emphasis on research and accused universities of producing research psychologists who were naive. Research psychologists countered with the charge that professionals were failing in the obligation to advance psychology as a science through research. As the amount of knowledge grows in the field of psychology, as the development of new practices requires longer training periods, and as research methodology requires more and more advanced study, the break between the profession and the science of psychology looms as more instead of less of a problem.

If there is a moral to be drawn from these developments in medicine and in psychology—one a profession and the other a discipline—it is that if a science is important to people, it is drawn into a profession; and if a profession is important to people, it is drawn into a science. Since psychology as a science produced knowledge with potential value to society, society demanded that this knowledge be applied in the service of humankind. Medicine as a profession offered services of such importance to people that society demanded that such services be the best possible and be based, therefore, upon the knowledge of a science. There were individuals in both fields who responded to such needs and demands of people and society.

An individual scientist may be investigating a line of research that turns out to be of such potential importance to humankind that the scientist shifts attack to that front, leaving the usual confines of the scientific domain and conducting research which then seems more professional than scientific. Albert Svent-Gyorgi, for example, began a pure research endeavor in studying the process of tissue healing. He discovered two substances, one which facilitated cell division and growth and the other which inhibited and shut down such activity once healing of tissue had been completed. The facilitation seemed to characterize the action of cancerous cells. Without the inhibitor substance, cell division and growth went wild. Because the inhibitor substance might possibly act to control cancerous cells, Svent-Gyorgi shifted his attention to cancer. In now attempting to study a problem of tremendous importance to humankind, however, he was concerned that since he now was attempting to be useful, he might become useless. Scientists believe that their research must be channeled by the problems of the science domain and not the problems of society.

A physician seeking a better treatment regimen for cancer might push research into activities that appear more scientific than professional. The need for more basic knowledge could conceivably foster research activities by a profession in the very areas that scientists are actively investigating. Hence, one could picture a scientist and a professional bumping into each other as they pursue their research—each going in different directions, each from a different starting place, and each with the same destination in mind. As they meet, each might turn to the other and say, "Turn back, I've already been there."

A profession improves in quality when it moves from an empirical basis for practice to a theoretically oriented practice, but such a move can often jeopardize the amount and quality of its useful application by practitioners. A science may find, as suggested by the phrase attributable to Svent-Gyorgi, that as it tries to be useful it may become useless. The trick is to know when to stop migrating, when to take the advice to turn back because somebody has already been there. All this, of course, exemplifies again the difficulties in balancing teaching, service, and research in programs of graduate study.

From one point of view, a certain amount of hostility is generated, within a science, against the scientist who migrates too far toward a profession; the same kind of hostility is generated, within a profession, against the professional who migrates too far toward the science. To deny that this is the case in physical education (or education, psychology, and several others) is quite foolish and naive. If a school were set up at a half-way house—the site where the scientist and the professional might meet, each going in different directions, each with the same destination—the product of such a school would likely be neither superior professional nor superior scientist, and would most likely suffer the hostility of both the science and the profession. It seems doubtful this individual would represent a superior product by any set of standards, and the appeal of a middle-of-the-road course is likely to find supporters only among the members of those committees who cannot agree on any course of action.

The changes sweeping across physical education today are healthy. Much like psychology, which was founded as a science and was forced into a profession as well, physical education, established as a profession, is experiencing the need to give birth to a science. Although such growing pains are difficult to live with, they represent an attempt to meet the demands of reality. The profession's gestation period for development of a well-formed discipline has been quite long and may even have been delayed too long.

Physical education is indeed ridding itself of its trade-like characteristics of the past and is moving toward an acceptable professional status. It is beginning to examine the basis of its own present practices on the strength of its own knowledge production and is expanding the usefulness and importance of its services to society. Some of its professionals are becoming so good that they are becoming less useful to the profession and more useful to the sciences. Those more useful to the profession are slipping into activities more scientific than professional. Those more useful, so to speak, are becoming useless. It is a healthy sign.

The danger now to be faced by physical education is not to realize that diversity in its ranks is to become the rule rather than the exception. Its attitude toward criticism must change as it accepts the fact of life that all it does cannot be defended by choosing up sides "for" and "against" physical education. Physical education must recognize that criticism is not a personal attack upon its dignity. A noted researcher in physical education once said that there were two major sins in physical education. One—the lesser of the two sins—was to suggest to someone how to do something better. The other sin—almost inexcusable—was to point out to someone in the profession that what he or she was doing was wrong.

Physical education apparently still lacks the maturity and confidence to accept criticism in a proper perspective. Critics are often classified as poor citizens, ingrates to the profession, or troublemakers who disrupt the honest toil of sincere and dedicated workers. During a recent meeting of the Board of Associate Editors of the *Research Quarterly*, for example, an AAHPERD staff member suggested that criticisms of articles published in the *Research Quarterly* were in bad taste, and questioned whether such critical articles should be published. It was stated that pointing out mistakes in published research was tantamount to airing the profession's dirty laundry in public. Although it was finally decided not to prevent publication of such articles, considerable discussion took place and strong sentiment was raised in favor of eliminating such critical articles.

The point of importance here is that the event exemplified the "good bunch" philosophy of physical education. Good bunch philosophy is apparently an offshoot of professional ethics, which holds that public criticism of colleagues in the profession is bad. As worthy as such an ethical code might be, it is difficult to see how it would apply to the case in point. If published research is full of mistakes and embarrassing blunders, how will future mistakes of the same variety be prevented if the previous ones are never identified? The criticism, if it is legitimate, can serve to call attention to the need for change and help correct a nagging but real deficiency. Suggesting that actual mistakes in the *Research Quarterly* never be pointed out seems to be analogous to the ostrich who reportedly hides its head in a hole when faced with danger. Ignoring deficiencies in physical education, whether in published articles appearing in the *Research Quarterly* or in the promulgation of out-dated practices, may preserve the egos of individuals, but egos cannot be as important as facts.

Barzun carefully differentiated between criticism and complaint and contended that criticism was not a personal attack but a means of forcing consideration of alternate courses of action. His understanding of the role of criticism was that criticism could "make two thoughts grow where only one grew before" (3, page 7). When a valid criticism is made of physical education, it is senseless to pout and contend that the critic is not a friend of physical education. If real deficiencies exist in physical education they should be rooted out and the identifier of the deficiency should be praised and thanked. For, so long as the critic forwards criticisms, there can be useful change and progress; and without honest criticism only stagnation and retrogression can prevail. False security and happy friends are not the ingredients of a true profession.

As the profession advances and as the academic discipline struggles into being, the opportunities and the need for sharp conflicts will increase. However, so long as the road connecting the profession and the discipline remains open there is hope; not only will disaster be avoided but the future of both profession and discipline will continue to hold promise. Presently those scholar-researchers moving toward establishment of an academic discipline appear aloof, snobbish, and ungrateful to the profession from which they were spawned. The profession—teachers, coaches, and administrators—seem, to the scholar-researchers, to be ignorant and unappreciative of the great contributions being made through research.

For some time ahead, physical education will see a division of labor appearing more marked than ever before. As a discipline of physical education unfolds, it will attract a particular and perhaps (to the professional) peculiar new breed of physical educator. Because of existing and growing commitments to society, the professional physical educator will be in even greater demand. The two groups will eventually interact with one another to produce changes that may please both, one, or neither of them. Whichever role a physical educator chooses, however, that individual should still be easy to identify. No matter whether the title be biokinetic engineer, physical activity scholar, exercise scientist, philosopher of sport, academic leader, administrator, or coach, the identity of the physical educator will be apparent.

For no matter how it is loomed, the thread of physical education will be visible in the fabric. If the thread cannot be found, we can be sure that the fabric must be some new synthetic and it is doubtful that it will wash well.

REFERENCES

1. American Psychological Association, Committee on Training in Clinical Psychology. Recommended graduate training in clinical psychology. *American Psychologist* **2**: 539-558; 1947.

2. Barham, Jerry N. Toward a science and discipline of human movement. *JOHPER* **37**: 65, 67-68; October 1966.

3. Barzun, Jacques. *Science: The Glorious Entertainment.* New York: Harper, 1964.

4. Boone, Richard G. *Science of Education.* New York: Scribner, 1904.

5. Cook, Stuart W. The psychologist of the future: scientist, professional, or both. *American Psychologist* **13**: 635-644; November 1958.

6. Flexner, Abraham. Is social work a profession? *School and Society* **1**: 901-911; June 26, 1915.

7. Henry, Franklin M. Physical education: an academic discipline. *JOHPER* **35**: 32-33, 69; September 1964.

8. Larson, Leonard A. Professional preparation in the activity sciences. *Journal of Sports Medicine and Physical Fitness* **5**: 15-22; March 1965.

9. Levy, Leon H. The skew in clinical psychology. *American Psychologist* **17**: 244-249; 1962.

10. MacCurdy, Robert D. Engineer or scientist? *Journal of Counseling Psychology* **8**: 79-81; 1961.

11. McGlothlin, William J. *The Professional Schools.* New York: The Center for Applied Research in Education, 1964.

12. Staley, S.C. Keys to advancement in physical education. *The Physical Educator* **18**: 83-88; October 1961.

13. Taylor, Calvin W., and Robert Ellison. Biographical predictors of scientific performance. *Science* **155**: 1075-1080; March 3, 1967.

Research Productivity in Physical Education

5

In these days of research and scientific study, we are being called upon to prove that Physical Education deserves its place in the curriculum. It is not enough for us to claim a number of "educational outcomes." We must prove that health and exercise instruction makes a definite contribution to organic vigor and establishes health habits that will endure.—F.W. Maroney. American physical education at the cross roads. *Journal of Health and Physical Education* 1(1): 20; January 1930.

A magical aura seems to surround any pronouncement concerning the need for research in physical education. Just as in the case of President Maroney's appeal quoted above, so also the idea of encouraging an increased production of quality research has always received rather unanimous acceptance and loud acclamation. Both emotional and intellectual appeals for more and better research have appeared regularly throughout our professional history. Each new appeal has seemed to be based genuinely upon irrefutable arguments, and each appeal has seen concerted efforts toward its fulfillment that were agreed upon by the vast majority of the profession. However, realizing this universally accepted goal for research has been a Sisyphean task.

For one difficulty, a working definition of the characteristics of needed research has eternally evaded those professing its virtues. Although the profession has consistently acknowledged the need for scholarly research efforts, it is still hard pressed to present a set of criteria upon which progress in this direction might be appraised. To some, the need for research has been translated into increased thinking and talking about the problems of physical education, in the expectation that recognition of a need will somehow result in satisfying it. All too often, however, those affirming the need for research have had very little to do with any actual production of scholarly research. Others have become entangled in sophisticated debates about research priorities and have campaigned diligently for one or more modes of inquiry as the optimum strategy. Educational philosophers, administrators, and curriculum experts have been admonished by scientific workers for wasted effort in policy making owing to an absence of facts with which to fashion their policies. Scientific investigators have, in turn, been accused of not recognizing the true pathways to absolute truth and of a failure to concern themselves with the pressing problems of the profession.

This chapter will attempt a partial assessment of the profession's commitment to scholarly research efforts. No graduate program can be formulated without some agreement as to what kinds of scholarly research efforts deserve emphasis and cultivation. The identification of needed scholarly research efforts is just as essential as an acceptance of their desirability. Some means for assessing the achievement of graduate study goals is, likewise, essential in order to ensure continuous progress in proper channels. Although the frame of reference to be employed as a means of assessment may be plagued with many acknowledged deficiencies, it may still manage to capture at least one valid aspect of the spirit of scholarly research productivity and commitment in the profession.

QUALITY IN GRADUATE PROGRAMS

Research is seen to be an essential feature of any quality program of graduate study. Although different emphases in courses of study must exist between preparation in a profession and preparation in a discipline, neither field can expect to be successful unless it accepts a strong commitment to research. In a discipline intent upon systematic organization of a knowledge structure in a particular domain, scholarly research represents the singular process by which it can accomplish its purpose. Although a profession has a different perspective on the value of knowledge, it may not completely negate responsibility for research, since it is obligated to examine the basis of its practices and continuously improve the quality of its services to society. If a profession ignored the necessity of research it would quickly begin to assume trade-like characteristics and fail in its commitment to humankind. Physical education, whether it be a profession or a discipline, must assume the responsibility for production of new knowledge through research efforts in its content domain. Thus, classification as a profession does not relieve physical education from a research commitment, and it seems allowable to ask whether or not this responsibility is being met.

There are many ways in which such a question might be answered, most of which would be bound to stir up heated controversy. Since the question as stated can elicit several different kinds of answer, perhaps we can ask simpler questions that require more direct and specific answers and upon which there is likely to be more agreement. As a beginning, let us consider another perennial academic question. Which universities are the best for graduate study? Such a question, of course, must be answered hundreds and even thousands of times each and every year by concerned students all over the country as they consider the prospect of graduate study. In the counseling of students in such matters, faculty members must often make evaluative judgments and suggest that some schools are better choices than others. In short, some graduate schools enjoy a good reputation and others do not; otherwise there would be no meaningful basis for making a choice by either students or faculty. The question is, how do good schools establish such a reputation? Naturally, good schools are assumed to be satisfactorily accredited and endowed with the power to award graduate degrees in the particular subject matter area of concern to the prospective graduate students. Beyond such obvious requirements, however, more concrete and visible criteria for assessment of quality in graduate study must certainly exist.

In 1966, the American Council on Education (ACE) published a report which compared the graduate departments of 29 academic disciplines roughly separated into five major fields—biological sciences, engineering, humanities, physical sciences (including mathematics), and social sciences (4). Only the fourth major study of its kind ever attempted, it far surpassed previous efforts both in depth and scope and has received rather widespread attention from the academic community. Conducted by Allan M. Cartter, the ACE survey included 106 leading institutions in the United States, represented by the 100 institutions which formed the Council of Graduate Schools in the United States in 1960 and six additional schools whose production of doctorates was considerable. Basically, the plan was to ask participants to subjectively rate graduate departments in their respective fields, using six major categories from "distinguished" down to "not sufficient to provide adequate doctoral training," with respect to (a) quality of the graduate faculty and (b) the effectiveness of the graduate program. Respondents were asked to consider items such as research and teaching facilities, curriculum features, quality of graduate students, faculty accessibility, and faculty competence in making their judgments. Small panels of experts were subsequently used to cross-check results in four selected subjects, and agreement was considered more than acceptable between the results of the major portion of the study and the more detailed cross-check analyses made.

Over 4000 returns were secured, representing 900 department chairpersons, 1700 senior scholars, and 1400 junior scholars. No graduate students participated in the study. Results of the study indicated that all three respondent classifications made similar judgments in their ratings, with only minor discrepancies. It was rather clearly shown that those graduate departments that were rated highly were to be found typically in institutions with the best libraries and the best salary schedules, with some 80 percent of the institutions located in only 13 states of the East, Midwest, and West Coast. Although there were many exceptions, good departments most commonly appeared in neat clusters representing logically related content areas at the same institution. An institution, for example, with a highly rated graduate department in chemistry seldom had weak graduate departments in physics or mathematics. A good graduate department apparently requires the nurture of good graduate departments in related disciplines, and all tend to prosper together or not at all.

Of particular importance for our purpose is the fact that the ACE study showed that the best graduate departments had faculties with the highest rates of research productivity in terms of publications. Such a finding is consistent with the notion that outstanding graduate departments have distinguished graduate faculties (among other qualities). Outstanding graduate faculties, in turn, exhibit impressive research publication records. Indeed, one analysis of the ACE study suggested that faculty members and graduate students alike could use the report as a "Consumer's Guide" to the academic marketplace (25).

The Cartter report and a later ACE study conducted in 1969 by Roose and Andersen (23) employed reputation or peer-rating methodologies. Such studies based upon prestige ratings are known to possess several characteristics which many deem important deficiencies: ratings are highly related to program size, and a halo effect often operates favoring departments located in prestigious universities. In response to such criticisms, the Council of Graduate Schools and the Educational Testing Service conducted a broader study which evaluated doctoral programs in chemistry, history, and psychology; considerably more data were collected than simple peer ratings. The 1975 study (5) included a number of programs which were also evaluated in the 1964 and 1969 studies. The results of the doctoral program ratings in the three studies were "strikingly similar" even though a considerably different methodology was employed in the 1975 study. In chemistry, for example, the correlation between 1964 and 1975 rankings was .98. Once again, research productivity and the quality of faculty research records were major determinants of doctoral program rankings.

Although more will be said shortly about research publication records, let us now look at one other aspect of the problem of assessing quality in graduate education programs. The ACE study suggested that ratings of departments varied little across department chairperson, senior scholar, and junior scholar respondents. Such a finding, however, seemed direct-ly related to the research publication rates, and could reflect agreement only upon the importance of research in determining an outstanding graduate department. However, what of teaching effectiveness? The ACE study apparently touched only indirectly on this topic in its sugges-tion to respondents to consider such factors as faculty accessibility, scholarly competence of the faculty, and teaching facilities. To help clarify the views of both faculty and administrators regarding the relative importance of teaching effectiveness and research competency in assess-ing the quality of graduate education, more direct evidence would seem necessary. Fortunately, more direct evidence to this point is available.

In a study involving 242 colleges and universities, questionnaire re-sponses from 6087 faculty members and administrators of various levels showed surprising agreement on the relative importance of several fac-tors related to promotion policies of university personnel (2). In general, faculty members as well as administrators both considered research ac-tivity and publication records as important factors in making decisions for promotion in rank. Teaching effectiveness was also considered highly important, but was rated as having successively less importance as pro-motion went up the scale from instructor to full professor. As the em-phasis upon teaching effectiveness declined, the importance of research activity and publication record increased. In general, the larger the in-stitution, the less is the emphasis given to teaching effectiveness and the more given to research and publications. As might be expected, those in-dividuals teaching only undergraduates, those with no publication records, and those with terminal degrees below the doctorate placed more emphasis upon the importance of teaching and less on research. An interesting finding was that Ph.D. holders rated unpublished research ac-tivity lower and publication record higher for all promotions than did the doctors of medicine studied.

Not unmindful of the hazards involved, it can be contended that the quality of programs of graduate study may be evaluated partially by the quality of the graduate faculty. Furthermore, the quality of the graduate faculty can be evaluated partially by their research productivity in terms of research publications. So to the major question of whether or not physical education is fulfilling its responsibility for research, we shall first ask about the research productivity in terms of published articles by (a) schools or departments, (b) individuals, and, to a smaller degree, (c) the entire profession.

It can be seen immediately that there are obvious deficiencies in con-sidering research productivity only on the basis of published research. Many research investigations probably never get published. Published research, however, has had the advantage of being evaluated by an editorial committee and presumably has been judged as worthwhile, important, and properly executed. Unpublished research may or may not share these advantages. Hence, published research has been scrutinized by a board of editors who represent the investigator's peers, are learned and competent in the research area, and have given an investigation the stamp of approval for the field of study.

Evaluation of research productivity on the basis of the number of unpublished master's theses, doctoral dissertations, and independent research reports that a faculty member has sponsored can similarly be questioned. Although a committee for the thesis or dissertation passes on its acceptability, the standards used by the committee members are suspect unless the committee members themselves have established credentials as researchers. Just as in the case of unpublished research by faculty members, the quality of sponsored theses, dissertations, and independent research remains in doubt.

Still another question may be raised about the relative quality of the published articles themselves. Some articles certainly represent classical milestones broadening the horizon of scientific inquiry, while others are of minor significance and even may have contributed to retrogression because of erroneous implications. Mere counting of published articles, therefore, cannot take into consideration the unequal caliber and importance of published research. Several studies have considered this specific point, however, and their results would seem to minimize the need for great distress over the quality versus quantity issue.

First of all, it seems senseless to debate quality when no quantity exists. With no publications, evaluating the quality of one faculty member's research productivity compared to that of others is a rather meaningless task. Before any qualitative appraisal can be made of research, some research product must be present. One of the often-mentioned criteria in a qualitative appraisal, for example, is that of creativity. In a study dealing with biographical backgrounds of space scientists, Taylor and Ellison (24) found that most of their biographical items were related to both research productivity *and* research creativity. This finding tended to corroborate the position taken by Bloom (3, page 251), who suggested that creative achievement depended upon a certain minimum amount of research productivity. In short, creative achievement could scarcely take place unless some research work had been accomplished.

Dennis (6) has likewise shown among psychologists that honors and awards most frequently go to those who are highly productive in terms of research publications. Honors and awards, election to office, and citations for service are seldom given to individuals with only a small number of publications. In psychology, a relationship exists between quantity of publications and recognition by fellow colleagues. Dennis also examined the bibliographies in widely used handbooks and advanced textbooks representing different areas of interest in psychology. His idea was that publications cited in these leading volumes represented valuable and enduring contributions to advancement in the field of study. Publications which were infrequently cited, then, were of less relative importance. Data on 401 bibliographic citations showed that cited references were the work of individuals with the greatest number of publications. Based upon number of publications, individuals in the top 10 percent accounted for 47 percent of the 401 bibliographic citations.

Similarly, Levy (14) has shown that 10 percent of a group of 781 Ph.D.'s in clinical psychology from 41 different schools accounted for 45 percent of the total number of publications produced by the group. Levy also demonstrated that a marked difference existed in the publication rates of graduates from the different schools. Graduates of some schools contributed far more published research than others, and, therefore, the number of graduates from a school was a poor guide for predicting research productivity by graduates. Golightly (11) compared Levy's data to the publication rates of faculty members at the same institutions. A rank-order correlation coefficient of 0.64 was found, suggesting that the publication rate of graduates from an institution is, to some degree, related to the publication rate of the faculty members. Productive faculties are, thus, more likely to graduate productive students while faculties that publish very little research tend to produce nonresearch-oriented graduates. Naturally, the quality of student input attracted to these institutions is an important factor in such a situation.

In psychology at least, quality and quantity of published research exhibit a fair relationship. In the limiting case of no quantity there can be no question of quality. Those individuals with the highest rate of productivity in terms of publications are most frequently cited in bibliographies of leading texts and reference books, suggesting an enduring importance and quality of their work. Those graduate departments whose faculty members are productive in research publications are more likely to produce graduates who will publish either as a result of training or because such departments attract quality students interested in research.

In physical education, the major vehicle for the publication of research is the *Research Quarterly*. As such, an analysis of the contributors to *Research Quarterly* would seem to be of some value. Needless to say, research productivity among physical educators is not limited to publications in this particular journal alone. Several other journals in our field of interest are published regularly in which contributions by physical educators are often present. Research papers are presented at state, district, and national conventions, with articles or resumes published in the proceedings. Research articles are being published by physical educators in journals outside the profession, for example, in such respected publications as the *Journal of Applied Physiology, Ergonomics,*

European Journal of Applied Physiology, Medicine and Science in Sports and Exercise, Perceptual and Motor Skills, Psychological Bulletin, and numerous others.

Some researchers in physical education believe that the *Research Quarterly* falls considerably short of being a high-quality research journal. Dismay is expressed over the fact that some institutions will not count anything in the *Research Quarterly* as a publication credit, that the quality of research articles is mediocre to poor, and that too much emphasis is given to statistics and experimental design in editorial reviews of manuscripts. Others say that the issues represent a hodge-podge of topical areas and that even if the articles included are of acceptable quality, the range of topics included resembles menus from a half-dozen restaurants. Still others complain that their areas—notably health education, history, and philosophy—are poorly represented.

Because of this situation, more than a few individuals have decided to publish their research more regularly, or even completely, in other journals. Unfortunately, such articles published elsewhere often represent the quality research that the *Research Quarterly* is accused of lacking. It is difficult to understand how the deficiencies in the *Research Quarterly* can be ameliorated if some of the best researchers publish elsewhere.

These and other qualifications must readily be acknowledged as deficiencies if we examine only the *Research Quarterly* for evidence of research productivity in physical education. The important fact still remains, however, that the *Research Quarterly* is the official research publication of AAHPERD and more adequately represents a sampling of the research areas existing in physical education than does any other publication. The *Research Quarterly* represents research in physical education to people outside the field, and an analysis of its content must certainly represent at least part of the research productivity in physical education.

Productivity of the Entire Profession

According to one report (7), 6,240 physical education staff members were employed in institutions of higher learning. About 33 percent ($N = 2,050$) were located in universities, 43 percent ($N = 2,690$) in liberal arts colleges, 21 percent ($N = 1,300$) in teachers colleges, and 3 percent ($N = 200$) in technological institutions. For comparative purposes, in all of higher education there were 157,000 full-time teaching faculty members, and psychology in particular had 3,800 faculty members. Of course, not all of the 6,240 physical education staff members employed in institutions of higher learning possessed a doctorate. Resick (21), for example, showed that for 145 out of 190 institutions offering an advanced degree,

Table 5.1

Articles Processed and Published
in the *Research Quarterly*, 1964 and 1974

Year	Manuscripts submitted	Manuscripts accepted	Articles published	Notes and comments published
1964	130	29	60	13
1974	337	59	46	9

a total of only 2,536 faculty members had responsibilities for professional preparation. Slightly over a third of this group (N = 962 or 38 percent) possessed a doctorate and over one-half (N = 1,427 or 56 percent) had a master's degree. Among institutions offering a doctoral degree, 53.1 percent of the professional staff had earned doctorates. AAHPERD's membership roster had over 7,000 faculty members from institutions of higher learning in 1971. There are 63 institutions with doctoral degree programs and 270 master's degree programs in the United States (10).

Such data do allow us some idea of the size of the faculty for physical education in our colleges and universities. Out of a total AAHPERD membership roster which has at times numbered over 50,000 members, let us assume that research productivity is to be expected more from the 7,000 or so faculty members in higher education than it is from other members of the association. If it seems necessary to do so, one might further delimit the responsibility for research productivity to only those at institutions offering advanced degrees or those possessing doctorates, or both.

The number of manuscripts submitted, the number of manuscripts accepted for publication, and the number of published articles or contributions to the notes and comments section of the *Research Quarterly* for two years a decade apart are presented in Table 5.1. For the data of 1964, it should be recognized that of the 130 manuscripts submitted, 66 were still being reviewed. Thus, the entry of 29 accepted is not to be interpreted as a true acceptance rate. Both years have similar uncertainties since some of the figures cited for articles submitted and accepted may represent cases in which an article was submitted, withdrawn, and then resubmitted; that is, submitted one year and then after revision resubmitted the following year.

The number of research investigations submitted to the *Research Quarterly* for consideration does not, of course, represent the sum total of scholarly research efforts by the profession. Even so, one must grudgingly admit that the figures do not seem overwhelming when one considers that the submitted manuscripts often include condensations of theses and dissertations executed for graduate degree requirements as well as research efforts by professional personnel. In 1977-1978, there were 4,638 master's degrees and 210 doctorates awarded in physical education (12). Of 59 articles published in 1973, 13 were either master's or doctoral degree studies. Psychology, on the other hand, with about half as many staff members in institutions of higher learning manages to publish almost a dozen journals offering research contributions from psychologists. Even assuming that each manuscript submitted and each article published was written by a different individual, the number of contributors to the *Research Quarterly* is not large. In 1964, the sum of total manuscripts submitted plus articles or notes and comments published comes to 203 contributions. The year 1974 shows an increase to 392.

Regardless of how one decides who should bear the responsibility for research productivity, the percentage of the total profession making contributions to the *Research Quarterly* is not impressive. If one considers all members of the national association and uses that number for the proper denominator, the percentage of active contributors would be quite infinitesimal. As we shall see shortly, the number of active and consistent contributors to the *Research Quarterly* is truly quite small. Many individuals publish once, perhaps an abstract of the master's thesis or doctoral dissertation, and then never again. If, as some individuals imply (18), AAHPERD's Research Council represents those "concerned with research" then only about one or two hundred in all of AAHPERD are "researchers." No matter how one slices up the cake, if workers in the field are going to make use of research being done to help improve their practices, then they are most certainly going to do it with the contributions of a very small minority.

At least two studies have been made that analyzed contributions in the *Research Quarterly*. Loucks (15) examined individual contributors, sponsoring institutions, geographical areas, and research areas. In a smaller follow-up study, Hertz (13) brought updated data on the 20 leading individual contributors to the year 1954. Both of these reports were used as a basis for methodology and a similar examination made in a third study by the present author. Contributions to the *Research Quarterly* were rechecked under a modified point system for the five time periods. Both authors and sponsoring institutions for articles published during 1930-1939, 1940-1949, 1950-1959, 1960-1969, and 1970-1979 were checked with a point system that allocated one full article point for each investigation published, and one-half of a point for a contribution to the notes and comments section. If an article was authored by more than one person, article points were divided equally among the investigators. Similar point allocations were made for sponsoring institutions.

Such a frequency analysis of contributions to the *Research Quarterly* is beset with more difficulties than one might expect. Many of the earlier issues of the *Research Quarterly* published the entire proceedings of both the men's and women's college-level physical-education association conferences. Articles published in sections devoted to the proceedings were identified as such in the *Research Quarterly* index and were usually followed by a listing of "regular" articles. At other times, only the proceedings appeared in entire issues. Inasmuch as Loucks had established the practice of counting such articles as regular *Research Quarterly* contributions, the precedent was followed in the present analysis. Loucks also employed the practice of giving publication credit to a committee chairperson if the chairperson's name were listed under the title. This was deemed inappropriate since many committee reports appeared without any such listing of the chairperson under a title one year while the next year would find the same committee reporting with a chairperson's name listed. In order to be consistent, all committee reports were excluded from the analysis. Even so, several minor discrepancies exist between the present analysis and Loucks' data for the same time periods. In several instances, Loucks' judgment was deemed inappropriate and a corrected count was presented. Whenever no suitable criteria for judgment seemed available, Loucks' original precedent was followed.

Contributions by School

Table 5.2 presents data on those schools that ranked in the top ten contributors for any one of the five time periods under consideration. The letters "SPS" stand for "school point score" while an asterisk appearing with the school's name indicates that the school offers a doctorate in health, physical education, recreation, or some combination of these subjects. As seen in Table 5.2, inconsistency rather than consistency seems to be the rule so far as a school's contribution record of articles published in the *Research Quarterly*. Several schools appeared within the top ten only briefly and then drifted far behind in later decades. Most of the records seem erratic with marked peaks and troughs, although one general characteristic seems quite in evidence: Of the top twenty schools in Table 5.2, only four do not offer a doctoral degree program. It may be of some interest to note that eight of the ten universities commonly referred to as the Big Ten appear among the top twenty schools. Ohio State is just out of the top twenty with a ranking of twenty-two, and only Northwestern University, which offers no doctorate, is missing.

Any explanation for the variability in performance by schools is naturally conditioned by many factors: Administrative changes, budget

Table 5.2

Leading Schools Contributing to the Research Quarterly (1930-1979)

Rank	School	First period 1930-1939 SPS	R	Second period 1940-1949 SPS	R	Third period 1950-1959 SPS	R	Fourth period 1960-1969 SPS	R	Fifth period 1970-1979 SPS	R	TOTAL
1a	University of California-Berkeley	9.00		26.41	2	33.83	1	53.25	1	19.58	2	142.07
2a	University of Iowa	46.83	1	24.50	3	28.00	2	15.00	12	9.42	12	123.75
3a	Springfield College	43.00	2	28.66	1	14.75	8	15.00	12	6.50	21	107.91
4a	University of Illinois	11.00	9	21.33	4	25.16	4	12.50	16	37.32	1	107.31
5a	University of California-Los Angeles	15.83	8	5		10.00		28.83	3	5.16		64.82
6a	Boston University	35.50	3	1.50		12.67	10	6.67		3.57		59.91
7a	Indiana University	2.50		10.33	6	27.50	3	10.25	19	9.33	13	59.91
8a	University of Texas-Austin	3.00		10.00	7	5.00		26.75	4	9.08	14	53.83
9a	University of Michigan	15.00	6.5			10.33		9.31		12.67	8	52.31
10a	University of Wisconsin	15.00	6.5	4.00		6.00		16.50	11	9.75	11	51.25
11	University of California-Santa Barbara					16.00	6	30.17	2	4.95	29	51.12
12a	University of Maryland			1.00		13.33	9	22.29	6	12.63	9	49.25
13	City University of New York	4.00		13.50	5	2.50		7.92		18.04	4	45.96

	Institution											Total
14[a]	University of Oregon	2.33		2.00	8	15.33	7	16.83	10	1.50		37.99
15[a]	University of Minnesota	10.00	10.5	8.00		6.83		5.33		4.58	33	34.74
16[a]	Teachers College - Columbia University	18.50	5	1.00		3.00		3.50		8.50	15	34.50
17[a]	Michigan State University	1.33		1.00		11.83		17.72	9	1.91		33.79
18[a]	Purdue University	1.00		4.00		3.56		14.67	13	6.92	20	30.15
19	Wellesley College	23.00	4	4.00		2.00				1.00		30.00
20	University of Florida			1.00		17.67	5	7.33		3.42		29.42
21[a]	University of Alberta							23.33	5	4.67	32	28.00
22[a]	Ohio State University							11.75	17	1.00		26.91
23[a]	Pennsylvania State University	10.00	10.5	2.00		2.16		12.46		12.80	7	25.26
24	University of California-Davis							20.00	8	4.83		24.83
25	University of California-Riverside					0.50		21.50	7	2.33	31	24.33
26[a]	Florida State University							2.00		19.00	3	21.00
27	University of Houston							.75		16.58	5	17.33
28[a]	University of Kentucky							1.50		12.92	6	14.42
29[a]	University of Massachusetts/Amherst							3.00		10.50	10	13.50
30	University of Kansas	2.00		5.50	10.5	.67		1.00		2.08		11.25
31	Yale University	3.00		6.00	9	2.00						11.00
32	Harvard University	1.00		5.50	10.5			2.00				8.50

[a]Doctor's degree offered

and allocation for research, salary structure, and program expansion or curtailment are among the more likely prospects. Wellesley College, for example, ranked fourth in the first time-period covering the years 1930-1939 and then contributed much less in later years. Circumstances surrounding the Department of Hygiene and Physical Education at Wellesley College allow some explanation for this marked drop in research production. Established in 1909, the department was actually a transplant of the Boston Normal School of Gymnastics, which was founded by Mrs. Mary Hemenway in 1889. After collegiate association with Wellesley, the department's able staff contributed greatly to the celebrated post-graduate program, which was the first to accept only students who had completed all undergraduate requirements for a major in physical education. After many distinguished contributions, however, the department was closed in 1953 when Wellesley College elected to return to being a strictly liberal arts college and abandoned any commitments to graduate professional departments.

Many qualifications and interpretations are possible for the data in Table 5.2, most of which can be questioned on some grounds or another. Newly established graduate departments may complain that even an enviable contribution record since inception would fail to qualify them for admission into the top twenty. Other departments may contend that their mission includes much more than the mere production of research articles for the *Research Quarterly* and point to noteworthy accomplishments in other areas: offices held in important professional associations, promotion of physical education programs and curriculum innovations, faculty members with distinguished service citations and awards, and the attractiveness of their graduates to prospective employers. Schools with enviable performance records in publishing, however, are likely to contend that the data constitute a reasonable "Consumer's Guide" to be used by graduate students in the selection of an outstanding school for further study. Other departments will continue to point out the errors in such an egotistical and unfair posture, pointing out the axiom that research is not all there is to physical education.

In a recent study (1), a distinguished group of leaders in the profession were surveyed to identify those institutions which in their opinion offered the outstanding doctoral programs in physical education. The top twenty doctoral programs, as ranked by the responses of 68 Fellows of the American Academy of Physical Education and 44 Directors of Graduate Programs in Physical Education, are presented in Table 5.3. It is obvious that the mean scores of these top twenty schools are very close, particularly in adjacent ranks where a difference of as little as .005 could be responsible for a change in rank.

Eight of the Big Ten universities (Minnesota was 22) and six West Coast schools earned rankings in the top twenty. Four eastern schools

Table 5.3

Top Twenty Doctoral Programs in Physical Education
as Ranked by Fellows of American Academy of
Physical Education and Directors of Graduate Programs

Rank	School	Mean score	Rank as contributor to Research Quarterly
1	Pennsylvania State University	1.420	23
2	University of Iowa	1.579	2
3	University of Illinois	1.600	4
4	University of California - Berkeley	1.629	1
5	University of California - Los Angeles	1.663	5
6	University of Michigan	1.771	9
7	University of Massachusetts	1.868	29
8	Michigan State University	1.874	17
9	University of Maryland	1.879	12
10	University of Wisconsin	1.889	10
11	University of Oregon	1.962	14
12	Ohio State University	1.972	22
13	University of Southern California	2.101	—
14	Indiana University	2.131	7
15	Stanford University	2.163	—
16	University of Texas	2.191	8
17	Washington State University	2.237	—
18	Purdue University	2.251	18
19	University of North Carolina	2.375	—
20	Columbia University - Teachers College	2.380	16

and two southern schools also made the top twenty. Thirteen schools which ranked in the top twenty as contributors to the *Research Quarterly* also ranked in the top twenty doctoral programs. Discrepancies between rank of doctoral program and rank as *Research Quarterly* contributor are apparent. Some discrepancies can be explained by a recent commitment of a school to a quality graduate program as in the case of Massachusetts, which initiated a Ph.D. program in the late 1960's. Although Massachusetts had a rank of 29 as a contributor to the *Research Quarterly* from 1930-1979, it ranked tenth for the latest period, 1970-1979, reflecting its new graduate program commitment.

The list of schools representing the top twenty contributors to the *Research Quarterly* and the list of schools of the top twenty ranked doctoral programs cannot be taken as lists of the *best* schools for graduate study without some qualification. Many of the schools have outstanding graduate programs in one or more specialties, but are not equally outstanding in all graduate program specializations that may be of interest to potential graduate students. Some schools have faculties that include highly productive researchers who do not publish as regularly in the

Research Quarterly as they do in journals more specific to their specialty. A potential graduate student, therefore, must be prudent in the choice of a graduate school and give careful consideration to the specialization available at a particular institution. On the other hand, schools on either list are schools with noteworthy programs and productive research records.

QUALITY IN GRADUATE PROGRAMS

Individual Contributors

One plausible explanation for the rise and fall of institutional contribution rates to the *Research Quarterly* involves the individuals actually doing the research. Ultimately, people are the originators of research investigations. Using the same point scheme as before, Table 5.4 presents the leading individual contributors to the *Research Quarterly*. Only individuals with ten or more authored or co-authored articles are included. Individuals who ranked in the top ten for the latest decade (1970-1979) are also included.

On the whole, individuals seem to exhibit more consistency as contributors than do schools. As might be expected, the names at the top of the list are well-known individuals with long and distinguished careers. After the first nine names, the number of articles (NA) published drops rather precipitously. In some respects the table resembles an intercorrelation matrix with only values above the diagonal appearing. Also, the ranking on the basis of number of articles rather than author point score (APS) would change the total rank in more than a few instances. The author point score may be unfair to individuals whose research specialty necessitates a team effort which results in multiple authorship and a lower author point score relative to number of articles. Previous analyses (13, 15) of *Research Quarterly* contributions used the author point score scheme, and the same protocol was employed here in order to be consistent.

Loucks (15) found in his analysis of 1,088 articles over the 20-year period of 1930-1949 that 779 different authors were sponsored by nearly 300 secondary schools and institutions of higher learning. In 1960-1969, there were 681 different authors from 193 schools, and in 1970-1979 there were 812 different authors from 223 schools. For the combined period of 1960-1979, only 125 authors and 126 schools contributed during both decades. The situation for the last twenty years (1960-1979) seems similar to the first twenty years (1930-1939) in that only relatively few individuals appear to be consistent contributors to the *Research Quarterly*. In one respect the list ought to provide some inspiration to graduate students and young people in the profession who are interested in research. Even based upon an entire half-century of the *Research*

Quarterly, fewer than a dozen publications could gain an individual into the top echelon of all-time contributors. Few other areas of study could offer such an opportunity and achievable goal.

A better understanding of the inconsistency in contribution records by schools might be realized if one were to plot, with respect to productivity, where individual contributors had been located during their careers. After all, if a school suddenly stops making contributions, it indicates only that faculty members at the school are no longer making contributions. In most cases, this can be attributed to the fact that personnel at the school has changed and productive researchers have either left the school for another position, retired, or died. In some other cases, productive researchers have accepted the challenge of other responsibilities and become efficient administrators or entered professional pursuits outside the realm of physical education.

Data on contributors to the *Research Quarterly* by schools and by individuals would seem to suggest that good schools are really defined by the presence of a good staff. After all, if a particular school possesses adequate resources for one faculty member to be productive, then the same resources are likely to be available to subsequent faculty members as well. The data seemingly suggest, however, that when a productive faculty member leaves, the school's contribution rate to the *Research Quarterly* is negatively affected. It would seem that placing a productive individual in a laboratory or department is more important than placing an individual in a productive laboratory or department. The best schools and programs undoubtedly attempt to do both: secure the ablest individuals and provide an optimum environment for research. One other comment on the record of individual contributors seems in order, although this information is difficult to interpret. The list of individual contributors seems to indicate that one institution seldom claims more than a pair of researchers at any one time. If cooperative research endeavors among physical educators is a desirable venture, it would appear that few institutions are capable of providing more than a pair of productive researchers for such enterprises.

Montoye and Washburn (19) completed an academic genealogy analysis of *Research Quarterly* contributors. All individuals who authored or co-authored five or more articles in the *Research Quarterly* were asked to identify the universities where they earned their advanced degree and to name the dissertation chairperson. Of the top twenty active contributors to the *Research Quarterly*, only two did not earn their doctorate at one of the top twenty ranked doctoral programs listed in Table 5.3. Seven of these top twenty active *Research Quarterly* contributors did their doctorate under the supervision of a chairperson who appears on the top twenty list of all-time *Research Quarterly* contributors. Although several of the top twenty active contributors did their degree work with chairpersons outside of physical education, it would seem that a sizable percentage achieved their status without benefit of sponsorship by a highly productive *Research Quarterly* contributor.

Compared to the total number of individuals in the profession, there are relatively few productive researchers. Such a situation is not unique to physical education, however, as Lotka (16) has proposed an "inverse square law of productivity" which has been shown to apply to many fields of study. Price (20) has suggested that the number of highly productive researchers in science is typically equal to the square root of the total number of contributors. In sport sociology, Loy (17) showed that these rule of thumb axioms were remarkably accurate in regard to sport sociology contributors. Of 100 sport sociology authors with two or more publications, Loy found ten who could be classified as high producers, ten being exactly the square root of 100. Price also suggested that one-half of all research contributions were accomplished by individuals with ten or more published papers. Loy found that the 19 authors having ten or more publications accounted for 56.5 percent of all published work studied.

HONORS AND AWARDS

Almost every scientific and professional society practices some form of public recognition for noteworthy achievement by its members. Whether the award be a simple certificate, a medal, or a cash prize of sizable proportions, it conveys the appreciation of an organization for a job well done. After a long period of time during which three separate committees selected recipients for various citations, AAHPERD established a standing committee designed to streamline and better coordinate the recognition activities of the association. The Recognition Awards Committee was created in 1964, and adopted a more formal procedure for nomination and selection of award recipients. Members of the Recognition Awards Committee were selected during the summer of 1964.

The Recognition Awards Committee consists of 24 members chosen on the basis of two men and two women from each of the six district associations. Every three years, the AAHPERD president appoints twelve new members to the committee so that at all times at least one member from each district represents each of the major interest areas of health, physical education, and recreation. Provision is made for the guidance of committee-member selection by the association president in that each district president may supply a list with up to eight names as recommended appointees. Any AAHPERD member may also make a recommendation for an appointment to the committee directly to the association president. Fair and adequate representation on the committee is thus provided for major interest areas in the profession. At the present time five major awards are bestowed by the association for noteworthy contribution to the profession: the Gulick, Honor Fellow, Anderson, McKenzie, and Mabel Lee.

Gulick Award

As an association, AAHPERD considers the Luther H. Gulick Award to be the highest honor it can bestow on any member for distinguished service. The award takes the form of a medal executed by R. Tait McKenzie and is presented annually at the national convention. No award need be given and usually only one award is made each year. The first year that the newly established Recognition Awards Committee was in operation, however, it managed to break a long-standing tradition and award two Gulick medals in 1965. The Gulick Award was established as a result of George J. Fisher's desire to follow through on an original proposal by Gulick himself for a cash prize to stimulate research among members of the Physical Education Society of New York City. Gulick proposed such an award in 1904 and created a fund of $50 from which cash prizes were to be made for the best article on physical education each year. A potent, if not singular, factor for Gulick's establishment of the fund was his wish to stimulate original study and research by members of the Society (8, 9). Unfortunately, there were no applications submitted in 1904 and no award was made that year or for any other year until Fisher's proposal in 1924.

Gulick may have obtained the idea of an award for worthy research activity from his duties at the 1904 St. Louis Fair. At that time, Gulick was president of the American Physical Education Association and accepted chairmanship of a committee in charge of a special meeting of the association to be held in conjunction with the Louisiana Purchase Exposition. On behalf of the association, six gold medals were accepted from Mr. James E. Sullivan, Chief of the Department of Physical Culture of the Louisiana Purchase Exposition, to be awarded for papers presented at the fair. Gulick appointed a committee to establish criteria for awarding the medals. Apparently, the committee held to high quality standards, for only one medal was awarded out of the six available. Furthermore, even this medal was awarded on the condition that the paper be further improved. After these additional improvements were made the medal was awarded to Dr. C. Ward Crampton (22). Crampton's paper entitled "Recent Investigations in the Effects of Exercise upon Blood Pressure, with Application of Results to Gymnastic Procedure" appeared later in the *American Physical Education Review* as a series of articles beginning in 1905.

It was during this same year (1904) that Gulick proposed his idea concerning an award for the best article on physical education to the Physical Education Society of New York City. Whether the two events were related or not is problematical. What was not problematical was Gulick's idea of an award for noteworthy research contributions of a scientific nature. Nowhere is such motivation more evident than in Gulick's activities in organizing the American Academy of Physical Education.* At the invitation of Gulick, a meeting was held on December 17, 1906 at Springfield College to ". . . consider a plan for the increase of interest in scientific problems connected with physical education." Minutes of this 1906 meeting stated that: "Those persons shall be eligible for membership who have done some good piece of research work related definitely to physical training." Following the typed sheet containing minutes of the meeting was another sheet with scribbled notes in Gulick's handwriting. In regard to a short phrase concerning the academy medal to be given annually was the comment " 'Gulick medal' conditions." On a second page of handwritten notations by Gulick was the statement "McKenzie and Gulick Com. on medal." It seems that C. Ward Crampton may have been suggested for membership on this committee—possibly because he had received a medal for his paper at St. Louis—since the letters "Cramp" were written and then crossed out at the beginning of the note concerning membership of the committee.

Several years later, a meeting of the academy was held on September 11, 1909, and a sheet of handwritten comments noted that the awarding of a medal was not to be adopted but that a ". . . certificate of excellence for all worthy theses" would be offered instead. The form of this certificate was approved at this meeting and it was decided that all Fellows of the Academy should sign each certificate. An original copy of the certificate, signed by all members present at the 1909 meeting, is housed with Gulick's papers at Springfield College.

The next meeting of the academy was held February 25, 1910 and the minutes contained the conditions under which the award was to be made. The two pages, apparently typed by Gulick himself, presenting these criteria are reproduced in Table 5.5.

Later in the year of 1910, a September 3-11 meeting of the academy was held at South Casco, Maine. Minutes of this meeting noted that "The committee on the extension of original work through the use of the diploma was created, consisting of Drs. Meylan, McCurdy, and Gulick." In addition, the report stated that ". . . the names of certain candidates for the diplomas, with their theses" had been presented at the meeting. The names of these candidates were not actually reported in the

---

*Materials and quotes presented from this point on concerning Gulick and the American Academy of Physical Education are taken from the collection of Gulick's private papers that is housed at Springfield College. In particular, one collection of papers and notes titled "Gulick: Letters, Notes, Papers on Founding and Early Meetings of The Academy of Physical Education, 1906-1911" contained information of greatest help.

Table 5.5
Gulick Manuscript Concerning Certificate
for Research in Physical Training

February 25, 1910.

ACADEMY OF PHYSICAL EDUCATION

The Academy of Physical Education was organized to bring [sic] together those who were doing original scientific work in the field of physical training, and to aid in the promotion of such work. Its membership is as follows. At the last meeting, held in the fall of 1909, it was decided to offer the diploma of the Society to persons contributing original studies of value. Each diploma is to be signed by each Fellow of the Association. Its size is fourteen by eighteen inches. The conditions of the award are as follows:

The subject must be one related to physical training. It must be based upon first hand observation of facts.

Each thesis should contain

(1) As complete a bibliography as possible of the subject, with comments as to the value of the chief references. This bibliography should give full title, author's full name, date of publication, name of publisher, size and number of pp.

(2) A concise statement of all the facts ascertained, arranged in some logical order. The authority for each fact must be given definitely so that any one else could readily verify it.

(3) A careful estimate and judgment of the significance of the facts and of their relation to each other.

(4) It should be written carefully in ink, on one side only of each sheet, in a book or on bound sheets having wide margins.

Candidates for the diploma should submit their work to me as executive officer. It will then be presented to those members of the Academy whose researches have most closely connected them with the particular subject under investigation.

There are no expenses in connection with the application for or the awarding of the diploma.

The securing of the diploma stands by itself and does not in any way involve or include fellowship in the Academy. The object is simply to promote original research, and to offer to all who are doing such work an opportunity for recognition by those who have been connected the most prominently with the advancement of original investigation and physical training.

---

minutes of the meeting available in Gulick's private papers. The titles of the theses submitted were: "On heart rate, blood pressure and scholarship correlation," "On college administration," and "On albuminurea." Whether any certificates were ever awarded is not known, and the original Academy of Physical Education faded out of existence during World War I.

The conditions and standards for the academy diploma, however, unmistakably called for original research and first-hand observation of fact. Unfortunately, it is not known what Gulick's sentiments were when he proposed an award for research at the Physical Education Society of New York City meeting in 1904. Gulick's actions in St. Louis and in the

Academy of Physical Education, however, would seem to indicate clearly that his motivation was to give an award to stimulate original research rather than to reward service of the form of dedicated working years. No more was heard of Gulick's proposal to the New York Society until after his death in 1918. In 1924, George J. Fisher presented a Luther H. Gulick Medal to Jessie H. Bancroft on behalf of the members of the Physical Education Society of New York City. His address on this occasion appeared in the *American Physical Education Review* (9) and stated that he and other members of the Society thought that "... it would be desirable to renew interest in the original idea of Dr. Gulick and at the same time to broaden the scope of the award so as to include recognition of meritorious service to the cause of physical education by the members." It would seem that some of this interest was prompted by the fact that the original $50 provided by Gulick had passed the $200 mark because of interest accumulations.

The first Gulick Medal was awarded a year earlier to the Gulick family and was accepted by Mrs. Gulick at a special meeting of the New York Society in 1923. After the New York Society disbanded in 1929, no further awards were given until 1939. At that time, the Health Education Teachers Association made an award to Jesse Feiring Williams. After making a second award, this time to Jay B. Nash in 1940, authority to present the Gulick Award was transferred to AAHPERD, and in 1944 an award was made to Charles H. McCloy. Up to 1981, 44 Gulick medals have been presented for distinguished service.

Honor Award

The Honor Awards of the national association are made in the form of a certificate in recognition of meritorious service, and no more than six are granted in one year. Honor Award candidates are chosen on the basis of their contributions to three major divisions of a criteria list: (a) offices held, (b) committee work, and (c) speeches, writing, and research. Up to 1981, 381 Honor Awards have been given dating from 1931, when the first award was given to Amy Morris Homans, who was then 82 years young. A complete list of Honor Award recipients is not published every year. The latest list appeared in the April 1978 issue of *JOHPER*.

William G. Anderson Merit Award

The William G. Anderson Merit Award was first given in 1949 to Mazie V. Scanlon. Originally, it was intended to honor the founder of the association by making an award in his name to individuals who best exemplified Dr. Anderson's devotion to his profession and to society. Since 1955, however, the award has been used more often to honor individuals outside the official AAHPERD structure. Before such action was taken, a trio of AAHPERD members had received both the Gulick and Anderson awards: E.C. Davis (Anderson Award in 1954 and Gulick Medal in 1965); Clair V. Langton (Gulick Medal in 1951 and Anderson Award in 1954); and Helen Manley (Anderson Award in 1951 and Gulick Medal in 1958). If the Recognition Awards Committee holds to its present criteria, these three individuals will be the only persons ever to have been awarded both the Anderson and Gulick Awards. A maximum of three Anderson Awards per year is set as a limit.

R. Tait McKenzie Award

The fourth AAHPERD award is the R. Tait McKenzie Award. Approval of the award was made by the AAHPERD Board of Directors in time to commemorate the first year following the R. Tait McKenzie Centennial. Mabel Lee, who must have set some sort of a record for distinguished firsts, accepted the first McKenzie Award at St. Louis in 1968. The award recognizes distinguished service to human welfare through the fields of health, physical education, and recreation. A description of the qualifications for the award appeared in the November-December 1967 issue of *JOHPER* and noted that individuals recommended were to be outstanding both within the profession and in outside relationships of an educational and community nature. Service to the profession was thus to be extended by interpreting the profession to other groups and associations.

Mabel Lee Award

In 1976, recognition of outstanding younger professionals was begun by an award named in honor of Mabel Lee. The first recipients in 1976 were Sharon A. Plowman and Mary G. Sholtis.

Distinguished Service Citation

In addition to these five awards a Distinguished Service Citation can also be awarded upon recommendation of the national president or recommendation and approval of the Board of Directors. The AAHPERD President's Citation is stated to serve two purposes: (1) to honor distinguished people, outside the fields of health, physical education, and recreation, who have made outstanding contributions to the profession or have given it unusual support; and (2) to bring the importance of health, physical education, and recreation to the attention of other fields by calling attention to the fact that some member of another field has made a significant contribution to physical education and at the same time to strengthen our relationship to these fields. According to stated policy, only individuals outside the profession are eligible to receive the President's Citation.

Such a short outline of the nature of the awards and honors that AAHPERD is empowered to confer enables us to understand the criteria upon which these honors are based. Because of traditional and continuing bonds with education, a major emphasis upon dedicated service, and the only recent rise of a move toward an academic discipline of physical education, it should not be expected that outstanding research would deserve and attract as much attention as it would, say, in a true academic discipline. Of more particular concern, however, is a test of the hypothesis that publication in the *Research Quarterly* is an effective path toward recognition of distinguished service and contribution to the profession. Again, bearing in mind the numerous deficiencies in use of the *Research Quarterly* as a legitimate representative of scholarly efforts by physical educators, let us see how major contributors to this journal have fared with honors and awards.

Of the 44 Gulick Medal Awards that have been presented for distinguished service, four of the top twenty major contributors to the *Research Quarterly* have been recipients. Two of the recipients were also presidents of the national association, however, and it would be difficult to say whether their research contributions or the office they held accounted for their Gulick Awards. Since the *Research Quarterly* only began publication in 1930, it could not be expected to have much influence upon early selections for the Gulick Award.

Whether the four Gulick Awards garnered by major contributors to the *Research Quarterly* represent a reasonable share of recognition is an indelicate question. To suggest that the Gulick Award, more than any other association award, should be awarded primarily for scholarly research contributions rather than for dedicated service to the profession would be an attempt to turn back the pages of time to Gulick's original motivation for such an award. Furthermore, many of the Gulick Award honorees have made numerous and outstanding scholarly contributions to the profession outside the pages of the *Research Quarterly*, while other honorees have made their mark through long and dedicated service of unquestionable value. Major contributors to the *Research Quarterly*, furthermore, have fared much better in the case of the Honor Awards. Of the top ten contributors to the *Research Quarterly* shown in Table

Table 5.4

Individual Contributors to the *Research Quarterly* (1930-1979)

Rank	Author	First period 1930-1939			Second period 1940-1949			Third period 1950-1959			Fourth period 1960-1969			Fifth period 1970-1979			Total	
		NA	APS	R	NA	APS	R	NA	APS	R	NA	APS	R	NA	APS	R	NA	APS
1a	Cureton, T.K.	12	10.33	3.0	15	12.16	1.0	6	4.50	11.0	6	3.67		3	1.16		42	31.8
2a	Henry, F.M.	2	1.00		5	4.50	9.0	18	15.50	1.0	13	7.08		6	2.58		44	30.7
3a	Slater-Hammel, A.T.				6	5.00	8.0	19	15.00	2.0	7	4.00					32	24.0
4a	Clarke, H.H.	6	5.50	7.0	2	2.00		13	8.42	3.0	13	6.33					34	22.3
5b	Karpovich, P.V.	6	6.00	6.0	10	7.33	3.0	4	3.00		11	4.92		2	0.75		33	22.0
6	Kroll, W.							2	2.00		17	14.00	2.0	7	5.00	4.5	26	21.0
7b	McCloy, C.H.	16	15.50	1.0	4	3.50		3	2.00								23	21.0
8b	Tuttle, W.W.	14	8.16	5.0	9	5.16	7.0	3	1.16		4	1.33					30	15.8
9	Berger, R.A.										25	14.50	1.0	3	1.50		28	16.0
10b	Affleck, G.B.	12	12.00	2.0	2	2.00											14	14.0
11a	Hewitt, J.E.	3	2.50		6	6.00	5.5				5	4.50					14	13.0
12	Singer, R.N.										13	10.50	3.0	5	2.33		18	12.8
13	Nelson, D.O.										9	7.75	7.0				13	11.8
14	Montoye, H.J.							4	4.00		17	4.63		4	1.17		30	11.6
15a	Scott, M.G.	2	1.50		8	6.33	4.0	9	5.75	4.0	1	1.00					13	10.8
16	Clarke, D.H.							2	2.00		11	7.67		4	2.50		16	10.7
17a	Espenschade, A.S.	1		1.00				1	0.50		3	2.50					13	10.7
18	Eckert, H.M.										8	5.75		5	4.50	7.5	13	10.3
19b	Carpenter, A.	4	4.00	9.5	6	6.00	5.5	7	5.83	7.0							13	10.0
20	Cozens, F.	10	7.33	5.0	4	2.50											14	9.8
21a	Irwin, L.W.	2	2.00		2	1.00		9	4.16		5	2.50					18	9.7
22	Smith, L.E.										14	9.58	4.0				14	9.6
23a	Larson, L.A.	4	2.00		9	7.50	2.0										13	9.5
24	Cratty, B.J.										12	9.50	5.0				12	9.5
25	Alderman, R.B.										10	8.25	6.0	1	1.00		11	9.3
26	Norrie, M.L.										8	7.25	10.0	2	2.00		10	9.3

Table 5.4 (Cont.)

#	Name	N	X̄	N	X̄	X̄	N	X̄	N	X̄	N	X̄	X̄	Yrs	X̄
27	Campbell, D.E.								7	6.50	4	2.13		11	8.6
28	Baumgartner, T.A.								6	4.00	9	4.50	7.5	15	8.5
29	Cowell, C.C.[b]	3	3.00				2	1.33	6	4.00				11	8.3
30	Rarick, G.L.[a]	1	1.00	3	2.00		3	1.33	4	1.58				15	7.9
31	Johnson, W.R.			1	1.00		6	3.99	7	2.82	4	2.00		16	7.6
32	Gutin, B.								4	2.50	4	2.00		15	7.5
33	Martens, R.								3	1.75	2	0.75		13	7.4
34	Pierson, W.R.						2	2.00	12	5.38	11	5.00	4.5	14	7.4
35	Nelson, R.C.						1	0.50	16	5.96	10	5.67	2.0	19	7.2
36	Jackson, A.S.								4	1.50				17	7.1
37	McCraw, L.W.			1	1.00		4	3.00	3	2.00	2	0.67		10	7.0
38	Whitley, J.D.								6	3.25	13	5.58	3.0	10	7.0
39	Skubic, V.			1	1.00				6	2.83	2	1.00		11	6.8
40	Mathews, D.K.					9.0	4	2.83	5	1.41	4	3.50		16	6.7
41	Rasch, P.J.[a]						11	4.92	8	2.29				15	6.3
42	Keogh, J.F.						7	3.83	8	3.58	2	1.00		11	6.1
43	Park, R.J.						1	1.00			6	6.00	1.0	6	6.0
44	Katch, F.I.								3	1.83	10	3.58		13	6.0
45	Falls, H.B.								4	2.33	6	3.00		10	5.4
46	Howell, M.L.						2	2.00	8	3.29	2	1.00		10	5.3
47	Ismail, A.H.								10	3.92	6	4.83		12	5.3
48	Williams, L.R.T.												6.0	6	4.9
49	Stull, G.A.						2	0.75	3	1.33	6	2.58		11	4.8
50	Katch, V.L.										13	4.42	9.0	13	4.7
51	Michael, E.D.								7	2.98	4	1.53		11	4.4
52	Bain, L.L.										4	4.00	1.0	4	4.2
53	Cotten, D.J.								6	2.50	4	.33		10	4.0
54	Weltman, A.L.										10	3.00		10	3.8
55	VanHuss, W.								9	1.85	1	0.25		13	3.0
56	McArdle, W.D.						4	0.50	4	1.33	6	1.25		10	2.9

[a]Retired
[b]Deceased

5.4, six have been so honored. Of the top twenty contributors, nine have been honored. Thus, only eleven of the top twenty individual contributors to the *Research Quarterly* have not received one of the 381 Honor Awards presented since 1931.

No one but an irascible ingrate would conclude that an outstanding publication record in the *Research Quarterly* qualified an individual for recognition only by others who publish in the official research journal of the association. Since membership in the AAHPERD Research Council is usually less than 150, research activities cannot be counted as a potent factor worthy of public recognition from an association numbering up to 50,000 members and sponsoring a vast number of activities and projects. In addition, many of the articles published in the *Research Quarterly* are acknowledged to be of poor quality and hardly constitute much of a contribution either to the profession or to knowledge. Researchers do not often seek or hold high and important offices in state, district, or national AAHPERD hierarchies. The only committee work that researchers are likely to undertake is that associated with the AAHPERD Research Council or Research Section.

At most, researchers identified by the unfortunate criterion of having been major contributors to the *Research Quarterly* represent only a small and quite inconspicuous segment of the entire profession. Indeed, even among many of those in the profession who consider themselves scholar-researchers, any identification with the *Research Quarterly* is painstakingly avoided on the basis that this journal does not represent much more than a biased sliver of the scholarly research activity within the profession. Fortunately, only a few are ever to escape the confines of such a closely knit Gehenna fraternity and attract attention on a national scale. If formal recognition seems necessary, it may be worthwhile to consider the establishment of an award within this group itself.

In proper perspective, therefore, graduate students and faculty members in the ranks of physical education who are interested in establishing a science of physical education should not expect that AAHPERD will ever give more than token recognition to scholarly and scientific research efforts. Indeed, becoming irked by a professional association for not acting like a scientific society is more than a little naive. A professional association must pay due attention to the fulfillment of an altruistic obligation by its members. One could argue, of course, that a professional association should recognize contributions to the profession to a much greater extent than it does contributions solely to the association. Such a criticism may or may not have validity when held against AAHPERD and the history of its awards. However, even if it were true that AAHPERD awards have gone overwhelmingly to the officers of the association (as some chronic complainers have charged), it would not be too unwholesome a deficiency since the vast majority of personnel involved in physical education see AAHPERD and the profession to be one and the same.

The realization that a professional association cannot be expected to behave like a scientific society may come only after many difficult years of strained relations between scientist and professional in physical education. Indeed, unless the move toward the establishment of physical education as an academic discipline is successful, there may be no need for such an inevitable confrontation, and dedicated researchers will continue to represent only a small and uneasy group complaining about not being appreciated. If, however, a major segment of the personnel in physical education manages to identify itself as concerned primarily with an academic discipline, then such a confrontation must certainly come to pass. What will happen when the scientists and professionals recognize themselves as distinct entities is difficult to predict and is left for wiser counsel than is available here.

REFERENCES

1. Baker, John A.W. *Determination of the Common Characteristics of Outstanding Doctoral Programs in Physical Education in the United States.* Unpublished dissertation. Iowa City: University of Iowa, 1981.

2. Balyeat, Ralph E. *Factors Related to the Promotion of University Personnel.* Cooperative Research Project S-017. Washington, D.C.: Office of Education, United States Department of Health, Education and Welfare, 1964.

3. Bloom, B.S. In *Scientific Creativity: Its Recognition and Development,* C.W. Taylor (ed.). New York: Wiley, 1963.

4. Cartter, Allan M. *An Assessment of Quality in Graduate Education.* Washington, D.C.: American Council on Education, 1966.

5. Clark, M.J. *Assessing Dimensions of Quality in Doctoral Education: A Technical Report of a National Study in Three Fields.* Princeton, New Jersey: Educational Testing Service, 1976.

6. Dennis, Wayne. Productivity among American psychologists. *American Psychologist* 9: 191-194; 1954.

7. Dunham, Ralph E., and Patricia S. Wright. *Teaching Faculty in Higher Education, 1962-1963: Primary Teaching Areas and Contract Salaries.* Report OE-53022. Washington, D.C.: United States Department of Health, Education and Welfare, 1964.

8. Fisher, George J., and Jay B. Nash. The Luther Halsey Gulick Award for distinguished service in physical education. *JOHPER* 16: 302-303, 362; June 1945.

9. Fisher, George J. Jessie H. Bancroft, Educator-author-pioneer-philanthropist. *American Physical Education Review* 29: 476-480; October 1924.

10. Forker, Barbara, and Warren Fraleigh. Graduate study and professional accreditation: applications to physical education. *JOHPER* 51: 45; March 1980.

11. Golightly, Carole, Donn Byrne, and E.J. Capaldi. The publication of psychological research among Ph.D. granting institutions: 1952-1961. Paper presented at the Southwestern Psychological Association, San Antonio, Texas, 1964.

12. Grant, W. In *Digest of Education Statistics 1980*, Vance and Lee J. Eiden (eds.). Washington, D.C.: U.S. Government Printing Office, 1980.

13. Hertz, Gil. Contributors to the *Research Quarterly*, 1930-1954. *The Physical Educator* **12**: 105-106; October 1955.

14. Levy, Leon H. The skew in clinical psychology. *American Psychologist* **17**: 244-249; 1962.

15. Loucks, Donald. An analytical study of the content of the *Research Quarterly*, 1930-1949. *Research Quarterly* **23**: 209-220; May 1952.

16. Lotka, A.J. The frequency distribution of scientific productivity. *Journal of the Washington Academy of Sciences* **16**: 317-323; 1926.

17. Loy, John W. The emergence and development of the sociology of sport as an academic specialty. *Research Quarterly* **51**: 91-109; March 1980.

18. Massey, Benjamin H. The physical educator as researcher. *Quest* **7**: 46-52; December 1966.

19. Montoye, Henry J., and R. Washburn. *Research Quarterly* contributors: an academic genealogy. *Research Quarterly* **51**: 261-266; March 1980.

20. Price, Derek J.D. *Little Science, Big Science*. New York: Columbia Univ. Press, 1963.

21. Resick, Matthew C. Professional preparation: graduate education patterns. *JOHPER* **38**: 51-55; April 1967.

22. Report of jury. *American Physical Education Review* **9**: 289; December 1904.

23. Roose, K.D., and C.J. Andersen. *A rating of graduate programs*. Washington, D.C.: American Council on Education, 1970.

24. Taylor, Calvin W., and Robert L. Ellison. Biographical predictors and scientific performance. *Science* **155**: 1075-1080; 1967.

25. Walsh, John. Graduate education: ACE study rates departments qualitatively. *Science* **152**: 1226-1228; 1966.

Research Laboratories in Physical Education [6]

Establishment of a research laboratory by itself cannot ensure an increased production of quality research in physical education. In fact, several areas of research in physical education require no special laboratory facilities at all. As Cureton (5) suggested, the true laboratories in physical education are the pools, playfields, gymnasiums, and camps. Prompted, perhaps, by the studies in the areas of tests and measurements, physiology of exercise, and motor learning, provision of special research facilities was eventually seen to be a logical necessity. As distinguishable research laboratories appeared in physical education, they represented reasonable indications of the intent to study certain problem areas under more controlled conditions than those available in the pools and fields. The absence of distinguishable research laboratories could be taken to indicate either the lack of interest in controlled study in such problem areas or the inability to secure adequate backing for their initiation. In either case, the absence of research laboratories signaled the inability of physical educators to study certain phenomena under appropriate conditions.

There are many problems in physical education that can best be studied under laboratory conditions. Because of the complexity of the factors capable of affecting the phenomena of interest, it is frequently desirable to isolate the phenomena to be studied and eliminate as many as possible of the extraneous variables that could confound the results of a study. The desired outcome in such experimental laboratory research is to effect careful observation, accurate quantification of the phenomena, and the control of relevant variables that could contaminate the observation and measurements. Instrumentation is used to make observation techniques more efficient and to minimize the reliance placed upon "human" evaluation of quantifiable phenomena.

Laboratory research can thus help isolate the research situation from unnecessary life variables by eliminating as many as possible of the extraneous variables that might influence the criterion variable under consideration. The danger in such purification of criterion measure assessment is that it may produce an entirely artificial situation unrelated to the real world. Artificial environments produced in a laboratory setting have come in for their share of criticisms, and "test tube facts" frequently are in contradiction to the real world. One of the most poignant observations on this question was made by Joseph Wood Krutch in his book *The Measure of Man*. In his book, Krutch suggested that the methods of inquiry being used in the study of humans were originally developed to study either machines or rats. His conclusion was that the current methodology used to study humans could only discover "those characteristics which the three do have in common."

Whether they are artificial situations or not, laboratory investigations still represent an essential and highly important component of scientific research efforts. In many instances, the laboratory situation constitutes the most efficient and most valid procedure to secure reliable data. In still other cases, laboratory research is the *only* way that such data and knowledge can be obtained. An astronomer, for example, faces considerable difficulty in any attempt to study the stars experimentally. The astronomer cannot arrange to move a solar system from one part of space to another in order to see what would happen. The astronomer can, however, concoct studies on motion and mass in an artificial laboratory situation. To the extent that the artificial laboratory situation demonstrates correspondence with actual phenomena in the real world, the astronomer comes close to bringing the universe into his laboratory.

A biologist wishing to study the effects of natural sources of radiation on living organisms might actually travel to different parts of the world and measure life forms in their natural settings. However, the biologist could also bring life forms into the laboratory and expose them to known and controlled intensities of artificially created radiation. The biologist could, in essence, speed up time and conduct studies that would take a lifetime to accomplish if one had to wait for these events to occur of their own accord in nature.

The initiation of research laboratories in physical education was beset with many obstacles. Physical educators tend to be extremely practical, concerned with the whole person, and desirous of affecting humankind in sweeping strokes of grandeur. They ask of research results, "What good is this to me in my daily teaching obligation?" They ask what applications of research can be made today, and they hold that tomorrow is too late for results. Demands such as these have tended to have the effect of forcing research in physical education to be extremely practical and of restricting the encouragement of "fancy" research laboratories for studying nonpertinent problems. Too often, however, the research endeavors allowable under such a set of demands have been evaluated by other researchers as being unscientific, unsophisticated, and just plain poor.

Insistence on immediate practical applications from research suggests an exaggerated desire for usefulness before sufficient knowledge of the pertinent parameters involved has been acquired. Sole emphasis upon practical research may place the role of a physical educator in a position analogous to the contrast between a florist and a botanist; a farmer contrasted with an agricultural engineer; or a first aider contrasted with a doctor of medicine. Many aspects of "scientific research" necessitate frequent use of the laboratory, and many of the practical problems in physical education demanding solutions may be studied at first only in the laboratory. Indeed, many of the phenomena of interest to physical education researchers can be measured only with rather sophisticated apparatus under standardized laboratory conditions. The appearance and growth of research laboratories in physical education thus reflects a wholesome recognition of the need to study certain pertinent phenomena.

ORIGINS OF RESEARCH LABORATORIES

Over the years, the establishment and development of adequate research laboratories have tended to depend primarily upon the productive research efforts of outstanding individuals already situated at a particular institution. In many cases, staunch research pioneers literally forced the acquisition of a research laboratory and equipment by first proving (often under most trying conditions) their own research capabilities and then demonstrating the value and need for this research. Such difficulties may be reflected partially in a comment from one of the earliest and most productive research pioneers: "My start in research in 1925 was in a horrible little room at Springfield College, poorly equipped and disgracefully budgeted" (15).

In more than a few instances, research laboratories were initiated despite the fact that administrative uncertainty existed about their appropriateness. Such caution, by the way, was exerted not only in higher administrative echelons, but in the departments of physical education themselves. Several researchers, for example, have told of harrowing experiences in pursuing their own research interests because of an argument that such research was not "physical education" research and that it did

Table 6.1

Physical Education Research Laboratories in the United States and Reported Dates of Origin

Springfield College (1920-1927)[a]	Louisiana State University (1957)[a]
George Williams College (1923)	Southwest Texas State College (1960)
University of California (Berkeley) (1936)[a]	University of Toledo (1960)[a]
University of Illinois (1941-1944)[a]	Temple University (1961)[a]
University of North Carolina (1946)	University of Montana (1962)
Indiana University (1948)[a]	Columbia (Teachers College) (1963)[a]
New York University (1948)[a]	Texas Woman's University (1963)[a]
University of Southern California (1950)[a]	Illinois State University (1964)
University of Texas (1950)[a]	University of Massachusetts (1964)[a]
Boston University (1950)[a]	University of New Mexico (1964)[a]
University of Florida (1951)	Southwest Missouri State College (1965)
University of Wisconsin (1951)[a]	Rice University (1965)
University of Kansas (1953)	Ball State University (1965)
University of Maryland (1953)[a]	Indiana State University (1966)[a]
University of Michigan (1953)[a]	Drake University (1967)
University of Oregon (1953)[a]	Herbert H. Lehman College (1967)
University of Iowa (1954)[a]	Western Kentucky University (1968)
Michigan State University (1954)[a]	University of Tennessee (1968)[a]
Texas A & M (1954)[a]	North Carolina State (1970)
University of Connecticut (1955)[a]	University of Virginia (1973)
Utah State University (1955)	University of Wyoming (1978)
State College of Washington (1955)[a]	University of Missouri
Brigham Young University (1956)[a]	University of New Mexico
University of Kentucky (1956)[a]	University of Utah
San Diego State College (1956)	Peabody College
Florida State University (1957)[a]	Syracuse University
Southern Illinois University (1957)[a]	Kent State University
University of Arkansas (1957)[a]	University of Colorado
University of California (Los Angeles) (1957)[a]	Southern Methodist University

[a]Offers doctorate degree.

not belong within the confines of a physical education school or department. The necessity of justifying research on a useful-knowledge criterion has short-circuited many an attempt at research by foolhardy dreamers.

In the face of numerous obstacles, however, physical education research laboratories were established. According to Donnelly's survey (6) which was conducted in 1958, three laboratories were established between 1920 and 1936. Another three laboratories were established between 1941 and 1948, and from 1950 to 1958, at least another 16 research laboratories have been established, and even this number may be an underestimate since it is not based upon an extensive survey study. Table 6.1 contains a list of research laboratories in physical education along with their reported dates of origin. Donnelly's list was updated to include the research laboratories now known to exist and to indicate several new schools now offering a doctorate degree program.

One can see that as many new research laboratories have been established since 1960 as had been established up to 1953. In less than a decade, more research laboratories came into existence than had been developed in over three generations following the founding of the association in 1885. An encouraging development is the fact that several research laboratories were established as an inducement to attract capable research personnel rather than to accommodate researchers already on staff. This suggests that a research laboratory may now be seen to be a necessary facility in any quality program rather than a desirable frill or appendage to essential activities.

Hunsicker's survey in 1950 (14) showed that out of 148 colleges and universities contacted only 16 reported specific physical education research laboratories, although an additional 12 schools reported having access to laboratories in other departments on campus. The physical education research laboratories ranged in size from a low of 120 square feet to a high of 5000 square feet with a median value of about 650 square feet. By 1958, Donnelly's survey showed that at least 28 research laboratories existed in physical education departments. Schools offering a doctorate-degree program reported a median of 2000 square feet of laboratory space (ranging from 405 to 3800 square feet), and a median of four separate rooms (ranging from one to seven rooms). In those schools not offering a doctoral program the figures were somewhat different, with a median of 1336 square feet being reported (ranging from 100 to 6500 square feet), and a median of two rooms being available (ranging from half a room to four rooms). Compared to the 1950 data, research laboratories in 1958 were about two to three times larger in median size.

A third study of physical education research laboratories was undertaken by the American Academy of Physical Education through its Committee for the Study of Facilities for Graduate Education. A report was released in May of 1965 concerning its survey of the 29 NCATE (National Council for Accreditation of Teacher Education) accredited institutions offering the doctorate in physical education, from which usable data on 22 schools resulted. Part of the results of this study are shown in Table 6.2, which contains information on the kinds of research laboratories, square footage available, and the approximate cost of replacing research equipment on hand.

In 1958, the emphasis fell into three broad categories, with the physiological area far ahead of the psychological and kinesiological areas. Table 6.2 shows that the situation was not much different in 1965 with 19 laboratories for physical fitness research reported, while kinesiology laboratories were reported in 14 schools, and 6 laboratories each reported in sport psychology and exercise therapy. Of some interest is the fact that separate laboratory rooms were now provided for historical, sociological investigations, and for administrative theory. The cost of

Table 6.2

Type and Amount of Research Space in 22 Institutions Offering the Doctorate in Physical Education[a]

Institution	Physical fitness	Kinesiology	Exercise therapy	Sports and exercise psychology	Sociological investigation	Administrative theory and practice	Historical	Teaching and learning	Philo-sophical	Other labs	Equipment cost
1	300										5,000
2	640	400								1,000	38,000
3	1,300	600		600						1,204	95,000
4	1,016	1,000						225		7,900	
5	2,862	1,682									39,224
8	1,000	833		500			150			350	52,000
9	1,300	1,260					144			950	55,000
10										2,250	55,000
11		850	1,560							2,250	15,000
12	3,500			3,040						800	50,000
13	1,000	800	1,700							1,700	85,000
14	1,320										
16										1,280	39,500
18	220	220	220	220							
19	300										
21	750	750		750						750	40,000
22	4,000	150	2,397							1,150	100,000
24	300	300									4,000
25	1,120										2,500
26	800	400	800	1,200							5,000
28	1,800	600	2,000		500						
29	2,000					450					65,724
Total	25,528	9,845	8,677	6,310	500	450	294	225	0	12,324	731,251

[a]All values are given in square feet except for the last column which is given in dollars.

Table 6.3

Relationship of Various Data
on Institutions Offering the Doctorate (*N* = 22)

Variable	1	2	3	4	5	6	7	8
1. Laboratory space		0.55[a]	0.06[a]	0.54[a]	0.64[a]	0.55[a]	0.26	−0.28
2. Equipment cost			0.72[a]	−0.06	0.59[b]	0.37	0.09	−0.33
3. Masters enrolled				0.53[a]	0.90[a]	0.61[a]	0.59[a]	−0.14
4. Doctorates enrolled					0.80[a]	0.37[b]	0.62[a]	−0.06
5. Total enrollment						0.61[a]	0.65[a]	−0.05
6. Masters completed							0.27	−0.23
7. Doctorates completed								−0.27
8. Doctorates offered								

[a]Significant at 0.01 level.
[b]Significant at 0.05 level.

replacing equipment averaged $43,015 in 1965 with a median of $39,750, whereas in 1958, the median value for replacement cost was $10,000. The 1965 data, of course, included only schools with doctorate programs, making the cost of equipment in the two surveys not directly comparable. No adjustment was made for any rise in costs because of inflation.

Besides square feet of laboratory space (all areas combined for any one institution), the 1965 committee report also included data on the number of master's and doctoral degree students enrolled, the number of such degrees completed for the school year 1964-1965, and whether the school offered a Ph.D. degree, the Ed.D., or P.E.D. These data were used to calculate rank-order correlation coefficients which are presented in Table 6.3. Not all 29 institutions included in the survey supplied full sets of information. Rank-order correlation coefficients in Table 6.3 were based on a number of 22 for all comparisons except those involving variable 2 (equipment cost), which was based on a number of 16.

Variable 8 represents a biserial *r* computed against other variables with a one score assigned if the institution offered the Ph.D. and a zero score if only the Ed.D. or P.E.D. was offered. Since ranks were used on other variables with a rank of one signifying highest, a negative correlation indicates that schools offering a Ph.D. ranked higher on the variable being considered. A positive r, on the other hand, suggests that non-Ph.D. schools enjoyed the higher rankings.

Although none of the correlation coefficients for variable 8 is significant, it is perhaps the most interesting of all the results. Negative correlations with laboratory space and equipment costs suggest Ph.D.-offering institutions "tend" to have larger and better equipped research laboratories, but this tendency is neither significant nor dramatic. Only three institutions offering the Ph.D. degree exclusively were reported (the other five Ph.D. schools also offered an Ed.D.) and their ranks for laboratory space were 2, 4, and 7 while ranking 4, 5, and 10 on equipment cost. The institution ranking first on both laboratory space (6547 square feet) and equipment cost ($100,000) offered both the Ph.D. and the Ed.D. degrees, ranked tenth on number of master's students, and sixteenth on number of doctoral candidates.

Most of the other relationships suggested are as would be expected, but there are several surprises. Equipment cost is apparently related to the number of master's degree students enrolled, but not to the number of doctoral candidates enrolled or graduated. An overall impression from the results suggests that master's-degree student enrollment is more important than doctoral enrollment so far as research laboratory size and equipment available in an institution is concerned. Again, based on statistically nonsignificant tendencies, Ph.D.-offering institutions and the number of students enrolled at both the master's and doctoral levels show no relationship (r's of -0.14 and -0.06), yet the number of degrees completed tends to be higher (r's of -0.23 and -0.27). This could suggest that the likelihood of finishing an advanced degree is slightly better at a Ph.D.-degree granting institution. Such a possibility does not mean that advanced degrees were easier to obtain, in any sense of the word, at the Ph.D. schools since information on the caliber of graduate work, student selection and attrition, and number of Ed.D. degrees awarded at Ph.D. institutions would be necessary to adequately consider this point. In the same respect, it should be noted that no evidence is suggested that indicates that advanced degrees were harder to obtain at the non-Ph.D. degree-granting institutions.

Regrettably, the schools included in the 1965 survey of research laboratories were not identified. Such anonymity is usually promised as an inducement for participation in a study that could cause embarrassment to an institution because of a poor showing. Several institutions, however, report research laboratory facilities that appear to be of high quality, and the overall improvement in number, size, and quality of research laboratories in physical education is certainly an encouraging development. As departments of physical education expand to become colleges of physical education, their plans for future development seldom fail to include an adequate research laboratory.

One of the encouraging developments with regard to research laboratories is that research in physical education is finding its way into undergraduate programs (25). Prior to recent times, research laboratories have always been linked to schools with developing graduate programs and research activity was deemed a responsibility of graduate faculty members. One of the notable exceptions to such a traditional pattern is the physical education research laboratory established at Southwest Missouri State College, Springfield. According to the chairperson of the department, the idea of a laboratory was nonexistent until Professor Gene Logan arrived on the campus in 1963. Logan found a rusty pair of calipers, a hand grip dynamometer of questionable vintage, and located an empty closet and machine room. He built a bicycle ergometer from discarded parts and a reaction-movement time apparatus. When Wayne C. McKinney arrived as chairperson in 1964, he talked a disbelieving college president into cementing the basement area of a nearby men's dormitory for use as a research laboratory. In the spring of 1965, the laboratory—some 3200 square feet of space—was opened as the Kinetoenergetics Laboratory under the direction of Professor Gene Logan.

As described in a *JOHPER* article in the February 1968 issue, the majority of the monies needed for the laboratory was obtained through usual departmental budget allowances and one small federal grant. The laboratory has two major objectives: (1) to enrich the professional preparation of undergraduate majors, and (2) to make provisions for undergraduate students and departmental staff members in the way of equipment for research activities either as part of regular course work or as a research endeavor per se. The *JOHPER* article describes the uses that are found for the laboratory and the benefits that have accrued from its existence. The staff at this school is noted for a number of scholarly contributions through both published research articles and several books. More significant, however, is the fact that such research endeavors are directed toward enrichment of the undergraduate major program, since no graduate program exists (or is desired by the staff) at the college. The department has made a commitment to quality undergraduate preparation and sees the use of a research laboratory as an essential feature of an ideal program. It would seem that when a staff that is dedicated to the pursuit and production of knowledge for the benefit of physical education is put together it serves as an effective catalyst for the initiation of a research laboratory and promotes a research-oriented attitude in its students.

HISTORICAL NOTES ON RESEARCH
LABORATORIES IN PHYSICAL EDUCATION

Most of the information presented in Table 6.1 is based upon Donnelly's survey of physical education research laboratories conducted in 1958. Since this survey was intended to elicit data only on existing research laboratories, it did not attempt to uncover any information on physical education research laboratories which might have once existed. At least two such research laboratories that were no longer in existence in 1958 deserve mention since they represented rather important milestones in physical education research endeavors. Some comment on each of these laboratories seems in order, particularly in view of the fact that one of them is a substantial candidate for position as the first physical education research laboratory in the United States. In addition, the dates reported for the University of Illinois and Springfield College research laboratories appear to possess some inaccuracy. Since establishment of accurate dates of origin holds some historical significance, it also seems worthwhile to consider this matter a bit further.

Illinois Research Laboratory

According to Donnelly's survey, the research laboratory at the University of Illinois was listed as having been established in 1941. At least three different sources, however, suggest a date of 1944 as being more exact. As is true with many laboratories, a kind of a prehistory exists prior to formal establishment and official designation of space and activities as constituting an actual research laboratory. One of these three sources is an article by Professor Thomas K. Cureton, who established the physical fitness laboratory in question. In an article published in the *Australian Journal of Physical Education* concerning research perspectives, Cureton (4, page 18) noted that: "Our own laboratory was established in 1944 at the University of Illinois, although graduate courses and laboratory-type graduate work has dated from 1941."

Confirmation of Cureton's statement is found in two separate master's theses (21, 22) completed at the University of Illinois, each dealing with historical aspects of the physical education program at this university. Each of the theses cite the physical fitness laboratory as originating in 1944 under the direction of Professor Cureton. Both of the theses cite a report of the University of Illinois Board of Trustees (42nd Report, 1941-1944, page 865) which officially established the laboratory on February 24, 1944. In view of such information, it would seem that a date of 1944 is more accurate as the date of origin for the physical fitness research laboratory presently in operation at the University of Illinois.

At any rate, neither of the two dates—1941 or 1944—takes into consideration the recognition of a previous research laboratory at the University of Illinois which had been established almost two decades earlier in 1925. The director of this earlier laboratory, Coleman R. Griffith, reported on the origin of his laboratory for research in athletics in an interesting *Research Quarterly* article of 1930 (8). One can see the presence of a prehistory again in the form of actual studies being conducted prior to (and perhaps leading to) establishment of a formal research facility. Griffith told, for example, of his early work beginning in 1918 with a "... series of informal observations" on some of the psychological factors involved in basketball and football. Such informal work continued on, and two years later "... for the first time, to the writer's knowledge, a piece of psychological apparatus was taken to the Illinois Athletic Field." The piece of equipment which Griffith used was a Sanborn reaction timer and he measured the reaction time of football players on the sidelines.

According to Griffith's account of the origin of his research laboratory, George Huff, who was the Director of Physical Welfare for Men, conceived of the idea for a research laboratory in athletics in the spring of 1925. Huff's idea was that such a laboratory, in addition to studying problems in the psychology and physiology of athletic activity directly, was not to ignore making contributions to "... pure psychological and physiological science." This aspect of Griffith's *Research Quarterly* article is verified in a report of the University of Illinois Board of Trustees (33rd Report, 1924-1926, May 16, 1925, page 227) in which the University of Illinois president, David Kinley, recommended to the Board that a request from George Huff, which called for establishment of research into the effects of physical training and athletics on participants, be approved. The board minutes also revealed that the proposal to conduct such research would be "... wholly at the expense of the Athletic Association except that the University would provide necessary laboratory space in the new Gymnasium." George Huff's recommendation was approved by the Board of Trustees, and on September 15, 1925 the Athletic Association agreed to "... cover the salaries and expenses of the proposed research into the effects of physical training and athletics on the individuals who participate therein, and to proceed with the appointment of persons to be in charge of such work on its psychological side and of the clerical help needed" (University of Illinois, Board of Trustees, 33rd Report, September 15, 1925, page 397).

In the fall of 1925, two large rooms were officially designated as a research laboratory in athletics. One room of 550 square feet was designated for psychological research and the other room of 500 square feet was to be used as a physiological laboratory and included a workshop and an animal rat colony from the Wistar Institute. Griffith stated that ". . . few other psychological laboratories devoted to a single group of psychological problems are better equipped than this laboratory for research in athletics." Although Griffith promised to describe the special apparatus available in his laboratory in a later article, he never published another article in the *Research Quarterly*. With the exception of a psychological laboratory then located at the Coaching School in Berlin, Germany, Griffith noted that his was the only other laboratory existing for the study of psychological factors in athletics.

Information about the research laboratory comes mostly from Griffith's *Research Quarterly* article concerning the lab and from the work produced in the laboratory by Griffith and others. In a March 1930 issue of the *Journal of Health and Physical Education*, for example, Griffith published an article entitled "Studies in the Psychology of Athletics" in which he cited work going on in several different topical areas. At that time, Griffith's research interests included studies involving the time it took a baseball batter to reach first base, errors in direction and distance in basketball free throwing, sleeping movements of basketball players as an indicator of stress and fatigue, and the Sargent jump as a measure of fatigue or physical readiness across a season of basketball. Griffith also cited a doctoral study in progress using rats to study the effects of severe exercise upon rate of learning, resistance to disease, and longevity. Results of two experimental studies, which were done in the Laboratory for Research in Athletics under the direction of Professor Griffith were reported in the *Research Quarterly*. The first, by K.J. McCristal, appeared in May 1933, and was an "Experimental Study of Rhythm in Gymnastics and Tap Dancing." In December 1933, an article by C.O. Jackson titled "An Experimental Study of the Effect of Fear on Muscular Coordination" appeared in the *Research Quarterly*. Both of these studies included title-footnote acknowledgment of Griffith's laboratory, and each investigation involved the use of special apparatus for data collection. Both McCristal and Jackson later became associated with the University of Illinois, Jackson as a distinguished faculty member and McCristal as Dean of the School of Physical Education, succeeding Dr. Seward C. Staley.

Griffith saw his research laboratory as being responsible for four major categories of activity:

(1) Records of various athletic skill performances from different sports were to be compiled and analyzed so as to reveal information about athletic skill learning which could then be utilized to improve upon pedagogical practices.

(2) Detailed observations of character and personality traits as well as shifting attitudes and moods which could not be measured by apparatus were to be collected and a psychological analysis made.

(3) Assessment of athletic aptitude or athletic talent was to be made for each individual athlete. Such an athletic talent profile was to include measures of quickness, power of attention, eye-hand coordination, memory ability, general alertness, and a paper and pencil test for a trait Griffith called "athletic alertness."

(4) Solution of any special problems involving psychology or physiology that may arise dealing with athletics. In all categories the opportunity for research by graduate students was to be provided.

In addition to such a wide scope of interest areas to which the research laboratory was committed, Griffith further expected to develop special new tests for the peculiar skills related to athletics. Griffith's *Research Quarterly* article (8) and an article entitled "Tests of Athletic Ability," published in the *Transactions of the Illinois State Academy of Science*, Volume 24, 1931, laid claim to the development of many such specially designed tests. Among the new tests or special apparatus developed, or both, were items such as: (1) an apparatus for reaction time to muscular load; (2) a test of baseball ingenuity; (3) a test of muscular tension and relaxation; (4) tests for four different types of serial reaction time; (5) tests for steadiness, muscular coordination, and learning ability; (6) tests for reaction time to light, sound, and pressure; (7) a test for measuring flexibility of coordination; (8) measurement of the muscular sense; and (9) a special test of mental alertness developed especially for athletes.

Although the Illinois research lab was established in 1925, it must be remembered that a graduate degree program in physical education at Illinois did not exist until 1942. Griffith, however, sponsored, through the College of Education, several master's theses that were easily classified as investigations dealing with physical education subject matter content. Thus, his research lab was sponsoring graduate research even though the graduate degrees were being awarded by the College of Education. Professor Thomas K. Cureton of the University of Illinois credits Griffith with sponsoring master's theses at Illinois before physical education was recognized as a graduate major in its own right. Writing in the mimeographed publication, *University of Illinois Thesis Abstracts, 1924-1953, in Physical Education*, Cureton noted that Professor Griffith was listed as the sponsor for seven of the theses before 1940 and that Griffith was probably also responsible for some of the eight other theses that were completed in the College of Education prior to 1942.

The research laboratory established by Griffith in 1925 went out of existence in 1932. This date coincided with both the establishment of a separate School of Physical Education at the University of Illinois and Griffith's resignation from the laboratory. Whether the events were related or not is not known. Since the laboratory was wholly supported by funds from the autonomous Athletic Association, discontinuation of the laboratory may have been made necessary by financial pressures for budget cuts due to the severe economic depression. Available school records at Illinois showed that student enrollment diminished from a high of 532 students in 1928-1929 down to a low of 349 students for the 1931-1932 school year. This drop in student enrollment was accompanied by a reduction in staff members from 25 to 18 over the same years.

At least two individuals on the Illinois campus in 1932 cited the need for economy measures as the major reason for dropping support of the research laboratory. One of these rather reliable sources, furthermore, suggested another factor of some potency as further contributing to such a decision. According to this individual, who shall remain nameless for obvious reasons, "The depression, plus the fact that Zuppke failed to see any improvement in his teams as a result of the research, eliminated a fine program." Zuppke, of course, was the football coach at the University of Illinois during the time-period under consideration. The depression could very well have been an important reason for the close of the laboratory, while Zuppke's alleged position may or may not have been involved. It may also have been the case, however, that Griffith elected to resign of his own volition and the resultant opportunity to economize by closing the laboratory was capitalized upon by a financially burdened Athletic Association. Griffith accepted a position in educational psychology and the directorship of the Bureau of Institutional Research in 1933, and he may very well have felt such a position represented a professional advance in his career too great to turn down. Even after his resignation and the demise of the research laboratory, however, Griffith apparently continued on with his practice of sponsoring graduate research through the College of Education. He was listed as the sponsor of a master's thesis done by Oliver M. Langhorst, which was completed in 1934 under the title of "An Experimental Study of the Use of Grading as an Incentive in the Performance of Certain Muscular Skills."

Griffith enjoyed a distinguished and productive career at Illinois. He was the author of five books in psychology* as well as the two classics in the area of sports psychology: *Psychology of Coaching* (9) and *Psychology and Athletics* (10). Prior to his formal association with the Illinois Athletic Research Laboratory, he had published several articles in

---

General Introduction to Psychology. New York: Macmillan, 1928; *An Introduction to Applied Psychology*. New York: Macmillan, 1934; *Introduction to Educational Psychology*. New York: Farrar and Rinehart, 1935; *Psychology Applied to Teaching and Learning*. New York: Farrar, 1939; *Principles of Systematic Psychology*. Urbana: Univ. of Illinois Press, 1943.

respected journals* dealing with problems of equilibrium, nystagmus, and rotation effects. Griffith was also a frequent contributor of articles to the *Athletic Journal* dealing with a wide range of practical aspects of psychological research in athletics. Article titles such as "Mental Stance," "Experiments in Basketball," "Types of Errors in Throwing Free Throws," and "Psychological vs. Tactical Fundamentals" suggest his strategy of applying a psychological method of inquiry to research in athletics.

During his years as director of the research laboratory in athletics, Griffith contributed articles to popular journals but also kept active in publishing articles dealing with more fundamental research as well. Before his death in February of 1966, he had published over 40 articles in a large number of different and respected journals. Although Griffith resigned from his position in the Athletic Research Laboratory in 1932, he continued on at the University of Illinois as a professor of educational psychology and as director of the Bureau of Institutional Research. In later years, his scholarly pursuits dealt almost exclusively with educational psychology and administrative problems related to an institution of university status. He eventually went on to become provost at the University of Illinois, capping off a brilliant academic and administrative career. The research laboratory he established in 1925, however, was no longer operative after his resignation in 1932.

The significance of the Athletic Research Laboratory as a factor of consequence in the development of physical education research is difficult to assess. It seems unfair to say that any research laboratory that failed to justify its existence and remain in operation was something less than a completely successful venture. Griffith's laboratory may very well have been established before the field of physical education was intellectually ready for such an enterprise. Then, too, the exact cause of the premature extinction of the laboratory remains unknown. Impact upon a profession is possible though any number of maze-like, ill-defined paths which, at best, can only vaguely be mapped. Many ingenious test-strategies and research insights ascribable to Griffith continue to be used and cited in current research, constituting ample evidence of the ultimate success of the endeavor at Illinois. Griffith's contributions in the area of sports psychology seem unique in a pioneer area and the quality of his research efforts was of undeniable excellence by any set of standards. In

---

*Concerning the effect of repeated rotation upon nystagmus. *Laryngoscope* **30**: 22-25; 1920; The decrease of after-nystagmus during repeated rotation. *Laryngoscope* **30**: 129-137; 1920; Experimental study of dizziness. *Journal of Experimental Psychology* **3**: 89-125; 1920; The organic effects of repeated bodily rotation. *Journal of Experimental Psychology* **3**: 15-46; 1920. An experimental study of equilibration in the white rat. *Psychological Bulletin* **18**: 100; 1921; Are permanent disturbances of equilibration inherited? *Science* **56**: 676-678; December 15, 1922.

the final analysis, however, the most significant aspect of the first Illinois research laboratory may very well be the fact that it was supported financially in toto by the Athletic Association. One can only regret that such a novel approach to academic athletics passed from the scene before a permanent marriage of athletics and research could have been consummated.

Springfield College

An established date of 1925 for the Athletic Research Laboratory at the University of Illinois earns it a place in history as one of the earliest physical education research laboratories in the United States. Based upon the dates of origin reported by Donnelly, only Springfield College in 1920 and George Williams College in 1923 appear to have predated the Illinois laboratory. It is not known upon what basis the George Williams College date for a research laboratory was established, but there is strong evidence that the 1920 date cited for Springfield College is in error. Part of this evidence appeared in an article by Professor Peter V. Karpovich in the 75th Anniversary issue of *JOHPER*, in which he gave a biographical sketch of a distinguished early leader long associated with Springfield College. In speaking of this distinguished leader, James H. McCurdy, Karpovich reminisced about his first encounter with Dr. McCurdy on the Springfield College campus:

> I came to Springfield College because I had heard about McCurdy's scientific research related to physical education. My first impression of the college was disappointing. There it was—a small school which could hardly be called an institution of higher learning. There were no laboratories to speak of, no research facilities. But there was McCurdy! (16, page 59).*

In later portions of the article, Karpovich quotes Dr. McCurdy as specifically stating that no formal research laboratory existed at Springfield. It is known that Professor Karpovich arrived at Springfield College in 1925 and completed an M.P.E. degree in 1929. Upon his appointment as professor of physiology in 1927, Professor Karpovich did not arrive upon the Springfield College campus until this facility was changed to the Physiological Research Laboratory in order to avoid confusion with the regular Department of Physiology on the Springfield College campus.

---

*Personal communication with Dr. Peter V. Karpovich, October 23, 1968.

Such a denial of a research laboratory at Springfield College in 1920 is, of course, based solely upon the personal recollections of only one prominent faculty member at Springfield College and is, thus, subject to some question. In addition, Professor Karpovich did not arrive upon the Springfield College campus until 1925 and it may very well have been possible that McCurdy had established a research laboratory in 1920 which no longer existed in 1925. This seems not to have been the case, however, for no mention is made, in a lengthy dissertation written about McCurdy at Springfield College, of establishment of a research laboratory under James H. McCurdy's direction. Atallah A. Kiddess' dissertation titled "A Study of the Work and Contributions of Dr. James H. McCurdy to Physical Education" was completed in 1958 and contained no reference to such a laboratory. This dissertation contained detailed accounts of McCurdy's accomplishments, both of major and of minor significance, and included many personal interviews with campus staff members as well as a meticulous search through private papers and correspondence of McCurdy and his colleagues. McCurdy was at Springfield College from 1895 until his retirement in 1935 and it seems doubtful that anything so significant as the establishment of the only physical education research laboratory in existence would have been overlooked. Based upon such evidence it seems reasonable to question the accuracy of a 1920 date and, instead, accept 1927 as a more valid date of origin for a research laboratory at Springfield College.

This then leaves the University of Illinois laboratory under Coleman R. Griffith and an unverified laboratory at George Williams College in 1923 as candidates for the earliest formal research laboratory in physical education in the United States. It is true, of course, that research work was being carried on by physical educators earlier than in the 1920's. Edward Hitchcock at Amherst College systematically collected anthropometric data on students as early as 1861 when he accepted a position as professor of hygiene and physical education. There is no evidence, however, that a formal research laboratory was ever officially established or recognized. The same is true for the work of William G. Anderson at Yale University, although it is known that Anderson had access to the Yale Psychological Laboratory. Some new information recently uncovered, however, fully authenticates the existence of a formal physical education research laboratory in 1892 that effectively predates both verified and unverified dates of origin ascribed to laboratories at the University of Illinois, George Williams College, and Springfield College. In addition, some vague clues exist in the literature suggesting that, around the same period of time, Dudley A. Sargent may have been involved with some sort of a laboratory facility.

Harvard College in 1892

There is fragmentary evidence that Dudley A. Sargent might have actually established a formal facility designated as a research laboratory in the Sanatory Gymnasium he operated at Church and Palmer Streets in Cambridge, Massachusetts. In his autobiography published in 1927, Professor Sargent stated:

> I have found that I could use my carriage-house gymnasium for a laboratory and conduct experiments that could not be carried out at Harvard because of the resultant publicity and curious on-lookers. For one thing we tested the swiftness of a blow in boxing: Dr. Fitz, instructor in physiology, worked out the problem with John L. Sullivan to demonstrate for him (20, page 204).

The carriage-house gymnasium referred to by Sargent was named, "contrary to appearance and surroundings," the Sanatory Gymnasium, which Sargent first operated to offer a program of physical education to Radcliffe College women. According to Leonard and McKenzie's *A Guide to the History of Physical Education*, the accommodations at 20 Church Street were secured by Sargent in 1883. This could indicate that Sargent had a laboratory facility available as early as that date. The reference to Dr. Fitz, however, definitely places the date of this cooperative study of John L. Sullivan by Professor Sargent and Dr. Fitz sometime between 1892 and 1894. George Wells Fitz received his medical degree from Harvard in 1891 and was an instructor in physiology and hygiene only during the years 1892 to 1894. More will be said of Dr. Fitz shortly, as he seems to have been a forgotten man in the histories of physical education that have been written and, yet, he was responsible for at least two significant contributions to physical education.

The study of John L. Sullivan referred to by Sargent, by the way, brought about a rather stringent admonishment from the editors of the old Triangle publication subsequently named *Physical Education*. In October of 1892, the editors of *Physical Education*, Luther Gulick and James Naismith, had this comment to make:

> Sullivan. Passing along a railroad news-stand a few days since, we were greatly startled by noticing a yellow covered book entitled: 'Life and Reminiscences of a Nineteenth Century Gladiator, by John L. Sullivan, with reports on Physical Examinations and so on by Dr. Dudley A. Sargent.' We made the purchase of the book and examined it critically. The first two hundred and eighty pages of it are about as arrogant a piece (sic) of egotistical writing as we ever had the misfortune to read. The last twenty pages contain illustrations of Sullivan in different positions, an anthropometrical chart by Dr. Sargent, and a discussion of Sullivan's physique by Dr. Sargent. We all expect so much from Dr. Sargent, both on account of his position at Harvard, his personal ability and standing that we can hardly believe that he knew where this article was to be placed.

Figure 6.1. George Wells Fitz (1860-1934). Head of the Department of Anatomy, Physiology, and Physical Training at the Lawrence Scientific School, Harvard from 1891 to 1899. Photograph from the Harvard (Class) Album, 1898.

No one in this country has stood more firmly than has Dr. Sargent in opposition to all that would lower the profession in the eyes of the public. It was surely due to a misunderstanding.

Whether or not Dudley Allen Sargent ever truly established a formal research laboratory remains questionable. If such a laboratory did exist, it seems likely that Sargent would have called attention to it, for Sargent was never known for his modesty in such matters. What no longer remains questionable, however, is the fact that a formal research laboratory in physical education was established at Harvard in 1892. This laboratory was initiated and directed by George Wells Fitz, M.D. (Figure 6.1) and must qualify as the strongest candidate for the first such physical education research laboratory in the United States. The facts concerning George Wells Fitz and this research laboratory were brought to light only recently. As discussed in Chapter 2 (see pages 51-59), George Wells Fitz not only developed the first formal physical education research laboratory, but he was also responsible for the first academic degree program in physical education in the United States. For reasons still mostly unknown, neither of these significant milestones in the history of physical education has ever been properly acknowledged. Details of the degree program were considered previously, and the present discussion will focus upon George Wells Fitz and the research laboratory that he established at Harvard University in 1892.

Fitz and His Laboratory

In September of 1893, George Wells Fitz published an article in the *Harvard Graduates' Magazine* entitled "Problems of Physical Education." Author credits noted that Fitz was then an instructor in physiology and hygiene at Harvard University and that the article was written in May 1893. The contents of this article have been overlooked, up to now, by historians of physical education. The first paragraph of the article read:

> Harvard's establishment of a laboratory for the experimental study of the physiology of exercise is a clear acknowledgment of the high educational claims of physical training. It is a distinct advance in the history of physical education, for though hitherto there has been much actual instruction in gymnasium and athletic work, and in measuring and prescribing exercise for students, little has been done in the study of the physiological and psychological effects of exercise. On the other hand, physiologists and psychologists have been little interested in physical education for itself, and their investigations have thrown but occasional, one might say accidental, flashes of light into its many dark corners.

Except for a few references to Dr. Sargent, the Delsartean system, and Ling gymnastics, the message in Fitz's analysis of the problems of physical education has as much validity today as it did when written over three-quarters of a century ago. Fitz noted that the people engaged in the work of physical education ". . . have been too busy with the practical side" to give attention to the more basic questions of exercise and physical education. The effect of this over-emphasis upon practical aspects was to perpetuate a continuous battle of opinions about practical problems. Fitz called for systematic scientific study of the effects of physical activity and exercise upon participants and an examination of the basic factors involved in physical activity per se. In the absence of such fundamental and basic scientific knowledge, Fitz could see only an eternal chaos, with far reaching hypotheses creating elaborate theories and systems of physical training in an intellectual vacuum.

To pursue such objectives for physical education, Fitz stated: "To that end, and for instruction in physiology and hygiene, the Physiological Laboratory was established in the Lawrence Scientific School a year ago." At least one acknowledgment of the establishment of this laboratory was made by an individual in physical education at the time. In July of 1893, Thomas D. Wood stated:

> We rejoice at the establishment of such workshops as the laboratory in the Lawrence Scientific School of Harvard University, designed for the experimental study of the physiology of exercise. Several new and important pieces of apparatus testify to the early success in this special laboratory. May such institutions be multiplied! (24, page 622).

Wood's message was essentially congruent with Fitz's article in urging the development of a science of physical education so that practices employed would be based upon knowledge and not fancy. In his paper, Dr. Wood quoted a passage from Fitz's article in the *Harvard Graduates' Magazine*, leaving no doubt of his knowledge of the development at Harvard University.

Further confirmation of the existence of this research laboratory is available in the annual announcements of the Lawrence Scientific School at Harvard University. A pamphlet entitled "Description of the Lawrence Scientific School, 1893," which is housed in the Harvard University Archives Library, contained this description of the laboratory:

> A large and well equipped laboratory has been organized for the experimental study of the physiology of exercise. The object of this work is to exemplify the hygiene of the muscles, conditions under which they act, the relation of their action to the body as a whole affecting blood supply and general hygienic conditions, and the effects of various exercises upon muscular growth and general health.

In *Views of Harvard*, authored by Hamilton Vaughan Bail (1, page 230), the date of 1893 is further verified since Bail commented upon a structure identified as part of the Lawrence Scientific School: ". . . and about 1893 a laboratory for physiology and hygiene was established in the east wing."

The strongest evidence for the existence of George Wells Fitz's research laboratory, however, comes from the many research publications by Fitz and his development of new and ingenious measurement techniques. Helen M. Petroskey's dissertation (17), "A History of Measurement in Health and Physical Education in the United States," credits Fitz with: (1) being responsible for the invention of the scoliometer; (2) probably being responsible for the first device for recording or measuring posture in this country; (3) designing one of the first instruments for measuring footprints and degree of flat-footedness; and (4) being one of the first physical educators to measure reaction time. From the outset, Fitz was dedicated to an objective and empirical investigative approach to the study of physical education. An incomplete list of Fitz's research publications with short abstracts of their contents follows and should give ample opportunity to appreciate the significance and quality of this man's work.

(1) Micro-manipulator for pure culture and microchemical work. *Science* **79**: 233-234; March 9, 1934. (See also "A new micro-manipulator." *Science* **76**: 72-75; January 15, 1931 and "comment on a Micro-manipulator" in the *New York Times*, May 20, 1934, VIII, **6**:4).

An instrument was described which allowed rapid selection of microscopic unicellular organisms for pure-culture work. Rapid chemical analysis of particles the size of 10-7 grams was made possible and a mount of the culture selections could be accomplished in 5-6 minutes.

(2) A clinical study of muscular cramp; a physiological cure. *Boston Medical and Surgical Journal* **195**: 854-857; 1926.

A method of treatment for cramp seizures by carbon dioxide retention was described which was reported to be "invariably effective" in almost 100 applications to muscle cramps of the thigh, leg, foot, abdominal wall, and diaphragm. Fitz related the practice of athletes to continue walking after strenuous competition as a possible aid in preventing a condition of hyperpneic alkalosis from developing.

(3) The physiologic cost of insufficient protective clothing. *Boston Medical and Surgical Journal* **170**: 648-651; April 23, 1914.

An examination was made of the claims made by manufacturers of special fabrics "who have bombarded the public with cleverly constructed statements of the vital superiority of their particular products." Fitz interpreted the research done by physiologists dealing with body heat and evaporation, and conducted a survey of several hundred prominent medical practitioners on the amount and kind of clothing recommended.

(4) A simple method of measuring and graphically plotting spinal curvature and other asymmetries by means of new direct-reading scoliometer. *American Physical Education Review* **11**: 18-23; March 1906. (Reprinted from the *Boston Medical and Surgical Journal* **153**: 572-575; November 23, 1905.)

Petroskey (17) credits Fitz with the invention of the scoliometer on the basis of this article. The scoliometer devised was made of a transparent celluloid sheet, 52 × 16 centimeters, marked off in 1-centimeter squares. The celluloid sheet was positioned in back of the figure and a graphic record marked on the sheet of the spine. The celluloid rectangle was equipped with two level-glasses set at right angles to each other to ensure proper alignment of the scoliometer both vertically and horizontally when positioned against a subject for measurement.

(5) A practical photometric method for case record. *American Physical Education Review* **10**: 292-306; 1905. (Reprinted from the *Boston Medical and Surgical Journal* **153**: 546-552; November 16, 1905.)

Although Petroskey (17) does not directly credit Fitz with inventing the first quantitative device for measuring posture in the United States, the method described in this article was the first to incorporate multiple camera exposures on the same plate. Each subject's photograph was also automatically identified by use of a numbered plate included in the photo. The technique also described the procedure for deriving ratios of subject size to image size on the photograph by use of a universal scale for direct image measurement off the photo, corrected for focal distances of the lens used and angles of the camera placement.

(6) The physical examination of school children. *American Physical Education Review* **6**: 212-216; June 1901.

Physical examination of school children was by no means a unique idea, but Fitz recommended several items on the examination which were quite unusual for the day. In addition to regular health and anthropometric checks, Fitz called for assessment of quickness and accuracy which could be determined by a child's "rapidity and accuracy in dotting spots on a sheet of paper"; a test of endurance by means of an ergograph; the effect of exercise upon pulse rate; and a test for nervous tone utilizing steadiness test items for the fingers and eyes.

(7) A location reaction apparatus. *Psychological Review* **2**: 37-42; 1895. (See also "What Nervous Tests Shall We Use to Complete the Picture of an Individual?" *Proceedings of the American Association for the Advancement of Physical Education* **10**: 89-109; 1895.)

An apparatus was constructed for measurement of the speed and accuracy with which a subject could touch an object suddenly presented in an unexpected position. Note was made of the applicability of such measures to activities such as tennis and fencing, where quick perception of a stimulus and accurate, fast responses were necessary for successful performance. Data were reported on over 200 subjects and an analysis made by sex, speed of response, and average deviation error score, which represented an accuracy response.

(8) A study of types of respiratory movements. *Proceedings of the American Association for the Advancement of Physical Education* **9**: 57-68; 1894. (See also the same article in the *Journal of Experimental Medicine*, New York, 1896.)

One of the first instruments for objective measurement of footprints was described. A flat surface marked by imbedded quarter-inch squares was covered with a thin application of ink. A sheet of paper was then softly placed over the board or flat surface. The subject then either stood or walked on the paper. Such a procedure kept the subject's feet clean of ink, and afforded foot impressions that could be measured for foot angles under either static (standing) or dynamic (walking) conditions.

This annotated list of Fitz's research endeavors is only representative of his work. He gave several major addresses at National Education Association conferences when he was president of the Physical Education Department of the National Education Association in 1899 and 1900. His name appears as author of the book *Principles of Physiology and Hygiene* (New York: Holt, 1908) as well as co-author with Henry N. Martin of the book *Human Body* (New York: Holt, 1910), which was a popular anatomy text of the day. Other articles included "A Simple and Accurate Method of Carbon Dioxide Determination, with Demonstration" published in Volume 9 of the *Journal of the Massachusetts Association of Boards of Health*; "A Leg-Apparatus for Spastic and Paralytic Cases" in 1895, and "Bed Posture as an Etiologic Factor in Spinal Curvature" in 1898, both published in *Transactions of the American Orthopedic Association*. In addition, the early issues of *Proceedings of the American Association for the Advancement of Physical Education* and the *American Physical Education Review* show Fitz to have been cited frequently for his reactions to scheduled papers as well as to have contributed several major papers of an administrative and philosophical orientation concerning the future of physical education.

Not much is known about George Wells Fitz since he has never been given much attention by historians. Unlike individuals such as Dudley Allen Sargent, Edward Hitchcock, Luther Gulick, James H. McCurdy, and other early leaders in physical education, no biography in the way of a doctoral dissertation is available for Fitz. Indeed, most of the well-known texts dealing with the history of physical education in the United States fail to mention Fitz even in a minor way.* It is known, however,

---

*Fitz, for example, fails to receive a single citation in any of these basic reference sources: C.W. Hackensmith. *History of Physical Education*. New York: Harper, 1966; Emmett A. Rice, John L. Hutchinson, and Mabel Lee. *A Brief History of Physical Education*. New York: Ronald, 1958; Deobald B. VanDalen, Elmer D. Mitchell, and Bruce L. Bennett. *A World History of Physical Education*. Englewood Cliffs, New Jersey: Prentice-Hall, 1953; Norma Schwendener. *A History of Physical Education in the United States*. New York: Barnes, 1942; Fred E. Leonard and R. Tait McKenzie. *A Guide to the History of Physical Education*. Philadelphia: Lea and Febiger, 1927; Fred E. Leonard, *Pioneers of Modern Physical Training*. New York: Association Press, 1919. In Arthur Weston's *The Making of American Physical Education* (New York: Appleton, 1962) Fitz is indexed only because Thomas D. Wood's paper on "Some Unsolved Problems in Physical Education" quotes a passage of Fitz's article in the *Harvard Graduates' Magazine*.

that Fitz was born in New York City in the year 1860 and that he was killed in an automobile/passenger-train collision on October 29, 1934 at Peconic, Long Island (*New York Times*, Tuesday, October 30, 1934, page 19, column 5). His development of the micro-manipulator (see reference in the preceding annotated bibliography) was important enough for the science section of the *New York Times* to have devoted several columns to Fitz's invention (*New York Times*, May 20, 1934. Comments on Micro-manipulator. VIII, page 6, column 4). Fitz served as editor of the *American Physical Education Review* from 1896 to 1900 and again from 1903 to 1906. In March of 1906, he withdrew as editor of the *American Physical Education Review* citing pressures of other literary work and ". . . his lack of sympathy with the present conduct of the Association" (7, page 36).

There is some evidence to indicate that Fitz was associated in some capacity with the Hemenway Gymnasium at Harvard University as early as 1888. An article by Fitz, "A Practical Photometric Method for Case Record," appeared in both the *Boston Medical and Surgical Journal* **153**: 546-552; November 16, 1905, and in the *American Physical Education Review* **10**: 292-306; 1905, which included the following footnote:

> The first multiple camera, a three-phase and the first automatic labelling device were designed and made in 1888 by the writer for use in photographing the students in Hemenway Gymnasium, Harvard University, where it has since been in constant use.

Records at Harvard University show that Fitz received his M.D. degree from Harvard Medical School in 1891. Thus, in 1888 he was evidently still a student and may very well have been an assistant in Hemenway Gymnasium and under the direction of Dudley Sargent himself, who employed such assistants. Fitz subsequently had an appointment as instructor from 1892-1894 and assistant professor from 1894-1899 in the Department of Anatomy, Physiology, and Physical Training at the Lawrence Scientific School of Harvard University. It was in conjunction with this department, furthermore, that Fitz's second significant contribution to the field of physical education originated. Under Fitz's direction, this department offered and awarded the first academic four-year degree in physical education in the United States. The department began in the school year of 1891-1892 and awarded its first bachelor of science degree in 1893, thus predating the 1898 date of the University of California and the 1899 date of the University of Nebraska, typically cited as the first such programs.

Such evidence as presented seems sufficient to accept the existence of both a formal physical education research laboratory in 1892 and an academic four-year degree program in physical education as early as 1891. To two such noteworthy and significant milestones in the history of physical education, however, only meager attention has ever been given. Thomas D. Wood's acknowledgment of Fitz's research laboratory was cited previously. A careful but by no means exhaustive search of the literature revealed only two other such acknowledgments in physical education circles. In June of 1892, the editors of the publication *Physical Education*, Luther Gulick and James Naismith, editorialized about the value of summer-school programs of physical training. The editors complimented the leadership and virtues of the Harvard University Summer School of Physical Education under Dudley Sargent's direction. At the end of this short page and a half editorial there appeared the following two sentences:

> Harvard has lately added to her courses one on physical training leading to the degree of B.S. This indicates the importance which is attached to that subject by that university.

A few months later, in October of 1892, these same editors commented upon the announcement that Oberlin College ". . . had just joined the ranks of the institutions putting in Normal courses of Physical Training." In this editorial, Oberlin was mildly admonished for offering a two-year course instead of a four-year course as was done at Harvard. Toward the conclusion of this editorial appeared this comment:

> We trust that the course at Oberlin will be most eminently successful, and that, in course of time, it may be extended so as to be equal to the other Normal courses on Physical Training, and a degree given for the course as it is at Harvard ("Normal Physical Training." *Physical Education* 1: 165-166; October 1892).

One must wonder how two such significant advances in physical education—establishment of the first formal research laboratory in physical education and the first academic four-year degree program—could have gone almost unnoticed by the profession. Outside of the isolated reference to Fitz's laboratory by Wood and the two instances of editorial comments in *Physical Education* the existence of both the laboratory and the program seem to have effectively been overlooked. The situation is somewhat incredible in light of the following points:

(1) One will note from the description of the degree program at Harvard (see pages 51-59) that Dudley Sargent actually taught courses in the department. Sargent was always proud of his accomplishments at Harvard, and in his book *Physical Education*, he called special attention to the prestige of Harvard University and noted with pride the place that physical education was afforded by so renowned a school:

> Perhaps no one thing contributed more to inaugurate this new epoch in America

than the building of Hemenway Gymnasium. The erection of this handsome, spacious structure at our oldest and largest institution of learning was one of the highest tributes that could be paid to the cause of physical education (18, page 126).

Yet nowhere in Sargent's book did he mention the establishment of the degree program or the research laboratory, which must have represented equally notable recognition for physical education by Harvard University. Sargent surely was aware of the significance of the degree program as he indicated in his chapter contribution to a book edited by the Dean of the Lawrence Scientific School:

> Perhaps the most important step that has yet been effected toward preparing young men for such positions of public service is that recently taken by Harvard University in establishing a four years' course at the Lawrence Scientific School in anatomy, physiology, and physical training. This course will embrace a very wide range of study and practical instruction in a great variety of athletic sports and gymnasium exercises. Upon its successful completion the student will receive a diploma of S.B., and be entitled to all the privileges and distinctions of graduates from other departments of the school (19, page 1140).

Bruce L. Bennett, in his dissertation on Sargent's life and professional contributions, noted that Sargent expected to be given faculty status for his role in the department (2, pages 81-82). For some reason, Sargent never did regain the faculty status he had lost in 1889, mostly because of his unpopular position on athletics. Fitz, of course, was appointed as an instructor and later as assistant professor in the department, while Sargent taught courses without any more faculty status than that afforded by the title Director of the Gymnasium. In a manuscript housed in the Harvard Archives entitled "Position Paper on Athletics" Sargent stated that, in his opinion, the degree program at Harvard failed because the practical work given in his summer school was not adequately recognized. This argument suffers some loss of credibility when it is remembered that all students enrolled in the degree program were required to attend the summer school from 1891 until at least 1896.

However, even if Sargent were slightly disenchanted with developments surrounding the degree program and his role in it, could it have so affected Sargent as to have him remain almost completely silent in his professional voice about the program? The short paragraph by Sargent in Shaler's book *The United States of America* (19) concerning the program was certainly not destined for consumption by individuals working in the physical education field. Surely, the fact that the first academic degree program in physical education originated at Harvard should have seen Dudley Sargent loudly acclaiming such an accomplishment in a number of places as evidence for the advancement of physical education.

(2) Several historical treatments of professional training programs for physical education as well as noted texts on the history of physical educa-

tion have failed to give any account of the laboratory or the degree program. Delphine Hanna, for example, published a paper in 1903 entitled "Present Status of Physical Training in the Normal Schools." Although it could be argued that her paper was concerned only with the present status of such programs, it seems incredible that no mention was made of the Harvard program at least as a historical footnote. Indeed, the first graduate of the Harvard degree program (James F. Jones) was situated at Marietta College from 1893 to 1899. Marietta College at Marietta, Ohio was in the same state as Oberlin College where Delphine Hanna was located and it seems incredible that Hanna would have been unaware of Jones' existence and activities at Marietta. Jones, of course, was in charge of the first Department of Physical Culture at Marietta, and such an event must have received some attention in the channels of communication available to so prominent a figure in physical education as Miss Hanna.

The same is true for Edward Mussey Hartwell's "On Physical Training," published as a Report of the Commissioner of Education 1897-1898, Volume I, Washington, D.C.: Government Printing Office, 1899. This account was written during the time that the Harvard program was still in operation and yet Hartwell failed to acknowledge or mention its existence. Hartwell's paper (page 563) almost pleaded for physiology and psychology to study the claims made by various systems in physical education because so much confusion existed among the battling systems—exactly one of the specific purposes stated by Fitz for his research laboratory and a prime objective for the degree program.

There is no question that Hartwell was aware of the program at Harvard and of Fitz's role in the department. In his presidential address contained in the 1892 *Proceedings of the American Association for the Advancement of Physical Education* (12, page 16), he specifically cited developments at Harvard in this area. His address discussed the many encouraging examples of the expansion and improvement of programs for professional preparation in physical education and he praised "the extensive courses in physical training that were being established at Harvard University." Indeed, E.M. Hartwell was the person who called upon George Wells Fitz to give a talk on the new program at Harvard during a symposium on professional training held in 1892 at the Philadelphia conference of the Association. Hartwell was also located in Boston as Director of Physical Education in the public schools at the time of the Harvard program's initiation and operation.

In this same line of thought, the failure of Fred E. Leonard to acknowledge the two significant developments at Harvard is also something close to extraordinary. Author of several texts and acknowledged as an authoritative historian of physical education, Fred E. Leonard was registered at the 1894 session of Sargent's Harvard Summer School of

Physical Education and for fourteen years served as Lecturer in Physiology and in History of Physical Education (23, page 410). Here was the noted historian on the same campus with the first academic four-year degree program and the first formal research laboratory and, yet, apparently unaware of their existence. To deepen this mystery even more, all students enrolled in the Department of Anatomy, Physiology, and Physical Training were ". . . required to attend a summer course of six weeks in which they will receive instruction intended to supplement the courses required to be followed during term-time." This practice of requiring academic-degree students to enroll in what must be Sargent's Summer School of Physical Education remained as a requirement from 1891 until 1896 when it was apparently dropped. At least no mention was made of the compulsory summer school attendance in the annual announcements of the Lawrence Scientific School's Department of Anatomy, Physiology, and Physical Training after 1896. All this means, of course, that academic-degree students were actually in attendance at Sargent's Summer School of Physical Education and that both fellow students and the long list of noted instructors in physical education from all over the country must have had contact with them. Also, like Delphine Hanna, F.E. Leonard was located at Oberlin College in Ohio, in the same state as the first graduate of the Harvard program, who was at Marietta College.

REFERENCES

1. Bail, Hamilton Vaughan. *Views of Harvard*. Cambridge: Harvard Univ. Press, 1949.

2. Bennett, Bruce L. *The Life of Dudley Allen Sargent, M.D., and His Contributions to Physical Education*. Unpublished dissertation. Ann Arbor: University of Michigan, 1947.

3. Bookwalter, Carolyn. Professional higher education. *American Academy of Physical Education* **3**: 102-112; November 1954.

4. Cureton, Thomas K. Why research? Professional perspectives: hindview, present, and future. *Australian Journal of Physical Education* **28**: 14-21; July 1963.

5. Cureton, Thomas K. Nature and scope of research in health, physical education, and recreation, Chapter Two, pp. 20-41, in *Research Methods Applied to Health, Physical Education, and Recreation*. Washington, D.C.: American Association for Health, Physical Education, and Recreation, 1949.

6. Donnelly, Richard J. Laboratory research in physical education. *Research Quarterly* **31**: 232-234; May 1960.

7. Fitz, George Wells. Editor's note and comment. *American Physical Education Review* **11**: 35-36; 1906.

8. Griffith, Coleman R. A laboratory for research in athletics. *Research Quarterly* **1**: 34-40; October 1930.

9. Griffith, Coleman R. *Psychology of Coaching*. New York: Scribner's, 1926.

10. Griffith, Coleman R. *Psychology and Athletics.* New York: Scribner's, 1928.

11. Hanna, Delphine. Present status of physical training in normal schools. *American Physical Education Review* **8**: 293-297; 1903.

12. Hartwell, E.M. President's address—The condition and prospects of physical education in the United States. *Proceedings of the American Association for the Advancement of Physical Education 1892*, pp. 13-40.

13. Hunsicker, Paul. Graduate preparation for research in physical education. *Proceedings of the College Physical Education Association* **63**: 83-88; 1959.

14. Hunsicker, Paul. A survey of laboratory facilities in college physical education departments. *Research Quarterly* **21**: 420-423; December 1950.

15. Karpovich, Peter V. Growth of research, pp. 55-56, in *Report of the WCOTP Committee on Health, Physical Education, and Recreation*. Washington, D.C.: International Council on Health, Physical Education, and Recreation, 1960.

16. Karpovich, Peter V. James H. McCurdy. *JOHPER* **31**:59, 112; April 1960.

17. Petroskey, Helen M. *A History of Measurement in Health and Physical Education in the United States.* Unpublished dissertation. Iowa City: University of Iowa, 1946.

18. Sargent, Dudley A. *Physical Education.* Boston: Ginn and Co., 1906.

19. Sargent, Dudley A. The physical state of the American people, Chapter XX, pp. 1122-1148, in *The United States of America*, Volume III (Nathaniel Southgate Shalter, ed.). New York: D. Appleton and Co., 1894.

20. Sargent, Ledyard W. *Dudley Allen Sargent: An Autobiography.* Philadelphia: Lea and Febiger, 1927.

21. Seidler, Armond H. *A History of the Professional Training in Physical Education for Men at the University of Illinois.* Unpublished thesis. Urbana: University of Illinois, 1948.

22. Seidler, Burton M. *A History of the Service Curriculum in Physical Education for Men at the University of Illinois.* Unpublished thesis. Urbana: University of Illinois, 1951.

23. Van Wyck, Clarence. The Harvard Summer School of Physical Education, 1887-1932. *Research Quarterly* **13**: 403-431; December 1942.

24. Wood, Thomas D. Some unsolved problems in physical education. *Addresses and Proceedings of International Congress of Education, Chicago* **31**: 621-623; 1893.

25. Marley, William P. The physical education laboratory in a general instructional program. *JOHPER* **46**: 34-35; October 1975.

The Dimensions of a Science

The words "science," "scientific research," and "scientific method" are widely used and possess great prestige. Few individuals active in the laboratory would want to be accused of being associated with non-scientific research because of the implication that nonscientific research is shoddy and of little importance. The scientific method, furthermore, is claimed by subject matter areas other than the traditional hard sciences. A Harvard law professor, for example, believed that law was capable of scientific study because if it were not, then he did not believe that anyone would continue to study law so vigorously (2, page 204). More than a few other subject matter areas are professing the need to examine and develop their scientific bases in order to ensure proper advancement.

If one were to ask for a specific definition of science or what the purposes of a science are, an answer would not come very easily. One is likely to stumble around mentioning words such as careful, systematic, unbiased, precise, and, eventually, scientific for a definition of science. The purposes of a science would be said to include the acquisition of knowledge, wisdom, understanding, making the unknown known, and the extension of the boundaries of knowledge. Owing to the amount of importance attached to science, it would be wise to consider science in more exact terms. Just as in the case of a profession, certain basic knowledge about a science is essential before intelligent discussion can take place. Perhaps with a better insight into the dimensions of a profession *and* a science one can make better value judgments concerning their proper emphasis in physical education.

DEFINITION OF A SCIENCE

A dictionary definition of a science is not a bad starting point. A science is defined first as knowledge, or a department of systematized knowledge. The definition goes on to include the ideas that a science is an endeavor which observes and classifies facts and, by induction and hypothesis construction, establishes general laws that are verifiable, especially as they pertain to the physical world. An important feature of a science is that the laws generated must be genuinely testable. The positing of a theory or a law that cannot be empirically tested in a precise way thus fails to qualify as an acceptable scientific theory. It is this feature of testability of theory and precise measurement that distinguishes the sciences from the quasi-sciences or the humanities. Verification of a law can be made, using acceptable experimental procedures, as many times as one deems necessary and by as many different individuals as is felt necessary, and the results should always remain the same, within established experimental limits of error.

Actually, there are two definitions of a science, and it is the presence of these two different concepts of a science that contributes to much confusion. As Conant has shown (3, pages 23-27), the *static* definition of a science is most congruent with usual dictionary definitions. A static definition of science emphasizes the discovery of new facts, incorporation of such facts into a well-structured body of knowledge, and the prediction of new facts within the system on the basis of general laws and principles. The *dynamic* definition of a science tends to minimize the importance of a well-structured knowledge and data domain and, instead, emphasizes the action of the workers in the area of study. A dynamic definition puts stress upon how content is studied rather than what content is being studied. Thus, we see two approaches to the definition of a science. One approach emphasizes the content in the form of organized knowledge while the other cites the methods employed to secure access to knowledge without stressing the nature of the knowledge secured.

Traditional and well-established subject matter areas gravitate, in general, toward acceptance of the static definition. Fields of study with less well-established domains of knowledge characteristically emphasize the dynamic definition when seeking recognition as a scientific area. Traditional sciences, for example, may criticize any claim that education is a science, on the basis that education has no definite, systematized, and unique body of knowledge. Education, on the other hand, may argue that the way it studies problems in teaching is scientific and, thus, education qualifies as a science. If teaching is a profession, then education is a science is another often used argument.

Although the various definitions of a science found in the literature are seldom identified as static or dynamic in the frame of reference used by the author, it is usually a relatively simple matter to categorize a definition as being either static or dynamic. One merely has to look for the emphasis present in the definition and then judge whether the major criterion seems to be one of subject matter content (static) or one of method (dynamic). Sometimes, of course, an author takes no chances and includes both the static and dynamic outlook.

Braithwaite, for example, typifies the static frame of reference in his treatment of science. According to him, the function of a science is to:

> ...establish general laws covering the behaviors of the empirical events or objects with which the science in question is concerned, and thereby to enable us to connect together our knowledge of the separately known events, and to make reliable predictions of events as yet unknown (1, page 1).

Lachman forwards a similar definition emphasizing the static definition frame of reference in his book dealing with the foundations of science in general:

> Science refers to those systematically organized bodies of accumulated knowledge concerning the finite universe which have been derived exclusively through techniques of direct objective observation (6, page 15).

Inherent in static definitions of a science, one can see the insistence that organized and cumulative knowledge be acceptable by scientists in all domains of scientific inquiry; that is, that reliable, organized, and accumulative knowledge in one scientific area possess identical structure or acceptance in another scientific area. A fact is a fact regardless of which scientific domain examines it. Two plus two of anything adds up to four whether it be molecules, molar teeth, or tangerines. A fact is never found to be true in one domain and completely false in another. Because of such a feature, an advance in knowledge in any scientific domain may be of importance to all branches of science. Principles of electricity developed in physics will not be refuted in a study of the nervous system nor will development of neurophysiology of the human nervous system employ principles antagonistic to principles developed in physics. Thus, science is a monolithic structure with facts discovered in any science available for use in any and all sciences.

Quite a different viewpoint of science can be seen in definitions geared to the dynamic frame of reference. Psychology as a field of study still experiences some serious challenges to its contention of being a behavioral science. This may partially explain one psychologist's definition of science when he contended that science cannot be defined in "terms of the subject with which it deals," and that:

> The definition of a science does not rest upon what is accomplished, but how it was accomplished. The important factor present when science is present and absent when science is absent is the factor, scientific thinking. To define science as 'any

body of organized knowledge which has been gathered through the use of systematic methods of investigation' is close to the true definition, but only if the emphasis is placed on the method of investigating and not the materials investigated (9, page 5).*

As might be expected, any claim by physical education that it is a science is likely to depend upon a dynamic definition of a science. Consider the following statement by a distinguished scholar in physical education:

> We can be scientific in our respective fields to the extent that we employ intelligent and persistent endeavors to revise current beliefs, weed out error, improve upon the accuracy of our beliefs, and search for the significant relationships between facts drawn from several disciplines previously mentioned. The *method*, not the content, defines the body of knowledge as a science. Physical education, health education, and recreation become scientific to the extent to which we apply the scientific method to phenomena that are their subject matter (4, page 286).**

Static definitions, with marked emphasis upon knowledge-data content and monolithic structure, imply domains and categories of scientific knowledge. Thus, traditional sciences have well-staked out territories of investigative efforts. Any field of study which concerns itself with the application of the data and principles from one or more of the traditional sciences to the solution of "practical problems" usually finds itself being accused of a parasitic ancestry and encounters heavy resistance against calling itself a true science. Engineering, for example, could not be classified as a true science if it merely applied the organized knowledge developed by physics to the problems of society. Medicine could not be a science if it simply applied the knowledge of physiology and other related disciplines to the treatment of illness.

Just how an area of study establishes itself as a true science would constitute an ambitious undertaking of quite considerable proportions. If the task could ever be attacked successfully, it would necessitate careful analysis of several imbedded controversies. Part of the effort would have to be allocated to the distinction between a pure and an applied science, what constituted a definable knowledge system, whether the knowledge system must be unique when compared to other areas of scientific inquiry, the hierarchy of the monolithic structure of science, and, sometimes, even who got there first and staked out the original claim. Deciding what constitutes a true science shall, instead, be left to those deeming it a necessary undertaking. The task of deciding, for example, whether biophysics merits identification as a true science shall be left to

---

*From *Introduction to Experimental Method* by John C. Townsend. Copyright 1953, McGraw-Hill. Used with permission of McGraw-Hill Book Company.

**From Cowell (4). Used with permission of American Association for Health, Physical Education, Recreation and Dance.

the true sciences of biology and physics. Although the arguments forwarded by biophysics might be of interest to us, the final decision may be centuries in the making and we can find more efficient use of the time available to us.

PURPOSE OF A SCIENCE

Implicit in the definitions of a science that have been considered is the purpose of a science. There are, however, some unforeseen difficulties in making the implicit explicit. Although a science is concerned with the production and accumulation of knowledge, it is more concerned with discovering relationships among such data and with developing an understanding of broader and broader systems. Accumulation of a thousand new facts is good, but formulation of a general principle that can explain all of the facts present and the thousands of new facts likely to come from the content domain is even better. Science is more than analogous to a reference librarian who merely catalogs various collections of facts for easy access. Understanding of facts and development of a coherent knowledge structure is demanded.

A science has as its function the discovery of facts, the provision of general laws depicting order and relationships among such facts, and the expansion of general laws to cover new facts not yet in existence.. A science is interested in the comprehension of the real world and in prediction. Control or manipulation of the world for the benefit of society is *not* usually held as an obligation of a true science. The engineer and not the scientist performs the function of control in the interest of society's benefit. This point of prediction rather than control exemplifies one of the basic differences between an academic discipline (or science) and a profession.

METAPHYSICAL FOUNDATIONS

If one were to study a scientist at work, one would find that some basic assumptions which are not truly scientific have been made by the scientist. Although most scientists would disavow any knowledge that is not capable of being validated empirically, their actual performance at work suggests an implicit acceptance of certain basic axioms that are not strictly amenable to empirical validation. Try as they may, scientists cannot escape the necessity of acceptance of these basic assumptions on the basis of belief rather than empirical proof.

Philosophers of science call these implicit basic axioms the metaphysical foundations of science. "Metaphysics" was a term apparently used by Andronicus of Rhodes around the year 70 B.C. in reference to an untitled book by Aristotle which presumably constituted a second or advanced volume of Aristotle's famous book *Physics*. Metaphysics meant next-beyond physics and seemed a befitting title. To-day the term metaphysics is taken to mean basic axioms in science that are not subject to direct empirical validation. Scientists, nevertheless, must accept the truth of such metaphysical axioms in order to pursue their work.

Physical Reality

The scientist accepts the existence and reality of time, space and matter. Philosophers sometimes debate the nature of physical reality as being something other than what human sensory systems are capable of perceiving; that is, a description of ice as frozen water which is cold may lack absolute truth since the description is dependent upon a vocabulary, similar sets of human experiences, and comparable sensory mechanisms for data acquisition. Sense-data may thus be questioned on the grounds that data are perceived by the senses. The philosopher points to the fallibility of human senses and suggests that "true" physical reality may be quite unlike currently held propositions. The scientist, however, holds that the physical and finite world actually exists and is more than a fan-tasy or an illusion of the senses.

Quantifiability of the Physical World

The scientist accepts the fact that if time, space, and matter exist as physical realities, then they must exist in amounts that can be measured. The existence of physical reality means that it can be observed and measured. In order to safeguard against the imperfection of the human senses, scientists insist upon careful and precise assessment in their quan-tification endeavors. Terms such as "big," "medium sized," or "small" are deemed inadequate because they lack precise meaning and could be interpreted differently by different investigators. Because of imperfec-tions and inadequacies in the human senses, special apparatus are frequently developed to provide impartial observation techniques. The adjective "sober" may have gained prominence in connection with scien-tific activities because of the notion that a drunk could not be considered a reliable and impartial observer of physical reality.

Consistency in the Physical World

The scientist accepts the principle of consistency in nature. Observations of the physical world that lead to the establishment of relationships between or among certain phenomena are held to be stable. Gravity results in objects falling to the ground. Gravity acts upon objects in this way all the time and not just during full moons or when the gypsy bands release a society from the curse of gravity-free environments. If, as in space travel, objects do not fall to the ground when released of support, an explanation of the event must be found that does not refute the existence (and law) of gravity. The trait of stability in phenomena also means that empirical events are both reproducible and predictable. If consistency in the physical world did not exist, the quest for knowledge would be meaningless since any knowledge established at one moment could not be relied upon to be the same the next moment.

Determinism

The scientist believes that any observable phenomenon is not only amenable to quantification and consistency, but that each phenomenon also has a definable cause. Something or somethings operated to produce the observed phenomenon. These causal factors, furthermore, can be observed, quantified, and are similarly stable or consistent in their actions. Spontaneous appearance of an event without cause is simply not accepted as a scientific explanation. Causality is searched for in the description and understanding of the physical world as science pursues its goals.

Intelligibility of the Physical World

Scientists embrace the notion that human beings are capable of observing and of understanding the consistency and determinism present in the physical world. The scientist holds that human intellect possesses the capacity to discover the facts and laws of nature so that they may comprehend and predict empirical events in the physical world. As a result, scientists deny the proposition that absolute truth is unrealizable to human beings and avoid revelation as an avenue toward the achievement of truth. Some critics contend that science has set up its goals so as to avoid some important questions that deal with an explanation of the physical world in regard to motivation. Thus, science avoids explaining why things happened on any moral basis and negates the responsibility of judging facts in nature as being good or bad.

History has shown that society sometimes places restrictions on what aspects of nature the scientist has a right to investigate. Some topics, it seems, are beyond the need for explanation or are outside the legitimate realm of scientific inquiry. Consideration of this interesting question is too enormous an undertaking to be pursued here, but some comments seem in order since they apply to physical education. Athletics, for example, seems to hold some mystique for our field. An inherent belief in determinism and consistency means that observable events can be measured and predicted. Yet many individuals involved with athletics tend to resist the contention that, knowing all pertinent facts, one could predict the outcome of an athletic contest. The feeling prevails that the human spirit cannot be measured and, since spirit is so important in athletic contests, scientific study of athletics is a waste of time.

At the same time, however, such an individual may keep track of batting averages, know when the hit-and-run play is likely to be called, and be likely to leave the ball park when there are two outs in the last of the ninth with the home team behind by ten runs. These actions, of course, denote an acceptance of some measure of consistency and determinism in sport. However, the contention that scientific study of sport could result in accurate prediction of outcomes is still likely to be viewed as impossible. The devotion of Americans to the underdog in athletics is well known. The will to win is called upon when the odds for victory are dismal. Success against overwhelming odds is prized more highly than victory over an inferior opponent.

The appeal and glamour of athletic activity is tied to the principle that the outcome is uncertain. Regardless of the number of physical facts attesting to the superiority of one opponent over another, the possibility of victory by the underdog is silently nurtured. According to Loy, one of the essential characteristics of games "is that they are marked by an uncertain outcome" (7, page 2). Is it too much of a nightmare to consider that a science of physical activity could make possible accurate predictions in sport? If a science of sport could establish the outcome of sport contests accurately before they were conducted, what would happen to athletics?

Operating Code in Science

In the conduct of their activities, scientists also adhere to a set of principles conducive to the fulfillment of the goals of science. Certain of these principles help to distinguish scientists from philosophers and theologians. Other principles help to channel their energies into avenues of work more likely to realize their task of comprehension and prediction of nature. Having implicitly accepted the metaphysical foundations of science, scientists cannot escape adoption of another set of general rules which guide their scientific endeavors.

Amorality

Scientists never judge the morality of a fact. A fact is neither good nor bad; it is either a fact or it is not. If the fact fits judiciously into a primitive theoretical framework, a new theory, or more generalized law, it is a better fact than one which seemingly has no such key position. Although scientists may sometimes describe a fact or theory esthetically (for example, a beautiful relation), they are referring to how nicely their new fact or theory exhibits the strength of enhanced comprehension or prediction in the knowledge system under development.

Thus, science disavows responsibility for the effects that its knowledge may have upon humankind. The concept of morality in science, or the lack of it, has been debated by many persons both in and out of the scientific field. Workers developing the atomic bomb during World War II are said to have frequently questioned the wisdom of their work. Was it right to be seeking the answer to a force so destructive that humankind might be in peril? In one sense, however, such questioning was done by the individual as a citizen of society, and not the individual as a scientist.

It would seem that the scientists' task is made less complicated if they can adhere to the principle of amorality. Since human beings seem incapable of existence as a scientist alone or as a philosopher alone, the achievement of perfect amorality seems less than likely. Scientific workers are, at the same time, both scientists and individuals of society. They are subject to interaction between these two roles in life and to further conflicts characteristic of all human beings. Their conscience, ambitions, personality, and human qualities and failings all serve to challenge and affect their activities as scientists. Through it all, however, scientists strive for moral neutrality in their scientific work, and usually exhibit such neutrality publicly if not privately.

The human desire to understand the complexity of life was not always confined to scientific inquiry. Neither was a quest for knowledge restricted to an understanding of nature alone; philosophers and theologians alike have also sought the absolute truth from the dawn of time to the present. Prior to the seventeenth century, the character of scientific explanation was primarily teleological in context. A divine purpose was accepted as the ultimate cause of any and all observable phenomena. Reason could accomplish only so much, after which divine revelation was necessary. The choice between the two methods of inquiry was difficult.

As the prominence and influence of natural philosophy grew, a mechanistic philosophy holding to physical cause and physical effect replaced strict teleological explanations. Such a transition was not easily accomplished. Science could ill-afford to claim itself to be against age-old traditional beliefs or to suggest new laws of nature that were incompatible with the laws of nature, human beings, and the universe as established by theological doctrine. One of the concepts employed by science in this predicament was the idea of useful knowledge as discussed in Chapter 1.

Amorality as an operating code in science is related in several respects to the metaphysical principle that human beings are capable of studying and understanding nature. In describing this metaphysical principle, we suggested previously that part of the mystique associated with athletics resists acceptance of the idea that accurate prediction is, or can ever be, possible in competitive contests. The attitude reflected in this position is related, in turn, to another attitude that was more prevalent in the past than it is today. This latter attitude implied that the scientific examination of certain topics was more than just impossible—it suggested such examination was wrong to the point of being tinged with overtones of sin. Remnants of such a belief are not yet completely dissipated even in today's age of enlightenment.

Around the turn of the century, one of the great leaders in physical education delivered a talk to a group of International Y.M.C.A. secretaries gathered at a conference in 1900, extolling the value of the scientific study of practical problems. The speaker was Luther Halsey Gulick and his talk to such a group was appropriate because of his association with Springfield College. As was true of many other early leaders in physical education, Gulick was active in a number of organizations. In his talk Gulick stated:

> ...let me say a few words on the relation of such study as this to dependence upon God's guidance and trust in Him, for some have thought that this scientific movement is an attempt to discover laws and principles that shall take the place of dependence upon God (5).

It is true, of course, that leaders in the Y.M.C.A. probably possessed stronger ties with a theological temperament than a comparable group of leaders in physical education circles. Gulick's remark, however, is certainly a good example with which to portray an attitude that questioned scientific research. Much the same as scientists had done centuries earlier, Gulick defended science against those who questioned its appropriateness as an acceptable method of inquiry. Some sentiment still exists, however, for the position that the scientific method lacks pertinence to the study of many of the human's problems, and more than a few people question its potential in the study of athletics.

Fallible Knowledge

Although facts should speak for themselves, the scientist knows that it is the human who observes, measures, manipulates, and evaluates these facts. Because of human fallibility, it is assumed that any data collected and interpreted must also possess similar characteristics of fallibility. The concept of fallible knowledge generates at least three other related operating codes in science which are closely related in meaning: objectivity, caution, and skepticism.

The Concept of Objectivity

Objectivity is closely related to the concept of amorality. The role of objectivity in science calls for a detached viewpoint and makes necessary the avoidance of any opinion or subjectivity in the interpretation of research findings. Preference for one interpretation of the data because of a personal viewpoint is to be avoided. One may ask whether such objectivity has resulted in the scientific style of writing research reports in the third person; that is, never use "I" or "we" in writing, always use the neuter "it," "the data showed," and avoid flowery or sentimental adjectives in description of results.

Caution

Caution is another by-product of the existence of a fallible-knowledge doctrine in science. The scientist is very cautious and must take great pains to minimize the acceptance of imperfectly validated "facts" as completely true. Any data forwarded as prospective new knowledge are ruthlessly evaluated in order to protect proper advances in the science. The accuracy of measurement techniques, conditions of the experiment, analysis procedures, and all other facets of the investigation are carefully scrutinized. If no mistakes are in evidence, the data are held in a scientific purgatory until the results are verified by other investigators and until the prospective new knowledge has been cross-validated beyond any question of doubt as to veracity.

Such caution in scientific endeavors is frequently distasteful to individuals who are looking for evidence to "prove" their point or to confirm a value-loaded opinion. Many physical educators, for example, prefer to believe that a proper program of physical activity is a deterrent to heart disease, and are dismayed to hear caution expressed against unqualified acceptance of this position. Even though dozens of investigations point to this conclusion, the scientific community still harbors many who consider that the issue is an interesting possibility, although still not scientifically proven.

Skepticism

Skepticism is another co-worker with caution in the operating code of fallible knowledge in science. Skepticism in science guards against the danger that dogmatists become unchallenged authorities on knowledge. Data forwarded as facts must be judged not upon the basis of who forwards them, but upon the scientific criteria for reliable knowledge. No individual, regardless of past successes and prestige, can ever be allowed to forward a preemptory set of data. All data are viewed suspiciously, regardless of origin, and are forced to face challenge, critical examination, and verification.

One of the safeguards, presumably due to skepticism, is the practice, by many scientific journals, of forwarding manuscripts to associate editors for review without including the author's name on the manuscript. The idea is that the work should be reviewed by the associate editors on the basis of its reliability and not upon the reputation of the author. At conventions, some students are amazed to hear seemingly discourteous questions raised about research papers. Some of these questions are pointed and are merciless to the feelings of the author. The intent of such questions is to help establish the validity of the findings, and accomplished investigators relish such attacks upon their work. If the work is no good, the author wants to learn of this sad end to the work. If the work is good, the barbed questions will be handled easily by the investigator and bring acceptance of the data. Good manners, strangely enough, are not in vogue when it comes to establishing the veracity of research findings.

Reductionism

Reductionism is perhaps the most important operating code in science since it gives origin to the principle of parsimony and to the need for theory utilization. Reductionism best embodies the major purpose of science because it defines the necessity for the continuous formulation of simpler laws that can account for broader expanses of data in the content domain. Simple, concise laws are more desirable than complex laws containing many qualifications and imperfections.

To accomplish reductionism in science, both parsimony and theory utilization become necessary adjuncts. Accumulation of a thousand isolated facts is not the end goal of science. Such facts must be welded together by a meaningful general law. The initial stages of a science find abundant use of theory construction as attempts are made to unify isolated bits of knowledge into a coherent structure. Parsimony demands that the simplest theory which accomplishes such a purpose be best since it guards against unnecessary complexity. Some authorities state that reductionism implies another metaphysical foundation of science. The idea is advanced that science endorses the theory that nature is simple, since reductionism seeks the simplest and most general description of nature possible.

A fine example of reductionism exists in the work done on fatigue curves in strength by physical educators and other exercise physiologists. Typical experiments designed to assess the patterns of fatigue curves commonly use some form of curve-fitting to smooth out minor complexities in the curve. The fitted curve is usually forwarded as an exponential equation or as algebraic in form. Information is then given concerning how well the fitted curve or derived equation correlates with the actual fatigue curve itself. The correlation is seldom perfect or error free, but the equation allows many curves to be described. One simple equation may be capable of describing any number of such fatigue curves—both those curves already in existence and those yet to be collected. Because the equations can be used to predict data on fatigue curves not yet in existence, one can see that reductionism is complementary to the goal of prediction in science.

Categorizing isolated facts into meaningful theoretical frameworks thus necessitates the development of theories. Such theories define relationships among facts and afford a means of viewing a vast jungle of facts in an organized, coherent way. The role of theory in science cannot be over-emphasized. Theory must not only serve to summarize a vast array of isolated facts, it must be capable of suggesting new facts and of stimulating the production of new theories capable of higher generalizations. The procedures by which such feats are accomplished involves the scientific method. More will be said of the scientific method in a later chapter.

Scientific Breakthroughs

The public is, by now, well conditioned to await with breathless anticipation the next major scientific breakthrough. With the dramatic developments in space shots and heart transplants, the layperson now expects amazing new discoveries to be announced with monotonous frequency. Yet many qualified scientists hold that there are few, *if any*, events that can be truly called scientific breakthroughs. Instead, these scientists point out that advances in science are achieved by a careful, piece by piece addition to the continuum of knowledge. When, as it so often does nowadays, the tip of this continuum of knowledge reaches a certain stage, new discoveries are imminent.

Thus, progress in science results more typically from slow and careful work which gradually broadens the base of existing knowledge. Such a concept implies that important advances in science rely more upon the preceding efforts in science than they do upon some exceptionally brilliant new effort. This does not mean, of course, that the interpretation of collected data may not be unique and brilliant, for this is the very nature of scientific thinking. What it does mean is that the accumulation of knowledge in science is slow and gradual. Seldom, then, are scientific breakthroughs ever achieved by any single brilliant research experiment. More often, events commonly referred to as breakthroughs represent the results of a long series of painstaking investigations conducted by a number of different scientists in a number of different scientific fields.

Because advances in science are based upon a knowledge continuum, each new research finding that is offered to the scientific community must pass through the filters of skepticism and caution. New information must be reliable, accurate, and true, or else it may cause needless confusion. Inaccurate research information masquerading as fact can give rise to false leads for further research, result in faulty and deficient theory, and inhibit research activities in the same area because it is thought that knowledge already exists. Because such outcomes can cause extended delays in the attainment of goals, considerable emphasis is given to the formal adequacy of scientific investigations. A piece of new information, regardless of how unimportant it may seem, is valued more highly if it is reliable than are contributions of seemingly major significance which are clouded with uncertainty as to their truthfulness.

Against such a background, it is understandable why science insists upon amorality. Facts cannot be disregarded or accepted on the basis of being good or bad. A fact, once established, exists and it cannot be politically denied its existence on the basis it is not a "good" fact. To ignore one "bad" fact could jeopardize the progress of the delicate knowledge continuum being generated and could derail scientific progress thus causing immeasurable delays. Only the veracity of a research finding comes under scientific scrutiny. The responsibility for moral scrutiny must reside outside the realm of public science.

With this borne in mind, it is also understandable why scientists expend such large amounts of energy in the study of seemingly unimportant and infinitesimal research topics. To build a knowledge system requires the use of sound building materials. When scientists attempt to synthesize a theory, they must be certain that the facts they are using are true. A layperson, however, may consider many research topics to be ludicrous and express public disdain and scorn at such apparently ridiculous investigations. The scientist knows, however, that the production of knowledge is slow and cannot be hurried. Only when research is evaluated from the vantage point of the science can the research be fully appraised, and even then, the time at which the findings are evaluated is a factor of major consequence since at any given time such an "evaluation" must depend upon, and be made within, the context of what is then known.

Priorities can be established, nevertheless, for the most likely prospects for productive research areas. Anytime that funds must be allocated, some system of priority rating must be practiced and choices made as to which potential research investigations should be supported. As will be seen later, criteria do exist for evaluating the importance of research topics. However, the history of science is replete with examples that amply illustrate the axiom that nature does not always follow the same set of criteria. What people may consider of poor priority as a research area may actually be of tremendous importance in a yet unrecognized frame of reference.

When Karl Jansky began his work in radioastronomy, he was unable to secure any grant support because it was stated his work "at the time had no obvious applications to practical matters." In one account of the significance of Jansky's work (8), it was pointed out that Jansky's findings could not be understood fully because this area of theoretical physics was not yet fully developed. Future advances in the knowledge of microwave spectroscopy, however, later illuminated in a most complimentary fashion the importance of Jansky's detailed findings. Today, radioastronomy is a field of study given high priority as a research area and Jansky is acclaimed as its famous pioneer.

Since facts often transcend the significance attached to them by humans, science must be free to follow research lines that may not be considered fruitful by some priority-assessing agency. Only the unbridled curiosity and imagination of the scientist can be depended upon in the long run. So long as the facts produced are contributions to and satisfy the inner logic of the content domain, they are worthwhile pursuing, whether their significance is apparent immediately or not.

Such free inquiry in science is commonly referred to as basic or pure research. Because of the apparent vagueness of purpose in basic research, it is often sarcastically criticized by those who consider practical and useful knowledge to be more essential. Charles F. Wilson, a former Secretary of Defense, was once quoted as saying that "basic research is when you don't know what you're doing." Although most scientists agree that support of basic research is essential to the advancement of science, it is often difficult to secure financial support for what appears to be an ivory-tower endeavor. Budget policies are often formulated by an economy minded public, and support of seemingly uncoordinated and purposeless research is quickly sacrificed in the name of avoiding waste. Unfortunately for basic research, its contribution to useful knowledge is often a long-range rather than an immediate prospect.

Applied research, after all is said and done, seems more efficient than basic research. In 1966, for example, the Defense Department released an interim report on its study of the contributions made by basic and applied research to certain technological innovations and to weapons systems development. Project Hindsight concluded that basic research had made only minor contributions, since 1945, to Defense Department goals in research and development. In general, the report made by Project Hindsight seemed to imply to most observers that technological innovation was best accomplished by direct research attacks upon the practical and pertinent problems associated with a specific technological goal. The report raised a wave of protest among scientists who cherished the principle that basic research was essential to unimpeded progress in science. Without continuous production of basic knowledge, these scientists claimed, technological advance would soon falter because of the neglect of basic science from which applied research receives its sustenance.

About two years after the Project Hindsight report, the National Science Foundation (NSF) released a study that strongly supported proponents of the pure-science ideal. The NSF study, "Technology in Retrospect and Critical Events in Science," concluded that basic research was far more important to technological advancement than Project Hindsight had allowed in its report. This study had randomly selected five recent technological advances from a list of 20 and traced back in time the critical events in science that were essential to the technological innovation. Each critical event was deemed to have been essential to the technological development; that is, without the existence of the critical event the recent technological advance could not have been made. Some 341 such critical events were documented for the five technological advances studied in detail. Of these 341 critical events, 10% were classified to be the result of development and application research, 20% were products of mission-oriented or applied research, and almost 70% were attributed to nonmission or basic research endeavors.

It was further shown that about 90% of the critical events emanating from nonmission or basic research had occurred a decade or more before realization of the actual technological advance. In the ten-year period immediately preceding the technological advance, however, mission-oriented and development/application research supplied the greatest percentage of critical events. There was also strong evidence to suggest that basic and applied research activities interacted with one another and stimulated progress in both mission-oriented and nonmission research endeavors. Peter Thompson's appraisal of the report which appeared in *Science* in January 1969 noted that the team of experts responsible for "Technology in Retrospect and Critical Events in Science" "...found strong justification for the idea that undirected research, with knowledge for its own sake as the only goal, provides a reservoir of understanding essential to subsequent technological innovation."

Research relevant to the practical problems encountered in the profession of physical education may thus seem worthy of the highest priority. Many critical problems in the profession, it seems, require a direct research attack in an attempt to offer immediate solutions. However, an inherent constraint exists in an operating code that permits only applied research activity. Unless a pertinent knowledge system developed by basic research is available, direct research attacks on practical problems may be neither possible nor successful. Many of the persistent problems plaguing the profession of physical education may survive countless applied research assaults because "critical events" necessary for a solution simply do not exist. Water is needed from the well of knowledge to put out the fires of practical problems. Who puts water in the well and what happens when the well goes dry?

If an enterprising student could manage the time, it would be interesting to consider the areas of basic research that have been cultivated in physical education. To do so would necessitate that the definition of basic research be settled first. Although this problem will be considered later, for the time being let us merely accept the usual definition of basic research, which holds that such research be done without any requirement that practical application of its results be imminent. With this definition accepted, one might ask: Has there been any basic research done in physical education?

Finding examples of basic research in the literature of physical-education that would satisfy the pure-science ideal would indeed be hard to do. In the first place, hard headed and practical physical educators tend to frown upon research investigations which do not produce useful knowledge. Useful knowledge, in this case, means information that can be applied immediately to the teaching of physical activities in a school setting. As evidence of this reluctance to accept basic research, one is invited to examine articles in the *Research Quarterly* and find how many fail to develop their potential contribution to useful application in athletics and physical education. Most such articles carefully devote a section to significance of the study which emphasizes immediate practical application. Indeed, manuscripts submitted to the *Research Quarterly* are often returned to the author with editorial comment on the need to relate the study to physical education and to show its significance to the profession.

Practical needs of the profession, then, do not tend to enhance a reasonable amount of respect for basic research in physical education. No matter how loosely one applies the criteria for basic research, numerous examples of basic research in physical education simply do not exist. Several researchers in physical education who are known as basic researchers rather than applied or practical researchers would not view their own work as truly basic. Whatever the cause for the apparent dearth of basic research in physical education, the situation gives good cause for the contemplation of another important and related question: What are the discernible areas for the basic research in physical education? The question has obvious significance for the movement toward an academic discipline of physical education. If a field of study has no examples of basic research can it ever be an academic discipline?

MONOLITHIC STRUCTURE IN SCIENCE

A community of scientists, it has been said, would constitute a more closely knit settlement than a community of philosophers. Walker (10, page vi) and others before him have suggested that science is a monolithic structure, cumulative in nature, which can be conceptualized as a tall building under construction. Nonscientific areas, on the other hand, are less than cumulative in nature and more closely resemble single family dwellings set wide apart as in a fashionable suburb. Contemporary philosophy, for example, has many competing theories bidding for universal acceptance. Science, on the other hand, displays a "self-consistent body of material accepted in practice by almost all scientists."

The monolithic structure of science forbids one area of science to refute an established fact in another branch of science. Facts about mass and motion established in physics, for example, are not denied by physical educators studying biomechanics. Instead, biomechanics researchers utilize established facts about mass and motion as they study problems in human movement. The sciences are, thus, mutually related and interdependent. An advance in one area can provide the basis for an advance in another area. Each area of science may, of course, structure a knowledge system in a slightly different way in order to suit its particular frame of reference. Such differences, however, are conceptual rather than factual, and any field of study which forwards a body of "knowledge" shown to be in open conflict with established facts is sure to be questioned as a scientific field of study.

Several classification schemes for the sciences have been forwarded in an attempt to portray the interrelatedness of all the branches of science. Usually such classification attempts make use of a sequential concept in which the more basic sciences assume a low-order category. Each successive level of the column, then, reflects a science composed of all (or most) of the lower-order levels or more basic categories beneath it. Thus, one finds physics at the base of one classification scheme since it deals with fundamental particles, atoms, and molecules. On the next category level one would find chemistry, followed by biochemistry, biology, physiology, and then zoology. The idea conveyed is that each successive higher-order category is dependent, in a large measure, upon the more basic categories beneath it.

Because of such interdependence of the sciences, it is not surprising to find that considerable overlapping exists among several of the sciences. Such an observation should be of special interest to physical educators intent upon the establishment of an academic discipline of physical education. The requirement that an academic discipline possess a unique content domain for its development loses some of its vigor when one considers the tremendous duplication of interest areas in the sciences. The relationship between the tenet of interrelatedness and the requirement of a unique content domain in science, furthermore, brings to light a concept that transcends the basic difference between a static and dynamic definition of science.

In those areas of study commonly called the life sciences today, one could find more than a few "distinct" disciplines studying the same content domain. The human eye, for example, comes in for close attention and study by anatomists and neuroanatomists defining structural characteristics, physiologists and neurophysiologists interested in function and neural transmission systems, psychologists concerned with perceptual processes, physicists working out optical mechanics, biochemists studying chemical constituents of vision, and zoologists developing a taxonomy of structural characteristics of the eye across several species.

In addition to these disciplines, one may also find the eye to be of interest to an ophthalmologist, an optometrist, and a reading specialist. Criminologists and mental health workers may be concerned about the eye in regard to facial features. Personnel placement managers may be concerned about the eye as it pertains to task performance prerequisites and job efficiency. Traffic control experts and state police officers find it necessary to consider the eye and vision in the context of accident control. School nurses and classroom teachers are found administering vision screening tests and cosmetologists contrive ingenious (and often expensive) ways of making the eye appear more beautiful to the beholder.

As a unique area of study, the eye seems to come into the content domain of many disciplines and more than a few professions and occupational groups. Which subject matter area then can legitimately "claim" the eye as its own unique content domain? The answer is, of course, that all these fields have a legitimate reason for studying the eye. Each, however, studies the eye with a slightly different focus of interest. The anatomist and physiologist may study the identical eye, but each looks at that eye from a different frame of reference. What the anatomist sees in the eye is not what the physiologist sees. Each of the basic disciplines, thus, considers properties of the eye in the context and from the perspective of its own knowledge-domain system. Facts established in one area of study are liable for use in any other area, and the tenet of interrelatedness is exemplified rather than refuted.

If physical educators were to decide to study the eye in the context of their knowledge domain, would they be accused of pilfering a content area already claimed by another discipline as its own unique field of study or demonstrating a lack of unique subject matter content in their domain and being forced to forage in other disciplines for topics worthy of scholarly research? Physical educators have been interested in the eye as it relates to motor activities and have researched several aspects of the role of vision in athletics. Among these are the role of peripheral vision in athletic performance, eyedness and batting skill, tests of eye-hand and foot-eye coordination, balance with and without vision, and the effect of blindness upon motor development and performance. Would topics such as these qualify for classification within an academic discipline of physical education, or are they merely extensions of the legitimate interests of other unique basic disciplines?

The answer is, of course, fundamental to any successful attempt at defining an academic discipline of physical education. As discussed previously (see Chapter 3), an essential argument in the establishment of an academic discipline of physical education involves the validity of using physical activity as the frame of reference and focus of interest. Whether such a posture will allow the acceptance of physical education as a full-fledged academic discipline depends upon many factors and, as yet, remains to be seen. Perhaps the strongest argument that can be raised in favor of an academic discipline of physical education would be the contributions that such a discipline could make to the scientific community. When other disciplines are found seeking the knowledge obtained in the field of physical education and the results of research investigations made by physical educators, one could claim some value for the physical activity focus of an academic discipline.

REFERENCES

1. Braithwaite, R. *Scientific Explanation.* Cambridge: Cambridge Univ. Press, 1955.

2. Brubacker, John S., and Willis Rudy. *Higher Education in Transition: An American History: 1636-1956.* New York: Harper, 1958.

3. Conant, James B. *Science and Common Sense.* New Haven: Yale Univ. Press, 1951.

4. Cowell, Charles C. The contributions of physical activity to social development. *Research Quarterly* **31**: 286-306; May 1960 supplement.

5. Gulick, Luther Halsey. Notes on International Secretaries Conference, Thousand Island Park, June 6-10, 1900. *American Employed Officers Conferences (Y.M.C.A.)*, Vols. 23-30, 1893-1902.

6. Lachman, Sheldon J. *The Foundations of Science.* Detroit: Hamilton, 1956.

7. Loy, John W. The nature of sport: a definitional effort. *Quest* **10**: 1-15; May 1968.

8. Southworth, G.C. Early history of radio astronomy. *The Scientific Monthly* **82**: 55-66; February 1956.

9. Townsend, John C. *Introduction to Experimental Method.* New York: McGraw-Hill, 1953.

10. Walker, Marshall. *The Nature of Scientific Thought.* Englewood Cliffs, New Jersey: Prentice-Hall, 1963.

Scientific Method in Perspective

The history of humankind reveals an eternal search for answers to essential questions. The earliest technique employed in this search for needed answers was probably that of trial and error. Humans simply discovered which materials were combustible and which things were edible. If serious errors were made, survival was threatened. If one individual survived better and longer than others, that individual came to be looked upon as an authority and a leader whose decisions could be trusted more than those of others.

Not all human questions could be answered effectively by the trial and error method. For such topics, reliance upon some form of mystical explanation was often the "appropriate" method. Although many of the explanations were of little empirical value, they were due some esteem if for no other reason than that of having satisfied the questioner. Currently, people consider the scientific method to be the most effective means of finding answers to their questions. If questions are asked that cannot be answered by application of scientific methods, the questions are simply ruled as not being legitimate questions for science. The questioners are then obliged to take their query elsewhere for satisfaction.

Basically, the scientific method comprises two major components: induction and deduction. Induction is a synthesizing process. Numerous bits of seemingly isolated occurrences of some particular phenomenon are observed. On the basis of this set of observations, a generalization is made. This generalization may not necessarily be true for all the occurrences of the phenomenon in question, but it seemingly brings some degree of order to the data under consideration. Deduction, on the other hand, starts with an inductive statement as a beginning point. If the inductive statement is true, then certain other things can be inferred from it. Analytic in form, deduction predicts the existence of other specific data which must exist if the inductive statement is, indeed, true.

Defects in either induction or deduction alone preclude either from being the sole vehicle for the scientific method of research. Regardless of how appealing it may appear, any inductive statement requires verification before it can be accepted as completely valid. The procedure for verifying inductive statements calls for deduction to be used. Deduction can only begin after some inductive statement is present. Strange as it may seem, it required several centuries for people to realize that a combination of the two methods might result in a better method for finding answers to questions. Today, of course, inductive and deductive cycles are used collectively and constitute the necessary procedures for science.

Observation of certain phenomena leads to an inductive statement. Induction is then followed by deduction and the veracity of the inductive statement is tested by using deduction to predict the existence of data not yet in evidence. If the existence of such other data is successfully verified, the inductive statement receives partial verification. As the collection of more and more deductively predicted data is shown to exist, not only is the original inductive statement verified more emphatically but a broader supply of facts is produced as the basis for another inductive statement. Thus, with a fuller supply of facts at hand, a more general or higher-level inductive statement may be composed. The validity of such a higher-level generalization may then be tested by further analytical, deductive predictions and data collection. The method of scientific inquiry is thus seen to be a combination of induction and deduction and is said to be self-correcting; for if the inductive statement is in error, the subsequent deduction and empirical data collected will uncover its deficiencies.

INDUCTION

An investigator seeks to give order and meaning to a particular set of empirical data. As a first step the investigator may try to discover meaningful relationships or similarities present in the data. Such a step may merely consist of categorizing the data into homogeneous groups or it may be correlational in nature. If a particular realm of inquiry is largely characterized only by taxonomy and correlations, however, it is usually considered an area of knowledge that is not very highly developed. Most model development is, in the beginning, correlational in nature and descriptive models rather than explanatory models are more common. Progress and advancement come by the establishment of higher-order principles from which lower-order principles and data can be accounted for, explained, and predicted. Such abstract constructs or hypothetical principles can thus serve as a theoretical system from which other constructs can be deduced.

To bring order to a mass of unorganized data implies the use of inductive reasoning. Beyond the idea that induction is to be used, however, there are no stereotyped procedures available that can be followed in the postulation of a model. Definite criteria for the value of an inductive statement do exist. These criteria result from the basic purposes of a science, and the inductive statement is obliged not to violate any of the metaphysical foundations and is, likewise, confined to the limits imposed by the operating code. Although such criteria necessarily affect the structure of inductive statements, they do little in the way of prescribing the method for accomplishing satisfactory inductive statements.

Inductive statements are highly esteemed if they postulate *archetypes* for the data system under consideration. An archetype suggests an original pattern in which all observations from the same knowledge domain can be embodied. A more prevalent term in use today is "model." The word "model" was originally used by Neils Bohr in 1913 in his description of the hydrogen atom. A model represents an inductive statement. Hence, the model has definite correspondence to observations present in a particular domain. Such a model need not be identical to the real world, and may be a form of abstraction. So long as it demonstrates correspondence to observations in the real world, can be used to make analytical deductions for verification in the real world, and fulfills criteria established by the purpose of the science, a model may be a much valued vehicle in a science.

One essential feature in this sequence is that the construct forwarded must be capable of verification or refutation in an empirical sense. Sometimes constructs or theories are forwarded which seemingly defy attempts to design experiments for their verification or refutation. According to Karl Popper (5), a philosopher of science, if a construct or theory is incapable of being tested empirically and either verified or refuted, it is simply not a scientific theory. Some form of ingenuity may be necessary to design meaningful tests of an attractive theoretical construct or to restate the theoretical construct in order to make it amenable to experimental testing.

DEDUCTION

Once formulated, the testing of a scientific theory or model follows a more definite and discernible pattern. The model or theory is made liable to experimental verification or denial. If the model is verified by many experiments, confidence in its validity is enhanced. If experimental evidence conflicts with the predictions of the model, then revision and modification of the model is necessary. The cycle of induction, deduction, and experimental testing begins again.

If the model (or theory) satisfactorily accounts for data already present, and successfully predicts the existence of new data, it can be called a scientific model or scientific theory. If all the data, both known and predicted, cannot be subjected to some process of experimental verification then the model is simply not scientific. A scientific model *must* be capable of empirical testing.

BASIC STEPS IN THE SCIENTIFIC METHOD

The scientific method is, therefore, a rather clear set of three basic steps:

(1) Suitable observation of pertinent empirical data is made and induction employed to postulate a summarizing statement in the form of a generalization, principle, or concise description.
(2) By analytic deductive procedures, the inductive statement is examined and predictions of new observations forwarded. Collection of suitable observations for the predicted and new empirical data is made.
(3) The adequacy of the inductive statement forwarded by step (1) is evaluated by the accuracy with which it accounts for the data upon which it was formulated and for its ability to predict the existence of new empirical data.

Completion of step (3) leads back to step (1) and the process continues through cycle after cycle until the finished theory or model is accepted as true and validated. Each cycle, furthermore, can be made on the basis of an expanded set of observed occurrences of the phenomenon under study. Usually only partial rather than complete verification or refutation can be made, but each cycle presumably leads to more accurate or more general statements, or both. Newer inductive statements then provide more yield from analytic deductive analysis with greater potency for verification or refutation.

Philosophers of science contend that step (1) represents an act of creation, which characterizes scientific thinking. Such scientific thinking cannot be made methodical, and few rules can be found to which it can be made to conform. Step (2) is called scientific research and is designed to test the adequacy of postulated theories. It is probably the step in the scientific method most familiar to the public and the one that involves the guided collection of data under rather standardized laboratory procedures. The term "formal adequacy" describes the validity of the research procedures employed in step (2) and includes such considera-

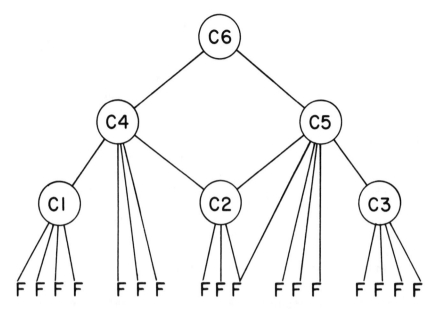

Figure 8.1. A schematic of a hypothetical model.

tions as experimental design, analysis of data, collection procedure, control of irrelevant factors, and laboratory instrumentation. Step (3) necessitates an interpretation of the collected data with regard to the research objectives. The entire process—steps (1), (2), and (3)—constitutes the scientific method.

One of the important advantages of a validated model is that it can relieve science of the necessity for conducting endless experiments. After a model has been successfully verified, it is no longer necessary to check all of its predictions in an endless repetition of experiments. As a validated model, it may be used in conjunction with other validated models in the inductive process to seek even higher level inductive statements and more general models. If validated models are composed of constitutive definitions (3, page 236), they can be used in such a search for interrelations among models rather than among single facts. The scientist can then work with broad theories in the inductive process rather than with a collection of seemingly isolated facts.

SCHEMATIC REPRESENTATION OF A MODEL

When a model becomes fairly well developed it possesses numerous connections among observed data and its theoretical constructs. Figure 8.1 depicts such a relationship. Depicted here are a number of empirical facts

(F). Construct 1 is capable of describing by straight lines the F's to which it is connected. The same is true for constructs C_2 and C_3. Note, however, that several facts are unaccounted for by C_1, C_2, and C_3. At the next level, construct C_4 is capable of accounting for C_1 and C_2 as well as some other facts that C_1, C_2, and C_3 failed to account for. Construct C_5 is similarly capable of accounting for C_2 and C_3. In addition, C_4 and C_5 mutually connect to and thus account for C_2. Construct C_6, the highest construct in this particular system, connects to C_4 and C_5 and, hence, indirectly to C_1, C_2, C_3, and all facts at the baseline.

The value of such a theoretical system is that an established system can account for and predict data *without* the necessity of actually carrying on an experiment or sets of experiments. Knowing the nature of C_6 and given certain data, one can predict the existence of other facts. Indeed, the theoretical system may predict the existence of facts and other lower-order constructs that the imagination and intellect of the scientist may not have considered.

As Margeneau states, the degree to which

> theoretical procedures or explanations are used or contrasted with correlational procedures or explanations represents one important criterion which characterizes a well-developed system of knowledge (3, page 27).*

In our terms, it constitutes a well-developed model.

MODELS IN PHYSICAL EDUCATION

Physical educators have generally shown a tendency to resist theory and abstraction. As a result, research that is not practical has occupied a position of minor importance. More value has, seemingly, been given to practical research that seeks to supply answers to the many everyday practical problems encountered by physical educators in the performance of their duties. Yet, only through research, construction of theory, and abstraction will such practical everyday problems be solved *efficiently*. For it is through theory and model development that answers to many questions are secured. Such models can suggest new questions as yet unasked by the practitioner and then supply possible answers to these questions.

To deny or minimize the importance of theory and abstraction in physical-education research endeavors is tantamount to a regression to earlier methods for resolving questions. As suggested previously, trial

---

*From *The Nature of Physical Reality* by H. Margenau. Copyright 1950, McGraw-Hill. Used with permission of McGraw-Hill Book Company.

and error, authority and tradition, speculation and argumentation can hardly be called efficient methods for problem solving or knowledge production.

There are several examples of model development in physical-education research that seem worthy of mention. One of these is the *memory drum* theory of neuromotor reaction advanced by Franklin M. Henry of the University of California in 1960 (2). Henry made note of present knowledge and data concerning neuromotor reactions and outlined some of the theoretical considerations pertinent to the construction of an appropriate model in the content domain. He then proposed a revised statement of the traditional theory, dealing with reaction time, which recognized new knowledge available about the human neuromotor system. It should be pointed out here that these actions by Henry constituted step (1) in the scientific method: that is, consideration of pertinent empirical data was made and induction employed to postulate a summarizing statement. In this instance, Henry modified an existing theoretical generalization on the basis of additional knowledge.

Henry's memory-drum theory postulated the existence of a nonconscious higher-nerve center that was capable of utilizing stored information to synthesize an appropriate sequence of nerve impulses. These nerve sequences activated neuromotor coordination centers, subcenters, and efferent nerves to effect the desired motor act. The nonconscious higher-nerve center was, itself, activated by incoming impulses either from the general afferent stimuli or from brain waves. The stored information to which we referred constituted a kind of neuromotor memory which was operationally defined to be the result of learned and accumulated experience-traces of optimum neuromotor coordinations to specific incoming stimuli. Thus, a rather substantial resource in the form of stored motor-memory was available for the synthesization of a neuromotor act dependent upon the kind of initiator stimulus received. Henry likened the system to an electronic computer that contains stored programs for neuromotor reactions. Upon reception of a stimulus, the appropriate neuromotor-control program is called into operation and a well-executed motor act is performed under its control. If no such program is available for the incoming stimulus, then an "unlearned complicated task is carried out under conscious control, in an awkward, step-by-step, poorly coordinated manner."

The form of the proposed model for neuromotor reactions is such that it allows any number of empirical and testable predictions to be made in the area of motor coordination. Indeed, the investigation reported by Henry in conjunction with his memory-drum theory tested the prediction that a longer reaction latency would occur with a complicated motor movement than with a simpler movement. This deduction holds, because a more complicated motor act would necessarily require more elements

of the stored neuromotor-memory capacity as well as more time for synthesizing the coordination of these elements and designating appropriate
nerve pathways for execution. A simple act, on the other hand, would require fewer elements of the stored neuromotor-memory system and an
appropriate motor act could be synthesized much more quickly. Henry
proposed to test this deduction by measuring the simple reaction time required for a simple, as compared with a more complex, motor act.

As Paillard (4, page 1693) has shown, the notion of a plan of movement for motor acts as a prerequisite to voluntary activity has been in existence for quite some time. In 1928, for example, Wacholder studied
voluntary movement and stressed the importance of *Bewegungsentwurt*
which embodied the thesis that a motor image or a plan for movement
must exist prior to any voluntary movement. Paillard cited other investigators who similarly theorized about such a "scheme of action" and
"intention directed towards a goal," which incorporated the tenet of
nonconscious centers for enactment. In addition, the construct has also
been forwarded that, once such a planned movement is begun, it is
dependent upon subsequent sensory input from the act itself to effect
successful completion. Without such additional sensory information, the
act would be poorly performed or even made impossible. This feature, of
course, represents an improvement over the simple and basic theory for
neuromotor reaction forwarded by Henry.

Henry's memory-drum theory for neuromotor reactions constitutes an
important attempt at model development in physical education. The
theory meets the requirement of being testable in an empirical sense and
has stood up quite well against the many investigations designed and conducted by Henry and his co-workers to test its validity. As these investigations accumulate and as additional knowledge from related fields
becomes available, the possibility of revising the theory may suggest
itself to some scientist. When (and if) such an attempt at revision takes
place, step (1) in the scientific method will be reenacted. To validate the
new theory steps (2) and (3) in the scientific method will be necessary.

Although seemingly self-evident, it may be wise to point out that the
actual investigations conducted to test the memory-drum theory would
appear rather "silly" to anyone who did not appreciate the theory
behind such studies. Henry, for example, required subjects to (a) lift a
finger off a reaction key when a gong sounded; (b) lift a finger off a reaction key when a gong sounded and then reach forward and grasp a tennis
ball hung by a string 15 centimeters above and 30 centimeters beyond the
reaction key; and (c) lift the finger as before and then move their hand
forward and upward, strike a tennis ball with the back of the hand,
reverse direction and go forward and downward touching a second reaction key, and finally change direction again going upward and forward
to strike down on another tennis ball. In each condition, the time be-

tween the sound of the gong and the movement of the finger off the reaction key was recorded. With the exception of the movement tasks required *after* the lifting of the finger in response to a sound, the three conditions were identical. If differences resulted in simple reaction time between the three conditions—as they did—then it would be concluded that the memory-drum theory received some degree of verification.

On the surface, the study might cause an individual who is ignorant of the theoretical construct being tested to shake his head in amazement at the trash being published in the *Research Quarterly*. The study would seem highly artificial, holding no promise of immediate practical application in the teaching situation, and of dubious value to physical education. What activity, after all, in physical education necessitates complicated movements forward, backward, and back again of the hand? Involved movements lengthen reaction time, so what? Unless readers of such investigations are aware of the theory behind such studies they would never be able to ask the proper questions. These studies are testing a basic model for the human being in neuromotor-reaction situations. The real questions deal with the topic of its effectiveness in this domain and not with the potential for application in the everyday teaching world. Knowledge must precede practice as much as possible.

What, then, of other models in physical education? How many theories (or models) can the reader list? Each issue of the *Research Quarterly* contains research investigations on a variety of topical areas. How often is the reader of these articles able to place the investigation within the knowledge structure of some theory and thus, appreciate its meaning? This knowledge structure, complete with theoretical constructs and prevalent models, constitutes the factual foundation for practices in physical-education activities. The reader of this book is invited to compile a list of models in physical education that help guide the practitioner in action. Such a list ought to be quite a lengthy one if the spectrum of professional responsibilities has anything to do with a requirement for a knowledge basis. Since physical education is eclectic, it must borrow some models.

A MODEL FOR PERSONALITY FACTORS IN ATHLETICS

As yet, no comprehensive model for personality factors in athletics has been forwarded, although there would appear to be a substantial number of studies available to serve as a basis for such an undertaking. Making sense out of all the facts at hand, in other words, the postulation of a model, awaits the efforts of some scholar. The mass of data and possible considerations in the area of personality factors in athletics provide substantial content for such an effort. The presence of much accumulated data, unfortunately, sometimes makes the initial formulation of a model as difficult as it would be were there a lack of data.

Under the aegis of the idea that even a poor model is better than no model, an attempt at developing such a model for personality factors in athletics might be justified. Such an attempt can serve, if nothing else, to exemplify the procedures likely to be followed in the development of a model. The model to be formulated here is purely hypothetical, and is not meant to be considered as a formal offering of a model to be put up for scientific scrutiny. In this case, the dynamic definition of a science will be used and the process of model development emphasized, rather than the data system itself.

A basic premise for personality research work in athletics has been that definable traits exist that are capable of differentiating athletes in one sport from those in another, or from nonathletes. Implicit in such work has been the idea that certain athletic activities develop or at least encourage the development of some personality traits. Contentions that athletics develop character, courage, or aggressiveness are examples of such a position. The major emphasis in much of the work on athletic personality has been on the identification of differences among various groups of athletes, and between athletes and nonathletes. Results from such studies would seem to suggest numerous differences. It would appear that when personality differences among athletes are demonstrated,the inference is drawn that such traits are related to success in a particular sport. Sometimes, the further inference is made that the presence of such traits in potential sport aspirants is desirable and that the cultivation of such traits would be beneficial to successful performance; that is, if basketball players score high on the femininity scale then the femininity trait is desirable in potential basketball players.

Certainly, factors demonstrated to be differentiators are suggestive of traits somehow linked to athletics. Demonstrating that such traits are linked causally to success in a particular sport, however, is quite a different matter. One might find, for example, that athletes in a particular sport differ on a trait from other athletes and from norms. If one could further show that this trait differed in some logical dimension between known levels of ability in the same sport, or that continuing participation in the sport augmented the magnitude of the trait, then some increased confidence might result in support of the thesis that the trait was related to successful participation.

However, there are several possible ways in which personality factors may be linked with athletics. First, it is possible that some set of personality factors exist which motivate individuals to select and participate in a sport. It may be true that those individuals who possess the greatest and most fortuitous combination of these salient factors continue in the sport and become successful. Thus, neophytes and successful veterans possess similar personality patterns differing only in intensity. Second, it could be true that there is no pattern which enhances initial entry into a sport, but that, either by modification of existing personality or attrition of inappropriate patterns, only those individuals possessing a suitable pattern persist and become successful. Under this alternative, neophytes possess dissimilar patterns but successful veterans possess similar patterns of personality. Third, both neophytes and successful veterans possess dissimilar, nondiscriminant patterns. Fourth, there is a similar pattern motivating entry of neophytes but participation or attrition results in a dissimilar pattern for successful veterans. Seemingly, researchers have often expressed preference only for the first alternative, expressing a note of failure if no significant differences are found or embarrassment if undesirable social characteristics are shown in athletes.

In addition to the previous factors mentioned in relation to entry, participation, and success, other factors suggest need for consideration in developing a model for personality factors in athletics. These factors could be thought of as interacting variables, lower-order constructs, or constructs of a higher order. So far as personality in athletics is involved:

1. Is there a difference between male and female participants?

2. Is there a difference between various classifications of sports, for example, team versus individual sports and combative versus noncombative sports?

3. If athletic activities attract or promise success to specific somatotypes, is it somatotype that determines the important personality characteristics and not the sport itself?

4. Are there any national differences in sports? For example, does basketball attract and develop similar personality characteristics in the United States, Russia, and Brazil?

The "answers" to such questions may be available in personality research already done. By viewing such data from any of the above frames of reference, a higher-order construct may be possible. The answers to these questions may be *implicit* in research done to answer other and different *explicit* questions. The researcher who seeks to postulate a model for personality factors in athletics may already have answers available in published research. If the researcher could ask the right questions and match them with the available right answers, a model could be postulated. Once postulated, studies to test the validity of the model can be planned. Studies done to test explicit questions of a lower order in the model can be used as evidence for or against higher-order constructs in the model. Also, the model may thus function to account for, explain, and predict the empirical data inherent in the realm of personality factors in athletics.

Let us assume that certain data and relationships do, in fact, exist and follow the development of a hypothetical model for personality factors

Figure 8.2. First stage of model development.

in athletics. Imagine that a set of eighteen studies on personality characteristics of athletes is available for our model construction. As a start, the scientist groups together all studies demonstrating similar personality characteristics. When this is done, five sets of facts (F) are obtained. Each set is composed of similar personality characteristics and each set is different from any other set. Set 1 comprises F_1, F_2, F_3, and F_4; set 2 comprises F_5, F_6, and F_7; set 3 comprises F_8, F_9, F_{10}, and F_{11}; set 4 comprises F_{12}, F_{13}, and F_{14}; and set 5 comprises F_{15}, F_{16}, F_{17}, and F_{18}. To begin, the model developer might start with the notion that there is a difference between individual sports as a group and those classified as team sports. The scientist would search through the available facts and collect for examination those facts about personality in individual sports and then bring together another set of facts dealing with team sports. Let us suppose that this has been done and that Figure 8.2 represents this first stage of model development.

Construct C_1 explains the relationship of facts F_1, F_2, F_3, and F_4. Imagine that $F_1,...,F_4$ represent data on personality traits of participants in tennis and golf. Construct C_1 merely summarizes the similarity between these facts and postulates that such traits are characteristic of participants in individual sports. Note that inherent in C_1 is the prediction that participants in individual sports other than tennis and golf will have similar personality traits. Construct C_3 summarizes similar data (F_{15}, F_{16}, F_{17}, F_{18}) on the team sports of basketball and baseball. Construct C_1 thus accounts for $F_1,...,F_4$ postulating an individual-sports factor for personality traits. Construct C_3 performs a similar function for team sports via $F_{15},...,F_{18}$. Unaccounted for, however, are the facts F_5 through F_{14}.

Next the model developer "sees" that F_5, F_6, and F_7 represent data on personality traits in wrestlers, boxers, and judo participants. Since these

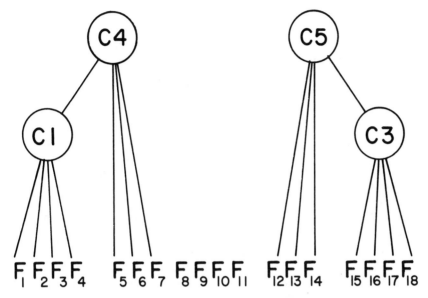

Figure 8.3. Second stage of model development.

data represent homogeneous traits, they are different from personality factors presently accounted for in C_1 or C_3. The model developer tries out the idea that another construct involving differences between a combative and a noncombative individual sport may be in order, and postulates C_4 to account for $F_5,...,F_7$. The modeler finds that C_4 adequately accounts for F_5, F_6, and F_7. In individual sports, then, it does make a difference whether the sport is combative or noncombative, so far as personality factors are concerned. With this success, the modeler postulates a similar construct, C_5, for team sports. At this point, the stage of model development is as shown in Figure 8.3.

It is seen that F_{12}, F_{13}, and F_{14} which were not accounted for by construct C_3 can be explained by C_5, which distinguishes between combative and noncombative team sports. Facts F_{12}, F_{13}, and F_{14} were data on football players—a combative team sport while $F_{15},...,F_{18}$ were data on noncombative team sports. Note that the postulation of C_4 and C_5 necessitated a revision in constructs C_1 and C_3. Another possible revision is that constructs C_1 and C_3, postulating team and individual sports, are more general or are of a higher order than C_4 and C_5 for combative and noncombative sports. Several possible rearrangements of the position of constructs and their linkage to facts might be in order. Such revisions, however, would be in the schematic representation of the model. The interested student is encouraged to create a personal schematic model for representation of the order and meaning of constructs. We shall retain the present schematic representation rather than invite confusion by realignments.

At this point, the model accounts for all facts except F_8, F_9, F_{10}, and F_{11}. Since such a situation exists, the model is not comprehensive. It suffers from the deficiency of not being able to account for F_8 through F_{11}. The model developer finds that these data represent facts about personality factors of participants in judo, gymnastics, horseback riding, and water polo. Supposedly, constructs C_1, (individual sports), C_3 (team sports), C_4 (combative versus noncombative individual sports), and C_5 (combative versus noncombative team sports) should be able to account for judo since it is an individual, combative sport; horseback riding and gymnastics are individual, noncombative sports; and water polo is a team and noncombative sport. But these facts (F_8, F_9, F_{10}, and F_{11}) are *not* explained by constructs C_1, C_3, and C_5. These facts are different from all others and seem to defy classification and accountability in the present model. Now what? The model developer studies these deviant facts, F_8, . . ., F_{11}, and it is realized that these facts are on *female* athletes. Aha! Then, perhaps, male or female makes a difference, and C_6, a sex construct, is postulated.

The scientist finds that by including C_6, a sex factor, the model can now account for F_8, which are data on female, individual-sport participants in the combative activity of judo; F_9, representing data on female participants in the individual and noncombative sport of gymnastics; and F_{11}, which represents data on female participants in the noncombative, team sport of water polo. The only deficiency left now is the unaccountability of F_{10}, data on female horseback riders. What can be done with these data? They do not "fit" into the model, and are a loose end. If the entire model is scrapped, some partial explanation of other facts is lost. If the decision is to modify the model to take F_{10} into account, how can it be done? One might just postulate a construct C_2 for horseback riders and acknowledge a deficiency in the model or lack of adequate data for further modeling. The present model is now represented in Figure 8.4.

The model has many advantages. It accounts for facts F_1 through F_{18} with the lone exception of F_{10}. Most models have such "loose ends" or conflicting data that do not fit. The history of science, however, has shown that only a new and better theory or model can overthrow a poorer one. If the presently postulated model can account for present facts, it has some advantages. We shall have to live with the disadvantages until a better model is proposed.

Investigators can then proceed to test the adequacy of the model in accounting for and predicting *new* data. Suppose a new fact F_{19} is produced. F_{19} concerns personality characteristics of participants in volleyball. Imagine, furthermore, that the personality characteristics of these

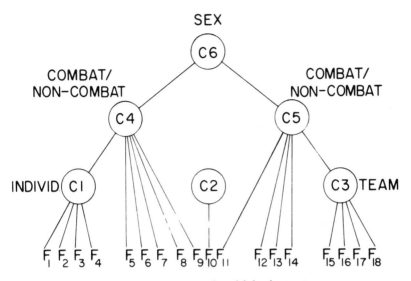

Figure 8.4. Late stage of model development.

male and female volleyball participants coincide with the data presented in our deviant F_{10}. F_{10} and F_{19} are now similar to each other, but different from all other F's in the system. The model developer now "sees" that maybe there are some athletic activities in which sex makes no difference. One incorporates this in C_2 which still stands by itself. It becomes a convenient catchall in which to assign unaccountable facts. Later, the nature of C_2 may be learned and a new construct forwarded.

Inherent in the model, via its constructs, are predictions of empirical data as yet unknown. Suppose someone asks what the personality characteristics are of female athletes participating in swimming. No data, imagine, are present as yet. The model, however, would predict that female swimmers should possess personality characteristics similar to those represented by F_9 since F_9 represents data on female (C_6), noncombative (C_4) individual (C_1) athletes. In the *absence* of any data, accepting the premise that swimmers' personalities were like F_9 would be reasonable. If a study were conducted and this were found to be true, further confidence in the validity of the model would result.

The researcher can now plan many studies with which to verify, refute, or revise the model. If the model is thoroughly validated it may be unnecessary to conduct new investigations. If an activity can be classified as being within the dimensions of the model, the personality characteristics of its participants can be predicted. Since the model would have been thoroughly validated with numerous correct predictions in similar circumstances, the predicted personality characteristics may be accepted *without* the necessity of actually measuring them.

Future development of the model may consider the relationship of the sex construct C_6 in the present model with sex constructs in *other* models. If some correspondence is suggested by a sex construct in occupational preferences and the C_6 sex construct in athletic personality, both models may be incorporated in a higher-order model. In a similar manner, the sex construct C_6 may be related to somatotype and sex characteristics. In this case, the somatotype construct may be introduced into the model domain, broadening the range of empirical data for which it can account, explain, and predict. As more and more separate models are shown to be interrelated, higher-order models can emerge. Each higher-order model is built upon lower-order models fashioning a monolithic structure. Thus, the interrelationships of an increasingly broad range of empirical data are encompassed. The use of models makes it possible to assimilate entire spectra of facts by the process of relating constructs instead of single, isolated facts.

OTHER POSSIBILITIES FOR MODELS

When physical education stops looking for simple answers to simple questions and seeks, instead, simple answers to complex questions, it will need to make fuller use of the scientific method. It is unfortunate but true that to postulate simple answers to simple questions represents a poor approach to employ as a means of advancement. A simple answer to a simple question asked because of some particular applied situation may have some immediate utilitarian value. Poor answers to trivial questions are more often the likely outcome.

An even greater tragedy occurs when investigations of important questions are conducted but the investigator is unaware of both the true meaning of the problem being studied and the requirements of an important answer. Franklin Henry (1) spoke of such a situation when he pleaded for better scholarship in research reports. Henry used the example of reaction time, reflex time, and speed in sprint running. These factors represent important scientific areas for research. His critique of an article published in the *Research Quarterly* in this area admonished the authors for not paying sufficient attention to prior research and of being unaware of the existence of a more powerful, more general model.

In a companion article, Slater-Hammel (6) pointed out the inevitable deficiencies that result in research investigations which are poorly conceived, with formal inadequacies, as well as investigations that are well-conceived but on rather meaningless questions. His criticisms were directed at research in the important area of strength development. Slater-Hammel's major objection was to haphazard combinations of important factors (such as number of repetitions, muscle loading, and recovery time) in such a manner as to doom the investigation to failure at the outset.

Implicit in both the Henry and Slater-Hammel articles are criticisms of the manner in which the scientific method was employed by researchers. Henry decried the absence of proper knowledge of previous facts and theories when investigators attempted to interpret their data. Postulation of a new model carried with it the responsibility of accounting for both old data and new data better than previous models. If researchers are unaware of or ignore previous facts and models, Henry argues, their new models can hardly be called sophisticated. Such research is either done in ignorance or ignorantly. Henry's criticisms are, thus, focused on step (1) (induction and the creation of a model) and step (3) (evaluation of the adequacy of a new model).

Similarly, Slater-Hammel's criticisms center around inadequate application of step (2) in the scientific method—the collection of new data on the basis of predictions inherent in the model. Investigations which suffer from basic inadequacies in experimental design cannot elicit knowledge essential to the verification or refutation of a model. A researcher must have the capacity to see implicit predictions inherent in the model and then to design an experiment to produce results that can be interpreted meaningfully in terms of that model. Thus, an investigation can be conducted that studies important predictions of a model but whose experimental design is inadequate; or an investigation can be conducted whose experimental design is formally adequate but is done on trivial, meaningless, or incorrect predictions inherent in the model being investigated. Both such events, according to Slater-Hammel, constitute "bad" research.

In essence, these two articles by Henry and by Slater-Hammel are critiques directed at one or more steps in the scientific method as employed by researchers in physical education. The ability to judge the merit of research demands knowledge of the scientific method per se. The student or neophyte researcher is often unable to judge the merit of research in the *Research Quarterly* because he or she suffers from inadequacies in knowledge of the scientific method *and* is unfamiliar with models in physical education research. The "average reader" of the *Research Quarterly* may not recognize good research when it does appear and is likely to call poor research good research.

The utilization of theoretical models and the scientific method for the advancement of knowledge constitutes the *modus operandi* in all the basic sciences. In more primitive and less defined knowledge areas, the so-called quasi-sciences that are bidding for recognition, a vigorous and massive effort is underway to search for methodological techniques with which to quantify phenomena in their content domain and strive for a sound knowledge structure. Unless the consumer of research efforts at either of these levels of science understands the goals being pursued, the research being produced will not be understood or appreciated. Simple research articles understood by the majority of all *Research Quarterly* readers could very well represent a research effort of questionable value. An article understood by only a small minority of readers, on the other hand, could represent a contribution to knowledge of tremendous significance that can be appreciated only when one understands the knowledge structure. Only knowledgeable readers can hope to evaluate the "importance" of research published in their field.

REFERENCES

1. Henry, Franklin M. A plea for better scholarship in research reports. *Research Quarterly* **31**: 234-236; May 1960.

2. Henry, Franklin M., and Donald E. Rogers. Increased response latency for complicated movements and a "memory drum" theory of neuromotor reaction. *Research Quarterly* **31**: 448-458; October 1960.

3. Margenau, H. *The Nature of Physical Reality*. New York: McGraw-Hill, 1950.

4. Paillard, Jacques. The patterning of skilled movements. In *Handbook of Physiology-Neurophysiology*. Washington, D.C.: American Physiological Association, 1960. Pp. 1679-1708.

5. Popper, Karl R. *The Poverty of Historicism*. New York: Harper, 1964.

6. Slater-Hammel, Arthur T. Research on muscle development. *Research Quarterly* **31**: 236-238; May 1960.

Unscientific Problems in the Development of a Scientific Model

9

Previous chapters outlining the general characteristics of science and the scientific method might lead many people to conclude that scientific research was an emotionless quest for hard facts through the use of rigid and standardized procedures. Facts are seldom hard and cold, however, and workers in science are endowed with enthusiasm and other human traits just as their counterparts in the arts. Indeed, the fascination and demands of science force scientists to call upon several "nonscientific" resources and act out a role quite foreign to the stereotyped images assigned to them by the public. In this chapter we shall consider some events in scientific research that are usually hidden behind the scenes and are seldom appreciated by the layman. To illustrate such unscientific problems in scientific research, the task of developing a model has been chosen in the hope that the quest for knowledge may be shown as a personal and warm challenge to the human intellect.

POSTULATION OF THE MODEL

At the outset, the model developer is at a particular disadvantage because no one knows which data are pertinent. The complete model, as yet unknown, may be highly complex with many interacting variables. The model developer may simply "guess" what data are relevant and make a selection of available data on that basis. Such guesses are naturally conditioned by many factors. Prior knowledge concerning similar phenomena, the insight or intellectual brilliance of the scientist, or simple chance may operate in the decision as to which data merit consideration. Once the data are selected, however, the model developer has a more difficult task. The model developer must provide order and meaning, account for, explain, and make predictions within the domain of the data. Accomplishing this feat is an entirely private matter. How the model was arrived at is not important; how the model fulfills its task is.

Many of the major advances in science have been made by individuals who, seemingly, jumped from an examination of the data to a sound explanation without following any visible steps of reason or logic. The fact that such intellectual leaps from data to sound theory have occurred so regularly in science accounts for the many attempts to forward some explanation of the phenomenon itself. Furthermore, the kinds of explanation which have been offered attest to the quite unscientific nature of the event that we have called model postulation. Eccles (6) terms such an event as due to insight. Dubois (5) describes them as dreams of reason, while Walker (16) calls the initial postulation of a model an act of creation. Larrabee (13) considered the initial postulation of a model to be a combination of past experience and imagination which he called disciplined imagination. Another philosopher of science disagrees with such quasi-mystical explanations and contends there is a logical pattern to be found in the establishment of new theories. Hanson (10) offers the thesis that sudden insights, when they occur, are analogous to the phenomenon associated with looking at reversible perspective figures so common in psychology texts on perception. A person sees one pattern which suddenly seems to reverse and another pattern is then seen. According to Hanson, sudden insight in science, alluded to by others as an explanation for the origin of theories, is nothing more than seeing the conceptual pattern as a whole or in a more efficient manner than before.

A fine example of the personal nature of such inductive leaps in science, from data to conclusion, can be illustrated by the comments Jacques Monod made concerning his research, which earned the Nobel prize in physiology or medicine. Monod relates his reading of an investigation on biosynthesis of protein from amino acids. The interpretation forwarded in the article was novel. Monod (14) stated that his belief about the solution to his problem was quite firm even though evidence for his belief was not available. But, Monod continued, a firm belief and strong inner conviction were necessary if a scientist were to have the patience necessary to establish the certainty of his beliefs. Later, Monod cites stumbling upon an important solution by accident while they were looking for something different. His early attempts at theory construction were far from being accepted, but his conviction had been established long before the absolute proof for the validity of his theory could be secured.

This particular aspect of the development of a model—its initial postulation—has been a topic of some concern for centuries. Many times, a major advance in science has come about through the discovery of a new way to account for facts already in evidence, rather than the sensational discovery of new facts. Such achievements intrigued people at a very early date and motivated them to search for an understanding of how such intellectual accomplishments were realized. If humans could understand the mechanism of intellect, it was reasoned, then humans could arrange for conditions to exist that were optimally conducive to intellectual achievement. In very early times, the problem was considered to be one requiring an analysis of thinking as a cognitive process. Philosophers sought to understand understanding, know knowledge, and explain explanation. Such work by philosophers is called descriptive epistemology. Although a philosophy of knowledge seems alien to scientific research, knowledge of the nature of mental processes is implicit in any attempt to understand the manner in which initial postulation of a scientific model is accomplished.

THE STRUCTURE OF KNOWLEDGE

Many of the explanations forwarded for knowledge and understanding in epistemology were based on obvious chronological sequences, from early and simple to later and complex stages. In his treatise "On Knowing," Aristotle (384-322 B.C.) sought to describe the phenomena. Aristotle observed that human beings were endowed with certain faculties for perception. When exposed to certain stimuli, these faculties or senses resulted in *sense-perceptions*. Other human faculties functioned to preserve such sense-perceptions as *memory*. After many such memories of similar sense-perceptions accumulated, humans had the capacity to classify them as *experiences*. Aristotle allowed that some living creatures below the status of humans were capable of "knowing" up to this level. The next levels, however, were thought to be uniquely reserved for human beings. Aristotle supposed that humans "must possess a capacity of some sort" which enabled them through *art* to derive a universal judgment about the many experiences they possessed. Such a universal judgment was, of course, accomplished by inductive methods through exercise of that "capacity of some sort." Aristotle also added the capacity for *reasoning* above this level of art and concluded that "intuition will be the originative source of scientific knowledge."

Centuries later, David Hume (1711-1776) wrote on understanding:

> But if you insist that the inference is made by a chain of reasoning, I desire you to produce that reasoning. The connexion between these propositions is not intuitive. There is required a medium, which may enable the mind to draw such an inference,

if indeed it be drawn by reasoning and argument. What the medium is, I must confess, passes my comprehension; and it is incumbent on those to produce it, who assert that it really exists, and is the origin of all our conclusions concerning matter of fact (12, page 32).

Clearly, the use of terms such as "art," "capacity of some sort," or "intuition" offered by Aristotle and a "required medium" offered by Hume are no better or worse than insight, dreams of reason, or acts of creation to explain the process responsible for the initial postulation of a model via induction.

The postulation of a model is often very unlike the commonly held conception of a scientific method in action, that is, guided by a formal, logical, and straightforward exercise of scientific thinking. Scientists are more often not logically perfect. They may, in fact, make large use of subjective opinions and hunches. They may jump about aimlessly in such efforts, flounder about in a sea of messy data, and contrive even messier experiments. Scientists may consider many ideas, some of which are contrary to known facts, but will persist in such dogged efforts rejecting the authority of logic, common sense, sound advice, and even be subjected to ridicule. Such stubborn strength and perseverance may even be characteristic of the gifted scientist and reflect ". . . the unusual and often deviant system of values of the independent thinkers" (7, page 170).

Hence, contrary to the public illusion, scientists may be unsystematic, illogical, emotional, hunch players, unfamiliar with the scientific literature, narrow-minded, and preoccupied with pet ideas labeled unimportant by learned colleagues. They may be viewed as dreamers with brains who need to be watched. If scientists are successful, however, the private maze-running will be reported publicly as a concise, formal, and straightforward scientific investigation. Albert Svent-Gyorgi once stated that the difference between the actual research activity—complete with deadends and ridiculous side trips—and the final report is a reflection of the investigator's personality (or honesty). The crucial difference between such a scientist and the village nincompoop, however, is that the scientist doggedly verifies hypotheses by experimentation. Science has a built in self-destruct mechanism called verification by experiment.

Consumers of research see mostly the finished product. Published research, however, represents only the successful endeavors of scientists. Hidden away in a researcher's file, one would find the unsuccessful research attempts—unsuccessful because of unworkable apparatus designs, faulty experimental controls, poor subjects, and poor ideas. These private files are seldom publicly exposed. It is mostly through personal contact, correspondence, visits to a laboratory, or informal conversations at conventions that the scientific researcher can be known as a recognizable human being instead of a logically perfect scientific computer.

None of this should suggest that the optimum method for postulating theories or models is to sit and wait for an inspiration. Although inspiration may be responsible for the end product, some things are necessary beforehand. In the first place the facts present in the model domain must be known. The model developer must have knowledge of these facts. The model developer must make preparation, by diligent attention to facts, become intimate with such facts, and think about these facts. The model developer must become familiar with prior attempts at model development in the content domain and be able to recognize the deficiencies and advantages in each. Conscious attempts at model postulation may not bring initial success, but knowledge of facts and attempts at postulation seem to be precursors to intellectual leaps, sudden insights, and divine inspirations.

The act of postulating a model or theory is step (1) in the scientific method and is typically referred to as scientific thinking. Whether such activity as demanded in step (1) is scientific or not can certainly be debated. More than in other steps, creativity is at a premium in the postulation of a model. It is usually here that "scientific breakthroughs" are given birth, here new ideas are born and later tested. Talent in scientific thinking, however inadequately defined, is an essential component and is as necessary to the scientific method as any other step or talent.

THE BLACK BOX IN SCIENCE

The preceding sections have shown several difficulties to be present when one attempts to be successful at step (1) of the scientific method. The hypothesizing or initial postulation of a model is not a straightforward procedure which can be programmed at will. There are similar difficulties in the succeeding steps, awaiting the user of the scientific method. The question of what "accounting for" and "explaining" means is at the root of one of these problems. Quite a historical controversy exists over the criteria upon which the accounting for and explanation of data (or nature) can be judged. In philosophy of science, the phrase "black-box theory of science" refers to several elements in this controversy. The black box theory of science exemplifies a basic problem of considerable significance in scientific research. What constitutes an adequate scientific explanation? Implicit in such a question is the need to examine the purpose of science itself, for until an adequate explanation of nature is achieved, science cannot be said to have fulfilled its goals.

Let us consider a situation involving the need for explanation and see if we can appreciate the issues involved with the black-box theory of science. When a six-year-old boy asks his mother where he came from, he may be satisfied with the answer that God sent him to earth from heaven. When an unsure father finally has a man-to-man talk with his adolescent son about the birds and the bees, he needs a little more detail in his treatment of sex. A medical professor lecturing on pregnancy and childbirth to a class of senior medical students would be likely to present an even more detailed account. A research scientist seeking new information on the genesis of life might make use of any and all such known facts in the search for new knowledge.

Now, each of these situations may serve as examples of different reference frameworks for organizing an explanation of sex. One might allow that the different explanations illustrated are not equally satisfactory as the best and most true explanation. Certain differences in the quality of the explanations seem in evidence, and it might be possible to rank the various explanations in order of their quality or degree of acceptability to science. The medical professor, for example, would undoubtedly present a fuller, more coherent, and intelligible presentation of sex than the father would in his talk about the birds and the bees. It would also be reasonable to expect that the research scientist's explanation would reflect an even higher echelon of sophistication so far as knowledge of sex is concerned.

Each of the situations described could be likened to developmental stages of knowledge or science, or both. Hence, the answer that "God sent him to earth" is analogous, in some measure, to the tribal medicine man's explanations of strange occurrences as being due to angry spirits. The unknown is explained away by allusion to an even greater but emotionally unchallengeable power. The father's advice would probably include enough carefully chosen facts of life to convince the young man of the advisability of ordering his sexual activities in accordance with prescribed social mores. The medical professor would present the cold facts of anatomy and physiology, including only enough reference to moral and spiritual issues to comply with medical and legal ethics. Of course, the epitome is reached with the research scientist. Although confronted with some seemingly unexplainable facts, the scientist remains firm in an adherence to a strictly objective, scientific, unbiased, and unattached explanation of the workings of nature in the subject matter domain of sex.

The philosopher of science, and the scientists themselves, are seemingly not all entirely satisfied with the last explanation as the true purpose of science. This dissatisfaction is embodied in the controversy over the black-box theory of science. Succinctly stated, the controversy involves the question of whether the nature or purpose of science is merely to describe factual situations or whether the boundaries of science also include the need to offer an explanation of these situations with an eye to the ultimate, value-loaded: "Why?"

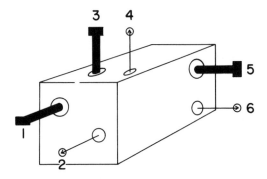

Figure 9.1. A black box.

Some scientists steadfastly claim that the true purpose of science is to describe nature in a strictly operational manner; that is, to describe only the process and its observable components. According to this position, science has no obligation to contemplate the meaning of these processes, only to describe them. Thus, as Bridgman puts it, "It is possible to analyze nature into correlations, without, however any assumption whatever as to the character of these correlations" (3, page 37). Such inquiries as—Is there a purpose to life? Why are some species of life short-lived and others long-lived? Is nature organized?—are all considered meaningless questions by operationalists.

Different kinds of explanations are thus possible even in science. Which kind of explanation is the most acceptable in science has been the basis for a long controversy that is still not settled. Our previous examples of different approaches to an explanation of sex served as a good introduction to this continuing debate. Now let us consider the classical example used to illustrate this black-box theory of science. Figure 9.1 shows a simple box, painted black, which has several different sized holes in it and several different sized pieces of string hanging out of these holes.

Now suppose we consider this black box as representing a set of empirical data and we want to account for, explain, and predict its nature. We note that it is rectangular and that small strings come out of the small holes and thicker strings come out of the larger holes. We pull string 1 out three inches and observe that string 3 goes three inches into the box. We pull string 3 out three inches and string 1 goes back into the box three inches. String 1 and 3 must be the same string merely going through the box! Good, strings 1 and 3 must be ends of the same piece of thick string. String 5, however, is thick and it has no corresponding thick string coming out of the box elsewhere. We pull string 5 out of the box six inches and note that string 2 recedes into the box six inches. When we pull string 2 back out six inches, string 5 recedes six inches back into the box. We conclude 2 and 5 represent ends of the same piece of string, going through the box, and that it is tapered, being thick at 5 and thinner at 2. Good, so far. Our explanation seems reasonable. Now we look at 4 and 6. If our explanations for 1 and 3 and for 2 and 5 are reasonable, what shall we expect for 4 and 6? Since 4 and 6 are both thin and come out of small holes, it would be reasonable to expect that 4 and 6 are ends of the same size string going through the box. We pull 6 out two inches. According to expectations end 4 should go into the box two inches. Unfortunately, end 4 remains where it is and number 2 goes back into the box two inches. End 2, however, we decided, was the other end of 5. Our explanation has hit a snag, or has it?

It is clear that by pulling all numbered strings in all possible ways we could describe exactly what happens. We would merely chronicle the results of pulling 1 out six inches, 6 out two inches, etc. If, in many such trials, the results were always identical for the same action we would have an adequate description of action (cause) and result (effect). Would such a description satisfy as an accounting for, explanation of, and prediction of the empirical phenomena, or would someone ask, "What is inside the black box?"

The black box could contain a complicated system of levers and gears and we might develop a blueprint of a gear system capable of "explaining" the results of pulling strings. It might well be, however, that a trained white rat is inside the box. Whenever a string is pulled the rat responds because of training by pulling another string. Geldard, speaking at a symposium on the principles of sensory communication, commented on the problem in the development of a model:

> ... There is much talk of 'black boxes,' some feeling safer when they get inside them whatever the complexity encountered, others concerned with more remote terms, either as a matter of preoccupation with broad psychophysical reactions or in the pretense that the box is empty (9, page 73).

A similar situation holds with our present black box and its holes and strings. If one could chronicle the action of myriad string-pulling and be able to predict the results perfectly, would this suffice as a model? Such a description might be called inadequate because it does not provide an explanation of what is inside the box. Faced with another black box, would our accounting of the first black box be of any use in accounting for the second black box? If not, our explanation seems inadequate since we cannot incorporate the new black box into our model. The principle of reductionism, one of our operational codes in science, would be unrealized.

Scientists may feign being unconcerned with and unobligated to making the why of nature and scientific facts compatible with some purpose for existence, but the intriguing question pervades the human consciousness anyway. The task of going behind stubborn fact to seek meaning and make these ends compatible may be ascribed to the philosopher, but the scientist will entertain the question even if its deliberation is excluded from formal research reports. Humans have always been compelled to look inside the black box and will not be satisfied with a mere description of what happens—human curiosity will always ask, "Why?"

Cold-fact scientists may proclaim the task of science as mere description and correlation, and then escape from further entanglements by a disguised retreat. Even in retreat, however, scientists play a waiting game, and, as soon as definite patterns become apparent in the data, they leap to the task and offer a more adequate explanation, unifying many facts with a deep satisfaction for such an accomplishment. For, as soon as scientists stop being photographers of facts and become committed to utilization of theory, they step into the difficult path channeled toward an end goal requiring an answer to "Why?" Such a path, representing in some ways a qualitative hierarchy of knowledge, is presented in Figure 9.2.

Supposedly, scientists would like to stop before arriving at the concept of nature. Unfortunately, as soon as they leave factual presentation, further progress is impossible without use of all the remaining steps. The fact that science must accept its metaphysical foundations in order to function is ample testimony to this argument. Unless scientists accept the fact that nature is intelligible to humans, that it is consistent, and that determinism is inherent in nature—why would science undertake any study of nature?

We can now better understand the difficulties in deciding upon what constitutes an adequate scientific explanation. The problem may be answerable only by mutual consent; that is, by accepting some forwarded position statement. In many respects, the controversy does much to exemplify the relationships between science and philosophy. One can see why some scholars contend that if science existed without philosophy, science would be a dull, sterile, and useless endeavor. Philosophy without the basis of a science would lack the factual foundation upon which to begin its quest for ultimate truth.

CATEGORIES OF EXPLANATION

Perhaps we can help resolve our difficulties with the black-box theory of science by some further attention to the question of what constitutes an adequate explanation. Philosophers have been concerned with knowledge, the meaning of knowledge, and related topics under the heading of epistemology, or the study of knowledge. Although scientific research is objective and deals with hard, cold facts, we did allow previously that

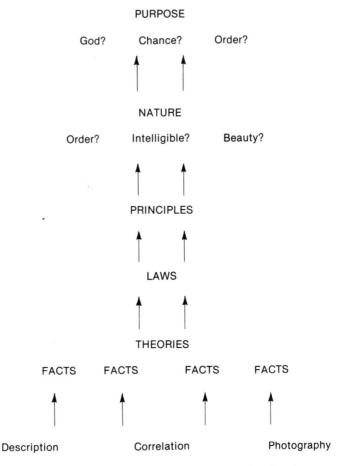

Figure 9.2. A continuum of levels of knowledge and explanation.

science had some unscientific or metaphysical foundations. We also accepted the presence of an operating code in science as well. Additional attention to another realm of a philosophical nature may not, then, upset scientific researchers too much. The black box and our problem of explanation may be settled or confused even more, but action of any nature might result in advances being made. Besides, there may not be any other alternatives.

Over a long period of time, different "explanations" offered have been analyzed and a kind of a classification scheme (model?) for explanations has been developed. The categories of terminology for explanations are not exact. Philosophy, after all, is not monolithic in structure as is science, and we are undisturbed by irregularities in philosophical "models" whereas irregularities in scientific models are inexcusable. One possible set of categories for explanations is as follows:

Description

Some believe that to describe accurately and completely constitutes an adequate explanation. Thus, the scientist is assumed to be merely a photographer of nature. Our example of the black box is one illustration of how a simple description might be used as a means of explanation. Very often, careful description of a phenomenon appears to be the only method of explanation possible. Such is the case for new frontiers of knowledge where very little framework for a knowledge structure exists.

Familiarization

In this category, if one can liken an unfamiliar fact with a fact (or facts) that is (are) familiar, explanation is achieved. If a new tropical fruit were discovered, the explanation that it was a cross between a watermelon and an orange might fulfill the requirements of satisfactory explanation. Knowing that the new fruit was a cross between two familiar fruits would, indeed, give us some indication of its properties since we have knowledge of the properties of watermelons and oranges. The use of analogies is a common method of using familiarization as an explanation as is the use of examples. (The student may ask where the knowledge about watermelons and oranges came from.)

Labeling

If one says that play has been universally observed in many cultures throughout the ages because play is instinctive, a natural need, or a drive, labeling has been used as a method of explanation (8, page 634). Our knowledge about play, of course, depends upon our knowledge about instinct, natural need, and drive. If our knowledge about instinct, natural need, and drive is poor—that is, if our explanations of these phenomena are unsatisfactory—we have gained very little by the use of labeling as a method of explanation. Labeling may be a convenient means of shifting ignorance from one place to another.

Teleology

Teleology represents a doctrine or belief that a fact is such because it fulfills an end or a purpose. A fact is a fact because it fits into the design of the whole. A teleological explanation implies purpose. As an explanation of empirical phenomena, it assumes a purpose for nature as a whole, some end-purpose and design being implicit. The vitalist doctrine that life is not determined exclusively by physical cause and effect but by the fulfillment of some master plan for nature as a whole is consistent with teleological explanations. The vitalist doctrine, and hence teleology, are in opposition to a strict mechanistic or physical cause and effect as explanation of nature. Entelechy, as well as vitalism and teleology, implies a nonmechanical cause as responsible for the phenomena in nature.

The following are examples of explanations saturated with teleological overtones:

A chicken crossed the road to get to the other side.

A top spins because it would fall over if it did not.

"I believe it was Epictetus, the Stoic, who was reported as saying, 'God gave man two ears, but only one mouth that he might hear twice as much as he speaks'" (4, page 99).

Aristotle began his treatise "On Knowing" with the statement, "All men by nature desire to know."

Teleological explanations do not occupy a prestigious position in science because of two major deficiencies: The first is that a teleological explanation implicitly connotes the ability of future events to act in their own behalf at an earlier date; in other words, the outcome is capable of anticipating itself and providing suitable conditions for its own genesis. Such an implicit feature of teleological explanations forwards the notion that an effect is capable of producing the cause, and is something less than tolerable to most scientists. The sun, for example, does not produce tides on earth because the beach wants to rid itself periodically of its debris; and the moon does not circle the earth so that all parts of the world can enjoy its presence at harvest moon festivals. In addition, and most importantly, if future events are endowed with the capacity to ensure their own genesis, then this capacity of future events merits endowment with some identity and some purpose. Since the future event allegedly arranges for its own realization, it has been endowed with possession of a master plan and the power to cause all empirical events to occur in accordance with this master plan. Typically, such a power has been called a god, the Creator, or Nature.

This last characteristic of a teleological explanation, the endowment of future events with a plan to control the destiny of all empirical events to its own ends, represents the second major deficiency. It is, of course, related to the first and is equally untenable to the majority of scientists. As attested to by the examples of teleological explanations previously cited, the kinds of explanations that a teleological approach can produce are often ludicrous and immediately recognizable as superstitious nonsense.

At about this time, most students would be ready to disavow the worth of teleology in their future research endeavors. Before making such a commitment, however, let us consider the role of teleological explanations for phenomena that are commonly studied by physical educators in their own scientific research endeavors. Afterward it will be interesting to see if a change was made in the evaluation of this category of explanation or not.

Example 1. Physical educators have frequently studied anxiety states in athletes prior to actual competition. The emphasis in such studies has been to collect data on parameters relevant to anxiety such as galvanic skin response, anticipatory heart rate, systolic and diastolic blood pressure, and questionnaire-type written tests as an index of emotional state of mind. Such pre-event data on athletes are then compared to actual competitive performances and conclusions are drawn regarding the relationships existing between the two categories. Several studies have shown, for example, that if no state of anxiety whatsoever exists in an athlete prior to competition, performance is less than optimal. In a similar manner, if pre-event anxiety is present at an extreme level, then competitive performance is, likewise, poorer than could be expected from the individual. Precompetitive anxiety, furthermore, is affected by continued experience in athletics, and the best performer eventually exhibits a level of precompetitive anxiety most conducive to superior performance.

Built into the frame of reference within which conclusions are formulated in such studies is the thesis that participation in an athletic event is capable of affecting the preanxiety state to be found in the athlete before the next contest; and, indeed, that different kinds of athletic events or the same athletic event at a different date are capable of affecting the preanxiety state differentially; that is, an unimportant contest would affect the preanxiety state differently than an important one, and some forms of athletics affect the preanxiety state more or less than others. If this is so, then is it the case that the athletic event acts to modify the preanxiety state in its participants so as to ensure optimum performance? Is an athletic contest a representative of a future event that is capable of controlling empirical events prior to its own existence and toward its own ends or not?

Example 2. A constant body temperature of 98.6 degrees Farenheit represents the balance, in humans, between heat generating (thermogenic) and heat-dissipating (thermolytic) mechanisms of the body. At rest, seldom will the normal body temperature vary more than one degree in any 24-hour period because of the effectiveness of this heat regulatory system. It is indeed fortunate that such a heat regulatory system exists, because heat due to metabolism alone would produce an increase of 4 degrees Farenheit in body temperature each hour if heat-dissipating mechanisms failed to function properly. Even the simple task of walking would double or triple the amount of metabolic heat produced by the body. The importance of thermolytic mechanisms to humans is readily appreciated.

Now, if an individual, without prior exposure to a hot and humid condition is made to exercise vigorously in such an environment, it would force the heat-regulatory system into operation. The hypothalamus is said to function as a physiologic thermostat and alter, depending upon thermal requirements of the body, the rate of heat-generating and heat-dissipating mechanisms. In the case of the exercising individual, modification of the rate of action of the heat-dissipating mechanisms is essential. Vasodilation of surface skin-vessels is effected to bring about an increased blood flow through the skin and allow a better heat transfer. Again, under control of the thalamus, an increase in sweat production occurs in an attempt to cool the body by evaporation. As we all know, however, the heat-regulatory mechanisms are apt to operate inefficiently in an individual who has not been previously "acclimatized," and heat stroke is a threat to life.

After acclimatization, however, the heat-regulatory mechanisms are decidedly more efficient. An individual who has been acclimatized to hot and humid conditions and begins vigorous exercise: (1) begins sweat production at a lower skin temperature; (2) produces more sweat per sweat gland; and (3) is capable of producing a greater sweat output in conjunction with a diminished loss of salt content in the sweat. The resultant effect is for work to be accomplished in a hot and humid climate with a lower heart rate and body temperature than was possible before acclimatization. The physiologist of exercise would refer to such a phenomenon as an example of the principle of homeostasis in which the body utilizes mechanisms necessary to restore the body to an optimal state.

Heat acclimatization by the body seems to demand a teleological explanation. Why do the mechanisms responsible for heat-regulation respond to exposure of the body to hot and humid conditions by developing an ability in the sweat glands to produce more sweat with less salt loss and to begin sweating at a lower skin temperature? Why should heat-regulatory mechanisms change so as to afford greater tolerance to the hot and humid conditions of the future? Why is it not reasonable to expect the heat-regulatory mechanisms of the body to fail even more dramatically when next exposed to the obvious trauma of excessive heat and humidity? Is exposure to heat representative of a future event capable of controlling and modifying bodily mechanisms so as to anticipate its future existence?

If the two examples used have had any effect upon the reader it was probably to cause reassessment of the value of teleology as a legitimate category of explanation. Such an effect is not surprising, since there are some individuals who present rather forceful arguments for the use of teleological arguments in biology. Ayala, for example, claimed that several kinds of teleological explanations could not be "reformulated in nonteleological form without loss of explanatory content" (1, pages 212-213). In fact, he contended that teleological explanations were absolutely essential in biology and actually constituted a distinctive feature of biology as a natural science when contrasted with any of the physical sciences. His paper in the *American Scientist* discusses the ways in which suitable teleological explanations can be used in biology without incurring either of the two major deficiencies of teleological explanations previously discussed. He argues rather effectively for this point as well as contending that teleological explanations in biology are completely compatible with mechanistic explanations. This argument, however, would require more space for consideration than can be given here. The reader, however, is challenged to concoct an argument for such compatibility and then read Ayala's paper to see how close to agreement the two arguments come.

Without too much difficulty, one can appreciate the attractiveness of teleological explanations; and an attitude toward nature somewhat compatible with teleology is not completely absent in literature familiar to physical educators. Eldred (2), a renowned neuroanatomist, asked ". . . why there should be more than one intrafusal fibre of each type in a spindle? It seems to me that just one nuclear-bag and one nuclear-chain intrafusal fibre could perform the same function as the two or more of each type we do find." Ragnar Granit answered, "One will have to ask the Creator" (2). A.V. Hill (11) expressed his disbelief of a then accepted theory that lactic acid was combusted each time it was formed merely to get rid of it. Lactic acid, he believed, must have some other important function since it represented a considerable amount of energy and combustion of lactic acid merely to get rid of it placed a heavy load on the circulatory and respiratory systems. According to Hill, ". . . the design of muscles is not so stupid as that."

Mechanism

A mechanistic explanation emphasizes the logical steps leading to the observed phenomenon. The occurrence of needed events is depicted in such a straightforward manner that the end result is anticipated by knowing its antecedents. In many respects, it amounts to a series of descriptive statements presented in some logical order such as spatial or temporal.

Cause-and-effect links are essential. Each effect must be shown to be the progeny of some cause. Such a scheme requiring a geneological tree to explain any event has been called causal ancestry. Each son, or effect, must have had some father, or cause. No bachelors are allowed. Hanson (10, page 65) suggests that the present-day esteem given to mechanistic explanations is due to the fact that the first important scientific theories came from astronomy and mechanics. Inherent in mechanistic explanations are the requirements for a regular succession of cause-and-effect links to form a causal-chain with which to explain observed events. Such an inexpugnable belief is, of course, determinism. Each present event must be correlated with pertinent antecedents.

THE USE OF EXPLANATION

Now consider an explanation of baldness. After each item included in the explanation follows a classification of the method used.

Baldness is hereditary (labeling). It occurs naturally (labeling) with aging (labeling) in men, but is seldom seen in women (description). Adherents of evolutionary theory point out that primitive humans possessed large quantities of hair over their body as protection against the elements (teleological or mechanistic?). As humans progressed to a higher form of life, their need for protection against the elements decreased and, hence, so has the need for hair covering the body (teleological) like animals (familiarization or teleological, or both). Since women do not grow bald, but men do, it is striking evidence that the male of the human species is far advanced over the female in intellectual maturation (?????).

If "explanations" of data resulting from scientific experiments are examined, they will be found to be classifiable under one of the categories of explanation presented. Which of the categories of explanations is (are) the best way to explain data? If the mechanistic category is chosen, remember one way that the black box could be explained. It is doubtful that the student was "satisfied" with an explanation that consisted of perfect predictions alone, no matter how accurate.

If mechanistic explanations are best and are achieved through the scientific method, we have another consideration. Karl R. Popper (15) contends that theories are nothing more than the residue left after a process of elimination. One hypothesis is forwarded but is refuted by experimental investigation. Another hypothesis which is not refuted by data is forwarded. Thus, by a process of elimination, satisfactory theories (and, thus, explanations of data) are developed; and the method of selection by elimination is nothing more than trial and error!

CHARACTERISTICS OF A GOOD EXPLANATION

During the sixteenth and seventeenth centuries, it was the common practice to examine evidence (or explanations) in "the natural light of reason." People would, under this scheme, judge the presence of innate truths by an appeal to intuition. Students may not accept an explanation as "good" if it is said to have stood the test in the natural light of reason. They might justifiably ask, " Just what is the natural light of reason?" Just what is a good explanation? There do not appear to be too many alternatives left.

Before having been subjected to the thorny issues of science, scientific research and scientific method, students might have felt that an explanation was "good" if it were sound, logical, accurate, meaningful, or clear. By now, students will look at such answers and think: labeling, familiarization, description, and dismiss these answers as unacceptable. The task of evaluating the adequacy of models is as much of a Gordian knot as was its initial postulation. Also, are not the issues involved in the initial postulation of a model [step (1) in the scientific method] similar or identical to those of evaluating its adequacy [step (3)]?

Hanson states, "Nothing can be explained to us if we do not help." Prior knowledge seems to be essential before a new event can be explained. New events are explained by backtracking through known cause-and-effect links, and constructing a causal chain. If any of the links are unknown, new causal chains are presented. If the explainer cannot find cause-and-effect links with which the person is familiar, there can be no explanation. An explanation, therefore, may require description, familiarization, labeling, teleology, and mechanistic methods. Aristotle's sense-perceptions, memory, and experiences may be prerequisites. An explanation must render intelligible the particular phenomenon under consideration. Such an explanation must not refute known facts, but must be compatible with them. Typically, the explanation proceeds from the known and travels to the unknown.

What, then, does constitute a reasonable explanation? The answer is quite simple—an explanation that is reasonable. If users of the explanation accept it as reasonable, it qualifies as a good explanation. Each portion of the explanation must satisfy users. No falsehoods can be present. In the end, a reasonable explanation *satisfies*. The more learned an individual, the more it will take for an explanation to satisfy. The kind of an explanation asked for and the kind of an explanation accepted as reasonable places as much responsibility upon the questioner as it does upon the answerer. Even the best mechanistic explanation may be enhanced by a little teleology.

REFERENCES

1. Ayala, Francisco J. Biology as an autonomous science. *American Scientist* **56**: 207-221; 1968.

2. Barker, David (ed.). *Symposium on Muscle Receptors.* Hong Kong: Hong Kong Univ. Press, 1962.

3. Bridgman, Percy Williams. *The Logic of Modern Physics.* New York: Macmillan, 1927.

4. Cherry, Colin. Two ears—but one world. In *Sensory Communication*, Walter A. Rosenblith (ed.). Cambridge, Massachusetts: M.I.T. Press, 1961.

5. Dubos, Rene. *The Dreams of Reason.* New York: Columbia Univ. Press, 1961.

6. Eccles, J.C. The physiology of imagination. *Scientific American* **199**: 135-146; September 1958.

7. Education for research in psychology. *American Psychologist* **14**: 167-179; April 1959.

8. Frederickson, Florence Stumpf. Sports and cultures of men. In *Science and Medicine of Exercise and Sports*, Warren R. Johnson (ed.). New York: Harper, 1960.

9. Geldard, Frank A. Cutaneous channels of communications. In *Sensory Communication*, Walter A. Rosenblith (ed.). Cambridge: M.I.T. Press, 1961.

10. Hanson, N.R. *Patterns of Discovery.* Cambridge: Cambridge Univ. Press, 1958.

11. Hill, A.V. The heat production of muscle and nerve, 1848-1914. *Annual Review of Physiology* **21**: 1-18; 1959.

12. Hume, David. Knowledge and induction. In *An Enquiry Concerning Human Understanding*, L.A. Selby-Biggs (ed.). Oxford: Clarendon, 1902.

13. Larrabee, Harold A. *Reliable Knowledge.* Boston: Houghton Mifflin, 1954.

14. Monod, Jacques. From enzymatic adaptation to allosteric transitions. *Science* **154**: 475-483; October 28, 1966.

15. Popper, Karl R. *The Poverty of Historicism.* New York: Harper, 1964.

16. Walker, Marshall. *The Nature of Scientific Thought.* Englewood Cliffs, New Jersey: Prentice-Hall, 1963.

Establishing Priorities in Research

At some time in the academic year, the typical graduate student realizes that it is time to get busy and start working on a thesis or dissertation. Such a task, added to a heavy schedule of courses and hours devoted to employment, is not easily accomplished. In some situations, the task is never completed and the student joins the "A.B. Legion"; *all but* the thesis or *all but* the dissertation. A student may confer with a professor and announce the desire to start work on a thesis or dissertation. The professor usually counters by asking what the student is interested in doing or how the student has been preparing for the study. Naturally, if he or she knew what was interesting or had done considerable preparing beforehand, there would be no need to confer with the professor.

A student may have read on some topic, however, and even be able to specify the area of interest. First attempts of this kind are a healthy sign. They are also almost always failures. The professor may question the student about specific ideas and deflate them very quickly—too general a topic, unimportant, already been done many times. So, back to the drawing board goes the student. Only now the student who made the initial attempt at finding a topic is even more confused.

Many universities emphasize that selection of a thesis or dissertation topic is the responsibility of the student. Students are told, sometimes harshly, that the ability to state and define problems worthy of research is a quality that they should possess as mature graduate students. One major university reportedly defers admission to doctoral candidacy until the student has outlined a specific dissertation topic and secured the approval of a graduate professor to sponsor the undertaking. Master's degree students, fortunately, are given more counsel and guidance for the thesis.

There is something painfully tragic about the trauma that finding a research topic represents. It has been pointed out previously that physical education is in desperate need of research. Few people in the profession do research; articles and talks from every corner of the profession present challenges and opportunities; and the unknown predominates over the known in almost every segment of the profession. Yet, the graduate students suffer because they cannot find a suitable topic for research. In a sea of ignorance, they cannot fathom what truth to seek.

Of even more tragic proportions is the possibility that the student's dilemma may be due to the education that was received in undergraduate school and is currently being received in graduate work. An undergraduate curriculum that emphasizes the mastery of "how to" and the acquisition of textbook facts is not very conducive to the fostering of research interests. Also, graduate courses taught by professors who do no research themselves completes the deadening circle. If graduate professors merely retail second-hand information already present in textbooks, and echo the thoughts of others that appear in articles, it is understandable why their graduate students cannot find research topics. In essence, graduate work fails to stir the student because it is not stirring.

In other situations, the responsibility for securing a research topic is justifiably put on the students' shoulders. When the research activities of a department are making noises, the students should have ears to hear. If the department is quiet, the student may have to "listen," through research publications, for activities going on elsewhere. One might even find it profitable to have the feet carry the ears to such a place.

FINDING A RESEARCH TOPIC

Most graduate-study programs require that a formal piece of research be successfully accomplished as part of the prescribed degree work. In some schools, the requirement of a master's thesis has been softened somewhat by allowing a suitable term paper to be deposited in the graduate office in lieu of a formal thesis. Other programs require a master's project which involves less breadth or depth than a thesis, but which is still considerably more than the usual term paper. Almost all doctoral degree programs stipulate completion of a formal dissertation or one or more independent study projects of an original nature.

Whether the research topic lies in the professional or the scientific domain, it needs to be identified before consideration can be given to evaluating its significance and planning the methods of study to be employed. To date, many research topics have been identified and completed. The origin of this research is sometimes spelled out in the research report itself, and an investigator may actually report how the topic was suggested. In other research reports, the original motivation to do the study may be implicit in the work itself, and it is often possible, with careful study of the investigation, to deduce the origin of the research topic. Finding a research topic might be made easier, then, if one were to consider possible sources of research topics in some organized classification scheme. Several such classification schemes for the origins of research problems have been offered from time to time and elements from some of them will be considered here.

Experience

The story is told of a promising physical educator who encountered a situation that prevented him from conducting himself as professionally as he deemed necessary. Try as he might, he could not conceive of an acceptable solution to this disturbing problem until finally he decided that drastic efforts were called for in order to overcome his professional ineptness. According to the fable, the troubled physical educator decided to improve his professional competency via further study. He went to graduate school and absorbed additional knowledge through formal course work and independent study over and above program requirements. His view of the professional responsibility that a physical educator shouldered was also broadened, and he even equipped himself with several research skills. He then went back to his teaching position and applied his new knowledge and skill to the solving of his original problem. Because of his improved professional competency, he now recognized other important problems hitherto unnoticed and set about working on their solutions as well. Each time a problem with which he was unable to cope successfully presented itself he sought counsel from his colleagues, pursued independent study, or returned to graduate school for additional work. This story, of course, is a fantasy.

Experience in one's profession can, undoubtedly, bring many potential research problems to the surface of consciousness, but only if practitioners know what to look for and what important questions they should ask of their experience. The student who comes to graduate school with a definite research topic in mind is still quite rare. Experience in the profession too often fails to illuminate possible research topics important enough to be worth the trouble of investigating or amenable to solution in a real world. More often, the situation finds a student expressing an interest in a particular area rather than a particular problem. Additional effort by the student often finds a more specific topic defined in one of two ways: (1) delusions of grandeur, and (2) delusions of minutia. Very seldom does the initial scramble for a research topic originating from experience fall into an in-between category.

Problems that graduate students with little practical experience suggest usually fall into the first category: delusions of grandeur. These young crusaders are ready to conquer age-old dilemmas in one sweeping charge right into the mouth of the cannon. The enormity and scope of the research topic that they are likely to suggest has made many a graduate professor's jaw fall in utter amazement. They suggest the need for an ideal curriculum, a physical training schedule to produce four-minute milers at the junior high school level, prevention of athletic injuries, selling physical education to the public, or the effect of athletics upon personality. Wise graduate professors listen patiently to the rough ideas being presented and then try to bring the topic down to reasonable proportions without dampening the student's obvious enthusiasm. Too often, however, the graduate student leaves the professor's office in a state of depression. After the topic had been delimited to the stage where it might have been feasible, the student was no longer interested in such a trivial problem. The professor, in effect, did not like the suggested thesis topic.

Experienced teachers bring with them the wisdom and success that only practical experience can provide. They have learned the folly of being idealistic and attempting to change the world overnight. Most of the topics that they suggest for research do not promise sweeping reforms of humankind or immediate salvation for the profession. Instead, they suggest problems in tune with the delusions of minutia category—topics of minor or trivial importance. One evaluation done at a major university brought to light several such experience-oriented problems. One veteran complained that women were never taught how to handle pep squads. Another success story decried the fact that men were never tutored on the intricacies of coaching girls' basketball teams. It is not surprising to learn that one master's thesis appeared presenting a program for the handling of pep squads and another developed a complete course-outline for the coaching of girls' basketball teams by men.

Somewhere between the delusions of grandeur and minutia, the world of reality and propriety must exist. Graduate work hopefully considers important problems in the profession and the means by which they can best be attacked. Careful counsel through graduate course work by well-informed scholarly faculties will surface those problems of major importance which deserve the highest priority for attack. Still further study will demonstrate the optimum techniques and strategies to be used in attempts to find solutions in these important but troublesome areas. Problems stemming from delusions of grandeur will be delimited while problems from delusions of minutia will either be eliminated or expanded to more meaningful dimensions. Such a result assumes that the graduate program and the graduate faculty are themselves not the victims of such delusions.

Experience is thus seen as an excellent source for identifying problems associated with the practice of a profession, if linked to an operative intellect that is capable of evaluation and priority setting. Experience, however, is more likely to surface professional problems than it is to suggest any topics of research aligned with an academic-discipline approach. Experience in the conduct of professional responsibilities cannot be expected to suggest the problems deserving highest priority in an academic discipline for the simple reason that research topics in a discipline are once-removed from the arena of professional activity. An academic discipline considers the research questions that are directly pertinent to the discipline and not to the profession. Rarely would experience in the conduct of activities inherent in physical education as a profession identify a set of topics suited for research in the academic discipline. Neither should the priority given research topics in a discipline be expected to match the priority given research topics in a profession.

Instead of talking about experience in terms of an individual, it would be better to speak of the collective experience of the profession as a whole. Activities of the profession taken as an entity are much more likely to suggest problems of major, rather than minor significance and, thus, qualify experience as an acceptable source of research problems. Experience, whether it be individual or collective, still must be examined intellectually in order to identify the criteria upon which to base priority ratings for research problems. Several suggested procedures for the identification of research problems in physical education are available in our professional literature. An examination of these procedures and the guidelines for their use will show them to be suitable only for identification of professional problems.

Professional Problems

Identification of professional problems can be achieved by simple application of the formula: Ideals minus practices equals problems. Larson et al. (10, page 43) substitute the word principles for ideals but the meaning is unchanged. These authors outlined a procedure for identifying problems in health, physical education, and recreation that is quite simple to understand. First, one must possess a description of the functions and goals of the profession. On the basis of an accepted set of functions and goals, one derives a description of the ideal practices for professional activity. Knowing what the accepted ideals are, one need only survey the existing practices in the profession. Whatever difference exists between present practices and ideal practices represents the problems facing the profession. Identified problems may then be ranked in order of importance, and used as a list of defined problems necessitating research or solution.

As a basis for establishing the functions and goals of the profession, these authors counsel reference to aims, objectives, and the philosophy of physical education. Since they reside at New York University, it is not surprising to hear them recommend the nine basic functions of a profession of physical education developed by Clark W. Hetherington. Hetherington, you will remember, was a leading exponent of the job-analysis technique and made use of it in designing the first Ph.D. program at New York University (see pages 67-71). The nine basic functions of the profession listed by Hetherington were:

(1) Interpretations (philosophy)
(2) Objectives
(3) Community organizations and auspices
(4) People—status, educability, and capacity

(5) Programs
(6) Leadership
(7) Administrations
(8) History and trends
(9) Professions

Bookwalter's approach to the selection of a problem is similar. What Larson et al. (10) call basic functions, Bookwalter terms problematical areas (3, pages 39-70). According to Bookwalter, potential research problems can be identified by going from the general to the more specific by means of: field analysis, problematical areas, differentiating factors or variables, and research methods. The basic scheme for this approach is represented in Figure 10.1. One simply chooses, as a starting point, one of the subdivisions under field analysis, carries the field-analysis topic to a problematical area, refines it by use of differentiating factors, and then selects a research method for its solution.

Application of the technique, Bookwalter states, shows at least 43 major areas under field analysis, 400 to 500 crudely estimated fields and subfields under the ten problematical areas. This gives approximately 5000 kinds of problem at this stage and at least 18 ways to differentiate these 5000 or more kinds of problem via differentiating factors or variables. When the research method is then considered, the number of potential research problems "illuminated" is in the millions.

The mechanical procedure for identifying research problems offered by both these sources, however, is definitely slanted to the profession. Little wonder, then, that the study of some 416 doctoral thesis topics for the years 1930-1946 reported by Cureton (7) showed considerable emphasis upon professional areas involving administration (12.8%), programs (25.5%), professional status (10.0%), and methods in teaching (5.5%). Just over one-half of the doctoral thesis topics were thus in the area of professional problems, suggesting considerable emphasis in an

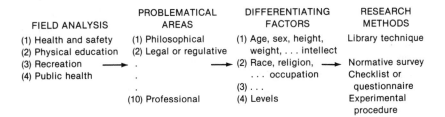

FIELD ANALYSIS	PROBLEMATICAL AREAS	DIFFERENTIATING FACTORS	RESEARCH METHODS
(1) Health and safety	(1) Philosophical	(1) Age, sex, height,	Library technique
(2) Physical education	(2) Legal or regulative	weight, . . . intellect	
(3) Recreation ⟶ .	⟶ .	⟶ (2) Race, religion, ⟶	Normative survey
(4) Public health	.	. . . occupation	Checklist or
.	.	(3) . . .	questionnaire
	(10) Professional	(4) Levels	Experimental procedure

Figure 10.1. Selection and definition of a professional research problem. (Based upon material from Karl W. Bookwalter, Selection and definition of a problem, in *Research Methods in HPER*, Chapter 3, pages 49-53. Washington, D.C.: AAHPER, 1959.)

attractive research area. Professional problems often constitute subject matter content for courses at the graduate level and almost universally, one finds courses offered with the word "problem" in the title.

The legacy of job analysis as a technique for the profession has been well utilized. Each of the two procedures outlined here for identification of research problems results typically in topics of concern to a profession rather than a discipline. The first technique, ideals minus practices equals problems, is a fine example of a residue technique. When one defines the residue left after subtracting practices from ideals one has successfully succeeded in identifying problems for study. Bookwalter's rationale can be likened to a progressive delimitation or zeroing-in technique. His system advises selection of a suitable research problem by a stepwise-reduction process from major to subsidiary considerations. Each of the two techniques share similarities in format, each has been successful in helping to identify professional problems for research study, and each has done its share to perpetuate a consideration of trivia in the profession.

If either the residue or zeroing-in technique proves too difficult for a graduate student, there is another attractive option. Because extensive lists of problems—both general and specific—are available in the literature, a student may find it easier to skip over the preliminaries and focus directly on a given topic. There are a few individuals in the profession, by the way, who have made a career of publishing articles that suggest problems for research and make strong appeals for scholarly research efforts, but who never find time themselves to do any original research work. The use of problem-identification schemes to select research topics in physical education reflects the same traditional approach to research used in education. To the extent that physical education has been molded by the influence of education, its own research methodology demonstrates the same characteristics. The basic rationale seems to be the identification of problems by (1) illumination of the difficulties practitioners encounter in their professional activities, and (2) differences between ideals and practices.

Inherent in such plans for finding research problems is the necessity to know what the basic functions and goals of the profession are. This task may or may not have been accomplished. However, if we accept the premise that basic functions and goals are known, we still must know what the ideal means of guaranteeing their achievement are before we can postulate ideal practices. Research in the area of professional problems is often conducted as if expedient solutions to emergency problems constituted truth. Such a view ignores the validity of such solutions. Taking a public stand on an issue may result in the solution of a professional problem by the achievement of group consensus of opinion. Such a solution, however, is only a policy agreed upon by the majority. It may or may not be a valid principle. As with any such pragmatic approach, value judgments may be confused with truth. As a profession, we have been prone to accept ideals postulated on the basis of beliefs or expedient solutions as being true without testing their validity. Given ideals, and knowing the status of present practices, problems that remain can be solved by manipulation of money, time, and people. Such an outlook probably explains why so many physical educators have administration as their end goal.

In 1961, long-time members of the American Academy of Physical Education were polled on what critical issues faced the profession (4). Members were advised to ". . . select sides and take a public stand." The critical issues presented were such that stands could be taken, since they all represented differences between accepted ideals and present practices. At the very best, some of the critical problems represented issues for which no accepted ideals could be agreed upon. The defect in such an approach is that too much attention is paid to residue problems and assessment of practices, while the bases upon which ideals are forwarded go relatively ignored. Please note that proponents of this traditional approach made no stipulation or requirement that any particular allocation of emphasis should be given to ideals, practices, or problems. In its operation, however, the end product is an over-emphasis upon the least important aspects. The emphasis is primarily upon the administration and mechanics of professional duties, housekeeping chores of a profession, internal policies and procedures of the profession, while attention to functions and development of ideal practices receives minimal emphasis. We operate as if we had all the basic truths and need only focus our energies on expediting their dissemination.

In testimony to this are the vast number of status studies which occupy library shelves of any university offering graduate degrees in education and in physical education. Status studies, of course, seek to assess present practices. Assuming that basic functions and ideal practices are known, status studies can be inserted into the ideals-minus-practices formula to show, by a residue process, the problems that exist. Typically, status studies conclude how well the profession is doing in the fulfillment of its basic functions and ideals.

Thus, analyses of teaching loads exist for the elementary level, junior high, senior high, and college levels. Similar analyses for the extra-curricular activities sponsored are available at these same levels. The whole series is then differentiated for male versus female teachers, experienced versus inexperienced teachers, athletic directors and coaches versus straight physical-education instructors, majors versus minors, master's degree versus nonmaster's degree, *ad infinitum*. Certification requirements, administrative practices, finances, budget, facilities, job analysis, equipment use and maintenance, curriculum, and so forth can also be studied at all levels and for all differentiating factors.

At one time, the widespread use of questionnaires in education research became almost intolerable. Whitney (17, page 139) stated that their almost universal use was probably due to neophyte researchers who considered questionnaire studies to be the quickest and most painless way to collect impressive batches of data. He called the questionnaire one of the worst devices for data collection that could be chosen, and he advised constraint in its use. There are, undoubtedly, many deficiencies in poor survey research whether the technique for data collection utilizes questionnaires, scorecards, check-lists, or personal interview methods. There are, similarly, many occasions where survey research is called for and constitutes the preferred technique. Even on these occasions, however, the survey research must be well done according to standardized and acceptable guidelines.

In moot testimony to the over-emphasis upon status-assessment research in physical education was the policy decision on surveys made by the AAHPERD Research Council. An announcement appeared in the *Research Quarterly* calling attention to a new section named "Notes and Comments" which would appear in the December 1954 issue. An innocuous statement was made that:

> . . . Readers should note that simple status surveys are no longer acceptable as regular Quarterly articles, by decision of the Research Council. Such studies will therefore be published in brief form (from 300 to 500 words) under Notes and Comments rather than as Quarterly articles.

For five years, until about 1959, this policy remained in effect, then it was somewhat relaxed. In 1959, surveys were, apparently, once again acceptable for publication, but it was stipulated that "emphasis should be on exposition and analysis" and that the study should indicate and justify the "significance of the findings for diagnosis, policy, or program."

Elimination of survey research is not being recommended here, since any profession will need to study itself and conduct such investigations.

Status surveys are necessary to secure information on employment conditions, teaching loads, certification standards, and similar parameters reflecting strengths and deficiencies. Data on such matters of internal organization are necessary in order to fashion an optimum environment for professional practice and, thus, serve society more effectively. The pitfall to be avoided is accepting the mistaken notion that such activity is *the* major research obligation of the profession.

The medical profession concerns itself with matters such as internal organization, but its major efforts in research are directed at development of ideal practices and the discovery of knowledge. Prime attention must go to the ideals and ideal practices. The most important problems in medicine, for example, are not linked to professional housekeeping, for example, dues, membership drives, recruitment of students, employment conditions, and the like. To be sure, such items require attention and deficiencies in this area could be disastrous, but they are not held to be *the* problems of the medical profession. The most important problems in medicine are linked to discovering a cure for cancer, developing a vaccine against rheumatic fever, new surgery techniques, and treatment regimens—all aspects of ideals and ideal practices. Medicine must pay attention to its housekeeping chores, but it does not focus on them; it focuses upon the discovery of knowledge and the development of new and better practices. As a profession, physical education has expended considerable effort in studying its housekeeping chores. It has paid great attention to the assessment of present practices and the description of problems. The solutions to its problems have too often been policy decisions established by consensus of opinion. Physical education has tended to accept ideals and ideal practices as settled issues.

Such a state of affairs has led to the inevitable consideration of less important problems. Residue and zeroing-in approaches to problem identification may be effective for the selection of topics amenable to solution by policy makers and administrative action. Consideration of the unknown rather than the known, examination of possible *new* ideal practices, and formulation of new ideals will be realized most efficiently only when scientific, rather than professional, approaches to research are emphasized.

Elimination of professional research is *not* being suggested here. Such research activities have been, and will continue to be, important concerns of the profession. Many situations demand immediate action and decision; requiring a high standard of precise knowledge before any decision is made is ideal, but not always possible. Indeed, problems requiring immediate decision probably owe their existence to the unavailability of precise knowledge. Major research activity, however, must be shifted to the realm of basic functions and ideal practices in order to ensure meaning and validity to professional research.

SCIENTIFIC PROBLEMS

Besides experience in one's profession, experience in the knowledge domain of one's academic discipline may also suggest problems necessitating research endeavors. As knowledge is acquired in an area representing some aspect of the present theoretical constructs and models, gaps and deficiencies in the system are readily seen. Once a firm foundation is acquired for some component in the subject matter domain, these deficiencies become immediately apparent even to those individuals of average intelligence. Such acquisition of knowledge may demonstrate that some accepted "facts" are not true or require considerable qualification, that some "facts" have been assumed true by agreement but never verified, or that some "facts" simply do not exist.

A model or a theory in some domain of knowledge in the discipline can suggest, via its deductive predictions, where research is needed. The absence of a model or a theory in some area of knowledge is equally potent in suggesting research possibilities. Looking for research topics, therefore, is made easier if one can discern the structure of the knowledge available, and the status of present models and theories. If practical experience can match itself with the model of structured knowledge systems, it is less likely to be improperly evaluated as to importance.

Professional research problems, according to the preceding sections, focus primarily upon assessment of practices against some defined ideal called a principle. Scientific research problems focus, instead, upon the ideals and the ideal practices themselves. Attention is upon the unknown, not upon the known. Models and a structured system of knowledge are sought with the idea that once validated models in crucial domain areas are achieved, ideals and ideal practices can then be postulated upon fact, not fancy or common consent.

To begin our consideration of scientific research possibilities, we shall first look at the many possible classification schemes for research experiments. A most common scheme, for example, is to differentiate between basic and applied research. Mostly, however, these efforts have been in vain, even though most people would wager that the two are easily distinguishable. Knowing the different types of scientific research that exist can help to clarify the kinds of scientific research that may be undertaken and to evaluate research that has already been accomplished.

The most consistent method employed to distinguish basic from applied research has been to use the presence of utilitarian goals as a criterion. If research is being done only to understand the laws of nature, with no thought given to the possible application of the acquired knowledge in the interest of society, then the research is usually said to be an example of basic research. Unfortunately, however, the identical piece of research might be done by an investigator whose motivation is wholly utilitarian. Thus, as Reagan (14) so aptly put it, the distinction between basic and applied research may depend upon "the psychological motivation of the man performing" and not upon the research itself. Unless one is able to judge the motivation of the investigator, one may not be able to distinguish the research as being either basic or applied.

Another deficiency in the basic versus applied dichotomy is the fact that mere passage of time may suddenly change the results of basic research into applied research, even though the motivation of the investigator remained constant and experienced no such transformation. Prior to the discovery that malaria was transmitted by the *Anopheles* mosquito, any research on the life cycle of the insect could well have been called basic. After the time of the discovery, however, the same research might have been classified as applied. Mere passage of time could, therefore, result in a research endeavor changing from the basic to the applied category. Actually, the only change that occurred was the importance of the research to society at that particular moment in time.

It would seem too tortuous an experience as well as a handicap to depend upon a classification scheme for research which simply dichotomized research investigations into only basic and applied categories. Unless we are ready to make complete reversals in our classification decisions due to passage of time as new psychiatric insights about the investigator's motivation are gained, a different frame of reference for classification of research undertakings seems in order.

This is not to discount the widespread usage of the terms basic and applied research, for these terms continue to have considerable meaning to a vast audience. In the words of the outstanding scientist J. Robert Oppenheimer, the arguments that basic science is a quest for new knowledge while applied science is a quest for new uses of knowledge "are disturbingly separate and unrelated arguments" (13, page 9). Rather than attempt a definite demarcation line between the two, it seems more intelligent to recognize their implicit characteristics and to seek a classification scheme for research investigations which avoids unnecessary deficiencies as much as possible.

Since we have expended considerable effort to formulate an understanding of science and research, the classification scheme to be presented here seems more adequate than a simple dichotomy of basic-applied. The classification scheme that follows assumes that the motivation of the investigator is in evidence, overcomes the dilemma of classification reversals due to mere passage of time, and is applicable to the research activities in any discipline area. Fulfilling these criteria, it, naturally, completely avoids the basic versus applied paradox and suffers from a set of deficiencies of its own. The reader can decide which classification scheme is the most appealing or can suggest suitable revisions. In either case, the process seems sure to help clarify thinking about research investigations.

TYPES OF EXPERIMENTS

Autotelic

Moore and Anderson (12) coined the term "autotelic" to describe ". . . activities undertaken by human beings solely because of their intrinsic interest." In their context, it was meant to apply to participation in social games simply because such games were enjoyable. The term "autotelic" is used here to apply to experiments which may have no specific goal other than satisfying the investigator's curiosity. Autotelic seems an apt description of such playing around. Moles (11) used the phrase ". . . no more directed than a child's fiddling with a toy . . ." to describe haphazard experiments.

Research done to satisfy an investigator's curiosity might be called basic or pure research, but this is not strictly correct. Basic research would have some goal—provision of facts in unknown areas and accumulation of data upon which to postulate models. Data accumulated from autotelic experiments may not even be in the fact domain of the investigator's research competencies. When asked why such research was done, the investigator might not have an answer. The investigator just had an idea to do it. The investigator had no guess as to what the results might be or even what significance such data might have. Upon completion of the experiment, the question might arise as to why the study was ever done.

Heymans, a distinguished Belgian pharmacologist, conducted an unplanned experiment that seems a proper example of autotelic research. An experimental animal had been used in a study that necessitated the denervation of one carotid sinus area. At the conclusion of the experiment, Heymans injected a potassium cyanide solution into first the common carotid artery with normal sinus innervation and then into the denervated artery. The potassium cyanide solution was apparently used because it ". . . was standing on the laboratory desk." Some very unexpected respiratory responses were observed which led to planned experiments to investigate the phenomena. The end result was the discovery of the chemoreceptors of the carotid sinus area. Heymans (9) noted that the initial experiment was ". . . a very foolish-looking trial," but suggested the value of a statement attributed to Darwin, "I like to perform foolish experiments."

Model Validation

Experiments that are designed to test the validity of postulated models constitute a second type of experiment. Such studies are, by design, goal oriented and assume the existence of some theoretical knowledge. They may seek to provide missing data in the domain, to verify by replication data already in the domain, or to expand the domain into other data areas. Expansion of the model domain may be into data areas for which models are not present, or it may seek links with data in areas which already possess satisfactory models. The linkage of such models may lead to more general models covering a greater expanse of data and thus help fulfill the goal of reductionism.

Model Oriented

Experiments performed to obtain knowledge upon which models may be postulated differ only slightly from "autotelic" research. The chief differences are probably the motivation of the researcher and the domain content in which the research is done. If the domain content is, or may be, related to models already in existence then the research would be model oriented. If the domain content, at the time, had no relationship to models already in existence and the research was done merely out of curiosity, it would be autotelic research.

Quite often on the frontiers of knowledge no intelligent questions can be asked and an investigator might be obliged to conduct studies in the content domain with something less than a specific plan. Model-oriented research is thus seen to include the attempt to discover new phenomena and to study the conditions under which such phenomena occur. The magnitude and limits of the phenomena, their characteristics and relationships to other constructs within the domain can be classified as model-oriented research. Only a thin line of demarcation probably exists between autotelic and model-oriented research but a difference does exist. Perhaps such a difference can be appreciated if one contrasts the Heymans example under autotelic research with that of a remark made by a professor at the Massachusetts Institute of Technology. Professor Edgerton had been conducting experiments attempting to photograph the ocean floor at a depth of several miles. When asked what he expected to find and what use his results might have, Edgerton replied, "If I knew, I wouldn't do it" (8, page 128).

Methodological

Development of testing techniques and equipment, experimental procedures, and analytic schemes constitute methodological research. Usually no new knowledge is discovered within the model domain. Contributions consist of improved methods of studying phenomena within the model domain. Construction of standardized attitude or knowledge tests, apparatus design, improved experimental procedures for the collection of data, and development of appropriate statistical analysis techniques are examples of methodological research contributions.

Methodological research contributions are generally of secondary importance to model validation and model-oriented research. Although methodological research contributions may expedite research and open new data domains, studies of model validation and model-oriented types have greater prestige. *The Journal of Applied Physiology*, for example, stipulates that submitted papers must deal with significant new research findings in some area of physiology. Articles dealing with methodological research are published under a separate heading of "Special Communications." In a similar manner the editorial policy of the *Research Quarterly* is to publish descriptions of new research apparatus or techniques in a section called "Notes and Comments."

In some circles of thought, any application of knowledge already available for the solution of some particular problem would be methodological. Some staunch academicians, for example, might consider most activities in the branches of engineering to be methodological research. A chemist sees no additions to knowledge in chemical science emanating from the work of chemical engineers. Physicists see their knowledge being used by civil engineers in the construction of bridges, but note few new additions to knowledge in physics. Engineers, according to such a viewpoint, are applied researchers. Few of their contributions are truly scientific advances. The advances made are technological, not scientific.

To an astronomer, the entire space program is methodological research. The physicist has seen available knowledge utilized in the development of space travel, but counts few new contributions to physics. After a recent space shot sent pictures of the moon back to earth, for example, several geologists and astronomers assessed the scientific importance of the pictures. Getting the camera there, taking pictures, and transmission of pictures back to earth were not scientific advancements. The pictures, which provided new data about the moon's surface, were scientific contributions.

Identification of problems worthy of scientific research studies could, of course, be suggested by experience. In the context of an academic discipline, however, the word "experience" has a different meaning than it has in a profession. Experience now refers to the collective activities of the academic discipline and not to the kind of experiences that a practitioner is likely to encounter in the profession. Research topics are more often generated from two major sources in a discipline: (1) productive scholars, and (2) the literature of the discipline.

Association With a Scholar

Historically, association with a scholar has been the foundation for graduate work in universities, having its origin in the German or European concept of a university. The presence of an outstanding scholar at a university is sought by administrators in the hope that the scholar will attract and produce students of a similar potential for scholarly achievement. Association with a scholar through course work, lectures, seminars, or assistantships is ideal; but even in the absence of a scholar at an institution, a student may become familiar with such individuals through their publications and public talks. Apparently, popular belief is that working directly under an established scholar is most ideal. Established scholars have demonstrated their knack of being able to identify the problems of greatest importance to the field. A "feeling" for research has shown the scholar to be skilled in choosing research activities that are satisfactorily located between the delusions of grandeur and delusions of minutia domains.

Personal contact with such a model may imbue students with a similar enthusiasm for research and help them to acquire the competence to pick the appropriate topics significant for study. One of the great values in association with a scholar is the possibility of "catching" the attitude toward the pursuit of knowledge. An established scholar has, evidently, been endowed with the right amounts of curiosity, disciplined imagination, and persistence to pursue new knowledge successfully. In the hope that such a scholar can pass on this gift to the next generation of scholars, administrators seeking to build strong departments at their university actively recruit such scholars. The best young minds seeking training also are attracted to these scholars.

Apparently both the administrators who seek productive scholars for their staffs and the bright young minds are making the right decisions. The prestige of a department is established by productive scholars, and the best students seek association with such departments and scholars. In 1960-1963 over 80% of the Woodrow Wilson Fellows and National Science Foundation Fellows, who were free to choose, decided to study in about 25 leading universities. These 25 universities were rated as leaders on the basis of the quality of their graduate faculties (6). The idea seems to be quite universal in the academic community that the best graduate education can be obtained only by studying under the best scholars. Coupled with the intellectual climate generated by serious and talented students drawn to such scholars, the environment would seem close to optimum for a program of highest quality.

Unfortunately, many graduate students in physical education are not as sophisticated in their choice of a particular school for graduate work as they might be. Too often, the choice of a particular graduate school may not have been greatly affected by consideration of what scholars are on staff or what the major course work and research emphases are at an institution. Such inattentiveness to rather major quality factors by prospective graduate students in physical education may be due in part to the lack of a definite goal in graduate study other than that of earning of an advanced degree. Geographical considerations, acquaintances, or the availability of financial assistance may have possessed greater potency than they should have had in the choice of a graduate school.

As both undergraduate and early graduate programs move to increased emphasis upon scholarly research, the situation is likely to change. As students acquaint themselves with the knowledge basis for physical activity and develop an intellectual curiosity in specific content areas, they are more likely to become sophisticated in their choice of graduate programs. Until then, it will not be uncommon to find that the intellectual interests of graduate students will be fashioned by the academic environment present in a particular school. An innocuous statement was once made that a student searches and searches again for a thesis topic until a graduate advisor agrees to sponsor such a thesis. Miraculously, graduate students discover that they are intensely interested in the same topical areas for research as their graduate advisors.

As might be expected, students who complete their graduate work under the supervision of a particular scholar assume the characteristics typical of that scholar, academic characteristics, if not personal as well. The growth of major research trends can sometimes be traced back to either one particular scholar or a group of scholars. Through classes, seminars, published research, and the sponsorship of theses and dissertations, research emphasis upon a particular area grows. Initially, a particular area of concern may be receiving little or no research consideration at all. Some individual begins productive work in this area, however, and affects both the kind and volume of research emphasis. The concept supposes some sort of school or identification of emphasis at a particular graduate school. Physical education has several such examples. It is no wonder that T.K. Cureton at the University of Illinois sponsored research on physical fitness or that Franklin Henry at the University of California (Berkeley) found so many students interested in neuromotor specificity. In a similar manner, it is not strange that so many students at Oregon became enthused about strength testing with H. Harrison Clarke around to sponsor such studies.

For those students whose interests and career goals are congruent with those of the staff and the academic environment at the school attended, the results will be pleasant and rewarding. For students who find themselves in a program unsuited to their aspirations, however, opposite results can be expected. It would seem of great importance for prospective graduate students to consider carefully the merits of the various graduate education programs available in physical education since the emphasis in such programs varies a great deal. Although most institutions possess some flexibility in their programs, they justifiably expect that students who enrolled at their institution did so because of their faculty and program.

Association With the Literature

Even if a graduate student has the opportunity of studying under a good professor, exposure to scholarly endeavors is still rather limited. A broadened exposure to scholars and knowledge is possible through the literature of the field. By becoming familiar with the literature, one is exposed to a good many scholars, both living and dead. (We are assuming, of course, that outstanding scholars have seen fit to publish their work.) Literature in a field of study contains the knowledge that human beings have produced in the search for truth. It represents a record of human successes and failures in the field and chronicles their activities, both shrewd and stupid.

A careful review of the literature can suggest many potential research problems because it results in knowing the present status of knowledge in a specific area. As the many investigations are read and studied, one sees the model or theory developed in a particular content domain. The absence of a model, gaps in knowledge, and the presence of conflicting research conclusions are equally effective in suggesting research topics. The importance of contemplated research can only be assessed when one knows the present structure of knowledge in the area of concern. Acquisition of this knowledge is accomplished by careful study of the literature. Through the literature, one is able to associate vicariously with scholars and reap the knowledge produced by such scholars.

Formally Adequate Models

Although association with a scholar or the literature may produce a definite research topic, the major problem that is faced is the planning of the actual study. The task is not so much in selecting an appropriate problem (hopefully), but in deciding how to execute the research. Formal adequacy is the stumbling block. Successfully carrying out an investigation that results in the addition of reliable data to knowledge already available requires formal adequacy.

Supposedly, graduate-level preparation develops the competencies necessary to plan well-defined and formally adequate research investigations. Inherent in any graduate-level course prescription is the acquisition of factual knowledge in problem-research areas and subjects that supply the tools with which to attack research problems. Any student who selects a research topic along historical lines, for example, would be expected to become knowledgeable in the subject matter of the area as well as to acquire the techniques of historical research. Certainly, a course in historiography would not be unreasonable. In the same manner, any student selecting an experimental study should consider the need for course work in subjects like statistics, experimental design, and laboratory techniques in order to gain the necessary competence to write an experimental research paper.

Judging by the experiences of many individuals in critical reading of master's theses, doctoral dissertations, manuscripts submitted for publication in the *Research Quarterly*, and articles published in the *Research Quarterly*, such a desideratum has yet to be adequately attained. Defects in student efforts are to be expected, tolerated, and perhaps even condoned. Similar defects in the performance of graduate-school products, however, are less forgivable. Critical reviews of the formal adequacy of *Research Quarterly* articles suggest many opportunities for improvement.

A beginner in research would do well to study the many articles published in the *Research Quarterly* that have critically evaluated the research published. These critiques point out the flaws in published research which need to be avoided in future research endeavors. After having studied these critiques, timidness by a beginner in research is understandable, and, in fact, desirable. Research must be carefully planned and executed so as to avoid either errors of omission or commission. The planning of a research study may, indeed, take very much more time than the actual collection of data. There is no substitute for such careful planning, and such planning is not simple to accomplish.

There is an available alternative to the original design of a study by a beginner in research. Although this alternative is not professionally attractive, it is certainly practical. The alternative amounts to the selection, as a model, of a formally adequate investigation already published in the content area. A beginner carefully searches the literature in an area of interest and then selects that investigation which most closely resembles personal research goals. Many worthwhile problems can be defined by broadening the base of previously executed and formally adequate research investigations.

As Weitz (16) suggests, major experiments might even be replicated as exactly as possible.there is certainly value in such cross-validation of results. One could more wisely, however, copy the basic experimental design and statistical analysis techniques while varying certain other parameters to fit the beginner's research goals more closely. The sample used might represent a different, more pertinent population; improved tests for the assessment of criterion measures might now be available; or more tests of criterion measures and more repeated measures for greater reliability might be used. The kinds of modification that could be made are countless. There is, after all, a finite number of experimental designs and analysis techniques. These designs and statistical analysis techniques, however, can be applied to an infinite number of research questions.

Identification of authoritative and highly capable investigators is easily realized by a careful and critical review of the literature. Some investigators may display a maturation in their own studies. Later studies may point out earlier inadequacies which are now being ameliorated via specified procedures. Such deficiencies, by the way, will not often be apparent or acknowledged in the early studies. If several recognized researchers are productive in similar research domains, their articles may offer mutual criticisms. Whenever "competing" theories, and their proponents, are present in a research domain, careful readers of the published work can harvest a multitude of benefits. Deficiencies in methodology, alternate analytic procedures, evaluation and criticism of interpretations, mistakes, and even bias may be pointed out.

Several such competing theories, and their proponents, exist in physical education. Warm-up is both beneficial to motor performance and is not; motor abilities are both specific and general; deep-knee bends are both harmful and are not; wheat-germ oil is both good and is not. The word-to-word and talk-to-talk combat on these topics is well known to those familiar with physical education research. The war still is not over, and campaign ribbons are still available.

Naturally, the copying of an experimental design from the literature is not the recommended procedure for ensuring formal adequacy of an investigation. One marked disadvantage is the restricting influence that such a practice can have upon the selection and execution of a research problem. All experimental designs and statistical-analysis procedures can be learned from appropriate course work in these tool areas. Copying model investigations hinders innovation and creative attacks on significant problems. Seeking the competence to plan a formally adequate investigation on a personal topic (whether this topic be autotelic or not) should never cease. Finding and executing the *first* research investigation, however, is the major battle. After the first well-done research, an individual would quickly see that the next several dozen investigations are suggested by the experience of the first research effort. The first study is like finding the end to a ball of yarn; once the end is located, unraveling it is not a difficult task.

EVALUATION OF A RESEARCH TOPIC

Intuitively, some research problems are judged to be poor and others as good. Given a set of possible research topics, most graduate students could identify the most absurd projects and do a reasonable job of selecting those topics of greater promise. When asked to state criteria upon which such judgments were made, however, a long pause punctuated by puzzled expressions and hand waving would precede any attempts at verbalization. Some topics for research are so ludicrous as to merit laughter. Other topics seem worthwhile, yet still seem less important than others. Surely, there must be some criteria upon which to evaluate the importance of a potential research topic.

Educationally oriented researchers are likely to use a set of criteria unlike that for a scientific-research endeavor, but some of the criteria will be similar. One of the first considerations mentioned is for the graduate student to weigh personal qualifications for the research study. If a student is to spend long hours of study and intensive effort in the performance of a research study, close attention should be given to a number of personal items. Bookwalter's list (3, pages 43-49) is certainly sound with respect to the fact that he takes into account interest, capacity, feasibility, availability of data, avoidance of personal bias, and personal returns such as satisfaction.

Introspection on the part of the researcher is a wise investment, since research is an intensely personal affair. Students might profitably avoid, however, strict compliance with usual lists of personal criteria for the evaluation of a potential research topic. Interest in the area, for example, is a laudable criterion. Ignorance of the area, however, might be the cause of paralyzing interest. Efforts in the area and resultant competency might give rise to interest. Capacity of the researcher must certainly be considered. The trap is seeking a study that can be accomplished with present capabilities and by not attempting to develop and acquire any and all competencies necessary for an important problem. Personal bias is to be avoided; yet, those areas in which an individual possesses the greatest interest might be those that are contaminated by large amounts of personal bias. The history of science shows many examples of individuals who harbored intense, stubborn, and highly prejudicial views on a certain topic. They pursued their aspirations and sometimes proved that their bias was the correct one. Only when personal bias leads to dishonesty is it a negative factor. Finally, the greatest personal satisfaction may come from completion of a research topic in the area of one's greatest interest, coupled with the realization that the stubborn bias one possessed was justified.

Personal criteria are important factors in the selection and evaluation of a research topic so far as the prospective researcher is concerned. These criteria, however, *are not* acceptable for evaluating the importance of the research topic as a contribution to knowledge. In this instance, criteria for evaluation of a potential research topic as a contribution to knowledge are dependent upon quite different considerations. The beginner in research should be careful not to confuse personal criteria with criteria originating from the needs of the knowledge domain. Criteria do exist with which an evaluation of a potential research topic can be made so far as its importance to the advancement of knowledge is concerned. Before we can begin our study of such criteria, we will first need to consider the meaning of formal and informal research endeavors.

Informal Research

This type of research endeavor may be thought of as a curious mixture of autotelic and model-oriented types of experiments. Researchers do not always know why they perform some experiments. The "hunch" experiment (studies apparently guided by blind insight), and even accidental discovery have, and probably will continue to have, an important place in the history of science. Insight may unerringly guide a researcher to meaningful experiments and the production of significant results. An explanation of the mechanics of such insight might parallel that of the process of induction. Science does not ask the researcher how a theory was formulated—it assesses the value of the theory. Similarly, science does not ask where the idea for a particular experiment originated—it assesses the value of the results.

Significant data resulting from experiments designed to elicit information in other areas also occurs. Some authors and scientists refer to such events as accidental. Accidental, however, implies that some fundamental error was made. Some discoveries have been recorded as resulting from an error being made. In such cases, accidental discovery is probably a legitimate description. When no fundamental error has been made, however, the term "serendipiditous" may be more applicable. Walter Cannon (5) coined this term to describe discoveries that were made while studying distinctly different topics. The ability of a scientist to *see* the meaning in data, of course, is the key factor.

An example of accidental discovery occurred when a shipment of Egyptian sand rats was delivered to the Joslin Research Laboratory in

Boston (1). The animals were fed the usual provisions, but investigators noted some startling results. Within a week, cataracts, obesity, and death caused by diabetes occurred in many of the animals. Further study pinpointed the cause to be a sudden change in diet. Egyptian sand rats, it was noted, were used to rough vegetables. A change to the synthetic laboratory meal laden with carbohydrates was found responsible. The remaining animals were saved by merely changing them back to their usual diet. Dr. George Cahill, director of the Diabetes Foundation Laboratory, said, "the phenomenon would be of value to investigators, particularly because of the speedy onset of the disease."

Jacques Barzun (2) criticizes science for not admitting more openly that scientific work is greatly affected by human temperament and emotions. "Mind encloses science, not the other way around," he states. His book cites many instances in which an individual as a human being, and not an individual as a user of the scientific method, was responsible for scientific discoveries.

A famous physicist and philosopher once said that scientists were "professionally trained to conceal from themselves their deepest thought" and to "exaggerate unconsciously the rational aspect" in their work. Moles (11, pages 99-100) cites the haphazard experiment—another likely term to describe our autotelic experiments—as being responsible for the discovery of penicillin. According to Moles, Fleming was "just playing about." In the "dogmatic method" a scientist postulates a theory without regard to any facts in its domain. So long as the theory is logically correct, the scientist is satisfied. The scientist then searches for data to which it might apply. "The method of contradiction," Moles goes on, "is used by scientists who have an arrogant personality." These scientists assume that accepted fact and theory are wrong and that just the opposite is true. Investigations are then designed to disprove the accepted, and verify their unaccepted or opposite theories.

All such examples of informal research are not uncommon occurrences in science. Unfortunately, such informal research is not likely to be considered important and significant *unless* the end results are important and significant. Curiosity, blind insight, hunches, and the whole array of possible autotelic experiments and informal research undertakings are allowable mostly on one's own time and expense. They are performed privately and sometimes secretly to prevent ridicule and embarrassment to the researcher. Informal research topics would not be acceptable in most settings as worthwhile topics for master's theses, doctoral dissertations, or research grant proposals.

Formal Research

Before the results are known, only formal research topics are likely to be judged to be worthwhile, important, and significant. Formal research topics have specific purposes, and the importance of these purposes can be judged. Formal research comprises model validation and, of course, certain model-oriented experiments.

The importance of model-oriented problems depends upon the importance of the model. If the model domain encompasses phenomena of significance, but facts within the domain are few, model-oriented research is of enhanced importance. If many facts are already available and the model domain is of little significance, the importance of model-oriented research is minimized accordingly. An investigator may contrive to make autotelic research into model-oriented research. If desired, the rationale for hunches and insight may sometimes be established. Doing so formalizes the problem, although the real motivation was informal. After the results of informal research are obtained an investigator may backtrack and give a rational basis for the experiment. The importance of model-validation research is judged in exactly the same manner as that of model-oriented research; that is, if the model is important and additional data can contribute to further development of the model then the research topic is worthwhile and important.

Our task, then, in evaluating the importance of a research problem is actually one of evaluating the model in whose domain it exists. Note that the importance of a potential research topic cannot be adequately (or at least consciously) evaluated unless one knows the model and the importance of the model. Fortunately, there are specific criteria upon which a model (or scientific theory) can be evaluated.

Criteria for Model Evaluation

A model, most naturally, is evaluated on the basis of how it fulfills its purpose. The purpose of a model is to account for, explain, and predict phenomena within its domain. Any list of criteria upon which to evaluate the adequacy and the importance of a model is, itself, implicitly based on several of the operating concepts and metaphysical foundations of science. The purposes of a model, therefore, are congruent with the purposes of science in general.

Since science accepts *determinism*, a model must postulate meaningful explanations for the occurrence of phenomena. *Consistency* requires the reproduction and prediction of the occurrence of such phenomena. Determinism requires an explanation through cause and effect, whereas consistency requires accuracy in the prediction of such effects. *Par-*

simony requires that the simplest explanation be preferred over complicated and intricate explanations having many assumptions and qualifications. *Reductionism* requires the formulation of generalizations. The more phenomena that a model encompasses, the more general it is and, thus, the more importance it possesses. The number of models necessary to understand nature must be reduced, not multiplied. Determinism, consistency, parsimony, and reductionism are all necessary and interdependent attributes of an adequate model or theory.

Sidman's list of criteria for theories (15, page 13) includes accuracy (consistency), inclusiveness (reductionism), and simplicity (parsimony). In addition, Sidman cites fruitfulness and relevance. Fruitfulness requires the model to suggest new avenues of attention. Hence, fruitfulness merely represents a requirement that the model lead to other models of a more general form. Fruitfulness is necessary if reductionism is to be achieved. Models that lead to the achievement of reductionism are, thus, fruitful. Relevance calls for logical adequacy. Apparently, Sidman requires that the models explain phenomena within their domains in a meaningful manner. Judgments of relevance will lead to consideration of what constitutes a reasonable explanation. Since we have already trudged through this maze with the black-box theory and methods of explanation, no further comments seem necessary.

Formal Adequacy

After the importance of a research problem has been established, an experiment must be designed to elicit the desired data. The data that the experiment will provide are important if they contribute to the achievement of the goals inherent in determinism, consistency, parsimony, and reductionism. The extent or degree to which the experiment provides such data is called the "formal adequacy" of an investigation.

The design of the experiment represents the plan by which answers to important questions are to be achieved. Note that formal adequacy is not the same as the importance of the research problem. Investigations that are formally adequate but which provide answers to unimportant questions may be conducted. Formal adequacy refers more to the validity and reliability of such answers, not to their importance. Lacking formal adequacy, however, data on important research problems would be worthless.

In judging the importance of a research problem, inclusiveness of the model was an important criterion. Generality in the formal adequacy of an experiment represents an extension of this factor into experimental design. The scope of the investigation as reflected in size and representativeness of the subject sample employed, number of phenomena measured, and the kinds of phenomena measured are the criteria upon which generality depends. However, generality is really determined by the extent to which reductionism participated in the evaluation of the importance of a research problem. A small sample, measurement of only one or a few of the important phenomena, and selection of phenomena less important in the model domain would minimize fulfillment of reductionism. The importance of the investigation would, therefore, be minimized.

Reductionism and generality are thus seen to be a common bond between evaluation of the importance of a research problem and its formal adequacy. Without generality in formal adequacy, the criterion of reductionism could not be satisfied. In a similar manner, the doctrine of consistency requires that accurate and reliable data be produced. If the investigation is not formally adequate, it will produce unreliable, inaccurate data. In short, the purposes of an investigation (its importance as established by evaluative criteria) must be fulfilled by attention to the formal adequacy of an investigation. Formal adequacy requires that the answers asked for be provided.

Thus, the importance of a research problem and its formal adequacy are complementary. Without one, the other is lost. The purposes of the investigation are established by consideration of its importance. Importance is judged by the contributions that it may make to the achievement of scientific goals. Once the purposes are established, achievement of the purposes is attained by planning experiments that are formally adequate.

Assuming that generality is achieved, validity and reliability are the most important criteria for formal adequacy. The measures secured must be *valid* assessments of the phenomena being investigated. In personality research, for example, valid tests must be used. There must be correspondence among the phenomena for which assessment is desired and the actual measures secured in an experiment. If invalid tests are used, desired measures of specific phenomena cannot be secured and the purposes of the investigation will go unachieved.

Reliability of the results is the second major criterion for formal adequacy. Accuracy of test measures is demanded by the doctrine of consistency; and, without reliability, no test measure can be valid. Reliability implies the reduction of error in measurements. Unreliable data destroys validity. In turn, the entire experiment lacks formal adequacy. Without formal adequacy, important research problems go unanswered. In experimental research, the design and analytic procedures require careful consideration. Collection of data must be done according to some overall plan. Analysis of data necessitates special competency. Experimental design and analytic procedures inevitably call for competence in statistics.

PROFESSIONAL AND SCIENTIFIC RESEARCH

Throughout this book, physical education has been referred to as both a profession and an academic discipline. A dual identity such as this makes it difficult to decide what content deserves inclusion and what matters would best be omitted. It has been suggested in various sections, however, that a profession and a discipline do exhibit some similarities in the problems that each face. Throughout, our thesis has been that physical education has concentrated too heavily upon professional dimensions and not enough upon academic-discipline responsibilities. Education as a profession has also been shown to have some growing pains of its own.

The kind of research endeavors to be encouraged in physical education likewise suffers from this dual role of profession and discipline. Criteria for a profession and for an academic discipline are not identical. Fortunately, the relationships between a profession and a discipline exist in greater numbers than one might expect. These relationships, as they affect research priorities, can be depicted graphically. Figure 10.2 is an attempt at this portrayal of professional and disciplinary research endeavors.

The representation in Figure 10.2 is given in terms of education in general because the figure was adapted from one originally developed at a conference in 1961 on strategies for research to be used for the improvement of instruction. One of the features bearing mention is that the arrows between any two of the research domains go in both directions. Thus, production of knowledge or recognition of needed research, or both may occur at any stage. Facts produced in a basic science may, indeed, be utilized for the betterment of instructional methodology. So too, may events in the schools suggest deficiencies in the knowledge structure of a basic science and in turn lead to advancement in knowledge. Figure 10.2 represents each research domain as a clearly separate block, but in the real world, the situation might be much closer to a fluid continuum having only vague lines of demarcation.

Relationships between a profession and a discipline are well depicted in this conceptualization of the research process, and there seems to be little need for further explanation. The reader is asked, however, to consider some intriguing questions based upon the figure: First, where would most of the research topics in a profession originate? Where would most of the research topics in a basic science-content relevant area originate? Which of the two (profession or basic science-content relevant) would produce the most important research findings? How certain are you of your answers? Do your colleagues agree with you or not?

One could argue rather vigorously that more important research topics would originate in the basic science-content relevant areas than anywhere

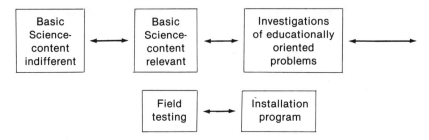

Figure 10.2. Relationship of research to a profession and a discipline. [Based upon Figure 2, page 98 in *Handbook of Research on Teaching*, N.L. Gage (ed.). Chicago: Rand McNally, 1963. Copyright by American Educational Research Association, Washington, D.C., 1963.]

else. It is here, after all, that adequate models for the knowledge structure are developed; and it is here where the more important research studies based upon sophisticated criteria so far as priorities for research are concerned will be conducted. However, what if the basic science-content relevant areas pursue knowledge in a direction away from educationally oriented problems? Must the profession wait for the basic science-content relevant areas to change their priorities, or will the profession decide to conduct its own research on educationally oriented problems within the content domain of the basic science? Should the basic science-content relevant areas be coerced into studying the knowledge structure closest to educationally oriented problems? If so, what might happen to the development of the basic science itself if it were forced to focus its activities on a different set of criteria for priority assessment?

Second, examine the blocks in Figure 10.2 once again and try to visualize the system in operation. Now imagine that you have been appointed as the Commissioner of Education for the United States. Part of your responsibility, of course, is to make sure that the education of our youth is the best that money can provide. Another of your responsibilities is to encourage research in education in order to improve continually educational practices. At the time you take office, you inherit a research and development program organized exactly as depicted in the figure. Your office finances and controls activities in each of the blocks, and the entire setup seems to be operating efficiently and effectively. Each of the constituent parts of the organization is staffed by highly capable individuals and all parts cooperate with each other.

Suddenly, however, you are faced with an unexpected and distasteful emergency. Because of certain financial difficulties you are directed to eliminate in toto one of the constituent parts. The directive is very clear. An entire block must be eliminated and you cannot make budget cuts across all the blocks in an economy move. The first block that is usually eliminated is that of the basic science-content indifferent area. This deletion does not seem to cause you too much grief since this block obviously contributes the least amount of useful knowledge anyway. Indeed, workers in this area have often caused trouble, claiming something about a pure-science ideal and denying any obligation to produce useful knowledge. Although you recognize the fact that the sciences form a monolithic structure, interdependent in nature with advances in one science often contributing to advances in another, you force yourself to live with your decision.

As if that were not bad enough, a new directive appears instructing you to delete another constituent block. As before, the deletion must be of an entire block. Which one would you delete? Most individuals would choose the field-testing unit for elimination, in the belief that the remaining blocks might still be able to function at some reduced level of effectiveness. Unfortunately, you continue to receive directives instructing you to delete, one by one, each of the remaining blocks. It has been the author's experience that rather lively debate occurs about which component would next be deleted so as to cause the least amount of deterioration in the effectiveness of the agency. The majority of students asked or required to delete components in the system usually decide down to two remaining blocks and then refuse to go any further, no matter what threats the instructor might use.

Usually, one of the two last remaining blocks surviving in this progressive surgery is that of the installation program. The arguments heard in defense of this component seem sound enough. Any advances produced must, after all, find implementation in the schools if any good is to come of them. If the Commissioner of Education is going to support research, there must be some returns in the educational setting. However, what now of the second remaining block? This block must fulfill the obligation of conducting research that will produce the knowledge for advances in educational practice. The choice is commonly between basic science-content relevant areas and the investigations of educationally oriented problems. Which of the two would you choose?

This exercise should serve to demonstrate that educational practice must replenish itself with a continuous flow of new knowledge. Without such a flow of knowledge, no advances in educational practice seem possible, and stagnation seems inevitable. Many people feel that the kind of research produced in the educationally oriented block would be most likely to bring about the most immediate results. Educationally oriented research seems to qualify as a kind of applied research, and could be conducted on the most immediate and stressing problems facing the profession. How long, however, can applied research be fruitfully conducted if the knowledge structure of the basic science-content relevant areas remains static? Eventually, the applied research in educationally oriented areas would "use up" all the knowledge available to science-content relevant areas. Then what would happen? What if applied research discovered that it could not solve some nagging problems in education because it lacked basic knowledge located in the basic science?

An installation program depends for its sustenance upon research and the production of new knowledge. Revision, deletion, or implementation of education practices must be based upon a sound knowledge-foundation. Administrators and curriculum experts can operate effectively only when research produces needed facts upon which to base decisions. The quality of the professional practices which society expects can be improved through professional research only up to a certain point, beyond that point, only scientific research producing new facts will allow for further advancement. The flow of new knowledge must be continuous for the best advances in professional practices to be realized.

The Case of No New Knowledge

Let us consider a hypothetical and far-fetched example of what might happen to a profession if it studied only itself and paid no heed to the production of new knowledge within its content domain. In 1885, as we have seen, the medical profession was not very highly esteemed. Medical education was short, admittedly poor, and schools were conducted on meager budgets. The state of knowledge in medicine was comparably deficient. With the appearance of the Flexner report, the status of the medical profession was drastically changed. Medical schools of poor quality voluntarily folded or were driven out of existence by persuasion or by licensing practices. The amount and quality of education required of physicians was notably improved, and the medical profession gained new respect from society.

These advancements in medicine could be attributed to the study of the profession itself; for instance, administrative and curriculum aspects were closely scrutinized, found wanting, and suitable reforms were initiated. Let us suppose, however, that medicine continued on (after reorganization) and always emphasized a study of itself without giving concurrent emphasis to the production of new knowledge. Let us suppose that medicine conducted only professional research—research designed to improve the profession; that is, studies of patient loads, licensing practices in various states, job analysis of city versus country physicians, grade-point averages and later success in medical practice, recruitment practices and salary structures, and the like were the only research investigations deemed immediately essential.

The result could be—hypothetically—that, by 1990, the medical profession would be organized excellently as a profession but would still be practicing medicine on the basis of knowledge available at the turn of the century. True, the ratio of physicians per 100,000 of population would be close to optimum because of the efficiency of medical-school recruitment and educational policies. True, the medical profession would be organized effectively to ferret out undesirables within the ranks. However, would the quality of medical services to society be optimum? Optimum methods for the treatment of polio may have been taught effectively, via the sound medical-school curricula, to the best students possible; but, would this be as desirable as the development of a vaccine to prevent the disease?

In all too many respects, the situation in physical education has tended closely to parallel this facetious, hypothetical example in medicine. The profession has labored for universal physical-education legislation, implementation of teacher certification laws, and education of the public about the values of physical exercise. Our undergraduate major curricula have stressed the role of mental health, the influence of the teacher as a model, professional responsibilities, and the acquisition of teaching methods. At the graduate level, the majority of our students are majors in administration, history and philosophy, or curriculum. Test and measurement research has dominated our "research" efforts. For several generations, we have debated grading in physical education and have constructed skill and knowledge tests for every possible grade level, geographic area, and level of student intelligence.

Let us imagine that the physical-education profession eventually becomes 100% successful in such goals. Let us imagine that physical education is required of every school child every day of the week of every school year. Let us suppose that teacher-student ratios and certification practices are optimum; that all our physical educators are as sincere, dedicated, loyal, and professional as possible. Let us suppose that our curriculum has been deliberated upon by the best minds in administration, history, philosophy, and curriculum construction and that there is unanimous agreement on *the* curriculum in physical education. Let us suppose that the public has finally been educated to realize the value of physical exercise and that the profession has an unlimited budget at its disposal.

What would happen then? Those fields manipulating available knowledge would have taken the profession as far as they could. So far as administration, philosophy, and curriculum development were concerned, the services of physical education would be most effectively administered. Further advances in the quality of services that physical education could provide for society would come only when new knowledge were made available.

Just as indicated in Figure 10.2, the implementation of a program depends for existence upon research and production of new knowledge.

Physical education, as a profession, has labored diligently to organize itself for effective service to society. The manipulation of available knowledge upon which to base its practices, however, may have outlived its usefulness as a process for effective advancement. Deficiencies in practices due to lack of knowledge cannot eternally be ameliorated by policy decisions and mutual consent.

Is a Thesis Necessary?

The graduate professor who has not heard a graduate student complain about the thesis requirement has probably not yet sponsored a thesis. A thesis is, after all, extravagant in its demands upon a student's time, disruptive of preplanned time schedules for the completion of a degree, characterized by a damaging set of limitations, hard to do, and financially costly. Unless the goal of a graduate student is a career in research, why should the student be required to do a thesis? Time could be better spent absorbing knowledge in additional course work or in the sharpening of skills as a practitioner. The student will have become familiar with research problems in the areas of health, physical education, recreation, safety, outdoor education, athletic training, adapted physical education, teacher education, and dance. Graduate course work will have provided at least a reading knowledge of statistics and the ability to read research articles and understand their conclusions. Although ready to admit the need for research, the student is reluctant to admit that a thesis should be required for *all* students. Why shouldn't just the students interested in research do research?

Indeed, why should there be a thesis requirement? Does it matter that this same student is adept at admonishing researchers for producing the "stuff" they do and is ready to suggest more practical and relevant research topics? Each time an assignment for a paper is made in a course, this student arranges a consultation with a graduate professor in order to ask for help in locating good references. Later, this same student may return to request an interpretation of some of the literature already provided. If the topic of interest is a personal one, the student will again be appalled at the lack of work being done and suggest that "they" ought to be doing research designed to help sincere and dedicated teachers and coaches with their nagging problems of the real world. Finally, the student is convinced that the academic prestige of physical education needs to be upgraded. Many teachers and administrators are "against" physical education, and the student calls for action to improve the image of the profession. Privately, however, he or she is convinced that the academic prestige of physical education is justifiably poor because the subject is just not "tough" in an academic sense. The student doubts the profession will ever command the respect accorded other areas and is thankful that most school districts have a single salary schedule for all subject matter areas. But a thesis requirement?

Is it the case that graduate students are naive and selfish? Is it true that their only interest in graduate work is to improve themselves, to earn a degree and qualify for a better position, to expect and demand from graduate study only what is useful to their immediate goals? Of course not. Complaints about a thesis requirement exist only at the early stages of graduate study because of a misunderstanding on the part of the student concerning the profession and its relationship to graduate study. The more mature graduate student sees that a thesis can be a contribution to the profession as well as a personal learning experience and realizes that not doing a thesis would be incredibly selfish. The student recognizes the needs of the profession as well as personal goals and needs, and he or she accepts the opportunity to make a contribution to the profession through a thesis. The mature student understands that graduate study exists not just to serve the individual but to prepare competent and productive workers to advance the profession as well. Indeed, such mature dedication and enthusiasm result in a determination to produce the best thesis physical education has ever seen.

REFERENCES

1. Accident in diet causes diabetes among sand rats. *Medical Tribune* **6** (98): 3; August 16, 1965.

2. Barzun, Jacques. *Science: The Glorious Entertainment.* New York: Harper, 1964.

3. Bookwalter, Karl W. Selection and definition of a problem. In *Research Methods in Health, Physical Education, Recreation.* Washington, D.C.: American Association of Health, Physical Education, and Recreation, 1959. Pp. 39-70.

4. Brace, David K. Critical issues facing physical education. In *American Academy of Physical Education, Professional Contributions No. 7.* Washington, D.C.: American Association of Health, Physical Education, and Recreation, 1961. Pp. 109-123.

5. Cannon, Walter B. *The Way of an Investigator.* New York: Norton, 1945.

6. Cartter, Allan M. *An Assessment of Quality in Graduate Education.* Washington, D.C.: American Council on Education, 1966.

7. Cureton, Thomas K. Doctoral theses reported by graduate departments in health, physical education, and recreation, 1930-1946, inclusively. *Research Quarterly* **20**: 21-59; March 1949.

8. Greenewalt, Crawford H. Basic research: a technological savings account. In *Symposium on Basic Research*, Dael Wofle (ed.). Washington, D.C.: American Association for the Advancement of Science, 1959. Pp. 127-132.

9. Heymans, C. A look at an old but still current problem. *Annual Review of Physiology* **25**: 1-14; 1963.

10. Larson, Leonard A., Morey R. Fields, and Milton A. Gabrielson. *Problems in Health, Physical and Recreation Education.* Englewood Cliffs, New Jersey: Prentice-Hall, 1953.

11. Moles, A.A. *La Creation Scientifique.* Geneva: 1957.

12. Moore, Omar K., and Alan R. Anderson. Some puzzling aspects of social interaction. *The Review of Metaphysics* 15: 410-425; March 1962.

13. Oppenheimer, J. Robert. The need for new knowledge. In *Symposium on Basic Research*, Dael Wofle (ed.). Washington, D.C.: American Association for the Advancement of Science, 1959. Pp. 1-15.

14. Reagan, Michael D. Basic and applied research: a meaningful distinction? *Science* 155: 1383-1386; March 17, 1967.

15. Sidman, Murray. *Tactics of Scientific Research.* New York: Basic Books, 1961.

16. Weitz, J. Let's do it again. *Psychological Reports* 2: 391; 1956.

17. Whitney, F.P. The questionnaire craze. *Educational Review* 68: 139-140; 1924.

Writing Up Research

After a topic for research has been chosen, it becomes necessary to prepare a thesis proposal that will adequately convey the important details of the contemplated research. The thesis proposal (or prospectus) is evidence that the research topic has been carefully studied and that a sound plan has been devised for its execution. In many schools, the thesis proposal must be approved by a thesis committee and then filed at the graduate office. At other schools, the proposal must receive approval only from the thesis sponsor, and may be a less formal endeavor. Most faculties assume the proposal to be a sort of informal contract between the student and the committee; that is, once the proposal is approved, both parties are obliged to operate within the defined limits. Thesis-committee members may require additional work, such as an increase in sample size, only if absolutely necessary, while students may not further delimit the scope of the study without consent of the committee.

A thesis proposal must establish the importance of the problem, in conjunction with a plan for the execution of the research, which promises a satisfactory set of conditions for success. In order to establish the importance of the research topic, the proposal must convey sufficient theory to suggest the potential significance of the study in terms of the model domain. This task usually requires an overview of related literature and the present state of knowledge existing in the topical area. The research topic is then related to such an overview of the topical area and its significance is explicitly defined. Once the importance of the topic is demonstrated, a plan for execution of the study is outlined in sufficient detail to guarantee formal adequacy for the collection of both valid and reliable data.

A good thesis proposal must convincingly demonstrate that the research problem chosen is important and that the research methodology has satisfactory formal adequacy. If the proposal fails to convince the thesis sponsor or committee on either of these points the study is in jeopardy. Even if the study truly possesses these qualities, failure of the proposal to communicate such points effectively may result in a potentially good piece of research not being approved or given proper support. The ability to write clearly and to present proposals that are both informative and persuasive, thus, becomes an essential talent to the prospective researcher. No matter how gifted an individual may be at identifying important research topics and planning their successful execution, the individual must also be able to communicate these talents to others. Failure in this case would force the individual to face the prospect of having such talents denied fruition.

Writing up proposals for research is not a responsibility peculiar to graduate students. Faculty members hoping to secure support for their own contemplated research must also write up formal proposals. Sometimes such a proposal is neither lengthy nor detailed as in the case where the proposal is presented for consideration by a departmental budget committee and the support being requested is nominal. At other times, the proposal may have to go into considerable detail and spell out all necessary specifics. If, for example, the proposal will find itself in competition with others for a large grant from some agency, it will have to be written with meticulous attention to details and must conform to all format standards required by the granting agency. Indeed, commercial agencies exist that offer the services of professional writers of research-grant proposals!

If all goes well and the research proposal is approved and successfully performed, the task of preparing the final report remains. Naturally, large portions of the proposal itself may be appropriate for inclusion, with only slight revision, in the final report. If the final report is being written as an article to be submitted for publication, it may be necessary, because of space limitations, to condense the initial proposal. The investigator must also present the results of the study, interpret and discuss the significance of such results, and draw meaningful and legitimate conclusions. Since the research investigation represents a considerable investment in terms of time, money, and intellectual effort, the final report should be done as well as the actual research itself. Unfortunately, this is not always true.

DIFFICULTIES IN SCIENTIFIC WRITING

Writing in a clear and persuasive manner is a task of considerable proportions that finds both the beginner and advanced researcher failing often. Woodford (16), for example, contended that too many articles appearing in scientific journals were very good examples of very poor writing. He commented that the typical scientific writer takes an inspiring and lively research topic and then "chokes it to death, embalms the remains in molasses of polysyllable, wraps the corpse in an impenetrable veil of vogue words, and buries the stiff old mummy with much pomp and circumstance in the most distinguished journal that will take it." Woodford's lament was not only that such writing was uninteresting, but that too often it was not clear and, thus, cheated its scientific audience from knowing exactly what was done and what results were obtained.

Editors of a scientific journal frequently find themselves in a quandary when considering an article for publication. Although the editors may be appalled at the poor writing in a manuscript, at the same time, they recognize that its contents exhibit a worthwhile scientific contribution. Some journals may encourage staff editors to suggest to authors the revision and modification of important sections of an article in an attempt to ensure adequate clarity. In so doing, the journal exposes itself to the danger of distorting the true meaning of a finding in an area of research unfamiliar to its staff members. Such journals are familiar with the wrath of an indignant author who has objected violently to the merciless mutilation of his or her masterpiece. Still other journals may decide to publish the article as it was submitted and let the reader struggle through deficiencies in writing. The position in the latter case is that the function of a scientific journal is to publish articles that are informative with no obligation to guarantee that such articles are also good entertainment.

Difficulty in writing is a widespread phenomenon and is hardly limited to researchers in any one scientific area. Poor writing was of enough concern in biology to result in the formation, by the Council of Biology Editors, of a committee to consider the matter of scientific writing and to make suitable recommendations to ameliorate the problem. The committee was responsible for the preparation of a manual entitled *Scientific Writing for Graduate Students* (15). It was noted in the manual that bad writing in scientific journals was all too common and that only a few universities saw fit to offer formal course work in scientific writing. The committee urged that a formal course on scientific writing be given at the graduate level which would take up the "requirements of scientific proof, the logical development of scientific argument, and precision of scientific expression." It was further recommended that such instruction be given by a scientist rather than an expert on writing. A major segment of the scientific community recognizes the difficulties caused by bad writing, and action to improve the situation is beginning to be seen in several quarters.

In many respects, the very nature of science seems against the production of scientific articles that are both informative and interesting. The growth of technical terms and special vocabularies has produced thousands of words which defy spelling and which are so hard to pronounce that they are referred to by initials.* Minute details about essential apparatus design and standardized data collecting techniques often require so much space that a truly adequate presentation is seldom seen. Instead, readers are referred to other articles by the investigators for coverage of such information only to find that these other articles refer back to even earlier articles and so on and on.

The scientist's frame of reference toward research work reflects itself in writing as well as in the laboratory. Scientists have been trained to avoid the theatrical arts in scientific endeavors, and such a scientific temperament understandably prevails in all science-related pursuits. The operating code for scientific work prescribes that it be amoral and objective. Therefore, scientists could not legitimately be expected to become involved subjectively with scientific work or forced to consider its status in a good-bad sense. For this reason, dramatic or flowery phrases laden with emotion are not considered appropriate in scientific writing. The detached viewpoint called for by objectivity results in avoidance of the use of the personal "I" or "we" in formal reports. Only the objective third person frame of reference seems suitably scientific.

Because of the operating code's requirement for caution and skepticism, scientists are obliged not to over-emphasize the importance of research endeavors. Horn tooting is simply not allowed. The more reputable and competent the scientist, the more likely it is that findings will be stated in rather neutral if not de-emphasized overtones. Scientists must guard against having a reputation be the reason for acceptance of results and must try to see that results speak for themselves. Many journals have a practice of blind review in which the author's name does not appear on the manuscript sent out to reviewers. The code of parsimony may even affect the writing style and find reported work stated in the simplest and shortest statements possible.

In short, the basic operating codes of science work against letting scientific research be written in a colorful and interesting style. Entertainment is not an obligation of scientific writing, sound presentation of results is. The work presented in scientific articles is to be judged on its

---

*One author referred to these tongue twisters as "vocables." See Jacques Barzun. *Science: The Glorious Entertainment*, New York: Harper, 1964, page 201.

merits as a contribution to knowledge and not upon its merits as an acceptable piece of literature. One must also guard against having deficiencies in the worth of a scientific contribution disguised or overshadowed by an elegant and charming writing style.

Although science editors of popular magazines may be highly skilled at translating technical jargon into easy-to-read articles for public consumption, these science writers are not the ones making new contributions to knowledge. Criticism of poor writing in scientific articles is of major concern only when the writing fails to present its findings clearly. Although it may be extremely desirable to have such essential clarity accompanied by an interesting style of presentation, such a style is not absolutely necessary and a criticism on this basis is not wholly legitimate. English professors and literary experts may be revolted by scientific writing, but their agony had best be ameliorated in ways that do no damage to scientific motivation. An important scientific contribution is not made less important because of a few split infinitives.

The unfortunate dilemma in scientific writing, however, is that clarity of presentation must include a clear way of depicting what the results were *and* the meaning of the results. It is here that the previously mentioned quality of persuasiveness becomes of paramount importance. Although the results should speak for themselves, they seldom do. If results did speak for themselves all that scientific journals would require would be a set of tables containing pertinent data. Results speak for themselves only when one appreciates the model domain within which they exist and how they "fit" into the structure of the model. The research report must so depict the setting that the results do come close to being self-evident.

Thus, the writer of a scientific report is caught between two horns of a dilemma. Brash showmanship and emotional theatrics might make a report interesting and entertaining, but it might also violate important operating codes in science. These operating codes have been of considerable value to science and they are not likely to be abandoned in the interest of good writing. At the same time, however, clarity of presentation and accurate reporting of the meaning of the results requires that some amount of persuasiveness be included. The results should not be clouded by theatrics, but neither should their true significance be lost because of improper modesty. It is difficult to choose between these two evils.

NEED FOR WRITING RESEARCH REPORTS

For many researchers the writing of a research report is a most distasteful task. Many prominent researchers even circumvent the necessity of writing up a formal proposal for a research study if they can. The plan for a research investigation is carried "in the investigator's head" or scribbled on scraps of paper stuffed in a manila folder. Once having completed a research problem and knowing the results, the researcher is prepared to move on and start additional studies. Preparation of a formal written report seems too time consuming and would prevent further, more advanced work on the topic. With the results of a research study in hand, the researcher is eager to take advantage of such findings and apply new insights, secured from their analysis, in tracking down new and promising leads. Rather than face the ordeal of putting his or her work down on paper, struggling with the problem of clarity and persuasiveness, the researcher may decide to do another study—a better study—and then worry about producing an article for publication.

No accurate estimate can be made of how many completed research investigations (in raw-data form) lie in filing cabinets, while new research studies are undertaken. By setting aside specific time periods during the year, some researchers force themselves to "take time out from research" and write up reports. Others have so many sets of data cluttering up their desk and files that their consciences literally force them to sit down and write up the results from at least one set of data. Still others write research papers only when forced to do so by an administrator who threatens loss of research support or by the pressure to publish in order to receive a promotion in rank or a salary increase.

Some researchers may decide not to write a research report fearing that an appropriate journal might reject it. To these authors, the research gathering dust in the files might be considered worthwhile, but if it were rejected for publication the blow might be too much to endure. These researchers might contend that writing up work is a bad idea because it is too advanced for their colleagues to appraise and understand properly. At one time such a posture was adopted by Mendel, who refused to publish any further accounts of his work because he was "deeply disappointed by the lack of response to his historic papers on heredity" (8).

Besides using all these arguments, a researcher may suggest that the publication of an article is of little value because so few people will ever read it, and even fewer use its results. This argument has some basis in fact. Less than 1% of the articles appearing in chemistry journals, for example, are ever read by any one chemist (1). A study by the American Psychological Association revealed that a similar situation held true for psychology, with research reports in psychological journals being read by only about 1 to 7% of a random sample of psychologists (10). No study has ever been made of the scientific habits of physical educators. An analysis of how many and what kinds of individuals associated with physical education regularly read the *Research Quarterly* would be of considerable interest. The methodology for such an undertaking is available in the cited references and requires no staggering amounts of sophisticated research ability.

All such arguments allowed, researchers still have an obligation to write and publish the results of their research endeavors. If the investigation was worth doing and it was executed successfully, the work should be offered to the scientific community for consumption. A science advances as contributions to it are made; and contributions are made only by communicating worthwhile research results. Any investigator who fails to communicate work exhibits an inexcusable form of selfishness— keeping work private rather than sharing it publicly. No possible argument can overshadow the simple truth that unless knowledge is communicated and shared it is really not knowledge. The only alternative reason explaining why some researchers do not publish is simple. Either they are doing absolutely no research or what they are doing is worthless.

TANGIBLE SUGGESTIONS

A novel usually has a hero or heroine, an antagonist or villain, and some supporting characters. The plot simply depicts the actions of these individuals under some set of circumstances. A moral may be present. Using only such basic building blocks, a novelist then writes the story. As we can all appreciate, such a guide to the writing of novels hardly seems overwhelming, and considerable variation in the quality of novels produced with such a guide is inevitable. The numerous ways in which a novelist fills in the basic plot are what make the difference, and the same idea can be developed by the same or different authors with tremendously different results.

Just as there is no absolute set of principles guaranteed to produce a good novel if the guide is followed, there is no simple method of writing a research report. Fortunately, however, there are some guidelines available which have been developed to help in the writing of an acceptable report. Such standards for research reports prescribe the adherence to specific rules for format, and require that certain topics be included. There are many variations in such standards for research reports, however, and many contend that there are more variations than consistencies. In order to ensure recognizable stability in format, over the years, some universities have adopted a school-wide manual as a standard guide for research writing. Some departments exercise the option to use the guide prescribed for publication of articles in pertinent research journals.

Two of the more popular style manuals are Campbell's *Form and Style in Thesis Writing* (2) and Turabian's *A Manual for Writers of Term Papers, Theses, and Dissertations* (14). Each year, in the October issue, the *Research Quarterly* publishes a short "Guide for *Research Quarterly* Contributors" outlining essential style requirements for submitted manuscripts. Scholarly journals have similar guides. The *Journal of Applied Physiology*, for example, publishes a two-page guide for its prospective authors. Any points not covered in the abbreviated guide are contained in the more detailed *Style Manual for Biological Journals* (13). In a similar manner, the American Psychological Association offers a style manual governing manuscript format for all of its publications (11).

These style manuals constitute excellent guidelines for the mechanical format of scientific papers, and their use can answer the many specific questions that arise in writing a report. For example, definite prescriptions are made for spacing on a page, form of bibliographical entries, footnote usage, size of figures, correct titles for tables, and dozens of other such mechanical features of actual reporting. Adherence to such rules helps guarantee uniformity in mechanical aspects of a report and enhances clarity.

Because most schools or departments make their own choice of appropriate style manuals, no material on style and format will be presented in this chapter. The student, however, will need to secure access to the designated manual of style and become thoroughly acquainted with its contents. It is a wise practice in many schools that requires all papers submitted to be in a standard form. Such a requirement allows the student many opportunities to practice using the chosen style manual and helps promote the possibility that the thesis itself will be in correct mechanical format. Although a professional typist may claim to know the correct format requirements, it is still the responsibility of the student to make sure that the thesis is properly typed and in correct form.

Thus, concrete guidelines are available for the mechanical features of a research report. Guidelines for the actual content of a thesis proposal and the thesis itself are, unfortunately, less specific. Although no foolproof set of guidelines can be established to guarantee a satisfactory write-up, there are some helpful hints available. The majority of these originate from a simple examination of good versus poor reports. As is well known, when some reports are read they seem to convey information smoothly and raise few questions about content. Other articles seem confusing and thoroughly unsatisfactory. If the features of a good report can be exemplified, they can be of considerable help to an individual struggling to produce an acceptable written report.

In the following sections, we will consider some of these features and attempt to illustrate with concrete examples both good and bad writing. Being aware of these features and applying the suggested criteria to the writing of actual reports, however, still looms as a difficult task. The very nature of some subject matter may require a unique and creative application of the criteria. Typically, each new report represents a different kind of challenge for the writer's communication talents. Several of the suggestions to follow, however, apply to most cases and have been found helpful in the past by many individuals.

Preliminary Considerations

Before looking at individual sections of the research report, several points of general writing strategy need to be considered. One of the most important points is the need to consider the reader. After a researcher has searched the literature extensively, planned a method of data collection and analysis, labored over the data analysis, and become drained of intellectual vigor attempting to interpret the results, the researcher often becomes so immersed in the research that perspective is lost. He or she fails to remember that anyone reading the report has not had the benefit of such a considerable background of study in the topical area. The researcher must guard against writing a report which only the researcher and God can understand. To do so requires that the report be written for others who are not as knowledgeable as the researcher. Although it often comes as a pleasant surprise, the completion of the research study represents quite an invaluable learning experience.

Beginners at research writing almost invariably fail to realize that their own level of knowledge and understanding was painstakingly acquired. They tend to forget the many hours of consultation and discussion with the thesis sponsor and the intensive studying of related literature that was suffered. Their initial drafts of a research report are so technical that even the thesis chairperson may have difficulty understanding it. The researcher knows everything that was done and why it was done. A section explaining an important point may be perfectly clear to the researcher but unintelligible to everyone else. In writing, therefore, the knowledgeable researcher must plan the writing carefully and consider how best to convey to the reader the desired information.

The reader must be pictured as being intelligent and reasonably well informed about certain areas of research, but not well educated about the specific research area being reported. A report must gear itself to some potential audience and avoid being so technical that it requires more knowledge on the reader's part than is reasonable. At the same time, the report must not be written in a manner which insults the intelligence of the reader. Presentation of facts essential for an understanding of the research conducted must be provided if it is reasonable to expect that such facts are not common knowledge. What this means, of course, is that the subject matter content of the research topic can greatly affect the writing strategy to be employed. Each new research report, thus, represents a new challenge to the author's writing talent; and an approach that was satisfactory for one kind of research report may not be satisfactory for another.

One of the best ways to test the adequacy of a research report is to have someone else read it. This sounds so simple a test that it almost seems ridiculous to suggest it. Yet, most graduate students will write a thesis chapter and never have anyone else read it before they formally submit it. No matter how hard the individual works at writing a clear report, it may still possess glaring deficiencies if it has passed the inspection of only the writer. If an individual would merely have a friend read the work carefully and react to it, many of these deficiencies could be identified. The writer might also ask this person certain key questions to make sure that the report has conveyed what it was intended to convey. Such questions could show that the significance of the report was misinterpreted by the reader or that the presentation of results gave too much attention to minor details and not enough to important findings.

Many established researchers write a research report as well as they can by themselves. The report is then set aside for a period of time during which time it is forgotten and ignored until it becomes relatively forgotten. When the report is again seen after this cooling-off period, the investigator often finds that the writing does not satisfactorily express certain points. The report, which, only a short time ago, appeared to be perfectly adequate is now seen as containing numerous flaws. Once the topic and the paper become less familiar, the writing does not seem so satisfactory. Another commonly followed practice is to forward preliminary drafts of a paper to colleagues working in the area and ask them to criticize the report. Finding colleagues and friends who will review a paper critically is not easy, for a careful review of a research paper takes time, effort, and talent.

Before writing ever begins, it is also a good idea to discuss the contemplated write-up with the thesis chairperson. This initial discussion on plans for writing may serve several useful purposes if the student comes prepared to discuss ideas and not just to ask for help. By this time, the student should be very intimate with the pertinent literature—even more so than the chairperson—and have definite ideas of how the paper should be organized. The conference with the thesis chairperson will reflect an exchange of ideas about the several ways that an actual write-up could be accomplished. The student might begin the conference by outlining personal evaluation of the important outcomes of the study. Establishing priorities is rather difficult unless one is very competent in an area, and what a beginner in the research area may consider to be of crucial importance, an experienced researcher might know to be of less scientific significance.

The student could very profitably present the set of critical points that will be emphasized in the final draft. If the thesis chairperson agrees with the priorities selected by the student, there will be less need for later revision. Many faculty members also use this prewriting conference to test the student's familiarity with the literature, and they may suggest the need to check more leads in the literature. Other faculty members take advantage of the occasion by recommending to the student certain areas of additional study and course work that will aid in successful completion of the study. One of the great advantages to the student can be the counsel received concerning what ideas do not bear additional study or development. Quite often, a student may be preparing to accomplish unnecessary tasks; the more experienced faculty member can head off such a waste of time by simply explaining why such activity is unnecessary.

After the preliminary conference, an initial draft of the research paper will be made. As suggested before, the student should ask another outside party to read the paper for clarity. Assuming that this has been done, the student is, understandably, eager to have it read by the thesis chairperson. Too often, this initial draft is something far less than acceptable. A good many graduate faculty members refuse to read "rough drafts" for a number of sound reasons. First, faculty members have been discouraged too often when they approved ideas in a rough draft and then saw the student react objectionably when a revised draft was returned for further revision. Rough drafts may contain appropriate ideas, but the approved ideas may not be properly developed and thus be unacceptable as a finished product.

A faculty member can never be sure what deficiencies in a rough draft the student is actually planning to eliminate by further work. Poor grammar, misspelled words, inaccurate reference citations, awkward wording, and a host of other deficiencies may be present in the rough draft. If a faculty member were to offer necessary reactions to all of these points an enormous amount of time would be required. If the thesis chairperson ignores minor deficiencies and reacts only to major defects, the student may misinterpret the lack of comment to mean approval. Later, when the student submits a revised rough draft, he or she is overwhelmed by the tremendous number of revisions necessary when nothing was said about them before.

The best procedure is probably for the student to submit the paper in finished form complete in all respects. A faculty member can then react legitimately to any and all deficiencies and can make careful and specific recommendations. If the number of such deficiencies is large, the student may expect the faculty member to return the paper with only a few general recommendations for major revision. Attention to more specific details would be reserved until glaring deficiencies had been eliminated. Students may justly expect to be able to use faculty members in writing papers, but must not abuse them by implicitly asking for too much help. Turning in typed pages with illegible scribblings as revisions, marginal notations, no bibliography, missing sections to be written later, smeared carbon copies, and one sentence paragraphs could only lead the thesis sponsor to believe that little effort had been given to the write-up.

SECTIONS OF A RESEARCH REPORT

At this point, it would be helpful to be reminded that a research report represents the end product of a scientific endeavor. If the investigation conducted were truly scientific, then it necessarily reflects the scientific method in operation. Prior to the consideration of the usual sections of a formal research report, a brief review of the scientific method should allow one to anticipate what sections a research report is likely to need. As we have seen previously, the scientific method consists of three basic steps:

(1) After suitable observation of pertinent empirical data has been made, induction is employed to formulate some theory or summarizing statement.

(2) The statement arrived at inductively is examined and predictions of new data extracted by analytic deductive procedures. Suitable observations for the predicted new empirical data are collected.

(3) The adequacy of the inductive statement forwarded in step (1) is evaluated, using as a criterion the accuracy with which it accounted for the data upon which it was formulated and the predicted new data collected in the present investigation.

Since a research report is a product of the scientific method, it will necessarily reflect the process itself. Any research report will, naturally, include all the basic steps in the scientific method. In practice, the order of these three steps sometimes seems confused due to a need to conform to certain format requirements. For example, some research-grant application forms and thesis designs require that a statement of the problem be given very early in the report. After the purpose of the study is stated, one is advised to discuss the significance of the study and to present a review of related literature.

In actuality, most research problems are not postulated until after a review of the literature has been made. It was the review of the literature that suggested the need for some work on a particular topic and the researcher chose from among many such possible studies the one thought to be deserving of highest priority because of its significance in the knowledge structure. Thus, the actual sequence in the research study was related literature, significance, and then formulation of the purpose of the study. Although the required format frequently calls for a mixed up order of the scientific method, the student should always bear in mind that all of the basic steps in the scientific method will eventually be included in the research report.

Table 11.1
Thesis Outline

Chapter One	Chapter Three (cont.)
Introduction	Measurement techniques
Statement of the problem	Experimental design and analysis
Significance of the study	procedures
Methodology	
Delimitations	Chapter Four
Limitations	Presentation of results and analyses
Summary	Discussion of results
Chapter Two	Chapter Five
Review of related literature	Summary of study
	Conclusions
Chapter Three	Recommendations for further study
Methodology	
Sample description	Appendix
Parameters measured and	
their selection	Bibliography

A typical thesis will, generally, contain five chapters arranged in a rather definite sequence and with specific subsections in each chapter. Although the suggested subsections within each chapter may exhibit considerable variation in the order in which they appear, there is rather good agreement as to what essential topics must be covered. A thesis proposal is not typically written in chapter format, but will necessarily concern itself with the same topics. In later sections, we shall consider differences between the thesis proposal and the formal thesis itself, but for now we will look at a skeleton outline of the thesis (see Table 11.1).

Each of these chapters is an important and necessary component of a research report and collectively they reflect the scientific method. Some universities may alter the number of chapters, but all of the components will still be represented. In areas of study that are not truly scientific, the thesis may appear to reflect something other than the scientific method. Historical and philosophical studies, for example, may be difficult to report using the subdivisions of a thesis presented above. Experimental investigations, however, can be reported efficiently with the format suggested.

In the following sections, some specific suggestions and concrete examples for the writing of a research report will be presented. Naturally these suggestions cannot apply to every report which may have to be written. The subject matter content greatly affects writing style and only intelligent effort can, in the end, produce an acceptable report. Many of the common mistakes cited, however, occur so frequently that just learning what not to do can help improve the quality of written reports.

CHAPTER ONE

Introduction

The first few paragraphs are highly important because they are the first contact with the reader, and will either create interest or dampen the desire to go on. These paragraphs commonly present information needed as quickly as possible, but not at the expense of stifling interest. Content dealing with the significance or importance of the study can safely be given later on. If the introduction can incorporate information needed to understand the topic, convey importance of the topic, and do this in a style that will arouse interest, the introduction can be said to be well done.

One of the common mistakes made in the introduction, however, is to present material that is too technical. Another hazard is overanxiousness in presenting material attesting to the importance of the topic. An introduction must be gentle and must gradually introduce the topic along with the necessary factual information. Consider, for example, the following paragraph which was submitted in a research paper on the patellar reflex:

> Sherrington first showed that the spinal knee jerk was a genuine reflex in 1893 (Fulton, 1949). Westphal and others (Fearing, 1928) did not hold to this theory because they contended that the time was too brief to permit such transit.

Even if the reader were knowledgeable in the area of patellar reflex research, this introduction is deficient in a number of respects. First, it is a very short paragraph and, thus, reflects poor writing. Second, the material contains a couple of jolts with the reference citations. Sherrington's discovery of the true nature of the spinal knee-jerk is cited as having occurred in 1893, yet the reference citation for this fact carries a date of 1949 and an author named Fulton. The second sentence says "Westphal and others" and then lists a reference citation alluding to Fearing. The use of secondary reference citations in this situation was certainly ill advised. Reference to a spinal knee-jerk and time too brief to permit such transit requires considerable background knowledge in order to be intelligible. To an uninformed reader, the term spinal knee-jerk could mean the spine did the jerking. Considerable information would have to be available to interpret the meaning of time in transit to underlying theory about reflexes. Thus, the introduction as written is certainly not very informative, is too technical, and fails in creating reader interest. As an introduction, it accomplished very little, perhaps because it attempted to do too much. It was not gentle enough for the reader to absorb.

In 1928, Franklin Fearing wrote an excellent article dealing with the history of experimental study of the knee-jerk (3). His first paragraph represents an excellent introduction to a difficult topic. To exemplify the notion of gentleness, information presentation, and interest arousal, Fearing's introductory paragraph is given here.

Perhaps no other reflex presents so variegated a history as does the knee-jerk. Because of the ease with which it may be elicited, the objective definiteness of the response, the relative simplicity of the neural mechanisms involved, and its usefulness to clinical neurology, it has been almost a constant object of clinical and experimental investigation since its discovery in 1875. The extent of these investigations is indicated by the comprehensive monograph of Sternberg,[2] published in 1893, in which over 500 titles are listed. The history of these investigations and those of the succeeding twenty-five years is of especial interest to students of neuromuscular phenomena, and offers data pertinent to their fundamental problems. These developments are concerned especially with methods of registration of muscular response, particularly as they relate to the technique of the study of reflex temporal relationships, and to the problems of inhibition and facilitation.

When Fearing's introduction is contrasted with the previous example, one can appreciate the difference that a good introduction can make to the reader. Fearing effectively portrayed the importance of the knee-jerk and the wide scope of its significance by referring to the amount of attention it had received in various interest areas. The knee-jerk's discovery date, 1875, was given, and an important reference source of over 500 titles suggested the enormous attention given the reflex in scientific literature. His last sentence gave a hint at what his paper considered deserving of priority emphasis when he called attention to the methods and techniques employed to measure neuromuscular responses. In later paragraphs, Fearing elaborated the more technical details which had to be understood, but the reader's initial contact with the paper was one which nurtured interest while still being reasonably informative.

Another introductory paragraph will be presented to illustate how a research report in the same topical area could be handled differently. In this paper, research was reported on the patellar reflex when subjected to Jendrassik and crossed extensor facilitation techniques (4).

Existence of the patellar reflex was independently discovered in 1875 by Erb (4) and Westphal (20) who immediately disagreed as to the causal mechanism responsible for the phenomenon. Erb considered it to be a true reflex while Westphal regarded it as a mechanical response of the muscle to a tendon stroke. The issue was still quite unsettled when Jendrassik (9) reported his discovery in 1883 of a facilitating effect upon the knee jerk if the hands were clinched immediately before the ligamentum patella was struck. Although the causal mechanism for the patellar reflex has since

been elucidated, some question still remains about the mechanism through which the
Jendrassik maneuver accomplishes facilitation of a reflex.*

In this introductory paragraph, different kinds of information were
used in an attempt to arouse interest and at the same time to be informative. The material presented called attention to the fact that the
patellar reflex was independently discovered by two different investigators who, at the time of discovery, disagreed over its cause. Fearing elected not to emphasize this point in his introduction, but it seems an
interesting point capable of drawing attention. A definition of the Jendrassik maneuver is included as well as informing or reminding an intelligent reader that the ligamentum patella is struck to elicit the patellar
reflex. We also learn that, although the original controversy over the
causal mechanism for the reflex had been settled, the mechanism for
facilitation due to a Jendrassik maneuver was still undecided. This point
suggests the importance of an investigation of the Jendrassik maneuver
even though no explicit statement was made about the significance of
research on the patellar reflex.

These two illustrations of reasonably satisfactory introductory
paragraphs demonstrate that several alternate approaches can be made
with equal success. Knowing the nature of the subject matter and significant points in an area allows any number of satisfactory introductions to
be written. Deciding which points to bring out in an introduction is not
so easy but the task is more difficult if not impossible if the writer is not
knowledgeable in the area. One suggestion for points to use is to ask
yourself what you considered to be the most interesting facts about the
topic. After all, what sparks one individual's interest could very well be
interesting to others.

Our comments about writing a satisfactory introduction bring to light
another important clue to successful writing: See how other authors have
handled similar tasks. An individual, for example, could write an introductory paragraph on the patellar reflex which incorporated strong
points of both of the examples used to exemplify satisfactory writing.
Even better, there are other points about the patellar reflex that could be
used to produce an introduction which would be superior to either of the
two examples. When the literature in a field is being studied, a student
would profit by making notes not only of the important facts but of the
method by which "good" articles presented necessary information as
well. Conversely, "bad" articles might be examined in an attempt to
detect the flaws in writing strategy that caused the poor effect.

---

*From Patellar Reflex Time and Reflex Latency Under Jendrassik and Crossed Extensor
Facilitation by Walter Kroll, in *American Journal of Physical Medicine* **47**: 292-301; 1968.
Used with permission of copyright holder, The Williams & Wilkins Co., Baltimore, 1981.

Statement of the Problem

Following the introductory paragraphs, most thesis formats specify that a clear statement of the problem should appear. Framing a short statement embodying the purpose of the study is more difficult than it might seem. Quite often, initial drafts contain long, complicated, and unwieldy statements because the writer has attempted to put too much into the statement of the problem. Rather than attempting to include all pertinent details in one statement, it is often better to forward a more general statement and subsequently to amplify the statement as needed in later material.

Consider the master's thesis which planned to give three different standardized tests to physical education majors. The idea was to assess value orientations held by (a) female and male physical-education majors, and (b) to study these majors at the freshman- and senior-year levels. One of the goals was to see whether any differences existed between the two sexes from freshman *to* senior years. Another feature of the study was to assess the amount of relatedness among the three different standardized tests all of which purported to measure value orientations.

Clearly, such a thesis problem has several substudies built into it, and any attempt at writing one statement containing all this information would be disastrous. Many (or most) well-planned studies will have a number of subtopics that deserve consideration embedded within their framework. In the above example, it would be unwise not to examine the relationships among the three tests administered, even though this was not the major purpose of the study. Although it is certainly true that a condensed version of the purpose of the study will not adequately present all the dimensions of the problem, the initial statement of the problem should not be expected to accomplish such a feat. Indeed, if a statement of the problem can succinctly portray all the dimensions of the study one might consider the possibility that the study lacks sufficient breadth. If the statement of the problem informs the reader of the broad, general purposes, it will suffice until the details can be filled in at a later point.

As a matter of fact, many of the published studies appearing in reputable scientific journals never formally present a separate statement of the problem. To check this, one merely has to glance over published articles and try to find an explicit statement of the purpose of the study. Absence of such a statement, of course, does not mean that a clear purpose was not present. What it does mean is that many writers choose to state implicitly the purpose of a study rather than to offer an explicit statement. Such a realization is often soul shattering to the beginner who has been drilled on the necessity of a clear statement of the problem being of classical importance to good research.

When an introduction handles its material satisfactorily, an explicit statement of the purpose is often unnecessary because it is already implicitly obvious. If the introduction, for example, develops the information about isometric fatigue curves and then notes that no such data have ever been collected on female subjects, would it be necessary to state formally that the investigation being reported, with a title of "Isometric Fatigue Curves in Female Subjects," was on female subjects and isometric fatigue curves? The section on methods or procedures would further clarify such additional details as they were needed. In a like manner, the several subtopics for consideration do not have to be presented explicitly if they are also implicitly expressed. If the study, for example, suggested that one of the major defects in previous studies on isometric fatigue curves was a failure to consider levels of strength, would it be necessary to state explicitly that levels of strength for isometric fatigue curves secured on female subjects would be assessed?

Several thesis guides, however, suggest that an explicit list of subproblems or hypotheses to be tested, or both, follow the statement of the problem. This suggestion is made in the hope that both the reader and the researcher will then be aware of the important subproblems present in the total research endeavor. If these subproblems are given, then the implicit portions of the research problem are made explicit. Few could fault such a practice, particularly with beginners in research. Published studies, however, seldom cite either such lists of subproblems or hypotheses to be tested unless the purpose of the material presented is easy to misinterpret. Too often, furthermore, lists of subproblems and hypotheses seem ludicrous, for they repeat self-evident information. The choice is a matter of value judgment and the student should be guided by the policy of the department or the preference of the thesis chairperson.

Significance of the Study

After an informative but gentle introduction and a clearly stated purpose of the study, a section is devoted to significance of the study, or sometimes, as it is also frequently called, the need for the study. The purpose of such a section is simply to convey the importance of the research and to establish the potential significance of its results. To accomplish this goal, several strategies are available, depending upon the actual significance that the researcher believes his or her study possesses.

Examination of many sections on significance of the study in various research papers leads to two major observations: (1) Any significance of the study section which is considered impressive is usually found with an introductory section possessing similar qualities; and (2) most studies in physical education discuss significance in the context of educational outcomes or immediate practical application rather than emphasize the scientific significance of the study.

The observation that satisfactory sections on significance are typically found in association with excellent introductions is no accident. Many good writers believe that a good introduction is essential to the production of a significance section containing impact and persuasiveness. It is in the introduction where sufficient interest is aroused and enough information is provided to set the stage for an adequate section on significance. Without these prerequisites of interest and essential information, the section on significance is likely to fail to be anything of merit. For this reason, good writers tend to view both of these sections as one continuous piece of writing. After an adequate composition, combining the introduction and the significance of the study, has been written, an attempt is made to split the entire piece into two smaller sections. Sometimes this can be done without any effort other than inserting the statement of the problem between the divided segments. Usually, however, some minor revision is necessary to ensure a smoother style of writing.

Thinking of these sections as one writing task serves to enhance their mutual dependence and helps ensure combined impact. By initially combining the two sections, a writer is better able to judge whether or not the flow of thought presented in the introduction is carried on and further emphasized in the section on significance. Too often, an introduction uses one set of facts to arouse interest and then, in the section on significance, emphasis is placed on an entirely different frame of reference. This commonly results in both sections being judged to be inadequate even though each may have been written satisfactorily if judged in isolation from the other. Anytime a writer cannot seem to find anything wrong in these two sections but is still dissatisfied with the combined impact, he or she would do well to consider the two as a single section and test their qualities of mutual dependence and single flow of thought.

Although most master's theses and doctoral dissertations require an explicit development of a section on the significance of the study, it is interesting to note that published research articles frequently fail to include such a specific section. Several recent issues of the *Research Quarterly*, for example, do not contain a single article with a specific section devoted to significance of the study. Instead, significance is developed implicitly either in the introductory material or in the review of related literature. Thus, just as in the case of a list of subproblems and hypotheses to be tested, if the significance of the study is already implicitly clear it does not have to be explicitly stated. The implicit versus explicit position is apparently applied differently to student research when compared with published research articles. Students are more often required to state explicitly even the most obvious matters, while more mature researchers are allowed considerable freedom when writing for publication.

The second major observation concerning significance of study sections was that physical-education research investigations seldom develop the scientific importance of the work against the theoretical structure in a knowledge domain. Instead, physical education papers tend to emphasize potential for immediate application of results against the background of accepted ideals for educational outcomes and objectives. The condition exemplifies the dedication of physical educators to professional commitments and the practitioner's difficulties as the primary criteria for conducting research. Unless the research produces useful knowledge for the immediate benefit of teachers, of what good is the research?

It would profit a student and many graduate faculty members alike to study the formats of sections on significance found in published scientific work and in theses and dissertations completed in academic disciplines. One of the first observations to be made as a result of this undertaking is that such sections are commonly nonexistent in these studies. When this section is present, it will be likely to deal with the knowledge structure and models in the content domain by pointing out conflicts in results of previous studies, noting the meager data available in the area, and the need for further work to verify existing theories. Sometimes the section dwells upon difficulties in the assessment of the phenomenon itself and then poses a new measurement strategy which is to be tested. In these cases, no mention is ever made of the importance of the phenomenon being assessed. Significance in terms of the application of the resultant data is only infrequently encountered. The research is deemed significant on criteria other than practical applications and benefit to society.

How, for example, would one develop the section on significance for an investigation in each of the types of experiments presented previously? Autotelic, model validation, model-oriented, and methodological categories each demand different writing strategies and yet, each would be written on the basis of criteria suitable for the evaluation of a model. How many studies mention reductionism, determinism, or improved accuracy in making predictions when development of significance is presented? One begins to see, it is hoped, that significance of the study means one thing in a profession and something else in an academic discipline. Recognizing this duality may help in writing an adequate significance section by channeling efforts in the right direction. Some studies are designed to contribute useful knowledge and others hope to make contributions to the knowledge structure. Requiring either of these classes of study to be judged with the same set of criteria for significance seems unfair.

Methodology

In a thesis prospectus, the section on methodology might very well be the longest and the most important of all sections. Methodology holds a key position in any research report, thesis, or dissertation. Unless an acceptable plan for the collection of data pertinent to the research question can be fashioned, great ideas for worthy research problems are seldom brought to fruition. All too often, grandiose research topics are miserable failures because of glaring deficiencies in the methodology. The research topic may have been succinctly stated and the significance of the study established beyond any question. When the time arrives, however, to specify the manner in which data pertinent to the research question will be collected, it becomes painfully obvious that the research idea qualifies as a delusion of grandeur.

A study proposing to assess the role of competitive spirit in athletic contests, for example, would certainly qualify as an important and highly significant research topic. The investigator could point out dozens of ways in which competitive spirit is involved in athletics and suggest that competitive spirit might even challenge physical condition and skill as the most important factor responsible for success in athletic contests. Worthy as the research topic may seem, however, deficiencies in methodology forebode failure. For quite some time now, competitive spirit has resisted the efforts of researchers who were intent upon measuring it reliably and validly. Unless a satisfactory technique exists for identifying and quantifying the trait of competitive spirit, how can any study purport to successfully examine its role in athletic contests? Thus, great research ideas involving competitive spirit must be considered as interesting but impractical until advances in methodology are achieved.

The principle involved is quite simple: Data pertinent to a worthy research topic must be liable to assessment. If not, no actual research problem can be said to exist, and the research question must either be modified or abandoned. Many worthy research topics are forced to remain unstudied because available methodologies for their execution are plagued with insurmountable deficiencies. Other research topics may be judiciously revised to permit the acquisition of reliable and valid data on a reduced scale. Such revision may, unfortunately, affect the original intent of the investigator and severely limit the significance of the modified study. Good research questions, however, must be paired with equally good prospects of providing good answers. Some important problems, thus, remain unstudied because satisfactory research strategies have not been developed to attack them. Lack of research in a particular area can reflect the presence of methodological obstacles and not lack of interest or professional oversight.

The requirement that data pertinent to the research topic must be amenable to reliable assessment is, of course, the requirement of formal adequacy in research. This does not mean that the only good research questions are those that can be supplied with good answers. It does mean that any investigation that seeks to provide data on a particular research question must be prepared to demonstrate the presence of formal adequacy in its experimental design. If a research question cannot be answered satisfactorily with current methodology, then the needed research is in the realm of methodology. In the case of competitive spirit in athletics, for example, the highest priority need is to develop a research tool capable of assessing the trait of competitive spirit. Unless reliable and valid assessment techniques are available, formal adequacy is impossible. Any investigation attempting to assess the role of competitive spirit in athletics would, in essence, be trying to assess the role of a nonassessable trait and would be doomed to failure because of a deficiency in formal adequacy.

Delimitations

The delimitations are those restrictions on the scope of the study imposed by the investigator to effect a workable research problem. If the research problem purports to measure the personality characteristics of participants in individual and in team sports, then some delimitation would be necessary. The investigator cannot hope to measure all participants in every individual and team sport, and neither can he or she expect to give every test designed to measure personality. A choice, or delimitation, must be made of both personality tests and of subjects to be included in the study. The investigator might decide to delimit the study to include only varsity golf and tennis athletes at one particular school to represent individual sport participants. Team sport participants might be represented by a delimitation to football and basketball players at this same school. Assessment of personality characteristics might be delimited to the use of one particular personality test. Note that each delimitation was imposed by the investigator.

Limitations

Restrictions on the scope of the study are inevitable and necessary. An investigator must delimit the study in order to pose a research problem that can be completed. Each delimitation of the scope of the study, however, leads to a limitation of the study. Some help in understanding the difference between a delimitation and a limitation of the study may come from considering the two concepts to be analogous to a cause and effect relationship. A delimitation is imposed by the investigator on the basis of certain legitimate reasons—cause. Because of this delimitation, a limitation—effect—of the study results. Thus, each delimitation of a study will bring about some limitation(s) of the study.

When the investigator cited above delimited the research problem to include only varsity golf and tennis players at one school, a limitation of the study occurred automatically. Although the research study purports to measure individual and team sport participants, the sample includes only golf and tennis players and football and basketball players at one school. To the extent that the sample fails to be representative of all individual sport participants at various other institutions and at different times, the study has a limitation. If the delimitation of sample composition had been to include golf and tennis players at more than one school, the limitation of the study in this respect would have been lessened. If the delimitation had been to include all golf and tennis players at every school in the country, the study would have been even less limited.

One might ask how the investigator could have delimited this study so as to incur the minimum limitation possible. To answer this, one would have to decide upon the best collection of data necessary with which to claim that individual sport participants were adequately represented. If every golf and tennis player at every school and athletic facility in the world were measured, would this have eliminated the limitation? Unfortunately, a definition of individual sports would include more than tennis and golf activities. Thus, even having measured every tennis and golf participant in the world, a limitation of the study would still exist. To the extent that tennis and golf participants *do not* represent all individual sport participants, a limitation is still present. Indeed, if the delimitation had been to measure every participant in every known individual sport all over the world, a limitation would still be present: How do these subjects represent those individual sport participants of the past and of the future?

Regardless of how one delimits the study in composition of sample, a limitation in the study will result. In a similar manner, delimiting the study to the use of a particular test instrument for personality also results in a limitation. One might ask again what the best set of personality data might be in order to minimize the resultant limitation. If only one instrument is used, then the study is limited by the extent to which this one test adequately assesses personality. However, even if every personality assessment technique available were administered, a limitation of the study would still result: How reliable and valid are these personality test instruments?

What, then, would be necessary in a research study on personality characteristics of individual and team sport participants in order to substantiate a claim of no limitation of the study? Every participant in every individual and team sport from all over the world would have to be included in the study. The personality tests given would have to possess perfect validity and perfect reliability. Even then, how would one evaluate the question of whether these "perfect data" satisfactorily represent the past and the future? Would one require the investigator to give these perfect tests to every eligible subject every year until the end of time? Must the perfect study await the development of a time machine capable of transporting the investigator back through the ages so that it would be possible to measure individual and team sport participants of the past as well as of the future?

These facetious comments should serve to illustrate an important characteristic of research: There is no perfect study. The limitations of a study on an important topic represent deficiencies in the research and constitute reasons for *not* executing the investigation as planned. If the limitations outweigh any potential contribution to knowledge, then the planned study must be modified or abandoned. Whether or not the potential contribution to knowledge of a study outweighs acknowledged deficiencies requires action by an experienced intellect. Even the most knowledgeable researchers, however, make the wrong decisions and undertake investigations that fail. One can only hope to minimize the incidence of failures by careful evaluation of the delimitation and limitation see-saw since elimination of all but perfect research studies is unattainable.

One other point is also illustrated by this consideration of delimitations and limitations of research studies: the importance of theory utilization, model development, and the pursuit of a stable knowledge structure. No single study can be expected to qualify as a perfect study with no limitations; neither can perfect data on all the facets of knowledge in a content domain be provided, regardless of how many endless series of studies are conducted. *Determinism* and *consistency* must be assumed in the content domain. As reliable facts are accumulated, generalizations in the form of theory and model development must be advanced. Unless *reductionism* is achieved, research on any one topic would be endless, without any possibility of visible progress. It is for these reasons that investigations are conducted in order to produce the most reliable knowledge possible, regardless of how small this amount of knowledge seems to be to the casual observer. The scientist knows that the production of one fact is better than the production of a thousand items of dubious reliability. Theory and model development depend upon the integrity of the knowledge used as building blocks. Grandiose research topics might appeal to the world-reformer but the scientist knows that progress is achieved by the careful and painstaking accumulation of reliable knowledge.

CHAPTER TWO

Review of Related Literature

Related literature is of importance on several counts. In the first place, the quality of a review is often assumed to be synonymous with the scholarly value of the investigation and to be an indicator of the amount of intellectual effort put forth on the part of the researcher. Second, unless one is aware of the relation of the planned investigation to knowledge already available, it is most difficult to convey properly the true significance of a study. Sections on significance of the study, for example, must cite certain key references in order to develop effectively the importance and need of the proposed research investigation. Third, the related literature chronicles previous research strategies in the investigative domain and affords a ready-made trial and error series with which to surface research techniques of greatest promise. Unsuccessful as well as successful research methodologies can be identified, and an optimum plan formulated for execution of the investigation that avoids pitfalls and capitalizes upon procedures of proven value.

The literature in a field simply represents the knowledge available in a particular content domain. If the knowledge system is relatively well developed, an organized frame of reference will exist with which to understand the mass of accumulated data; that is, well-developed theoretical constructs and models will exist. Viewing knowledge through the lens of a satisfactory model will not only help to focus attention upon pertinent data, but will also provide the understanding necessary to appreciate the significance of contemplated research endeavors. Gaps in knowledge and deficiencies in current theory can portray effectively the need for certain research on some priority basis. Without a coherent model, however, the importance of contemplated research is more difficult to assess. As we have suggested previously, criteria do exist for evaluation of a model, and, thus, for formal research endeavors. In the absence of a satisfactory model for guidance, data of almost any variety may or may not be of importance.

A review of the related literature thus has a very simple obligation: It must effectively portray the status of knowledge in the particular content domain under consideration. The vast accumulation of knowledge must be organized for optimum assimilation and understanding by the reader. Any review of the literature that describes research investigations without some attempt at synthesis and generalization implicitly declares that no theories or models exist in the knowledge domain. A string of paragraphs giving abstracts of research articles arranged either in chronological order or alphabetically by author's last name can only be interpreted to mean that a unifying theory is absent. A satisfactory review of the literature, thus, must do more than just present a description of accumulated bits of data. It must seek to organize the data into a meaningful entity from which analytical deductions, attesting to needed research, are almost self-evident.

In essence, a review of the literature constitutes step (1) of the scientific method. If other scholars have already made inductive attempts at formulating theories, the reviewer may proceed to describe the various efforts at definitive models and contrast and evaluate these models. By use of the criteria for a model, the researcher may call attention to the adequacy and inadequacy of current theories and point out areas of agreement and disagreement. Assessment of current theory can define the areas of highest priority research needs and indirectly, but effectively, further cultivate the significance of the contemplated research endeavor. Only through such an understanding of the overall knowledge domain can the importance of a research proposal be appreciated. Any review of the literature which fails to present a coherent and organized knowledge scheme and then to show the strategic location of the proposed research in such a system accomplishes less than what is expected of it.

If a research topic is proposed in an area devoid of organized theory, the literature review presents different problems. An investigator may declare the intention of formulating an original model. If such an obligation is assumed, one can expect to find little help so far as suggestions for procedure are concerned. Step (1) of the scientific method is an inductive process that is, apparently, subject to few methodological laws. A review of the literature which forwards no organized model for understanding when no such model exists is excusable, since the formulation of a satisfactory generalization is by no means an ordinary feat. If, however, an organized model does exist and the researcher ignorantly presents a review lacking in coherence, the act is quite inexcusable.

Let us consider one example of a writing strategy designed to present an acceptable review of the literature. The knowledge system dealing with factors responsible for fatigue due to serial or sustained muscular contractions still lacks a definitive model. Although considerable data have been accumulated, two opposing theories on fatigue exist at the present time. One theory posits the cause of muscular fatigue to be located in the central nervous system, while the other holds that the site of fatigue is peripheral and is due to chemical changes in the muscle itself. Knowing that these two major theories exist would aid in any consideration of the vast amount of data and conflicting reports in the literature. A reviewer might choose to amplify upon each of the major theories and then, in independent sections of the review, report the evidence in favor of each theory. Evidence against each of the theories might then be developed and some attempt made at conciliation of the opposing models.

In addition to the above strategy in organizing a literature review, another writing strategy might also be used. Consider the contribution that the following paragraph makes in the area of strength and fatigue research (5):

> Investigative approaches to assessment of isometric endurance have in general included manipulation of (a) force of contraction, (b) contraction time or duration, (c) number of contractions, and (d) recuperation time allowed. In analyzing the results of such experiments the conceptual factors of relative and absolute endurance are additional requirements. Analysis of isometric fatigue curves induced by holding a maximum contraction for a fixed period of time (16, 18), for example, represents a varying force, a fixed time, and no recuperation. Assessment of isometric endurance in terms of the time some percentage of maximum strength can be held (13, 15) is thus viewed as a fixed force, variable time, one contraction, and no recuperation. Approaches involving the maximum number of times an isometric contraction can be made with load equal to some percentage of maximum strength (8) or serial isometric contractions of maximum force with intertrial recuperation periods (5) could be similarly classified.*

Inclusion of information about the two major theories of fatigue served to orient the reader to the knowledge domain under consideration. An analysis of research strategies aimed at providing pertinent data for advances in the knowledge domain is also advantageous. The paragraph just quoted offers insight into the research methodologies employed in the area of strength and fatigue. It allows the reader to see another facet of consistency in research papers—that of methodological approach—even though these same research papers may offer opposite conclusions as to the cause of muscular fatigue. When coupled with an outline of the two major theories, the synthesis of methodological approaches in fatigue research affords a coherent and organized frame of reference with which to consider the hundreds of seemingly unrelated research investigations present in the knowledge domain. To some degree at least, the reader would better "understand" the research domain.

If the review of literature can provide an intelligently organized approach to the research domain under scrutiny, it advances toward acceptability. If a summarizing critique can also be provided which effectively evaluates the status of knowledge, explicitly cites deficiencies and strengths in current models, and suggests research priorities, it fulfills its obligations. Against such a background, the importance of the proposed research investigation is more easily seen and appreciated. Writing strategies, however, are dependent upon the inductive talents of the

---

*From Kroll (5). Used with permission of American Association for Health, Physical Education, and Recreation.

writer, and each research domain may provide any number of suitable approaches for achievement of a satisfactory review of the literature. A string of isolated facts will not suffice as an acceptable literature review. Beyond that, both step (1) of the scientific method and the review of the literature depend for fruition upon the creative talents of the investigator.

CHAPTER THREE

Methodology

As suggested previously, the section on methodology must establish the formal adequacy of an investigation. Valid and reliable data must be collected according to an acceptable plan that will fulfill the requirements for a satisfactory answer to the previously established worthwhile research question. Regardless of how important the research is and how significant a part of the knowledge structure it is, lack of an acceptable research methodology precludes any prospect of success. Whether in a thesis written by a beginner or in research conducted by a reputable investigator, the manner in which data pertinent to the research question are collected is of critical importance. Useless answers to important questions can be provided if the research methodology is faulty. Conversely, if rather unimportant research questions are asked, even the best methodology cannot salvage the research endeavor. Thus, as much care must be given to the methodology as to the selection of a significant research topic.

In addition to fulfilling the requirement of formal adequacy, an acceptable section on methodology satisfies a basic principle of scientific work. That principle involves the notion of *replicability* and the opportunity for other scientists to reproduce a research undertaking exactly in order to *verify* findings. In the language of statistics, cross-validation of results is a synonymous term implying that the results show *consistency*. Because of space limitations in scientific journals, detailed information concerning methodology is frequently missing. Reference is more often made to use of standardized and commonly accepted data-collection techniques described in detail elsewhere. Although published articles may seem to be frugal in methodological descriptions, the absence of details is by no means an indication of unimportance or oversight. In most thesis and dissertation research, however, every detail of the research methodology is presented, making replication of the research by others a simple task.

Sample Description

The number of subjects used, procedure for subject selection, and pertinent information about the subjects should be included. The size of a sample is important because of its relation to inclusiveness and generality, both of which are part of the criteria for model evaluation. Coupled with a description of the procedure for selection, the sample size gives information about the representativeness of the sample. Referring back to the study on individual and team sport participants, for example, if only one school were included, then the representativeness of the study would be limited no matter how many subjects were secured at that school. Similarly, information on whether the subjects were naive about the study purposes, and how many subjects failed to complete the study and were lost helps give further insight into the problem of a representative sample.

Sample size also affects the "precision" available in statistical analyses and is important to any evaluation of the experimental design employed. Precision refers to the size of the error term used in testing for statistical significance. The size of error terms can be partially controlled by consideration of the intrinsic variability of the criterion measure and appropriate selection of sample size to reduce the error term. A well-planned investigation will have a sample size that provides precision sufficient to demonstrate statistical significance when differences of practical significance are observed. (See, for example, *Experimental Design in Psychological Research* by Allen L. Edwards, pages 97-100 for the procedure for planning sample size.) A description of sample-size determination may be included under the sample-description or experimental-design sections of the methodological chapter. Strange as it may sound, a sample may be too big as well as too small and well-planned investigations will include sample-size determination to ensure both efficiency and validity.

A description of pertinent information about the subjects is included in order to provide the opportunity for a consideration of the study from other perspectives. Another investigator, following insight into the problem area, may want to know the age, height, weight, or general body configuration of the subjects. Another researcher may be interested in the subject matter major or educational level of the subjects, while another may seek information on handedness of the subjects. No list of pertinent information to be included in this section can be formulated since the nature of the research domain determines pertinence. Whatever factors seem pertinent in the research domain, whether part of the current research question or not, should be included if at all possible. If nonathletes were used, how was nonathlete defined? If athletes were used, what sport did they represent? How proficient were they? Were the data collected in-season or out-of-season?

Parameters Measured and Their Selection

Criterion measures must be identified and some rationale for their selection presented. Information should be provided on why the particular tests or parameters measured were chosen over others. Hence, a selected test might have been evaluated as possessing greater validity or better reliability than other potential tests. Parameters or tests which have been standardized or shown to be measurable under the conditions expected, or both, merit preference over assessing techniques of dubious reliability and validity. If either less valid or less reliable tests must be used because of other considerations, the reason for such a choice should be presented honestly. Time limitation or the need to maintain subject motivation, for example, might have disqualified some of the best tests because of their length and difficulty. Limitations of the study due to criterion-measure assessment techniques should be acknowledged openly, and evaluated as to importance.

Measurement Techniques

After the basis for selection of suitable criterion measures and their assessment techniques has been established, the researcher must describe the manner in which data were collected. Information on apparatus design, instrumentation, time of data collection, instruction to subjects, number of trials or measures secured, and method of recording data is commonly included. If a new piece of apparatus were built, an adequate description must be included. New instrumentation may necessitate the inclusion of a circuit diagram. Pictures of equipment and disposition of subjects during data collection can help communicate necessary details. In short, this section should contain all information necessary for another investigator to replicate the study exactly as it was done by the present researcher.

The nature of the research problem again dictates the kinds and amounts of information to be included. If strength of the elbow flexors was measured, for example, one would need to describe the posture of the subject during a trial, the angle at which the limb was positioned, test instrument used to record strength, length of time allowed for exertion, number of trials and time between trials, subject motivation controls, and any other points pertaining to the measurement situation. In the case of a standardized test, most of the controls necessary for satisfactory data collection might be cited in the test manual, offering a convenient check list of essential points to be covered. Only an intellectual familiarity with the research domain can ensure adequate consideration of essential measurement-situation conditions. Thus, an analysis of related literature again looms as an important step in the conduct of a successful research investigation.

In addition to these tangible and rather visible items of concern there is a somewhat less concrete item of considerable importance in methodology. Many kinds of criterion measure require more than possession of factual knowledge about measurement techniques for adequate assessment. The additional ingredient is the ability of the data collector to administer the technique properly; that is, there is an art or "feel" to some forms of data collection. Just as a surgeon must be skillful as well as knowledgeable, a researcher must not only be aware of the procedure for data collection, but must also be adept at the art of the technique. Unless such skill is coupled with factual knowledge, the data collected may be unreliable and invalid even though purportedly collected according to prescribed procedures.

The beginner in research is often required, therefore, to show evidence of an ability to collect data on criterion measures satisfactorily. A common practice is to include a sort of dress rehearsal in which the planned study is actually conducted on a small scale. Such pilot studies, as they are called, can illuminate unforeseen difficulties in the methodology and can allow practice time for the investigator to develop data collecting skills. Evidence can then be given on the reliability of data collecting skills. A research study conducted by a beginning researcher in a respected laboratory and under the direction of a reputable investigator might be accepted as satisfactory without definitive evidence of proper methodological skill. Implicit trust in the honesty of the researcher in this case is an obligation as well as a compliment. Skepticism in science, however, makes provision of concrete evidence of the researcher's capabilities preferable to the invoking of implicit trust.

Experimental Design and Analysis Procedures

In order for the data to give reliable information pertinent to the research question, attention must be given to the experimental design and analysis procedures. Once having settled upon the research question, criterion measures, and the techniques of criterion-measure assessment, it is necessary to decide upon the pattern of data collection to be followed. This pattern or blueprint for data collection is essential if data are to be free of contamination by irrelevant research factors and amenable to satisfactory analytic procedures. Too much research in physical education, unfortunately, exemplifies poor experimental design and faulty analysis. It seems as though considerable attention has been paid to the definition of worthy research questions and the sharpening of measurement techniques while design and analysis considerations have gone relatively unnoticed.

Although experimental design involves the application of statistics, statistical techniques and design of experiments are not synonymous terms. Experimental design has as its purpose the provision of data pertinent to the research question in the most efficient and economical manner possible. It concerns itself with methods for increasing the accuracy of an experiment and considers such topics as sample size determination, intrinsic variability of the criterion measure, number of treatments to be used and the range of their manipulation, and number of replications needed. Appropriate analytic techniques are selected after the basic design of an experiment has been formulated. Design and analysis problems may interact in the formulation of a final plan, but to suggest that selection of analytic techniques constitutes the design of an experiment is rather naive.

It would be an injustice to make any recommendations on experimental-design and statistical-analysis procedures in this small section. Both topics constitute essential research tools and require intensive study. Competency in these areas can come only from careful and extensive formal study. Course work, independent study, consultations with an authority, and experience in application are all required to achieve satisfactory knowledge and familiarity with these essential research tools. To suggest to a beginner that the appendix at the end of a textbook on tests and measurements would provide a sufficient background in the subject is sheer nonsense. Neither can it be said that the student could "pick up" what competencies are needed by independent study of such topics pertinent to the research. The researcher should be prepared to develop competence in using these research tools during the program of graduate study. Even then, with at most one to four courses in the various subjects, the student will still need access to a knowledgeable individual. Consultation with an expert in statistics is invaluable, but no consultant can be expected to lay out the entire design, select appropriate analytic techniques, and then tutor the researcher in the calculation and interpretation of results. Only with an adequate background of preparation can one hope to conduct satisfactory research, free of glaring deficiencies in design and analytic procedures. A careful review of the literature may bring to light design and analytic techniques that appear to be satisfactory and may offer some help in making the right decisions. Some benevolent thesis chairperson may assume a major portion of the burden and ensure adequate design-decisions. In the end, however, only competence in and knowledge of the use of the tools can ensure that correct and sophisticated decisions have been made.

CHAPTER FOUR

Presentation of Results and Analyses

In this section, the raw data collected are subjected to the planned analytic procedures and presented to the scientific audience in meaningful form. Since the analytic procedures were designed to provide reliable information pertinent to the research question, it is often helpful to begin the chapter with a condensed presentation of the research problem, data collection procedures, and plan of analysis. It is helpful, in other words, to review the dimensions of the study before presenting complicated tables, figures, and charts. The simple practice of merely citing what criterion measures are to be analyzed is of great help in organizing the presentation of data analyses. Subsections in the form of subheadings aid in breaking down the total analysis scheme into more coherent and meaningful units. Since research problems generally involve several different research questions, the section on analysis can be divided into subordinate topics of more manageable proportions without undue difficulty.

The related literature is an important source of ideas for methods of clear presentation of data analyses. Published articles employing the same or similar analytic techniques can provide valuable clues for strategies of data presentation, while the mechanical format for tables, figures, and charts can be secured from standard reference texts on such topics. Highest priority should be given to the goal of writing a section on results that gives proper emphasis to important aspects of the study and presents needed information with clarity and persuasiveness. Hence, data and material irrelevant to the important research question should not be allowed to mask the essential results of the study. Detailed presentation of raw data on each subject or long tables containing information which can be condensed after analysis are not usually included in chapter four in order to preserve a conciseness consistent with clarity. Such material, if the researcher and chairman believe it worthy of preservation, can be included in the appendix. In published research, extensive data lists and preliminary-analysis tables may be made available to interested readers upon request, but are not customarily included in the article itself. If the author prefers, such materials may be deposited with an appropriate documentation institute where it can be obtained by interested individuals for a small fee.

Just as in the introductory and significance of the study sections, the researcher must be concerned with a suitable writing strategy to ensure proper emphasis is given to the most relevant parts of the study. Lengthy tables and uninterpretable figures may have to be relegated to the appendix in order to ensure clarity and suitable attention to essential points. Several points of interest may have to be omitted because their inclusion might serve to cloud the more important results of the study. Exclusion of such materials frequently distresses the investigator who spent long hours of toil to obtain them. It is painful, for example, to simply report that no correlation coefficient among the 22 criterion measures was significant and to delete the table presenting the impressive intercorrelation matrix. Yet, the table of correlation coefficients offers no information that is not contained in the short, one-sentence declaration of no significant correlation. The test of all material for inclusion, however, is whether the material contributes to an understanding of the study or not.

Discussion of Results

One common difficulty likely to be encountered by the researcher comes from the necessity of presenting *and* interpreting the results given in the preceding section. Results are presented along with the interpretation of the analytic procedures and the researcher finds it difficult not to go into some discussion of the results. When the time comes for a discussion of the results, the writer is often devoid of any additional comments. Foolproof guidelines to ensure satisfactory separation of the two sections are not available. Indeed, many researchers circumvent the necessity of presenting separate results and discussion sections by combining the two topics into one unit.

Whether or not the two sections are kept separate or are combined into one unit, the commonest mistake of beginning researchers is a failure to discuss adequately the meaning of the results. It seems almost a rule of thumb to find massive amounts of data in the tables, figures, and charts given in the section on presentation of results, followed by a complete void so far as interpretation is concerned. Yet it is in the discussion of results that the researcher demonstrates true insight into and scholarly understanding of the knowledge domain as it relates to the study results and previous research in the literature. The discussion of results represents step (3) in the scientific method and is as important as—indeed, more important than—either of the preceding steps.

Having formulated an important research question after intensive study of the knowledge domain, the investigator fashioned a study with excellent formal adequacy and proceeded to collect data both reliable and pertinent to the research question. The analysis condensed the enormous amount of isolated data into meaningful terms upon which judgments of relevance to the research domain could be made. How, then, do his answers fit the research questions asked? What concordance is shown between the data and the theoretical constructs present in the content domain? Do the results verify existing theories or point out deficiencies and the need for revision of currently accepted theory? After the long hours of intellectual struggle and meticulous data collection, the drudgery of data recording and analysis, arduous efforts at clear presentation of the analysis, and the interpretation of dozens of statistics, the simple question should be asked—so what? After all of that, what does it all mean in the context of the knowledge domain as a whole?

One of the simple checks on the adequacy of a discussion section is to review the sections on the statement of the problem and the significance of study. Are the important research questions that were asked satisfactorily answered in the discussion section or not? How have the results of the study contributed to better understanding of the significance of the study factors? The data collected and results from the analytic procedures contribute additional and *new* bits of information within the knowledge domain. Should not a researcher feel obligated to make some attempt at viewing the new conglomerate of data in the knowledge domain and to try to evaluate the potency of current models? In so doing, the researcher will have come full cycle through the scientific method. Step (3) will have led to step (1) of the scientific method, and a new inductive generalization might be formulated for consideration by other scientists. It would, therefore, allow the researcher to make recommendations for further study based upon a new—and hopefully better—vantage point in the knowledge domain. It would—one can only hope—provide leads for further research efforts and help draw the investigator into further research.

CHAPTER FIVE

Summary of the Study

In a thesis or dissertation, Chapter five includes a summary of the entire study starting with the introduction, following through with condensed material on all other sections, and ending with a list of results. Since each of the previous chapters were concluded with a summary, the composite summary in Chapter five should not be too difficult to write. All that is usually needed is to revise the sequence of individual chapter summaries by incorporating some transitional phrases or sentences for enhanced continuity from one summary to the next. The final summary would allow an interested reader to skip over the first four chapters and read the last for a grasp of the total study. With such an overview, the preceding chapters could be examined with a better idea of the complete research endeavor.

Many scientific journals, however, do not permit a summary or conclusion section to be included in manuscripts submitted for publication. Such material is considered as repetitive of information already presented and is, thus, deleted from any article considered for publication. In place of the summary at the end of the article, such journals commonly require a short abstract of the study which is situated at the beginning of the article. The abstract thus serves the same purposes as a summary and allows journal readers to grasp quickly the essentials of an article published in the journal without reading the entire article. Preparation of an abstract requires a considerable talent since presenting essential information about an investigation in some 150-200 words is not an easy or enjoyable task.

Conclusions

The conclusions presented should represent broader statements about the knowledge contributed by the study than the list of results included in Chapter four. Although each conclusion must be defensible by reference to results from Chapter four, it is not necessary to qualify and cite quantitative evidence for each conclusion. These conclusions might very well reflect the essential points developed in the discussion, where the strategic significance of the study was pointed out in terms of more general theoretical constructs. It goes without saying that the conclusions should relate to the basic research questions stated for the study. Unfortunately, too many conclusions stated in research conducted by beginners seem to have no connection to the statement of the problem presented in the first chapter. Thus, one of the critical checks on the acceptability of the conclusions is whether or not they constitute answers to the research questions originally posed.

Recommendations for Further Study

How sad it is to find recommendations for further study considered by graduate students as an unimportant "mop-up" task that can be handled before lunch on the day of the final orals. At least this seems to be the case if one judges the typical set of recommendations in theses and dissertations. Perhaps the poor quality is to be expected since the recommendations are one of the last tasks of the researcher and by then intellectual vigor is almost exhausted. Yet, a truly adequate and carefully thought-out set of recommendations for further study could very well constitute one of the more important contributions that could be made. After the intellectual struggle is over, the researcher has knowledge of the

topic that is possessed by no one else in the world. Results are known only to the investigator until these results are released via some form of
publication. The insights developed about the research domain and the
clues to improved research strategies might enable the researcher to suggest research possibilities of far greater significance than the knowledge
contributed by the study itself.

As suggested in the section on discussion of results, some attempt to
relate the results of the study to knowledge in the content domain seems
an implicit obligation of the researcher. This is no more than the last step
in completing the cycle of the scientific method of research. Having
taken the precarious step of inductive leap from data to possible theory
[step (1)], the researcher is provided with an opportunity to make suggestions even beyond this step. Recommendations for further study represent step (2) in the scientific method and call for the researcher to suggest
research strategies designed to test the inductive insights forwarded in
step (1). The analogy has been used before in this book. Once having
found the end of the ball of yarn, new ideas for research can be pulled
out, with each tug bringing the researcher closer and closer to the beginning and the achievement of knowledge and understanding.

Rather than representing a culminating stroke of genius, however, the
recommendations for further study section too often seem lifeless and
uninspired. In fact, the drained investigator frequently takes the opportunity to second guess the results and gives the impression that the study
was filled with many inexcusable deficiencies. No investigator should try
to alibi honest weaknesses in the study, but neither should apologies be
made for a legitimate undertaking that somehow failed to provide the
definitive results expected of it.

Comments suggesting the need for more subjects in a future study
simply imply that the present study was inadequately planned; that is,
determination of an appropriate sample size was expected in any well-
planned experiment. Failure to find an expected significant correlation
between two of the criterion measures may have been due to the absence
of a real relation and not due to a poor sample. If the study lacked formal adequacy, it should not have been undertaken. If the limitations of
the study outweighed the importance of the study and possible contributions, it should have been revised or abandoned. Having established
these conditions previously, the researcher is under no obligation to explain any apparent lack of success.

PUBLICATION OUTLETS
FOR PHYSICAL EDUCATION RESEARCH

Although the *Research Quarterly* is the official publication vehicle for research in physical education, it is by no means the only outlet for scholarly research. Several journals exist that are either directly or indirectly associated with physical education. These journals afford the opportunity to disseminate research results of interest to physical educators. In fact, it is quite difficult to choose the most appropriate journal for a particular research article because physical educators have contributed to a great number of different publications. The wide interests of physical education researchers have served to spread scholarly contributions across a broad spectrum of journals, both learned and not so learned. Any scholarly-research endeavor worthy of execution, it is to be hoped, is worthy of submission for publication in order to transmit the knowledge discovered to the scientific audience.

For our purposes, only those publications that have rather strong ties with physical education and those associations with sizable physical education memberships have been singled out for comment. No mention is made of publication outlets at the state or regional level. Those state associations publishing a journal, for example, and the proceedings of district AAHPERD conventions are not considered, although they certainly represent legitimate research outlets. Neither is much consideration given to foreign physical-education periodicals as cataloged by McCloy (7) and by Montoye (9), or to current periodicals published in Canada and the United States as listed by Redman (12). It is realized that scholarly-research reports and articles often appear in these periodicals, and their exclusion should not be taken to mean that they have no value as publication outlets.

Several of the publications listed require membership in a particular organization before the publication outlet can be utilized, while others do not. For example, only AAHPERD members or individuals sponsored by AAHPERD members can present reports at research section meetings and can have an abstract published in the research council sponsored *Abstracts of the Papers Presented to the Research Section.* Other journals published by membership organizations, however, accept manuscripts from nonmembers without prejudice. Those publications to which nonmembers have limited access, however, usually have strong bonds with physical education and are considered worthy of mention.

American College of Sports Medicine

On April 23, 1954, the American College of Sports Medicine was founded by a group of ten individuals representing physicians, physical educators, and physiologists. One of the expressed purposes of the organization was:

To promote and advance scientific studies dealing with the effect of sports and other motor activities on the health of human beings at various stages of life.

Other stated purposes reflected the desire of the organization to provide for an adequate exchange of knowledge and experience among the many sciences and disciplines concerned with human fitness and sport. It decried "professional isolationism" and vowed to encourage cooperative efforts, involving concerned disciplines in the study of a broadly defined sports medicine area.

The American College of Sports Medicine (ACSM) is affiliated with the Federation International Medicine Sportive (FIMS) and has used the Federation publication *The Journal of Sports Medicine and Physical Fitness* as its formal publication outlet for a number of years. This journal publishes all papers in English with summaries in English, French, and Spanish. Articles appearing in the journal have been devoted to "The medical aspects of sport and physical training for the purpose of improving and maintaining health." Nonmembers may subscribe to *The Journal of Sports Medicine* for $50 a year. Journal offices are maintained at Minerva Medica, Corso, Bramante 83-85, 10126 Torino, Italy.

In 1966, the American College of Sports Medicine began publication of its *Newsletter*, which now appears quarterly, in January, April, July, and October. Now titled the *Sports Medicine Bulletin*, it contains information of general interest to the organization members and is currently under the editorship of Carol L. Christison. In addition to regular annual conferences, ACSM sponsors many regional meetings as workshops, provides the service of a speakers bureau, and is generally active in many pursuits related to sports medicine.

A publication entitled *Science and Medicine in Sports* was first issued in March 1969 as the official journal of the American College of Sports Medicine, with Bruno Balke, M.D., of the University of Wisconsin serving as editor-in-chief. The new journal was ". . . to emphasize the interdisciplinary forum of this quarterly journal" and sports medicine was defined as having ". . . its roots in the basic, clinical, pathophysiological and psychological sciences closely related to man's engagement in sports, games and other activities of sufficiently stressful nature." Six section-editors were appointed representing athletic medicine, clinical medicine, biomechanics, growth and development, physiology, psychology and sociology. In 1980, the name of the journal was changed to *Medicine and Science in Sports and Exercise* and a "blind review" adopted. Information about publications and the ACSM is available from the American College of Sports Medicine, 1440 Monroe Street, 3002 Stadium, Madison, Wisconsin 53706.

American Corrective Therapy Journal

From its beginning in 1946, up until 1966 this publication was called *The Journal of the Association for Physical and Mental Rehabilitation*. Starting in 1967, the publication was renamed *The American Corrective Therapy Journal* reflecting a name change of the sponsoring organization to The American Corrective Therapy Association. Corrective therapy was an outgrowth of the work of physical reconditioning units developed by the United States Armed Forces during World War II. The association was formally organized in October 1946 by a group of corrective therapists at the Veterans Administration Hospital in Topeka, Kansas.

Since its inception, the American Corrective Therapy Association has had strong bonds with physical education. Throughout its literature, corrective therapy generally links itself with adapted physical education and even with steady growth as a profession itself, it has not diminished its close relationships with physical education. A physical educator (Thomas K. Cureton of the University of Illinois) is a long-time member of the advisory council as well as a contributing editor with H. Harrison Clarke of the University of Oregon. For a number of years, the editor of *The American Corrective Therapy Journal* was Jack Leighton of Eastern Washington State College. The office of editor is now held by another physical educator, B. Robert Carlson of San Diego State University.

An analysis of *The American Corrective Therapy Journal* over the years 1946-1964 showed that seven of the top ten contributors to the journal were associated professionally with physical education and corrective therapy (6). The reporting of actual empirical research undertakings accounted for about one-fourth of the content emphasis over these years. About three-fourths of the journal content dealt with professional and philosophical problems of the association as it sought its identity. Much greater emphasis appeared for physical (74.8 percent) than for mental (25.2 percent) topics.

The American Corrective Therapy Association is affiliated with AAHPERD and has been amply represented in AAHPERD's therapeutics section. A good number of the adapted physical educators employed in school settings are also certified corrective therapists and participate actively in both AAHPERD and American Corrective Therapy Association functions. Although the corrective therapy journal understandably reflects its paramedical orientation, articles dealing with strength, physical fitness, personality and physical activity, and similar topics of interest to both corrective therapy and physical education appear regularly.

It is interesting to note that, among the top ten contributors to the American Corrective Therapy Association journal, one finds some familiar research names in physical education. Thomas K. Cureton,

Charles H. McCloy, and H. Harrison Clarke rank among the top ten contributors to the corrective therapy journal and also rank among the top ten contributors to the *Research Quarterly*. Such a finding is in line with previous consideration of the quantity versus quality controversy—productive researchers are highly productive and do quality-work as well.

Completed Research
in Health, Physical Education, and Recreation

Starting in 1959, *Completed Research in Health, Physical Education, and Recreation* combined the activities of two research council committees. Prior to 1959, the theses abstracts committee had been reporting abstracts and reference citations for master's theses and doctoral dissertations, while the committee on annual bibliography of completed research covered research published in periodicals. *Completed Research* affords research exposure by giving paragraph abstracts of completed theses and dissertations. Although this does not constitute full-fledged publication of research, it does allow a thesis or dissertation, which may not qualify as a publication in the *Research Quarterly*, to be publicly referenced and a short resume of its contents given.

The Federation Internationale d'Education Physique Bulletin

The FIEP publishes its bulletin out of offices in Lisbon, Portugal. Sections of the publication are dedicated to general subjects, scientific, school, and recreation-work topics. A special feature of the journal is to publish many articles with full translations in English, French, or Spanish. American physical educators are frequent contributors. "Treatment of World News" is an attractive section, and each quarterly issue customarily carries reviews and abstracts of books and foreign physical-education journal articles.

National Association for
Physical Education in Higher Education (NAPEHE)

At the invitation of Amy Morris Homans, six directors of physical education in New England women's colleges met at Wellesley and formed the association eventually known as the National Association for Physical Education of College Women. A comparable organization for men was founded in 1897 as the Society of College Gymnasium Directors, which later became known as the National College Physical Education Association for Men. In June 1978, after years of distinguished achievements, these two organizations voted to merge and form the National Association for Physical Education in Higher Education (NAPEHE). The Proceedings of the annual conference, which customarily includes research presentations, are published by Human Kinetics Publishers of Champaign, Illinois.

Quest

This journal offered its first issue in December 1963 as a joint venture of The National Association for Physical Education of College Women (NAPECW) and The National College Physical Education Association for Men (NCPEAM). One is not quite sure what the specific purpose of the publication was to be from the account in "From the Editors" appearing in the first issue. Apparently, *Quest* came into being because ". . . the number of supporters swelled into a veritable command" for the ". . . need of a challenging professional publication." Throughout the introduction, however, words and phrases like "manuscripts that mentally challenge," "persons courageous enough to present them effectively," and the promise that *Quest* ". . . will be neither vassal to expediency and mediocrity, nor the tool of any group or organization. If it is to be free to attempt the high summons with which it is challenged it must move along paths of its own choosing" served to suggest considerable freedom in choice of goals.

To date, the vast majority of manuscripts published in *Quest* must be classified as philosophical, historical, and professional. *Quest* has, indeed, demonstrated itself to be a mentally challenging publication. Issues such as "The Leisure Enigma" (Monograph V, 1965), "The Nature of a Discipline" (Monograph IX, 1967), and "Toward a Theory of Sport" (Monograph X, 1968) have dealt admirably with topics of paramount importance. Indeed, after seeing the results, one must, in retrospect, consider the initial introduction in 1963 to be a fairly adequate description of things to come.

Sports Psychology

During April of 1965, the First International Congress of Psychology of Sport was held in Rome, Italy. At the Rome Congress, the International Society of Sports Psychology was formed, with Dr. Ferruccio Antonelli of Italy being elected as its first president. Delegates to the Rome Congress from Canada and the United States met informally to discuss the formation of a sport psychology society in North America. Arthur T. Slater-Hammel of Indiana University having been elected vice-president for English speaking countries of the International Society and Warren Johnson who was elected monitor-at-large subsequently traveled to Barcelona, Spain and attended a meeting of the managing council of The International Society of Sports Psychology in September, 1966.

An organizational meeting of The North American Society for Psychology of Sports and Physical Activity (NASPSPA) was held on March 17, 1966 in Chicago just prior to the AAHPER national convention. The some 55 individuals present agreed on the value of organizing a North American society in sports psychology. A steering committee of nine individuals was selected at the Chicago meeting to decide on the formal details of the organization. After a meeting of the steering committee, the following officers were elected:

A.T. Slater-Hammel, Indiana University, Chairman
Bryant J. Cratty, University of California, Los Angeles, Vice-Chairman
Roscoe C. Brown, Jr., New York University, Secretary
Warren Johnson, Maryland, Representative to the International Society
Gerald Kenyon, Wisconsin, Editor of the Newsletter

A full day meeting was agreed upon by the steering committee to be held in Las Vegas prior to the AAHPER national convention. In January of 1967, the first edition of the *Sport Psychology Bulletin* appeared, and following the March 8, 1967 meeting in Las Vegas it was decided to form the NASPSPA as a nonprofit corporation, the purpose of which shall be "to encourage and promote the study of psychology of sport and physical activity through meetings, investigation, publications, and like means of co-operative endeavor." The North American Society for the Psychology of Sport and Physical Activity (NASPSPA) was officially incorporated under the laws of the state of Indiana on March 13, 1967. The NASPSPA was officially affiliated with the International Society of Sports Psychology (ISSP) and accepted the responsibility of convening the Second International Congress in Washington, D.C. from October 29 to November 2, 1968.

The first official officers of the newly formed North American Society for the Psychology of Sport and Physical Activity were:

President: A.T. Slater-Hammel, Indiana University
Vice-President for National Affairs: Bryant J. Cratty, University of California, Los Angeles
Vice-President for International Affairs: Warren Johnson, University of Maryland
Secretary-Treasurer: Roscoe C. Brown, New York University

Publication Director: Gerald S. Kenyon, University of Wisconsin

An executive committee, in addition to the above officers, also included:

Richard Alderman, University of Alberta
Donald A. Bailey, University of Saskatchewan
Jack R. Leighton, Eastern Washington State College
Leon E. Smith, University of Iowa

An official journal of the International Society of Sports Psychology to be published twice a year (spring and autumn) was planned, with all papers to appear in their original language (English, French, German, and Spanish). The *Sport Psychology Bulletin* is circulated to members of NASPSPA as a medium for the exchange of information and ideas with respect to both the society and sport psychology itself. No rigid schedule for the *Bulletin*'s publication exists at the present time but it is hoped that a formal publication vehicle will be developed as an outlet for research in sport psychology.

Statutes of the International Society of Sports Psychology exemplify the purposes of its organization:

(a) to support and promote scientific research and relations between scholars within the framework of sports psychology;
(b) to call periodic international congresses;
(c) to attend to relations with similar national organizations and international ones of medicine, psychology, sports medicine and kindred sciences;
(d) to take part actively in information and documentation services with respect to Sports Psychology;
(e) to encourage the establishment of national Societies within the framework of this International Society.

In 1967, the number of accepted applications for membership in the International Society was approximately 650. Counting membership in various affiliated national societies, the total membership is around 900 with 38 countries represented. The mailing list for the North American Society included approximately 100 names from both Canada and the United States. Membership in the North American Society is available to professionally qualified persons who are interested in sports psychology.

Over 100 participants registered for The Second International Congress of Sports Psychology held in Washington, D.C. in 1968. Insight into the interest areas being developed can be achieved by the list of topical areas for which papers were evaluated:

Sport and emotional health

Perception and motor learning

Psychological problems of
superior athletes

Personality dynamics of athletics
Research methodology and design
Social psychology of play and
   sport

Sport and play for atypical
   children and adults
Actions and interactions of
   sport, spectator, and athlete

Implicit in the organizational framework of both the International Society of Sports Psychology and the North American Society for the Psychology of Sport and Physical Activity is the principle of an interdisciplinarian study of sport and physical activity. In this notion, the societies share much with the American College of Sports Medicine which also involves several disciplines in its attention to sports medicine. Of great encouragement to research personnel in physical education is the fact that physical educators find themselves associated with respected researchers from other disciplines in both organizations. Indeed, the membership of physical educators in both organizations is seen to be essential if proper consideration is to be given the content areas of sport and physical activity under consideration. Such an arrangement creates ample opportunity for physical educators to identify themselves as capable of respectable scholarly endeavors and fosters a rise in the esteem with which physical education may be viewed by other disciplines and professions. Intelligent scholars in any discipline bear no prejudice against physical-education research if such efforts are legitimate contributions to knowledge. It is amusing to hear some staunch AAHPERD supporters criticize membership in these organizations by physical educators as contributing to a splintering of AAHPERD unity, while at the same time campaigning for better public relations and education of the public and other disciplines to our value.

Research Section

At each national convention sponsored by the American Association for Health, Physical Education, Recreation and Dance (AAHPERD), meetings of the research section afford opportunity for the presentation of research investigations. Almost continuous reporting is now necessary during the convention to accommodate all the submitted papers. Simultaneous meeting of two sections is sometimes necessary to present close to 100 separate research papers each year. Because of the need for attendance at other meetings, many individuals are unable to attend all the research section meetings of interest to them. The Research Council, in cooperation with AAHPERD, now publishes one-page abstracts of all papers presented at research section meetings in *Abstracts of Research Papers*. This publication is usually available at the AAHPERD convention for a nominal charge.

Papers for presentation at research section meetings are screened on the basis of one-page abstracts submitted by the authors. Hence, no critical review of the quality of the research papers submitted is ever made. The quality of the research presented understandably varies from poor to excellent, but by and large, the research quality is seldom embarrassing. After each paper is presented, or at the end of a meeting, time is usually available to allow questions from the floor. Some lively discussions have occurred in the past, and both audience and participants have profited from the insightful criticisms and comments which resulted. Although understandably serious and sober in atmosphere, research section meetings have had their share of humorous events. At one convention, Dr. Leon Smith from the University of Iowa rose to present his paper, which was the last paper scheduled on the very last day and hour of the convention. In attendance at the meeting were only the section chairperson, Dr. Smith, and the individual who had just presented his paper. Looking around the large room, Dr. Smith began his talk with the words, "Fellow scientists."

The Foil

A professional organization for women majors and minors, Delta Phi Kappa publishes *The Foil* semiannually in January and May. As an official publication of this national professional physical education fraternity for women, *The Foil* is primarily comprised of the organization's business matters. However, feature articles appear, and the organization biennially awards a research grant to a woman who has completed some research investigation of unusual excellence. One of the requirements of this research award is that the recipient agree to have a research abstract published in *The Foil*. As a research publication outlet, *The Foil* must be considered a limited access journal.

The Physical Educator

Published four times a year in March, May, October, and December, *The Physical Educator* contains a wide variety of material for the profession. It is the official publication of the professional fraternity in physical education Phi Epsilon Kappa, which is affiliated with AAHPERD. Regular features of the publication include "In The Editor's Corner," "Teaching Techniques," "Elsewhere in the World," "Teachable Dances," "Book Reviews," "Recent Articles" (abstracts), and "Noteworthy People in the Profession." Manuscripts are considered in the areas of health, physical education, recreation and safety, as well as articles in other pertinent related fields.

Since 1940, *The Physical Educator* has published articles of interest to the profession. Each issue is both informative and enjoyable since poems, satire, and articles of professional challenge and scholarly insight are included. News of professional developments as well as literary quotations from the ages make the publication a close friend to the profession.

In 1955, the *Index and Abstracts of Foreign Physical Education Literature* was sponsored and published by Phi Epsilon Kappa as a service to the profession. The national office was established as a depository for foreign journals in the areas of health, physical education, and recreation and an exchange plan extended to editors of foreign journals. A concerted effort was made to provide complete English translations of research articles originally published in other languages. Many abstractors and translators have given many hours of service to make issues of the *Index* an invaluable aid in tracing foreign physical education literature.

Motor Skills: Theory into Practice

This relatively new publication includes articles which pertain to the application of knowledge and research to sport and movement instruction. Issues to date have included articles dealing with the processes by which theory can be interpreted into actual physical education practices, specific application of research concepts to the teaching of motor skills, and syntheses from research on sports or teaching principles.

Journal of Motor Behavior

Pioneered by Richard Schmidt, the *JMB* publishes articles which contribute to a basic understanding of motor behavior. One of the strengths of the publication lies in its contents, which reflect various perspectives of analysis: psychological, neurophysiological, biomechanical, developmental, and clinical. Authors from various disciplines publish regularly in the *JMB*.

Journal of Sport Psychology

Begun in 1979, the *JSP* is a multidisciplinary journal examining the influence of psychological variables on sport performance and the influence of participation in sport upon psychological variables. Papers dealing with theory, review of the literature, position papers, and original reports of either basic or applied research in sport psychology are solicited. The *JSP* is published by Human Kinetics Publishers.

Journal of Sport Behavior

Sponsored by the United States Sports Academy at the University of South Alabama, the *JSB* publishes original and theoretical papers dealing with the study of social behavior in games and sports.

Journal of Human Movement Studies

The *JHMS* is an international journal concerned with the development of human movement as a field of study. Relevant areas of interest include aesthetic evaluation of human movement, physiological determinants of movement behavior, movement in a societal context, personality and movement behavior, techniques for the analysis of movement, and comparative studies in movement.

Journal of the Philosophy of Sport

Published by the Philosophic Society for the Study of Sport, the *JPS* publishes articles containing detailed and discrete treatments of topics relevant to the philosophy of sport, philosophic discussions, synthesis statements, critical notes, and critical reviews of current or classical works and literature in the philosophy of sport. The *JPS* is published by Human Kinetics Publishers in Champaign, Illinois.

Journal of Sport History

The *JSH* is published under the auspices of the North American Society for Sport History (NASSH) three times a year. Scholarly articles pertaining to all aspects of sport history are included, as well as articles that are hypothetical and theoretical sport historiography. Issues also contain literature surveys and book reviews. The editor is Jack W. Berryman at the University of Washington.

Journal of Sport and Social Issues

Sponsored by the Institute for Sport and Social Analysis, the *JSSI* publishes original and theoretical papers dealing with studies of social behavior that focus on such problem areas in sports as minorities, racism, rights and health aspects, national and international politics. The editorial office is located at the University of Nevada, Las Vegas, and the editor is James H. Frey.

Review of Sport and Leisure

Successor to the *Sport Sociology Bulletin*, the *RSL* contains research, theoretical, and philosophical articles relevant to sport sociology, sport psychology, and professionals in leisure service. Benjamin Lowe of Governors State University, Park Forest South, Illinois, is the editor and publisher.

Journal of Teaching in Physical Education

The founding editors of the *JTPE* noted that "a scholarly publication of this nature has been needed for several years," and received an enthusiastic response from teacher educators, allied professionals, and in-service physical educators. An introductory issue of the journal appeared in the spring of 1981 and is to be published three times a year. Articles considered appropriate for the *JTPE* include research articles, discussion articles, and research abstracts which relate directly or indirectly to teaching, or teacher education, in physical education. The *JTPE* editorial office is located at Douglass College, Rutgers University, and the co-editors are Michael W. Metzler and Mark S. Freedman.

REFERENCES

1. Ackoff, R.L., and M.H. Halbert. *An Operations Research Study of the Scientific Activity of Chemists.* Cleveland: Case Institute of Technology, Operations Research Group, 1958.

2. Campbell, William Giles. *Form and Style in Thesis Writing.* Boston: Houghton Mifflin, 1954.

3. Fearing, Franklin. The history of the experimental study of the knee-jerk. *American Journal of Psychology* 40: 92-111; January 1928.

4. Kroll, Walter. Patellar reflex time and reflex latency under Jendrassik and crossed extensor facilitation. *American Journal of Physical Medicine* 47: 292-301; 1968.

5. Kroll, Walter. Isometric fatigue curves under varied intertrial recuperation periods. *Research Quarterly* 39: 106-115; March 1968.

6. Kroll, Walter. Contributors to the APMR Journal. *Journal of the Association for*

Physical and Mental Rehabilitation **19**: 190-193; December 1965.

7. McCloy, Charles H. An evaluation of foreign physical education literature. *American Academy of Physical Education* **3**: 90-99; 1954.

8. Merton, Robert K. The Matthew effect in science. *Science* **159**: 56-63; January 1968.

9. Montoye, Henry J. Foreign physical education periodicals. *The Physical Educator* **11**: 70-74; October 1954.

10. *Project on Scientific Information Exchange in Psychology.* Washington, D.C.: American Psychological Association, 1963.

11. *Publication Manual of the American Psychological Association.* Washington, D.C.: American Psychological Association, 1957.

12. Redman, Aletha B. A classified list of current periodicals in the fields of athletics, health, physical education, and sports published in the United States and Canada. *The Physical Educator* **13**: 14-18; March 1956 and **13**: 54-59; May 1956.

13. *Style Manual for Biological Journals.* Washington, D.C.: American Institute of Biological Sciences, 1966.

14. Turabian, Kate L. *A Manual for Writers of Term Papers, Theses, and Dissertations.* Chicago: Univ. of Chicago Press, 1967.

15. Woodford, F. Peter (ed.). *Scientific Writing for Graduate Students: A Manual on the Teaching of Scientific Writing.* New York: Rockefeller Univ. Press, 1968.

16. Woodford, F. Peter. Sounder thinking through clearer writing. *Science* **156**: 743-745; May 1967.

Back to American Physical Education

12

Throughout this book, our major thesis has been the need to develop research activities and graduate study programs that can foster the growth of a knowledge structure for physical education. We advanced the idea that professional education has unwittingly sapped physical education of the motivation to develop its own identity and of the strength to plot its own destiny. An allegiance to education has allowed only stunted development within the borders of educational dogma and has restricted activity on the part of physical educators to problems defined by education rather than by physical education itself. Now that education has come in for its share of criticism and drastic reforms are being considered, physical education finds itself floundering in uncertainty. To the general public and the academic community, sincerity and dedication alone no longer seem a sufficient argument for acceptance and support.

Abandonment of the historic ties with education was *never* recommended in our consideration of physical education and graduate study. Leaders have recognized that a place in the school curriculum was a desirable goal from the beginnings of organized physical education in the United States. An alliance with education and mutual concern with teacher preparation, educational advancement, and professional problems should be permanent and welcomed commitments on the part of physical education. A profession of physical education, comprising dedicated and able teachers, deserves freedom from scurrilous attacks and unwarranted jeopardy to its existence. Recognition of real deficiencies in the profession, however, must take place and changes made when warranted. No professional ethic should be interpreted to mean guaranteed insulation from valid criticism, whether that criticism originates from within or without the profession. A profession exists for service to society and must be capable of reacting to its changing needs.

However, in addition to a professional commitment and the preservation of the strong bonds with education, physical education must face up to another commitment. Whether physical education is only a profession or is both a profession and an academic discipline, its research efforts must be as much in evidence as its avowed dedication to good works. Only through research can a profession examine the basis of its practices and improve the quality of its services to society. Such research must deal with more than extensive study of its housekeeping chores alone; it must be prepared to discover knowledge essential to its progress as a learned profession. An academic discipline must, similarly, produce new knowledge in order to forge a sound knowledge-structure and bid for recognition as an accepted member in the community of scholars. Regardless of how one chooses to think of physical education, research is essential to its progress and existence.

As we have seen, physical education has not been characterized by excessive research activity. Teachers in the public schools shun the responsibility and consider it an unrealistic obligation irrelevant to most of their professional tasks. Graduate students plead for exemption with the argument they are preparing for school positions and qualify for a release from a research obligation on the same basis as the school teachers. Faculty members at colleges and universities have different alibis. Coaches are busy coaching, staff members point out that they are committed to a specialty in folk dancing or team sports, and administrators see their role as one of facilitating research by staff members. Finally, the spotlight falls on faculty members in charge of graduate courses who quickly pass the responsibility on to the person in charge of research. This person may choose to suffer silently the slings and arrows of unethical colleagues or can proudly accept identification as a researcher. Such an individual can point to chairmanship of the research section in the state association or to a talk on research given to the majors club as evidence of research skills and interest. Such an individual is, of course, developing several dozen ideas for monumental research endeavors that will avoid the blunders pitifully committed by poor researchers who do not care about the quality of the work they publish.

As a professional association primarily geared to an educational orientation, AAHPERD has not been overly impressive in its commitment to research. It has, of course, condoned and encouraged the idea of research; but responsibility to a broad spectrum of professional activities has prevented any vigorous priority evaluations from being made. For whatever reason, AAHPERD, by refraining from priority setting seems to have become an innocuous, pleasant, and ineffective association which continually strives for equal representation of all its far flung commitments. Typically, equal representation of diverse-interest groups in the association has resulted in perfunctory actions with predictable outcomes. By the time all of the separate voices are heard and accommodated, any policy arrived at is so diluted by compromise that it is of little value.

The recent surge of emphasis upon research, development of innovative new graduate programs, and movement toward the establishment of an academic discipline has brought over-due attention to deficiencies in the knowledge structure of physical education. Since the vast majority of professional physical educators seem to profess intense and legitimate reasons for not doing research, perhaps the only recourse left for a research-conscious segment of the profession is to establish an academic discipline. At least the responsibility of doing research in an academic discipline cannot be denied, and a separation of the profession from the discipline could offer some positive outcomes. A profession, unfortunately, has an obligation to research, and dichotomizing physical education seems fraught with its own set of inherent deficiencies.

The academic discipline cannot be expected to conduct research guided by a set of criteria appropriate to the profession. Prospects of knowledge useful for immediate application to important professional problems will grow dimmer as the academic discipline matures in its own right. Establishment of an academic discipline of physical education will simply not erase the research obligation of the profession. Knowledge generated by the discipline may certainly be of value to the profession, but to require the discipline to solve professional problems is naive. The profession cannot exempt itself from a research obligation by pointing to the existence of an academic discipline nor can the discipline allow itself to be molded by professional goals.

OLD PATHS AND NEW PATHS

An old proverb says something to the effect that it is better not to retrace old paths which were unsuccessful, but to walk new ones regardless of how painful and slow the new route may be. The current suggestions for new paths include a recommendation for the establishment of a scholarly and research-oriented academic discipline of physical education. Is this really a new path? We have previously developed the position that the original founders of American physical education pursued the goal of a place in the schools for physical education and concerned themselves with professional preparation of teachers. Early leaders however, also saw the need to develop a knowledge structure upon which teaching practices and physical activity could be based. Thus, the need to provide services to society was recognized as an obligation which had to be coupled with an equally important commitment to the development of a science of physical education.

George Wells Fitz at Harvard in 1891 and Thomas D. Wood at Stanford in 1892 established academic degree programs which explicitly recognized the dual responsibility of physical education. Luther Gulick contended that neither teacher training nor medical education alone was adequate preparation in the new profession of physical education. Both the Harvard and Stanford programs attempted to produce a physical educator with strong scientific and research-oriented training. Fitz's research laboratory at Harvard, the first in physical education, was developed to supply essential information for the practice of physical education. He noted that workers in physical education "have been too busy with the practical side" to concern themselves with research. As a result, Fitz contended that knowledge seemed "to have very little to do with the development of any system of physical education." The goal of the Harvard degree program and research laboratory was a simple one—to prepare capable physical educators imbued with the scientific spirit and to develop a knowledge basis for the profession.

Both Fitz and Wood saw that the then raging battle of the systems represented an issue of much more significance than most people realized. They argued that debate and an exchange of opinions over which system deserved endorsement was wasteful and ignorant. Opinion as the basis for decision was seen as an inappropriate operating code for physical education and unworthy of perpetuation. They believed that claims made by proponents of any system should be supported by factual evidence, and each man initiated programs designed to supply physical education with scientifically oriented, research conscious, and productive physical educators.

As it turned out, decisions were made about the most appropriate system for American physical education. No case can be made for the position that such decisions were based upon sound scientific knowledge rather than upon policy statements arrived at by mutual consent. Perhaps the precedent set has been too much for physical education to overcome. Does modern physical education solve its own battle of the systems any differently now? Can the profession of physical education now boast of a knowledge structure upon which decisions are made? Does fact or fancy constitute the operating code in modern physical education? Let us consider an example or two of modern practices in physical education which are not uncommon and see whether fact or fancy guides professional practice.

Example 1

One of the accepted educational concepts perpetuated in the profession is the obligation to meet student needs. There is evidence, of course, that motivation, interest, and attitudes are important in learning and merit proper attention in education. Difficulty arises, however, when an irrefutable principle is used in situations to which it has no relevance. One of the ways that the unquestionable principle of student needs is abused is in physical-education curriculum development. The idea of student needs is interpreted to mean that student interest is an important and high-priority criterion in selection of activities to be included in approved curricula. An expression of interest on the part of students in some particular activity is taken as evidence of a student need, and swift consideration is given to incorporating the activity into curriculum offerings. Who could question the decision to allow for student needs?

Let us imagine what a hypothetical application of the student-interest axiom might look like in actual practice. The director of a required program at a college notes that judo is sweeping the country in popularity. On an activity preference list, a sizable percentage of incoming students express a desire to receive instruction in judo and the director believes that it is time to take cognizance of student interest and consider the addition of judo instruction to the course offerings. A curriculum committee might be asked to make a recommendation to the department. Being democratic, a student representative is appointed to the committee, and after due deliberation the committee approves of judo. The wrestling and gymnastic facility is available and a competent instructor is assigned to handle the new course on judo. Enrollment in the wrestling and gymnastics sections has been small for several years so judo classes are added in place of these unpopular activities.

The decision is a resounding success. Judo sections fill to capacity, student groups congratulate the physical education department for its innovative flexibility, and the college administration is happy with the responsiveness to student demands. The wrestling and gymnastics instructors learn to live with their unpopularity and attempt to develop a broader range of professional competencies. Because of better than expected student acceptance, a judo club is established and more judo sections scheduled for ensuing semesters. The prospect of judo as an intercollegiate sport is entertained, a faculty-staff judo night is arranged, and the activity is a smashing success as an intramural sport.

Is it unfair to question the validity of this apparent success and the operating code by which it was achieved? If not, let us at least examine the mechanics by which this new activity was so successfully introduced into the program. First, it would seem that student interest was the most important factor in identification of the activity as a potential addition to the program. Should student (or public) opinion be the prime mover for entrance into a program? The curriculum committee must have considered the various reasons for the inclusion of judo in the program. What were these reasons? What facts about judo were used to evaluate the contributions judo could make to the objectives of physical education? Is judo as desirable an activity as the ones it replaced in the curriculum?

Some people would argue that a profession has an obligation to assess the merits of any activity on the basis of factual evidence before allowing it to be introduced into the program. Is public opinion and committee sanction based upon heresay evidence the operating code in curriculum development? It goes without saying that a profession is often forced to make decisions without the benefit of the kinds of evidence needed for intellectually guided action. However, how long are such opinion-guided, student-interest operations to continue? When will the demand for factual evidence grow to the point that research is insisted upon to allow future professional decisions to be based soundly upon fact and not fancy?

Example 2

If the judo example seems strained and far-fetched, consider the current furor over movement education. What evidence supports the claims made by proponents for the outcomes of movement education? Even less than systematic observation shows that movement education is being explained and demonstrated in clinics and at conventions across the country. Teachers in attendance take notes, ask for additional materials, and work diligently to develop curriculum outlines. The idea of movement education appeals to some. Others do not believe it to be appropriate beyond the earlier grade levels. The pro's and con's of movement education are debated, while numerous believers incorporate the system into their program and disbelievers cling tenaciously to traditional and proven physical-education activities.

Is movement education being debated professionally with an operating code unlike that employed during the battle of the systems era? Does solid factual evidence about participation outcomes and contributions to objectives determine which activities are to be included in a curriculum? There are countless examples of professional decisions being made which are based upon inadequate knowledge. Isometric exercise programs, for example, were incorporated into conditioning programs long before adequate knowledge existed. Even after the German researchers corrected their earlier findings, programs in existence and new programs continued on the basis of faulty and premature principles. Exercise fads are adopted by the profession almost as injudiciously as by the uninformed public. Rather than guiding the lay public, the profession seems to be guided by the public, students' needs, and so forth.

BACK TO AMERICAN PHYSICAL EDUCATION

Can one's imagination be asked to predict sensibly what physical education would be like today if the original motivation in 1891 for a science of physical education had survived? Suppose, for example, that Fitz's efforts for a scientific basis had been nurtured along the proposed path. Suppose that the principles inherent in his B.S. degree program had been extended to graduate study programs. Suppose that science rather than educational dogma had captured the allegiance of physical education. Suppose that the products of first doctoral programs in a Fitzonian academic discipline of physical education had been productive for several generations. Suppose, if you can, that sincerity and dedication had been applied to the pursuit of knowledge, or that physical education were being criticized because it mimicked its academic brethren and overemphasized research at the expense of teaching.

Fortunately or unfortunately, whichever the case may be, physical education did not continue with a dual commitment to develop both a service-oriented profession and a research-oriented discipline. Its energies were, instead, devoted almost exclusively to the establishment of a profession aligned with education, and the quest for a science of physical education was abandoned. Attention to knowledge-generating research was hardly feasible when little enough time was available in professional preparation programs to develop essential skills called for in an educational setting. When graduate study became available, it focused upon education and the physical educator in a school environment. Job-analysis techniques defined professional responsibilities and identified the subject matter for professional graduate programs. All in all, the development of practitioner competencies and finding solutions to allied professional education problems absorbed the time and intellectual strength of physical education.

Somehow, the motivation for coupling the practitioner track with a research-oriented science of physical education failed to survive. The persistent demands for immediate solutions to practical problems arising from professional service commitments allowed little time for an objective examination of the validity of accepted practices. Research and scholarly activity were directed to problems identified by practitioners in educational tasks. The value of any contribution was tested by how well it worked in a practical situation. In such an environment, the need to survive prevented any encouragement of efforts to nurture a science of physical education. It would take time to accumulate enough knowledge to structure a theoretical framework for physical activity and such time could simply not be spared by a profession so occupied with its work.

Perhaps the time has once again arrived to consider the wisdom of a commitment to a science of physical education. After three-quarters of a century devoted to professional aggrandizement, physical education may, at last, be able to afford the time for research. Administrative practices, curriculum designs, philosophical issues, and professional house-keeping chores have had the benefit of our complete attention. If physical education is to continue as a profession, it must fulfill all of the criteria for a learned profession. Altruism is laudable and essential; but practices must be guided by the intellect as well as by good intentions. We can hardly expect to exempt ourselves forever from the development of a knowledge base with the argument that we must provide useful services. Reacting to emergencies with workable solutions supplied by majority vote cannot eternally be the operating code for physical education.

NATURE AND NURTURE OF RESEARCHERS

Whether it be a profession or an academic discipline, physical education is in dire need of productive researchers. However, is physical education capable of finding enough research talent for its needs? Those of you now in graduate school should look around at your colleagues and ask yourselves how many of them have voiced a desire for a research career. Have you? If physical education cannot depend upon advanced graduate study to supply its need for researchers, where can it turn? Even if a supply of research talent can be recruited, will our graduate programs cultivate such a resource and develop productive researchers? Once having found and trained researchers, will physical education nurture their talents and allow them to be productive? Because of an exaggerated desire for usefulness, the profession has built up a resistance to scholarly excellence and it may require rather extraordinary efforts to break out of the traditional restraints that shackle quality research efforts in physical education. The anti-intellectual sentiment in physical education is even more of a problem because its existence is denied by the profession.

Identification of Research Talent

Input into graduate study programs is a major factor in determining the quality of the end product. Since graduate students come from undergraduate programs, it seems safe to say that research talent will have to be identified and nurtured at the undergraduate level. This does not mean, of course, that students with other undergraduate backgrounds may not be attracted to graduate programs in physical education; but their importance as a major source of research talent will be minimal for some time. Physical education must depend upon the undergraduate major program as a reservoir of talent for research-oriented graduate programs.

Now, the question raised by this situation is whether or not an undergraduate program geared to the preparation of a practitioner can be depended upon to fulfill the talent needs for researchers. By design, these undergraduate programs will emphasize educational goals and objectives, devote considerable time to the development of essential practitioner skills, and generally seek to enhance the professional aspects of physical education. With this much emphasis on the "how" of physical education, there is likely to be less than enough attention given to the "why" of physical education to develop interest in a research-oriented scholarly approach to a discipline of physical education. As we have seen, undergraduate programs fail to promote enough interest in research to satisfy the research needs of a profession much less an academic discipline.

Career goals generated from a professional undergraduate program are, understandably, in the realm of the profession. Teaching, coaching, and administration are the usual choices, while the number professing academic discipline or research goals will be small unless some attempt is made to nurture such interests. Although many undergraduate programs could benefit by an increase in the amount of theoretical work, it is doubtful that professional programs could survive the onslaught of a deluge of academic-discipline courses. The infusion of discipline-oriented courses could dilute the effectiveness of teacher-preparation courses and retard, rather than advance, the profession of physical education. The profession, meanwhile, must decide whether its preparation programs contain sufficient academic depth to justify their existence and claim to status as a learned profession. Finding the proper balance between professional methodology and discipline-like scholarship emphases will continue to perplex curriculum designers of both undergraduate and graduate programs.

There is hope that an improvement in professional preparation programs so far as academic depth is concerned will result in a greater supply of academically capable and research-oriented students for graduate programs. Those content areas deemed important to the profession can spark the research interest that can be kindled in later graduate study. Other recommendations to increase the reservoir of research talent include a plan to provide two tracks in undergraduate programs, one for the practitioner and the other for the scholar. The wisdom of a five-year program in teacher preparation has also been debated in which a bachelor's degree is taken in the usual four years and the fifth year is spent in education. Such a plan would preserve the integrity of both a discipline-oriented undergraduate major and the fifth-year program of professional education.

Physical education is, of course, one of the very few entities that claims to be a subject matter area and yet is frequently housed in colleges of education. A subject matter department more often prepares its majors in the discipline area and then transfers the student to the department of education for the acquisition of professional teaching competencies. Physical education, on the other hand, assumes both of these responsibilities. As a result of such a dual identity, physical education has not been able to claim much success in its role as a developer of the knowledge structure in physical activity. Its success in producing outstanding teachers remains debatable, although there is more evidence to argue positively on this issue than there is on the question of a knowledge structure.

Development of four-year academic-discipline-oriented programs at the undergraduate level would undoubtedly be the optimum strategy for producing research-oriented graduate students. Several schools have already initiated such programs that are free of any commitment to prepare the major for a professional career in education. The University of Massachusetts, for example, offers four-year tracks in exercise physiology, kinesiology, sport history, sport philosophy, sport psychology, and sport sociology. Graduates from this program can elect a fifth year of study to qualify for teacher certification, but the goal of the program is to prepare scholars in these areas of the academic discipline of physical education. Thus, the discipline track is not meant to represent a model for professional undergraduate training. The philosophy is not vocational, but scholarly. The major question yet to be answered is whether sufficient numbers of academically talented students will elect the discipline track over traditional teacher preparation programs.

The practical and vocationally oriented viewpoint in physical education is admirably reflected in the typical reaction to proposals for academic-discipline concentration at the undergraduate level. A common question asked by traditional physical educators—see if you did not ask it yourself—is what a major in a concentration such as sport history can do after graduating. The fact that physical educators choose a professional career in teaching seemingly welds their attitude to a vocational outlook. Their temperament forces them to think of a college degree as preparation for gainful employment and the notion of a pure-science ideal or the pursuit of knowledge on nonutilitarian grounds is quite unthinkable. An academic discipline of physical education might be accepted but only on the grounds that it will serve the profession. How then, does the English department justify a degree in literature? Why are degrees offered in chemistry when chemical engineering is available as a career choice? For an interesting experience, go over to the English and chemistry departments and ask them to justify their existence.

The very nature of dedication to a profession can work in opposition to the development of an academic discipline. Convincing a pure-bred professional that basic research is essential is a difficult task. Convincing a physical educator sold on the importance of services to society that an academic discipline of physical education should not be obligated to produce useful knowledge alone may not be possible at all. The simple axiom repeated throughout this book is that the criteria for a profession cannot be used to evaluate or develop an academic discipline. Neither can the criteria for an academic discipline be applied to the legitimate responsibilities of a profession. At best, we can hope that an understanding of the differences in objectives between the two may allow an uneasy truce to exist until such time as the discipline matures to the point where it can offer a knowledge structure which makes possible useful applications by the profession.

Cultivation of Research Talent in Graduate Study

Researchers capable of producing the quality work needed are not likely to be supplied by undergraduate training alone. Regardless of the quality of the undergraduate program and of the academic talent of the students, advanced graduate study will be necessary to train capable researchers. The nature of these graduate programs was discussed previously in the section on basic models for graduate study, where both professional and disciplinary curriculum strategies were considered. In addition to the arguments brought out in that context, the following points also deserve mention.

1. *The criterion of practical experience.* Many graduate departments in physical education require that the candidate for admission to a doctoral program have at least two years of successful teaching experience. Such a requirement apparently means that doctoral candidates must be mature (at least two years more) and have had practical experience in a school system. Unless a doctoral degree recipient has had such practical experience, how can such an individual be expected to teach satisfactorily at the college level? How can such an individual give instruction to prospective teachers in the undergraduate program without having actually taught? It seems obvious that the experience requirement is an inheritance from professional programs of education, for no self-respecting academic discipline impedes graduate study by a talented scholar until a little experience is gained.

The training required to do scholarly research is not enhanced by several years of teaching in the public schools. Practical experience, is, perhaps, important in graduate professional programs although proof for such a policy has never been abundantly available. At least so far as the production of talented researchers is concerned, the requirement of practical teaching experience works to delay the start of a research career. Certainly the academic discipline of physical education should seriously question such a requirement. Professional graduate programs might also do well to consider the advantages of an experience requirement against the loss of productive research years.

Consider the program offered at the University of Wisconsin Laboratory of Experimental Design. This graduate program was designed to train educational researchers competent in statistics, experimental design, and research methodology. According to Julian C. Stanley, who is director of the laboratory, young doctoral candidates are sought so that ideally they can complete the Ph.D. before age 30 and preferably before the age of 25. Too young? Graduate study in the basic sciences is encouraged immediately after the bachelor's degree is completed. The idea is common in most disciplines that contributions will most likely be made by those with the best preparation; hence, a direct path to the Ph.D. without stop-offs for experience or intermediate degrees is the preferred plan. Why, then, should doctoral candidates in an academic discipline of physical education be required to show several years of practical experience in a profession before they are admitted or allowed to complete a Ph.D. degree?

2. *Content versus method emphasis.* The heritage of the job-analysis technique for identification of course content at the graduate level must be reappraised in the light of its net return to the advancement of the profession. To be sure, identification of professional responsibilities imposed by society must be honored and curricula designed to develop essential professional skills. A professional must possess the necessary competencies to function effectively and fulfill the service obligation to society. But to the extent that graduate training in such programs has served solely to perpetuate practices of dubious validity and sap intellectual vigor, the job-analysis technique has been a dismal failure as an effective means of designing strong professional curricula.

Job-analysis techniques may show that a professional has to supply press releases to the news media, do typing, take notes at committee meetings, and prepare a budget. This does not constitute a legitimate reason for demanding that the professional take courses in journalism, typing, shorthand, and accounting. The tasks performed by a professional must be appraised on the basis of whether they constitute legitimate responsibilities that enhance rather than dilute professional effectiveness. The tasks performed may be necessary and even important, but do they merit time for acquisition at the graduate level? What priority should such tasks be given in comparison to factual knowledge or research training?

Physical education has often confused worthwhile services with competencies worthy of priority emphases in preparation programs. Any task expected of a teacher has been taken to be a legitimate reason for the provision of training time in the curriculum. This attitude accounts for the continued revision of professional curricula, the perpetual arguments over which and how many physical activities are to be required of the major, and the widest possible assortment of course titles in order to blanket a diverse set of identified teaching responsibilities. Regardless of what choices are made, graduates of the program still possess inadequacies and the program undergoes another revision. Is it time to realize that no program can equip a major with all the competencies necessary in professional service? Is it time to expect that some competencies can be developed by experience on the job? Need we take class time to discuss letters of job application, conduct mock job interviews, plan P.T.A. fairs, and frame policies for pep squads? Method is essential in a profession, but does knowledge to guide the practices deserve a higher priority than it now receives?

3. *Research tools and research emphasis.* The scientific method requires familiarity with the status of knowledge in the content domain *and* the necessary methodological research skills to conduct meaningful experiments. This means that a graduate program must provide both a knowledge base and formal experience in using the tools of research. The ability to ask important research questions would be wasted unless coupled with the talent to plan formally adquate studies to supply acceptable answers. Some graduate programs require students to take the majority of their course work in a related discipline or in a composite of related disciplines. Other programs have decided upon a double graduate major, one in physical education and the other in a related discipline. Still other designs call for minors in related disciplines while some programs allow the student to take all work in the home department. The selection of appropriate research tools and the amount of emphasis required will call for many difficult value judgments to be made. About the only definite guideline available is that sufficient mastery of research tools must be achieved to permit the production of formally adequate research.

Regardless of the choices made from such perplexing alternatives, the major factor in a successful program will probably be the climate for research which exists in the home department. Unless the physical education department provides an academic environment and demonstrates that research productivity is a high priority objective, the graduate products are not likely to be imbued with a research spirit and the drive to do research. Graduate faculty members must themselves represent satisfactory models of productive research scholars. They must be active in research, committed to the pursuit of knowledge, and insist upon research excellence in their students. Students must have the opportunity to do research, to work cooperatively with faculty members on research projects, and generally to immerse themselves in a research environment of the highest possible quality.

Based upon our analysis of the research productivity of physical educators, it may be difficult to provide a rich research experience in more than just a few schools. It may be necessary to rely heavily upon a quality research experience and environment in departments of related disciplines until a better supply of physical-education researchers can be secured. Graduate students may have to be counseled and honestly advised as to the opportunities for research that exist in various schools. Some schools offering graduate degrees might consider deletion of their programs until such time as adequate support and personnel can be secured. Indeed, some schools might be encouraged by the profession to concentrate on a quality undergraduate program and to abandon ineffective graduate offerings of doubtful quality. Of course, this may be impossible to accomplish because it necessitates agreement on criteria, priority assessments, and harbors the possibility of professional discourtesy.

Nurturing Productive Research Talent

Assuming that efforts are successful in identifying and training quality researchers, will physical education give sustenance to their endeavors? Many researchers in physical education presently find it necessary to consider research an avocational task. Their assigned responsibilities in a department absorb the major portion of their time and leave little formal time for research efforts. They look forward to week-ends, vacation periods, and stolen evenings from their families as opportunities to involve themselves in scholarly work. Yet, in the very same departments they can see time allotted for administrative duties, coaching responsibilities, committee memberships, and supervision of equipment rooms. If time can be spared in the professional work day for these assignments, what place on the priority list must research occupy?

Naturally, the policies of an institution will dictate certain priorities for staff assignments over which individual departments have little control. If research time does not exist as a legitimate function then research-conscious individuals will have to work on their own time, attempt to change the policy, or seek greener pastures. Universities, however, typically reduce the teaching load for graduate faculty members. This reduction in teaching responsibility partially reflects the notion that the course content of graduate work requires more time for development. It also reflects time allotted for the sponsoring of theses, dissertations, and other student research endeavors. But one of the more important reasons for the load reduction is to allow time for research on the part of the faculty member. This would be interpreted by some shallow thinkers to mean that any faculty member who is afforded a reduced teaching load is committed to make research contributions.

If the faculty member instead elects to use this time to further improve the quality of his or her teaching, serve as an officer in a professional organization, or volunteer for extra assignments, can this be faulted? Basically, a very simple decision has to be made. If research is needed and important to the profession, can other worthwhile endeavors be substituted in place of research? Who could criticize a graduate faculty member for toiling over a course outline or developing audiovisual aids for class materials? Who could deny that chairmanship of a committee or an office in a professional association was important? Who would not approve of a graduate faculty member who acted as a consultant to school superintendents, evaluated curricula in the public schools, or conducted clinics in lifetime sports? The answer is that such pursuits are all important, essential, and worthy of time being spent on them by any faculty member. But has the graduate faculty member fulfilled all that was expected? Should that individual deny some requests for time in order to devote some time to research?

This is treacherous ground, isn't it? It almost seems as though a recommendation were being made for a faculty member to slough off teaching and service responsibilities in favor of a research commitment. Teaching and service, however, are not the only obligations of a graduate faculty member. The point is that a graduate faculty member who devotes all professional time to teaching and service is not doing anything wrong; he or she is just not doing everything right. A faculty member has a threefold obligation, one of which is research. One simply cannot be two-thirds dedicated and slice research off the list. If research is not produced by the graduate faculty, who will commit themselves to it? Can teaching and service be the only contributions necessary for the advancement of physical education?

We come now to the administrator, who is plagued with the responsibility of providing the best possible program. There are many problems for the administrator and few visible rewards. A research atmosphere must be provided to nurture the researcher. In addition to the mechanical obstacles of securing financial support and satisfactory facilities for research, there is another perplexing problem. An administrator is more likely to be imbued with professional attitudes than with the value system of a disciplinarian or researcher. The administrator must be concerned with equitable teaching loads, staff harmony, criteria for salary increases and promotions in rank. There is likely to be some difficulty in communicating with the researcher whose outlook and value system is quite different. The researcher as an academic disciplinarian and the administrator as a professional are likely to disagree sharply on the priorities to be assigned to teaching, service, and research.

The full-fledged researcher in physical education will be uncomfortable in a setting where teaching and service are *the* obligations of a faculty member. A commitment to research can make the researcher stand out as different in most traditional physical education departments. While other staff members toil at the honest labor of teaching and counseling of students, the researcher will be fooling around with funny gadgets in the laboratory. While colleagues boast of winning the conference championship or awards for teaching excellence, the researcher will be revising a rejected manuscript. Requests for released time from teaching responsibilities will be politely questioned while working colleagues become irked with such a lack of interest in students and physical education.

Both the administrator and the researcher will find it difficult to defend time and resources allotted to research. Available staff resources are commonly inadequate to cover teaching and service responsibilities. The researcher is often asked politely to assume a larger share of the professional load. With colleagues burdened by excessive teaching and service loads, the researcher's conscience will force acceptance of more nonresearch responsibilities. George Wells Fitz's comment on the situation back in 1891 may have been right. Physical educators may simply "be too busy with the practical" to allow any research commitment. Regrettably—but undeniably—the talented researcher will be impaled on the twin horns of teaching and service functions. There is simply too much real and essential work to be done in physical education to allow a commitment to research. The researcher will accept more teaching and service responsibilities, such performance will be reinforced and rewarded by colleagues and administrators, and research productivity will be characterized by good intentions.

Fitz had a dream for a science of physical education. His program at Harvard lasted less than a decade, was criticized by no less a hero than Dudley Sargent, and Fitz slipped into oblivion so far as physical education was concerned. The current dreamers see an academic discipline of physical education or, at the very least, a vigorous drive for new intellectual strength in the profession. But will it last any longer than Fitz's dream? Can the traditional insistence on practical matters so characteristic of our profession today be expected to nurture the ideal of a solid knowledge structure for physical education? Or are we just too busy being sincere and dedicated to develop an intellectual base to guide our practices?

You could make a difference.

Index